RULES OF THE ROAD

RULES
OF THE
ROAD

*The Automobile and
the Transformation of
American Criminal Justice*

SPENCER HEADWORTH

STANFORD UNIVERSITY PRESS
Stanford, California

Stanford University Press
Stanford, California

Printed in the United States of America on acid-free, archival-quality paper

ISBN 9781503630413 (cloth)
ISBN 9781503636187 (paper)
ISBN 9781503636194 (electronic)

Library of Congress Control Number: 2022048571

Library of Congress Cataloging-in-Publication Data available upon request.

Cover design: David Drummond
Cover photograph: Shutterstock
Typeset by Elliott Beard in Utopia Std 9.25/13.5

For my parents

CONTENTS

RULES OF THE ROAD

Introduction

It is difficult to overstate the automobile's importance in American society. According to the Census Bureau, over 85% of employed Americans use private automobiles to get to work.[1] Motor vehicles are similarly essential means of transportation for family responsibilities, errands, and recreation—to say nothing of the US economy's dependence on trucking.

Technological innovations, of course, are fundamental to the story of automobiles in America.[2] However, the rise of what legal scholar Gregory Shill calls "automobile supremacy"[3] owes to much more than the evolution of the internal combustion engine and the emergence of the assembly line system. Economic and business developments were crucial, with manufacturers finding strategies for mass marketing cars and finance companies offering the installment plans that facilitated both mass production and mass marketing.[4] From there, a cumulative series of public policy and urban planning decisions cemented private automobiles' preeminence among modes of transportation.[5] Particularly since postwar suburbanization,[6] most of the country's infrastructure for transportation to work, school, and places of worship prioritizes private vehicles. Along the way, law has reinforced automobiles' status as the top transportation priority,[7] entrenching access to a car as a functional necessity for Americans across the socioeconomic spectrum to hold down a job, shop for groceries, care for relatives, participate in politics and civil society, and do most other activities outside their homes.

Thus, as it has to varying degrees elsewhere, automobility has emerged as a defining characteristic of the American socioeconomic system. At a basic level, the term *automobility* denotes the use of automobiles as a means of transportation. Merriam-Webster dates the word's first known usage to 1896.[8] Scholars point to historian John Burnham's 1961 article "The Gasoline Tax and the Automobile Revolution" as an early example of the term's use in academic writing.[9] In the early 2000s sociologist John Urry further popularized the term in sole-authored publications and in collaboration with sociologist Mimi Sheller.[10] In its more developed academic use, automobility refers to automobiles' predominance among means of transportation, the various systems and institutions that enable and sustain that predominance, and an accompanying set of attitudes and sensibilities.[11]

Rules of the Road uses automobility's prominence in American life as a lens for understanding the past, present, and possible futures of US criminal justice. As the book's substantive chapters explain, alongside building the world's foremost car culture, the United States also built the world's most car-centered criminal justice system. Cars played key roles in the evolution of criminal law, the emergence of modern criminal justice institutions, and the ongoing story of individual rights and systematic inequalities in criminal justice policies and practices.

Cars transformed the lived environment. Governments made unprecedented investments in roads and highways. Planners refashioned existing cities to accommodate automobiles and designed new residential, commercial, and industrial developments around driving. Within only a few decades of automobiles' introduction to the US market, daily life had come to substantially depend on cars, with driving integral to where Americans lived, what they did for fun, and how they made ends meet.

Through reshaping Americans' physical surroundings and daily lives, cars also reshaped crime and criminal justice. The proliferation of automobiles foregrounded traffic and its attendant problems as new subjects of regulation, a responsibility that fell to criminal justice authorities. The chaos—and carnage—that the flood of automobiles wrought on city streets constituted a pressing public safety problem and precipitated a new regime of regulation and legal accountability centered on the driving privilege. Cars also directly or indirectly created new crimes—from jaywalking and speeding to auto theft and vehicular homicide—and became prominent means and methods by which people committed preexisting types of crime.

These changes precipitated a fundamental reorganization of criminal justice around the imperatives of a motorized society. In the twentieth century the patrol car and driver emerged as "the basic police technology."[12] The vehicle stop soon became the primary site of direct interaction between the public and criminal justice authorities. Notably, the car-based policing system exposed middle- and upper-class people to unprecedented levels of law enforcement attention. In previous decades police energies were overwhelmingly directed toward poor and marginalized people; the new world of traffic enforcement and vehicle patrol, however, meant that better-off people were far likelier than before to find themselves subjected to law enforcement activity.[13] Yet roadside encounters were also a new site where social inequalities manifested, as the massive racial disparities in vehicle stops and associated experiences dramatically demonstrate.[14]

Readers who have lived in the United States likely have some degree of personal familiarity with the close relationship between cars and the criminal justice system; as either drivers or passengers, most of us have either been pulled over or experienced the concern that we might be. The value of this book's "car-window view" of US criminal justice, however, goes beyond this personal relatability. Understanding the modern history, current configuration, and foreseeable future of criminal justice requires grasping how myriad car-related cultural, economic, political, and geographic factors have dramatically affected the conceptualization, enactment, and enforcement of criminal law.

With automobility as their common thread, the chapters that follow address multiple key issues and debates in twentieth and twenty-first century criminal justice. As in many aspects of human affairs, priorities and preferences in the administration of criminal law often reduce to choices between competing values. For instance, in the autocentric US criminal justice system, vehicle stops and searches offer a compelling case study of the tension between protecting individual liberties and empowering legal authorities. The Fourth Amendment protects the people against unreasonable searches and seizures. Over the years courts have decided which types of government actions run afoul of this protection and which do not. In *Carroll v. United States* (1925), the US Supreme Court established the "automobile exception" to search warrant requirements, ruling that vehicle stops necessitate giving officers comparatively wide latitude to conduct searches without obtaining warrants. Moving forward, vehicle stops remained a crucial context for considering the appropriate balance between protecting citizens from arbitrary or overbearing exercises of state power and government's interest in granting authorities broad discretionary power. These sorts of tensions also manifest in other dimensions of the criminal justice system, for instance, prosecutors' sweeping discretionary authority in the context of deciding what to charge when impaired drivers cause fatalities.

Relatedly, *Rules of the Road* addresses the issue of privacy. Surveillance technologies are powerful resources for criminal justice authorities; *Rules of the Road* examines multiple surveillance methods and their implications for citizens' privacy. In our autocentric society, prominent examples include GPS location tracking, traffic enforcement cameras, and automated license plate readers. These tools can be immensely helpful in investigating crimes and supporting prosecutions. Yet they also raise significant Fourth Amendment issues and broader questions about the appropriate extent of authorities' information-gathering power.

In addition to questions about how to best balance authorities' power and citizens' rights, *Rules of the Road* engages multiple dimensions of the wide-ranging discussion about the allocation of criminal justice resources and the most desirable priorities and goals for the criminal justice system to pursue. The modernized police departments that emerged amid the intense motorization of the early twentieth century developed as generalists, with broad authority and diverse responsibilities. Notably, new obligations related to traffic enforcement fell to police departments, a crucial development that shaped law enforcement organizations in the subsequent decades. Debates about what police departments should look like and what police officers should do continue to involve questions about how policing resources should be directed, with traffic duty as a particular point of consideration.

Other dimensions of autocentric criminal justice discussed in this book address similar prescriptive questions about what the criminal justice system should do and how it should do it. Vehicle stops and searches, for example, emerged as a prominent criminal justice tactic during the national prohibition of alcohol and continue to feature prominently in the war on drugs.[15] Both Prohibition and the war on drugs offer opportunities to consider the costs and benefits of approaches to intoxicating substances that use criminalization and aggressive enforcement relative to "legalize and regulate" approaches. A conspicuous outcome of the war on drugs is a major increase in incarceration rates; in addition to these more familiar types of criminal punishments, *Rules of the Road* discusses collateral consequences, that is, penalties that are not part of formal sentences but nevertheless result from criminal proceedings. From the car-window view, driver's license suspensions connected to non-driving offenses are a particularly impactful version of such consequences.

The car-window view is also useful for thinking through major changes in criminal law and its enforcement. New laws criminalizing intoxicants and policies of aggressively enforcing such measures, often on the nation's streets and highways, are important examples. More fundamentally, cars themselves changed what cities looked like and patterns of antisocial behavior. Policymakers and officials responded in turn, devising new laws and enforcement strategies that corresponded to the sweeping social changes brought about by automobility. For example, expanded opportunities for criminal activity cross-ing conventional jurisdictional boundaries engendered an expanded role for the federal government in criminal justice, an area that had typically been state governments' domain. In an increasingly interconnected country, this "federalization" continued in subsequent decades, especially via the leading role the federal government took in pursuing the war on drugs.

The war on drugs has also contributed heavily to the enormous inequali-ties in criminal justice system involvement for people of different racial and ethnic backgrounds and social classes. Many readers will be familiar with the huge racial disparities that characterize mass incarceration. *Rules of the Road* highlights car-related factors that contribute to systemic inequalities in differ-ent groups' exposure to law enforcement attention, criminal charges, and as-sociated penalties. For people who could afford them, automobiles made daily commuting much more feasible, enabling suburbanization. As the twentieth century unfolded, local, state, and federal officials consistently prioritized in-frastructure projects focused on cars and their drivers. At the same time, many opportunities to buy suburban homes were difficult or impossible for Amer-icans of color to access. Moreover, urban road-building projects around the country cut through existing neighborhoods, particularly minority neighbor-hoods, displacing hundreds of thousands and damaging quality of life, prop-erty values, and economic opportunity for those who remained. These policy and planning decisions directly contributed to worsening residential racial segregation and structural inequalities. These socioeconomic conditions, in turn, directly contributed to pronounced differences in the rates at which people from different backgrounds are exposed to stops, searches, arrests, criminal charges, and criminal punishments.

As the book describes, vehicle stops are a primary site of racial disparities in criminal justice. These roadside encounters are by far the most common way that people interact directly with police. A prodigious body of research shows that drivers of color, especially African Americans, are disproportionately likely to be pulled over. These motorists are also more likely to experience intrusive elements of vehicle stops, such as intensive questioning, handcuffing, and searches. As Charles Epp, Steven Maynard-Moody, and Donald Haider-Markel compellingly demonstrate, these disparities are driven by police officers' dis-proportionate tendency to target drivers of color for investigatory stops.[16] In these stops, traffic code violations serve as pretexts to detain and scrutinize se-lected vehicles and their occupants. Deciding whom to pull over is an exercise of the discretion that characterizes the working lives of law enforcement offi-cers and other street-level bureaucrats,[17] including the 911 operators who make pivotal decisions about the allocation of emergency response services.

Given the revenue that citations generate, vehicle stops are also a significant context for considering the role of money in criminal justice policy and practice. In this vein, *Rules of the Road* explores critiques of automated traffic enforcement that highlight the revenue these systems generate for both governments and the private companies that administer and maintain them. The book also discusses civil asset forfeiture laws, which authorize law enforcement agencies to seize and keep personal property based on officials' assessment of probable cause to believe that the property in question is connected to illegal activity. On this matter, too, the car-window view is relevant: Most forfeiture actions begin with vehicle stops, and automobiles themselves are frequent forfeiture targets.[18] The idea of "policing for profit" in autocentric law enforcement has attracted substantial controversy and stands as one of the numerous contentious topics in contemporary criminal justice.

PLAN OF THE BOOK

Rules of the Road proceeds roughly chronologically. It begins around the turn of the twentieth century, in the earliest days of automobile travel in the United States, proceeds through cars' rise to predominance throughout the twentieth century, and moves on to emergent issues of the twenty-first century. However, each chapter connects the past with the present, emphasizing connections between historical developments and current issues in criminal justice. Along the way, the book attends to how cars shaped American criminal justice and draws on specific car-related contexts to address broader themes and issues. Each of the twelve substantive chapters opens with an introductory "road map"[19] laying out its key points. The chapters proceed as follows.

Chapter 1 describes the huge impact that cars had on American society and their key implications for criminal justice. This chapter uses motor vehicle theft as a case study in how lawmakers and law enforcement agencies—as well as other interested parties—reshaped criminal justice in response to the new circumstances of the automobile age. Chapter 2 continues with a discussion of law enforcement agencies' rapid bureaucratic and technological evolution during the modernization and motorization that characterized the United States in the early twentieth century. When combined with motorized police forces, advances in communication technology—particularly the radio—enabled the centrally coordinated policing systems that we recognize today.

Chapter 3 focuses on a pivotal era for US criminal justice: Prohibition. Efforts to enforce the Volstead Act led to key developments that would shape criminal justice for decades to come, including the rise of vehicle searches and landmark Fourth Amendment rulings from the Supreme Court. As their utility for transporting contraband during Prohibition suggests, automobiles offered historically unprecedented freedom of personal mobility to those who were able to access them. But, as Chapter 4 details, poorer people, racial and ethnic minorities, and women faced significant obstacles and resistance in seeking to avail themselves of the autonomy that cars provided. As jurisdictions adopted driver licensing and examination requirements in the first half of the twentieth century, age emerged as a primary factor in formal determinations of who should be considered fit to drive. Chapter 4 links considerations of age in driver licensing to the broader history of juveniles' treatment in the criminal legal system, with both contexts demonstrating the evolution of young people's legal privileges and accountability under the law.

Chapter 5 highlights how cars reshaped American life in the mid-twentieth century. This includes a discussion of the suburbanization that automobile commuting made possible and what it meant for the distribution of resources and opportunities in the country's metropolitan areas. Vehicle patrol's corresponding rise to predominance changed the face of policing, driving new debates about the relative merits of foot patrol, vehicle patrol, and other policing strategies. Building on Chapter 5, Chapter 6 focuses on the discretionary decision making that plays key roles in both police rapid response and vehicle patrol. This account notes key court rulings that affirmed police officers' broad authority to conduct stops and searches based on their own judgment. It also notes the major racial disparities that characterize citizens' roadside interactions with law enforcement.

Chapter 7 addresses the relationship between the United States' federalist system of government and a socioeconomic context in which cars—among other factors—have rendered state borders considerably less meaningful. As automobility made interstate crime more feasible, federal authorities took on a larger role in criminal justice. Chapter 7 discusses drug trafficking and human trafficking as two contexts in which interstate activity—and federal involvement—are particularly prominent. These are also both contexts in which moral entrepreneurship campaigns have played important roles. Chapter 8 addresses another such context: drunk driving. This chapter describes the grassroots campaign that fundamentally shifted drunk driving's treatment in the criminal justice system. It goes on to discuss the role of prosecutorial discretion in contemporary cases involving impaired motorists who cause fatalities.

Chapter 9 engages with the topic of collateral consequences of conviction. In keeping with the book's theme, it focuses especially on policies that revoke or limit driving privileges as penalties for legal violations unrelated to driving safety concerns. Like many collateral consequences, these policies extend the impact and duration of criminal justice involvement far beyond formal sentences. And, in the case of license suspensions imposed for failures to pay fines and fees, they elevate the role of the criminal justice system as a source of revenue generation. Chapter 10 keys in on revenue generation through criminal justice interventions in the form of civil asset forfeiture. Although seizing property believed to be connected to lawbreaking has a long history, this practice has grown far more commonplace and impactful in the war on drugs. Civil forfeiture proponents argue that the power to seize property is crucial to damaging criminal enterprises and undermining their profitability. Detractors, on the other hand, contend that these policies create undesirable incentives for law enforcement agencies and violate property owners' due process rights.

Chapter 11 deals with automated traffic enforcement, another area of auto-centric law enforcement activity that has attracted controversy related to revenue generation. Many road safety advocates praise the use of camera systems that automatically detect red-light and speeding violations and cite violators. In addition to allegations that these systems chiefly serve to fill government coffers rather than promote safer driving, critics have suggested that automatically generated citations raise due process problems and that these camera networks function as systems of general surveillance. Surveillance and privacy concerns are also central to Chapter 12, which focuses on location tracking in the criminal justice system. Location-tracking technologies are powerful tools for law enforcement officials, particularly in a motorized society. Chapter 12 describes how both radio frequency and GPS trackers have helped authorities keep tabs on people and their vehicles, including the key roles these tools have played in numerous criminal investigations. At the same time, the far-reaching surveillance capabilities that contemporary location-tracking tools provide raise significant issues regarding individual privacy and constitutional protections against government overreach.

The book's Conclusion opens with a look at two recent happenings: the onset of the COVID-19 pandemic and the 2020 murder of George Floyd and associated protests against police violence and racism. Both events' implications for criminal justice continue to reverberate, with several notable dimensions directly related to the close connection between cars and the criminal justice system. After recapping some of the book's main themes, the Conclusion closes with a few notes about what we might expect in the near future of American criminal justice.

ONE

Revolutions per Minute

The Automobile and a National Transformation

The interconnected development of automobility and criminal justice in the United States began around the turn of the twentieth century. Cars' introduction and rapid spread revolutionized transportation. In turn, this sea change in how Americans got from place to place spurred corresponding revolutions across myriad other domains, from patterns of daily life and the nature of the built environment to the law and criminal justice organizations. Highlighting key ways that cars reshaped the nation, including fundamental reconfigurations in law enforcement, this chapter first describes the dramatic impact of cars on American cities. The proliferation of traffic laws and traffic enforcement offers a case study of how policymakers and criminal justice institutions respond to changing technological and social circumstances. Beyond the problems of automobile traffic itself, cars also rapidly became involved in various types of crime. Motor vehicle theft is particularly notable as a novel form of crime that arose alongside automobility. Efforts to combat car theft shaped the history of US criminal justice, including serving as a key factor in the Federal Bureau of Investigation's growth into a large and powerful agency.

Lawmakers passed numerous statutes in response to automobile-linked crime, with multiple measures targeted specifically at car theft. Most notable among these is the National Motor Vehicle Theft Act of 1919. Commonly known as the Dyer Act, this law made it a federal crime to transport stolen vehicles across state lines. The Dyer Act and its enforcement illuminate key aspects of how automobility caused major shifts in American criminal justice, as legal authorities sought to respond to new types of offenses and patterns of offending. Subsequent pieces of federal legislation—including the Motor Vehicle Theft Law Enforcement Act of 1984, the Comprehensive Crime Control Act of 1984, and the Anti-Car Theft Act of 1992—illustrate how criminal law evolves over time. These later measures exemplify authorities' efforts to directly target various activities involved in car theft or conducive to its profitability, such as carjacking, maintaining chop shops, and manipulating car titles. Early car theft laws demonstrate governmental responses to dramatic changes in technology and society. In turn, ongoing legal responses to this issue demonstrate how criminal laws propagate and diversify over time.

MOTORING MANIA

The emergence of the United States as the world's foremost car culture began in the late nineteenth century. In 1895 entrepreneurs filed more than 500 automobile-related patents, and the periodicals *Motorcycle* and *Horseless Age* hit newsstands.[1] On Thanksgiving Day of that year, the *Chicago Times-Herald* sponsored the first official automobile race. The first sale of an American gasoline-powered car followed shortly thereafter, in February 1896.[2] Brothers Charles and Frank Duryea built the vehicle, a two-cylinder car with a half-dozen horsepower known as the Runabout. Working out of Springfield, Massachusetts, the Duryea brothers based the Runabout on the model that Frank drove to victory in that first automobile race on Thanksgiving in 1895.[3]

The Duryea brothers' sale of their first Runabout was the initial drop of what soon became a torrent. American manufacturers rapidly outpaced their European competitors, becoming the world leaders in automobile production by 1907.[4] Americans were also buying cars at an unmatched clip: In the first three decades of the twentieth century, the number of registered vehicles in the United States went from a few thousand to over 23 million.[5] According to President Warren G. Harding, by 1921 "the motor car [had] become an indispensable instrument in our political, social, and industrial life."[6]

The early twentieth century marked the onset of automobility: the use of cars to get from place to place and, in fairly short order, cars' rise to predominance among transportation technologies. However, turn-of-the-century America was not prepared for the explosive growth in car ownership and driving. Thoroughfares were flooded with scads of new drivers who generally lacked relevant training, experience, and licensing, and in many cases were only minimally familiar with cars and driving. Moreover, these neophytes found themselves operating in an environment that was poorly equipped to handle them. The designers and builders of the country's existing infrastructure had not accounted for cars. Streets and avenues intended for pedestrians, horses, and horse-drawn carriages were muddy, rutted, and often not large or capacious enough to properly accommodate motor vehicles, especially in the numbers in which they began to proliferate in the nation's cities.

Moving forward, an interdependent historical relationship developed between the construction of solid-surface roads and the widespread adoption of cars. There is something of a "chicken or egg" character to this relationship: Cars create demand for better roads, but better roads also encourage more people to buy and drive cars. Motorists were not the first constituency to advocate for better roads. In the late nineteenth century bicyclists in the Northeast pushed for road improvements.[7] So did farmers in the South; the popularity of railroads decreased traffic on rural highways and siphoned off funding for their maintenance, and railroads charged farmers handsomely to carry their freight.[8] Local politicians representing agricultural areas also wanted to improve their roads, hoping to slow the trend of their constituents moving to cities.[9]

Although the process of road improvement looked different in different places, it is clear that the advent of the automobile proved a singularly impactful influence on road building. Urban bicyclists and the rural "good roads movement" had seen some success, but the early twentieth-century boom in automobile manufacturing and sales launched a new era of street and highway construction.[10] Indeed, enabling easier driving by improving roads was the foundational objective of the American Automobile Association (AAA). Formed in 1902 in Chicago, AAA launched its long-standing lobbying campaign in its inaugural year, throwing its support behind legislation that would provide federal funds for highway improvement.[11]

The deep connections between cars and the criminal justice system manifested at this early stage of the country's commitment to the automobile. Especially in the South, governments used incarcerated people's labor as an inexpensive way to improve roads. A 1901 report from the US Department of Agriculture (USDA) described putting incarcerated people to work on road-building projects as having "passed the experimental stage [and] become a part of the accepted practice" across the South, including Alabama, Arkansas, Florida, Georgia, Kentucky, Louisiana, Mississippi, North Carolina, South Carolina, Tennessee, Texas, and Virginia.[12] This report, appearing in the *Yearbook of the Department of Agriculture* and penned by a special agent in the USDA's Office of Public Road Inquiries for Southern Division, reflects the push from agrarian interests to use incarcerated people as a captive labor force for road improvements, even before the widespread adoption of internal combustion vehicles.[13] The USDA report echoed southern politicians' fiscal arguments for using "convict labor," noting that an incarcerated person "do[es] this work without compensation and at a cost actually less, in many cases, than that of his keep in the county jail."[14] Summarizing his review of the numerous jurisdictions adopting the practice, the USDA special agent noted, "It has been . . . the general verdict from the various counties in the Southern States where convict labor is employed in road building to any considerable extent, that in both efficiency and cheapness it is decidedly superior to such free labor as is ordinarily available there for this work."[15]

Southern states' use of incarcerated people in road-building projects is particularly infamous, as both a cheap labor source and an instrument of racial control over the Black population.[16] The practice, however, was not limited to the South; automobiles' growing prevalence resulted in incarcerated people being put to work on road-building projects nationwide. In 1914 the *Proceedings of the Academy of Political Science in the City of New York* dedicated an issue to the topic of "Good Roads and Convict Labor." National Highways Association president Charles Henry Davis wrote the issue's foreword, decrying prisons that "hold men in abject slavery, in idleness worse than death. Without sun. Sometimes without light. With foul air and fouler companions."[17] Davis argued that roadwork, by comparison, promised better conditions and better outcomes for people convicted of crimes, as well as larger social benefits, particularly counteracting illiteracy by making it easier for rural children to get to school. Pressed with new demand from swelling ranks of motorists and persuaded by fiscal arguments, by the mid-1910s authorities all across the country were using incarcerated people to build roads. Beyond the early-adopting southern states, this included state and local governments in Arizona, California, Illinois, Iowa, Kansas, Massachusetts, Michigan, Minnesota, Missouri, Montana, New Jersey, New Mexico, New York, Ohio, Oklahoma, Oregon, Pennsylvania, Utah, Vermont, and Washington.[18]

The exponential growth in automobile traffic required governments to overhaul their road systems, and they often relied on people involved in the criminal justice system to do so. As authorities soon learned, the arrival of cars also necessitated attention to how all those new drivers comported themselves on the highways and byways. Particularly in the earliest years, regulation and oversight of automobile traffic was catch-as-catch-can. Police departments were not organized or equipped for traffic enforcement. At a more basic level, their jurisdictions lacked relevant laws to enforce. Thus, as the Wild West era on the Western frontier drew to a close, a new, figurative Wild West emerged on roadways across the country. Characterized by rapid technological innovation, widespread vehicular adoption, and more than a little chaos, this period birthed a novel set of conflicts, conundrums, and dangers.

Under these conditions, congestion from car traffic quickly became a considerable problem, particularly in dense cities with growing populations and burgeoning economies. In the emerging economic hub of the Midwest, for instance, Daniel Burnham and Edward H. Bennett created their celebrated 1909 Plan of Chicago with an eye toward facilitating the passage of pedestrians, horse-drawn vehicles, and streetcars.[19] However, even these forward-looking planners failed to adequately account for the looming wave of automobile adoption. Chicago's inundation with automobiles created debilitating congestion; in the mid-1920s Chicago's downtown Loop may have had the worst automobile traffic of any place in the world.[20] These issues led local authorities to largely abandon the Burnham Plan in favor of an automobile-centered approach to city planning in the 1920s.[21]

Cars' sudden ubiquity also created new conflicts on—and about—the streets themselves.[22] Before cars' proliferation, city streets were much more mixed-use spaces. They were thoroughfares for pedestrian and vehicle traffic but also spaces where children played and pushcart vendors hawked their wares.[23] Early instances of road rage manifested as clashes between pedestrians and motorists. These clashes, in turn, reflected a broader struggle about what constituted legitimate use of the street as public space. Adapting infrastructure to accommodate cars required not only physical reconstructions of streets but also social and cultural reconstructions of how people conceived of streets and their purposes.[24]

Cars clearly presented new risks to health and safety. Between 1913 and 1932 deaths from car crashes increased 500%. Twice as many Americans died from car collisions than from World War I during the year and a half the United States was formally involved in the conflict.[25] In a development particularly relevant to criminal justice considerations, cars swiftly surpassed crime as a threat to life, with several times more people dying annually from crashes than from crime within a few years of widespread automobility.[26]

The rapid accumulation of deaths and injuries precipitated considerable outcry. "Road hog," "joy rider," and "speed demon" emerged as new terms for aggressive and dangerous drivers. Before cars, walking predominated as most city-dwellers' means of transportation, and many deadly incidents involved cars striking pedestrians. Newspapers depicted automobiles as "speed-monsters" or "juggernauts" crushing everything—and everyone—in their path.[27] City governments and advocates for cracking down on dangerous drivers frequently focused on children killed by cars. In 1923, for instance, St. Louis erected an enormous downtown monument bearing the inscription, "In Memory of Child Life Sacrificed on the Altar of Haste and Recklessness."[28] Judges and juries, too, tended to favor pedestrians in legal cases involving automobile accidents.[29]

The rhetorical and legal contest over pedestrians' and cars' rightful place in the street was far from one-sided, however. Businessmen in the automobile industry and organized groups of motorists pushed back, seeking to assign pedestrians more responsibility for their own safety in roadways and to strengthen both norms and legal requirements that pedestrians cross streets only at right angles and at intersections.[30] The term *jaywalker* was crucial to streets' reinvention as places where cars reigned supreme. Building on *jay* as an epithet for "a country hayseed out of place in the city," *jaywalker* referred to a rural person unfamiliar with the "proper" way to negotiate city streets.[31] With its clear connotations of unsophistication and lower social class and status, the label proved effective. Although advocates for pedestrians resisted the term, it caught on and became a key part of redefining streets as places where cars belonged and pedestrians did not, except in limited and transitory fashion. Cities across the country proceeded to adopt ordinances to regulate pedestrians' movements on streets, with jaywalkers subject to police whistles, fines, and arrests.[32] Continuing their pattern of lobbying for car owners' interests, motorists' organizations were vocal advocates of these laws' passage and aggressive enforcement.[33]

The socially constructed idea that streets are primarily cars' domain—and that pedestrians use them at their peril—now seems natural or commonsensical to some Americans and objectionable to others. The law has largely come down in favor of prioritizing motorists among street users.[34] Laws targeting jaywalking are part of this legacy. Police have wide discretion in deciding whom to stop and charge for jaywalking violations. Today, cities across the country demonstrate stark patterns of racial inequality in jaywalking enforcement, with Black pedestrians ticketed at rates far exceeding their proportion of the population.[35] Motor vehicles strike and kill thousands of pedestrians every year; with the majority of these incidents occurring outside intersections, allegations of jaywalking continue to offer a resource for explaining—and perhaps justifying—pedestrian deaths.[36] Laws pertaining to jaywalking, however, are only one of the ways that authorities responded to the new exigencies of the automobile age.

TRAFFIC AND TRAFFIC LAW

Before cars, city dwellers relied on walking, horses, horse-drawn vehicles, and streetcars. As urban populations grew in the late nineteenth century, dense city centers experienced growing congestion, but lacked formalized traffic codes to help manage the problem. Indeed, the very ideas of "traffic" and "traffic congestion" were not things to which city governments attended until the advent of the automobile.[37] Orderliness on the streets depended primarily on "common sense" and adherence to customs, especially the "keep to the right" practice, and interpersonal exchanges constituted the primary mechanism for social control of traffic, with police sometimes arbitrating conflicts arising in thoroughfares.[38] Although informal means of regulating non-automotive traffic may have generally sufficed for large swaths of the country, they proved increasingly inadequate in the tightly packed downtowns of late nineteenth-century America.[39]

Cars' emergence exacerbated congestion problems in urban areas and created new dangers elsewhere. Early on, local governments hoped that automobile regulation based on the honor system might prove effective. They posted signs intended to cajole or shame people into driving slowly and carefully. Demonstrating this approach, a 1915 billboard in Fresno, California, implored:

MOTORISTS ATTENTION!
YOU ARE ON YOUR HONOR
FRESNO COUNTY HAS NO SPEED COPS
DRIVE SO THEY WILL NOT BE NEEDED
SPEED LIMIT 30 MILES PER HOUR—Board of Supervisors[40]

As traffic volumes swelled and deaths and injuries piled up, it became apparent that a laissez-faire approach to vehicular regulation was inadequate in the automobile age. Cars' speed was the most significant factor. People certainly could be—and were—killed by being run over by horse-drawn wagons or streetcars, but automobiles constituted a far greater danger to pedestrians and other vehicles.

Motorists were also comparatively isolated and anonymous. For drivers of fast-moving cars, streets increasingly constituted spaces for just passing through, and engagements with other street users were fleeting. Cars' physical characteristics compounded this issue. Glass and steel encased motorists, separating them from other street users in new ways, especially after closed automobiles surpassed open-air cars in popularity in the 1920s. These aspects of automobility created problems for modes of traffic regulation that relied on communication, adherence to norms, and a certain degree of interpersonal accountability. Cars insulated drivers from the social space of the street and thereby substantially liberated them from mechanisms of informal social control.

As cars wrought conflict, chaos, and carnage in American cities, the need for formal regulations became apparent. New York City led the way in establishing systematic rules to govern automobile traffic, adopting reformer William Phelps Eno's "Rules for Driving" in 1903.[41] State and local governments around the country soon followed suit, enacting a host of laws pertaining to road safety and establishing limits on how drivers could legally use cars.

However, the various state legislatures and city councils creating this new legislation faced the sorts of problems that commonly plague legal responses to new and fast-developing technologies. Cars were novel machines with rapidly growing capabilities. It was unclear how to best conceptualize how they fit in alongside pedestrians and other vehicles. Authorities in different jurisdictions— and sometimes different people and factions within jurisdictions—could not agree on what was most important to regulate, how to tailor rules to address emerging problems, or how to enforce this almost entirely new category of law. Even interventions that seem almost obligatory with the benefit of hindsight were not necessarily evident to the earliest lawmakers. Not until 1911 was the first line painted down the center of a road (in Wayne County, Michigan, home to Detroit), with other cities beginning to adopt the practice around 1915.[42] And, although "keep to the right" had long been a widespread norm, it took years for governments across the country to formally institute the rule.

These circumstances were less than ideal for motorists. Given the limited social experience with cars and lawmakers' uncertainty about how to approach their regulation, the laws themselves were often unclear, poorly worded, and confusing. This made it difficult for even dutiful drivers to ensure that they maintained compliance behind the wheel. Interjurisdictional inconsistencies in traffic laws further complicated things. With cities, counties, and states creating laws through idiosyncratic processes and in response to locally specific circumstances, the rules of the road varied considerably from place to place. Early motorists encountered differences in how fast they could drive at different times and in different conditions; differences in how to legally overtake other vehicles (if at all); and differences in how laws pertaining to cars would be enforced (if it all). Even if they made sincere efforts to drive legally, it was easy for drivers to find themselves on the wrong side of the law. There was some irony to this situation. Automobility made it far easier for people to spread out geographically. In cars they could visit other cities and states much more readily than they could using horses, trains, or boats. At the same time, however, discrepancies in traffic laws tinged these interjurisdictional adventures with confusion and rendered them potentially legally perilous.

With experiments in motorist self-regulation failing, governments needed ways to implement their new traffic laws. Signs and signals communicating rules to drivers were part of the formula. "Silent policemen"—posts at the center of intersections to deter corner-cutting left turns—were one early innovation, first introduced in New York in 1904.[43] Traffic lights adapted from railroad signaling devices followed a decade later, pioneered in Cleveland in 1914 and adopted elsewhere subsequently.[44]

The lion's share of traffic enforcement responsibility fell to law enforcement agencies. Cities seeking to (re)instate order on their streets began using police for traffic regulation around 1910.[45] In these early efforts authorities largely sought to reestablish the pre-car status quo. They blamed urban streets' bedlam on automobiles' speed and emphasized protecting pedestrians through curtailing motorists' pace. With many collisions occurring at intersections, city governments that were dedicating policing resources to traffic problems focused first on assigning "cornermen" to manage traffic at crossroads.[46] These allocations of police resources to traffic problems were just one early development; as cars continued to proliferate, their implications for crime and criminal justice did as well.

CARS AND CRIME

In addition to precipitating new traffic responsibilities for police departments, automobiles had a host of other consequences for law enforcement. Cars' widespread adoption had profound implications for criminal offending, transforming the types of issues criminal justice authorities faced and necessitating reconfigurations of the law enforcement enterprise.

First, cars quickly became popular tools in the commission of numerous forms of crime, including burglary, robbery, kidnapping, and the transportation of stolen and illicit goods. Automobility collapsed physical space, creating more opportunities for crimes across larger geographic areas. For crimes such as burglary, automobiles made it easier to abscond with more property, more quickly. Indeed, "getaway cars" made it easier for lawbreakers of all sorts to avoid apprehension, frustrating law enforcement agencies. For instance, in 1922 police in Chicago complained that they could not keep up with cars spiriting suspects away at up to 60 miles per hour.[47] Recognizing such issues, the chief justice of the United States, former president William Howard Taft, wrote in a 1923 letter that "the automobile is the greatest instrument for promoting immunity of crimes of violence that I know of in the history of civilization."[48] Another contemporary observer noted that "the motor vehicle has ushered in a new era of crime and police problems."[49]

Recognizing cars' destructive capabilities, people also began using them as weapons. In Philadelphia, for instance, in 1925 police arrested nearly 9,000 people for using vehicles as an instrument of assault and battery.[50] Like many aspects of the relationship between cars and the criminal justice system, this weaponization has both persisted and evolved over time, and cars as implements of violent force continue to feature in high-profile incidents. For example, in 2017 James Alex Fields Jr. used a Dodge Challenger to ram a crowd of counter-protestors at the Charlottesville, Virginia, Unite the Right rally, killing Heather Heyer and injuring numerous others. Beyond Charlottesville, vehicle rammings have become more prevalent as terrorism tactics in the United States and abroad.[51] Police shootings of drivers also often involve allegations that motorists used or attempted to use vehicles as rams against officers, as in the 2021 shooting of Andrew Brown Jr. in North Carolina.[52]

Automobiles also caused lawmakers to create entirely new categories of criminal offending. Jaywalking, discussed earlier, is an example of a comparatively minor type of infraction resulting from cars' proliferation. Laws pertaining to vehicular homicide—discussed at length in Chapter 8—arose later in response to growing concerns about drunk driving fatalities. From the earliest days of automobility, however, motor vehicle theft constituted a particularly notable form of car-dependent crime.

More or less as soon as people started buying cars in significant numbers, people started stealing them. *Horseless Age* first reported on automobile theft in 1902.[53] Cars' attractiveness for theft was plain. The new machines were both valuable and self-transporting, making them lucrative targets that functionally abetted their own taking. And, especially early on, they were easy to steal. Compared to competing steam-powered and electric vehicles, the first internal combustion cars featured minimal security devices or none at all.[54]

Early car thieves demonstrated particular interest in getting their hands on costlier high-end models with greater resale value.[55] However, the nature of automobile theft as a category of criminal offending changed substantially with the rise of standardization in automobile manufacturing and the corresponding rise of mass production. Standardization and the assembly line system offered enormous benefits to automobile manufacturers, allowing them to build cars faster, cheaper, and with a less-skilled workforce than was needed in the previous craft production model.

Mass production also had specific implications for car theft. As most famously implemented by Henry Ford and the Ford Motor Company, mass-produced cars engendered substantial "democratization" of automobile ownership because of their comparative affordability, opening purchase opportunities for less wealthy people. In turn, more cars on the road translated into more opportunities for theft. Ford's limited security measures did not pose major challenges for would-be thieves. Early Model Ts had just two types of brass keys to operate their battery-magneto switches. Beginning in 1919, Ford offered a lockable electric starter as an option; however, these starters used only twenty-four different key patterns, and starter plates and their matching keys were stamped with the same code, making it short work for an enterprising thief with a ring of keys to identify the correct one.[56]

In general, standardized cars were easier to steal than their craft-produced predecessors. If you could steal one Ford, you could steal any Ford. The same soon became true of other makers adopting mass manufacturing. Mass-produced cars were also notable for their uniformity; in the case of Fords, this uniformity extended all the way to paint jobs, with Henry Ford quipping that "any customer can have a car painted any colour that he wants so long as it is black."[57] Particularly given the era's poor record keeping and lack of standardized vehicle identifiers, this uniformity made it harder for authorities to spot stolen cars and easier for thieves to abscond with them.

Mass-produced cars were also easier to sell, either whole or in parts. The mass market for automobiles entailed greater demand for used cars, both domestically and internationally, which ill-gotten vehicles could help meet. Further, with interchangeable parts, thieves could more readily disassemble stolen cars and sell them off piece by piece; this precipitated the "chop shops" and "car theft rings"[58] of the mass production age. Capitalizing on mass-produced cars' relative indistinguishability and their parts' interchangeability, groups of thieves who stole multiple cars of the same model could even swap out various parts to produce new "Frankenstein" cars ready for resale.

For all these reasons, car thieves shifted their focus from expensive models to popular, widely owned cars. They could learn how to steal these models quickly and easily. They knew they could readily sell them and their parts, with so many other cars on the road requiring the same components. Moreover, they knew that it would be harder for authorities to catch them engaging in these kinds of activities than it would be to apprehend them driving off in more recognizable cars or trying to sell higher-end specialized vehicles or parts.

With automobiles easy and profitable to steal and stolen cars hard to find, auto theft rates exploded. By 1920 it was estimated that 10% of all cars manufactured got stolen. By 1925 between 200,000 and 250,000 cars were stolen annually in the United States.[59] The wide availability of mass-produced cars also made it common to combine auto theft with other types of crimes; for instance, one could commit a conventional robbery and then steal the victim's car to both assist the getaway and increase the spoils.

Law enforcement's initial response to the issue of automobile theft was unsystematic and generally ineffective. In substantial part the impediments to successful government interventions in this area reflected the broader limitations that characterized police departments of the time. US law enforcement is notably decentralized, with powers and responsibilities diffused across myriad

municipal, county, state, and federal agencies. This situation created new difficulties when cars came on the scene, as law enforcement agencies confronted
far more cases involving activities that crossed jurisdictional boundaries and
thus required interjurisdictional coordination to resolve effectively. Automobile theft was a prime example, with cars stolen in one jurisdiction swiftly finding their way elsewhere. (As discussed later in the book, subsequent decades
have seen substantial moves toward interjurisdictional communication and
collaboration. However, US law enforcement, like other aspects of the American government and legal system, remains notably decentralized compared
with its counterparts in Europe and elsewhere.)[60]

Given police agencies' relative isolation from each other, they often failed
to transmit theft reports to other areas, curtailing the likelihood that thieves
would be apprehended and stolen vehicles recovered. And interjurisdictional
communication—or lack thereof—was not the only issue. Because of poor
record keeping, many thefts were not documented at all. When they were, records were often missing key information that could help identify stolen cars
among seas of nearly identical mass-produced vehicles, such as serial numbers
or unique characteristics.[61]

Weaknesses in law enforcement responses to automobile theft helped drive
significant developments in US criminal justice, including the August Vollmer-
led push for better police record keeping, discussed in Chapter 2, as well as a
series of impactful statutes and regulations. However, notable early efforts to
counteract car theft came from private sector actors outside formal law enforcement, namely, insurance companies. Insurers focused particularly on facilitating stolen vehicles' recovery. To this end, in 1912 eleven companies formed
the Automobile Protective and Information Bureau.[62] This group created and
distributed notices about stolen cars containing information that would allow
local police departments to identify and recover them; these "wanted posters"
included images of cars cribbed from advertisements and listed their color and
details about their equipment.[63]

These initiatives relied on local police using the distributed information
and making meaningful efforts at recovery. To help incentivize such efforts, the
Automobile Protective and Information Bureau offered rewards of $25 to $100
for recoveries of stolen cars.[64] These rewards seemed to help. In New York City
a 1914 report from the district attorney's office indicated that some detectives
assigned to auto theft had done nothing to pursue car thieves before insurers
began offering rewards. Once the rewards were on the table, increased enforcement activity led to police finding cars, making arrests, and in short order collecting $10,000–$15,000 in rewards.[65]

Demonstrating an interest in reducing their reliance on police departments' active investment in fighting car theft, in 1912 the National Automobile Underwriters Conference established the National Automobile Theft Bureau (NATB). Through this organization the car insurance industry created its own private police force, as well as an information clearinghouse designed to compensate for perceived shortcomings in law enforcement agencies' collection and distribution of the records needed to recover stolen vehicles.[66] At a time when police agencies were still getting up to speed on the burgeoning phenomenon of automobile theft, NATB staff possessed special expertise on car thieves' modi operandi and best practices for identifying ill-gotten vehicles. They put this expertise to work in efforts to standardize auto theft records and train police in the investigation and resolution of these offenses, as well as encouraging police agencies to create their own specialized car theft units.[67] As this description suggests, these efforts significantly blurred the boundary between the public and private sectors, creating questions about how and where we should delineate between the interests of the business community and the interests of the government. As noted in later chapters, these sorts of questions have recurred throughout US criminal justice in the twentieth and twenty-first centuries.

Government actors also undertook their own initiatives to understand and mitigate the new phenomenon of auto theft. Working with their partners in the insurance industry, criminal justice authorities identified different categories of car thieves: "joyriders," primarily young people, and "professionals," who often had experience or expertise in building and repairing cars.[68] Basic security devices such as locks were often sufficient to deter teenage joyriders, but more determined and sophisticated professionals, often working in groups, necessitated more robust law enforcement interventions.[69]

Facing high rates of auto theft and difficulties catching car thieves, state governments endeavored to enact legal changes to alleviate the problem. These changes included title laws requiring owners to have car titles on record, more systematic license and registration laws, and beefed-up criminal justice record keeping, which enabled better, more reliable statistics on automobile theft in their states and better records on other types of crimes.[70]

State officials also urged the federal government to get involved. The decentralized and siloed character of US criminal justice impeded interagency systemization and coordination, and beleaguered officials looked to federal authorities to help respond to crimes that increasingly crossed the boundaries of municipal, county, and state jurisdictions.[71] These problems were particularly acute in the case of motor vehicle theft, which was almost inherently interjurisdictional. Cars were easy to move between states, especially in the densely populated Northeast, and without federally coordinated criminal justice responses, taking a stolen car from one state to another impeded law enforcement efforts significantly.

The most notable statutory response from the federal government came with the 1919 passage of the National Motor Vehicle Theft Act. Also known as the Dyer Act for its sponsor in the Senate, this law made interstate transportation of stolen vehicles a federal crime.[72] Under the new law, those who moved vehicles across state lines faced significant penalties: up to ten years imprisonment plus fines. Recognizing the difficulties that law enforcement agencies faced when thieves transported stolen vehicles outside the jurisdictions where thefts occurred, the Dyer Act led to extensive and consequential federal law enforcement activity related to automobile theft. In so doing, it also constituted a landmark development in the federal government's involvement in law enforcement activities in general. As discussed further in Chapter 7, this role would continue to grow and evolve over the twentieth century and into the twenty-first.

The Bureau of Investigation (BOI) took the lead as the chief enforcement agency for the new law. (This was the original name of the Federal Bureau of Investigation [FBI]; the agency was known as BOI from 1908 to 1932, the United States Bureau of Investigation from 1932 to 1933, and the Division of Investigation from 1933 to 1935, until settling in as the FBI.) Enforcement of the Dyer Act was slow at first, but over time prosecutions grew. "In 1920, Bureau agents investigated 1,480 car thefts, leading to 1,056 arrests. By 1940, FBI investigations resulted in 4,153 stolen vehicle recoveries and 2,340 convictions."[73] Altogether, "in the first two decades of the Dyer Act, the FBI recovered more than 56,000 motor vehicles valued at $32 million."[74]

Beginning in the 1920s, the BOI realized that the Dyer Act would become a key weapon in the arsenal of federal law enforcement. The law gave federal authorities a crucial new jurisdictional hook, providing them with jurisdiction in cases that had previously been the sole province of state and local law enforcement agencies. As cars became ubiquitous, so did criminal cases involving cars and those spreading into expanded geographic territories. This geographic diffusion, in turn, continued to engender federal activities and helped the FBI develop into a large and powerful agency.[75]

In addition to advancing systematized nationwide law enforcement strategies, the Dyer Act proved useful in building criminal cases involving multiple offenses. Many of the people whom bureau agents arrested were also alleged to be involved in other crimes (such as burglary, robbery, and bootlegging) or already had outstanding warrants in other cases. Federal actions to break up auto theft rings also tied into broader efforts to counteract organized crime, and federal prosecutors used Dyer Act violations as a strategy for charging, convicting, and incarcerating people they believed to be participants in bigger criminal enterprises.[76]

In the 1930s the Dyer Act gave the bureau a legal basis to join efforts to arrest infamous outlaws like Pretty Boy Floyd, Bonnie and Clyde, and John Dillinger; because these investigations involved allegations of crossing state lines with stolen cars, the Dyer Act gave federal authorities jurisdiction to involve themselves in the cases. Take Dillinger's case: Facing trial for the murder of an East Chicago police officer during a bank robbery shootout, Dillinger was jailed in Crown Point, Indiana. On March 3, 1934, he effected a brazen escape. Producing a pistol, he secured the guards' keys—as well as two machine guns—and made his way to the jail's garage. (Contemporaneous reports described Dillinger's weapon as a wooden pistol he had carved days earlier, reportedly "to the amusement" of jail staff, blackened with shoe polish; some historians contend that someone smuggled a real gun to him.) Upon reaching the garage, Dillinger reportedly asked the attendant, "Hey lad, what's the fastest car in the joint?" When the attendant indicated the sheriff's Ford, Dillinger commandeered it, compelling a deputy taken hostage to drive him, another escapee, and the garage attendant, now a hostage as well, away from the jail.[77]

Dillinger's choice of destination proved pivotal. He directed the deputy to drive west, toward Chicago. By crossing the state line into Illinois in the stolen car, Dillinger violated the Dyer Act and thus became for the first time the subject of federal investigation and pursuit. Within five months bureau agents tracked him down and killed him outside Chicago's Biograph Theater.[78]

The Dyer Act also led directly to the downfall of Bonnie and Clyde, who faced similar allegations of stealing getaway cars to facilitate other forms of violent and property crime. Indeed, a 1934 letter to the Ford Motor Company seemed to attest this very thing.[79]

Tulsa, Okla
10th April [1934]
Mr. Henry Ford
Detroit Mich.

Dear Sir: -
While I still have got breath in my lungs I will tell you what a dandy car you make. I have drove Fords exclusively when I could get away with one. For sustained speed and freedom from trouble the Ford has got ever other car skinned and even if my business hasn't been strickly legal it don't hurt enything to tell you what a fine car you got in the V8–
Yours truly
Clyde Champion Barrow

Purportedly from outlaw Clyde Barrow of Bonnie and Clyde notoriety, this missive sang the praises of the V8 Ford as a getaway car. Although there is some debate regarding the letter's authenticity, sending it would have been in character for the self-promoting Barrow. The sentiments also fit with the couple's documented preferences in purloined transportation; in the early 1930s bureau investigators tracked Bonnie Parker and Clyde Barrow across the country through their stolen Fords. This investigation resulted in a federal warrant for the pair's arrest for violations of the Dyer Act. The subsequent manhunt culminated on May 23, 1934, just a few weeks after the letter was sent from Tulsa, when a posse of law enforcement officers gunned down Parker and Barrow in Louisiana.[80] Naturally, they were driving a V8 Ford.

Alongside joining high-profile manhunts under the auspices of the Dyer Act, the bureau was also developing scientific and technical tools to aid in curbing car thefts. The law enforcement resources that the bureau created in this early period would prove essential assets to the agency's central role in building federal coordination in criminal justice. In 1924 the bureau founded the National Division of Identification and Information, including a fingerprint database, establishing a new centralized repository for cataloging information about individuals who had attracted law enforcement attention. In 1930 they began keeping systematic statistical records on crime, a forerunner to the Uniform Crime Reports (which include auto theft as an "index crime").[81] And, in 1932 the FBI Laboratory was created. Again evincing cars' influence on these major developments in criminal justice, two of the lab's first collections were samples of automobile paint and tire treads to use in identifying cars involved in criminal activity.[82]

To fully systematize efforts to track stolen cars, authorities needed a single standardized identifier linked to each vehicle. Vehicle identification numbers (VINs) emerged to fill this niche. VINs were introduced in the United States in 1954.[83] But, in their incipient form they were not organized according to any common standard, meaning that different manufacturers used different formats, if they used VINs at all.[84] The federal government pushed for greater standardization of VINs with Federal Motor Vehicle Safety Standard 115. Taking effect at the beginning of 1969, this standard mandated that all road-going motor vehicles have VINs "sunk or embossed" in a visible location behind the windshield's left side.[85] Although now mandatory, VINs were still not standardized. The VIN hodgepodge would persist until 1981, when the National Highway Traffic Safety Administration (NHTSA) standardized the format, requiring that all on-road vehicles sold contain a 17-character VIN, excluding the letters O, I, and Q to avoid confusion with the numerals 0, 1, and 9.[86]

In subsequent years the federal government remained active in efforts to counteract car theft. The Motor Vehicle Theft Law Enforcement Act of 1984 aimed to reduce theft rates and facilitate the tracing and recovery of stolen vehicles and parts.[87] The legislation reflected Congress's response to perceptions that car theft was growing increasingly professionalized. The NHTSA implemented the 1984 act by issuing the Federal Motor Vehicle Theft Prevention Standard, which required manufacturers of cars the agency designated as "high-theft" to include VINs on engines, transmissions, and twelve major body parts. This measure targeted professional chop shops, which broke stolen cars down into parts for resale. Without inscribed VINs, authorities had no way to track components after they had been separated from stolen cars. The 1984 act made it a crime to tamper with VINs and empowered authorities to seize and forfeit cars and car parts on which VINs had been modified or removed.[88] It also authorized US Customs to require that exporters of used motor vehicles submit proof of ownership containing the VIN before exportation.[89] The Motor Vehicle Law Enforcement Act also provided new leverage for federal prosecutors by applying federal racketeering law (namely, the Racketeer Influenced and Corrupt Organizations [RICO] Act of 1970) to illegal trade in stolen cars and parts.[90] RICO prosecutions allow authorities to obtain harsher sentences than would otherwise generally be available.

Aiming to impede sales of stolen cars through legitimate venues, the Comprehensive Crime Control Act of 1984 criminalized counterfeiting or forging car titles.[91] Several years later, the Anti-Car Theft Act of 1992 criminalized both carjacking and running a chop shop. This law also bolstered vehicular record keeping and interstate information sharing. Further, it imposed new obligations on state departments of motor vehicles and automotive businesses to look up VINs before completing different types of transactions.[92]

Despite these numerous interventions, motor vehicle theft remains a significant problem for the country's criminal justice authorities. In 2018 the FBI recorded nearly three-quarters of a million auto thefts in the United States, representing total losses of more than $6 billion.[93] The rise of motor vehicle theft and evolving multifaceted attempts to control it prominently exemplify cars' dramatic impact on crime and, correspondingly, on criminal justice. Auto theft, however, is just one example. Altogether, the emergence and rapid proliferation of cars is perhaps the best example in US history of the pressures and problems that lawmakers, law enforcement, and citizens alike face when adapting to major changes in technology and society.

THE TRANSPORTATION TRANSFORMATION

In 1974 renowned sociologist and criminologist Donald Cressey argued "that three inter-related conditions are among the most significant events in the history of organized police. These are the arrival of the automobile and its affluent drivers, the correlated introduction of new methods for control of motorists, and assignment of the enforcement authority to police departments."[94] Cars' widespread adoption created unprecedented changes. In turn, governments faced new questions about how to exercise their police powers in their changed circumstances. (In US constitutional law the "police power" does not refer narrowly to law enforcement authority but broadly to the state's authority to create and enforce rules to protect the public's health, safety, and general welfare.)[95]

The country's experiences in the early twentieth century and beyond demonstrate adaptations in criminal justice policies and practices in response to technological and social change. Things set in motion early on—cooperation between the business community and legal authorities, an expanded role for the federal government, and many other examples discussed later—set the tone for the criminal justice system's emergence in its modern form. As the car's centrality to daily life and economic activity continued to grow, the criminal law and the agencies that enforce it evolved alongside. As the next chapter explains, automobiles precipitated numerous changes to criminal justice organizations and their policies and practices. These changes reflect authorities' responses to the new challenges of a modernizing and motorizing society. Changes to criminal justice, however, are not just responsive; they also affect the broader social world, feeding into the ongoing dynamic relationship between our predominant mode of transportation and our methods of policing, prosecution, and punishment.

TWO

Calling All Cars

Police Modernization and Communication

The early twentieth century was a pivotal period in the modernization and motorization of both US society and US police departments. Two figures in particular help illuminate how criminal justice organizations developed in this era. The first, August Vollmer, was a pioneering police administrator who championed reshaping police departments to be rational, efficient agencies focused on the goal of crime control. A primary point of emphasis for Vollmer was motorizing police forces to work in a rapidly motorizing world. The second key figure is the German sociologist Max Weber. Weber, a penetrating and prescient analyst of human organization, detailed bureaucracies' crucial role in modernizing and rationalizing societies. Vollmer's applied interventions and points of emphasis coincide remarkably with Weber's abstracted theorizing. Modernized, motorized society presented a host of new challenges for criminal justice organizations. Vollmer's priorities for reform were the blueprint for remaking police departments across the country in response to the emerging exigencies of the early twentieth century. And, as the close correspondence with Weber's ideas indicates, Vollmer's vision for modernized, motorized police departments exemplifies many of the key features of bureaucratization and rationalization as broader phenomena.

The onset of automobility held key implications for the historical development of US police organizations. Of the multifarious ways that cars affected law enforcement, one of the most profound was the emergence of traffic duty. The assignment of traffic enforcement to police departments helped those organizations develop into the generalist agencies we recognize today, with broad

jurisdiction to handle a range of different forms of lawbreaking and other problems. Cars were also centerpieces of the technological developments that characterized major changes to police departments in this period. This included
laying the foundations of the patrol car and driver themselves as "the basic
police technology."[1] When combined with wireless communication via radio
technology, patrol cars enabled the rapid response models and systematic policing strategies that characterize contemporary US police departments.

MODERNIZED POLICE DEPARTMENTS
FOR A MOTORIZED SOCIETY

American society industrialized and urbanized dramatically in the late nineteenth century. Between 1870 and 1900 the populations of the country's ten
biggest cities more than doubled.[2] Civilian police agencies had operated in
US cities since the mid-1800s but "were notoriously inefficient, powerless, and
often corrupt."[3] These underdeveloped and poorly organized departments focused primarily on dealing with public order issues and were ill equipped to
confront serious crime. Automobiles' arrival added to the mix a passel of new
public safety concerns and implications for criminal offending.

These circumstances engendered a push for major changes to the country's
police departments. Early twentieth-century reforms birthed the modernized police departments we recognize today. These modern departments are
characterized fundamentally by a primary focus on crime control, as well as
professionalized officers, refined bureaucratic structures, comparatively sophisticated methods, and paramilitarization.[4]

The standard-bearer of police modernization and professionalization was
August Vollmer, who took command of the Berkeley, California, police force in
1905. Vollmer has garnered the title "father of American policing" in recognition of the major changes he brought to policing in Berkeley and of his reforms'
pronounced influence on police agencies across the country.[5] At the core of all
these reforms was Vollmer's fundamental emphasis on making the police a rational, efficient enterprise focused on the objective of controlling crime. Upon
taking the reins in Berkeley, one of Vollmer's first moves was a clear symbol
of the organization and discipline he intended to bring to his police force: He
obtained funding to buy his deputies uniforms and mandated wearing them.[6]
Today, of course, police uniforms are ubiquitous, and the practice may seem
commonsensical. However, the introduction of uniforms for metropolitan
police forces was controversial.[7] Americans scorned symbols of monarchic and
autocratic power; when uniforms started popping up in eastern cities in the
mid-1800s, the new "bluecoats" evoked the "redcoats" whom the country had

fought for independence less than a century earlier. For their part, some officers saw uniforms as gaudy or insufficiently masculine. From a more critical perspective, the adoption of military-style uniforms embodied the influence of the American military's expanding imperial activities.[8] Along with contemporaneous changes to police organizations and operations, uniforms' symbolism presaged police militarization as a phenomenon of growing consequence and controversy throughout the twentieth century and into the twenty-first.

Vollmer also had clear ideas about whom he wanted in his new uniforms. He pushed a much more selective process of officer recruitment than had conventionally been the case in US policing, seeking out smart and capable candidates with college educations. He aspired to raise the police to the same social status as "teachers, doctors, lawyers and engineers"; to make the job more attractive, prestigious, and competitive, he made many of his officers full-time employees, increased their salaries, and offered pensions.[9]

Beyond selecting more qualified and educated candidates, Vollmer broke new ground by having the department itself train the officers. In Berkeley he established the country's first police academy and encouraged extensive training in police work as a science.[10] Vollmer's vision of a scientifically grounded and methodical approach to law enforcement involved first building on principles of established social and physical sciences and then developing new concepts and techniques specific to "police science."[11] Vollmer was an influential early advocate of using laboratories to analyze evidence, and his department pioneered such law enforcement technologies as the polygraph.[12] (Here, too, Vollmer's legacy is complicated, with aspects of the police science he championed garnering criticism as unreliable, invalid, or pseudoscientific. In 1998, for instance, the US Supreme Court held that despite a general "aura of infallibility" surrounding lie detector tests, "there is simply no consensus that polygraph evidence is reliable," and polygraph results are typically inadmissible in court.)[13]

Aligning with his emphasis on systematizing and rationalizing law enforcement, Vollmer was also a staunch advocate of improving record keeping, which to that point had been generally inconsistent or nonexistent in police departments.[14] As discussed in Chapter 1, robust records were especially important for investigating emerging twentieth-century forms of crime, such as automobile theft, which required authorities to have documentation of registrations, serial numbers, and other pieces of information that could be used to locate and recover stolen vehicles. The new offices, resources, and responsibilities of Vollmer's modernized police agency required increased organizational capacities. To meet this demand, Vollmer stressed the importance of bureaucratization, with a developed division of labor, specialized officeholders, and a clear chain of command. In Vollmer's bureaucratized police department, this arrangement entailed military-style ranks and hierarchies.

In both the staffing and the operation of the police department, Vollmer stressed the importance of independence and apoliticism. It was crucial, he argued, that officers not be hired or assigned to leadership positions as political favors or patronage to particular communities or interest groups. Similarly, he emphasized that police organizations needed to operate independent of political agendas or direct pressure from political figures. Law enforcement, he argued, should be a largely self-contained enterprise, motivated by a detached analysis of what would most effectively control crime, not the vicissitudes of political fortune or the whims of powerful people. Like many of Vollmer's reforms, these may seem like obvious or even essential priorities for law enforcement agencies. However, before the professionalization and modernization that Vollmer spurred, many police departments awarded jobs to people based on their connections and operated in large part as functionaries of local political elites.[15]

VOLLMER AND WEBER

Vollmer's reforms for policing track closely with key ideas advanced by the German sociologist Max Weber about the development of bureaucracy and bureaucracy's role in advancing rationalization in human affairs. Pioneering the formal study of bureaucracy and bureaucratization was one of Weber's many germinal contributions to social science. Chapter 11 of Weber's magnum opus *Economy and Society*, which was published shortly after his 1920 death, is dedicated to the topic. Weber broke new ground in identifying and analyzing the key characteristics of bureaucratic organizations, and he saw bureaucracies as the linchpin of the societal rationalization that is arguably the primary theme of his entire oeuvre. He should not be taken as an uncritical champion of bureaucratic organizations, however. Weber recognized the form's potential to reduce "every worker to a cog in this [bureaucratic] machine and, seeing himself in this light, he will merely ask how to transform himself from a little into a somewhat bigger cog, . . . an attitude you find . . . increasingly among our civil servants."[16] As Weber famously argued in *The Protestant Ethic and the Spirit of Capitalism*, the advancing rationalization of society threatens to surround the individual in an "iron cage," according to first translator Talcott Parsons, or a "shell as hard as steel," in a more literal translation of the original German.[17] For Weber, bureaucracies constituted both the setting and the mechanism of rationalization. Recognizing their potency for facilitating outcome-oriented, depersonalized action, his pathbreaking analysis of bureaucracies highlighted both their centrality to modern, rationalized Western societies and their potential to curtail autonomy, limit individuality, and stifle creativity.

Despite his reservations about some of the implications of bureaucratization, Weber's account of bureaucracies' ideal-typical characteristics demonstrate how the form engenders efficiency and effectiveness in organizational action.[18] In turn, the parallels between Weber's breakdown of bureaucracies and Vollmer's agenda indicate a noteworthy alignment between the German sociologist's abstracted analysis of what makes bureaucracies so good at what they do and the German American bureaucratic leader's vision of how to build a rational, legitimate police department suited to the mission of contemporary crime control.

In Weber's theory of bureaucracy, as in Vollmer's approach to reforming the Berkeley police, clear hierarchies are essential. Leaders' role is to direct the organization and to distribute tasks and responsibilities to subordinate officeholders as official duties. As emphasized in Vollmer's positions on selectivity and training, appointments in Weber's ideal-typical bureaucracy are based on qualifications. Hires for entry-level roles are based on credentials and competencies, and higher-ranking roles in the bureaucracy are awarded based on skills, qualifications, and experience. Here again, the connections to Vollmer's reform agenda are clear; in Weber's archetypical bureaucracy, as in Vollmer's police department, jobs—especially leadership positions—are not awarded through political patronage or nepotism. (Interestingly, the word *nepotism* itself is derived from a practice associated with the Catholic Church, operating on the basis of what Weber would categorize as "traditional authority" rather than the "legal-rational authority" that characterizes rationalized and bureaucratized society. Now used to refer generally to favorable treatment toward relatives, the word *nepotism* comes from the Italian *nepotismo*, from *nepote*, meaning "nephew." In 1667 an Italian published a book detailing popes' preferential treatment of their nephews. [Given their vows of celibacy, popes did not—officially—have the sons who would otherwise typically enjoy such spoils.] *Nepotism* subsequently emerged in English usage, referring to special favor shown to any family member.)[19]

Weber's theory of bureaucracy offers no room for appointments based on personal relationships or political considerations. Instead, everything is rule driven, disconnected from officeholders' individual preferences and predilections. Weber's bureaucracy is decidedly hierarchical, with superiors holding power to direct subordinates. Crucially, however, the distribution of responsibilities to organizational subordinates is not driven by bureaucratic leaders' whims or caprice. Rather, it is essential that organizational activities are driven by sets of rules and regulations, which are at least relatively transparent. These

rules can be changed, of course, but they are changed through formal procedures, which are themselves rule driven, not by dictate or fiat from bureaucratic superiors.

This type of orientation is also pivotal to the apoliticism that Vollmer wanted
from his police department and the model that would influence police departments nationwide. Vollmer stressed that police priorities, strategies, and practices should not change wholesale as a result of shifts in the political winds but
should instead be based on solid principles of good police work and the "science" of effective crime control. Weber's account of rule-driven bureaucratic
action also echoes in Vollmer's emphasis on scientific methods. Vollmer strove
to develop a set of best practices for how police departments should operate effectively and efficiently, foundational rules to guide both big-picture strategies
and day-to-day operations.

Weber's ideal-typical bureaucrats are dispassionate in the execution of their
official duties. They make decisions based not on emotion or (again, in principle) on what they believe to be most advantageous for them personally, but
based on objective analysis and on what best serves the interests and advances
the goals of the organization. The bureaucracy's shared rules and principles
should constitute the basis for officeholders' action, which should proceed
without bias against or preference toward any particular person, group, or
agenda outside the bureaucracy's stated purpose and function. This type of
orientation figures prominently in what Vollmer wanted from his professionalized police force, whom he thought should be united around the shared goal of
crime control and shared rules of police science.

Weber and Vollmer were also on the same page about record keeping. For
Weber, bureaucratic action should fundamentally revolve around "the files,"
the written rules that govern the bureaucracy's operation and the records of
bureaucratic action. Through documenting organizational action and recording work products, the files reduce duplication of effort, promote efficiency, and
inform future action. For Vollmer, record keeping helped bring the police department into the modern age, facilitating a systematic approach and enhanc-
ing its effectiveness as an enterprise dedicated to the mission of controlling
crime.

For Weber, all these features were essential to the bureaucracies that he
saw as key mechanisms of the rationalization of society. As Weber observed
Western societies—right at the time Vollmer took over the Berkeley Police
Department, in the early twentieth century—he identified a move away from
traditional models of authority and social organization and toward elevating
efficiency and dispassionate logic as the organizing principles for basically all
of social life. Weber saw societies leaving behind traditional structures of au-

thority, especially religion, and instead focusing on the kind of dispassionate, allegedly value-free forms of social organization that would reach their zenith in the model of bureaucracy he developed. For his part, Vollmer advanced a vision of how to modernize and professionalize police organizations that closely paralleled Weber's points about what makes bureaucracies such effective vehicles of goal-directed action.

One of the main places that Weber identified growing rationalization was in the world of commerce and business. Here, he saw the profit motive becoming something like a universal value and bureaucratic business organizations helping to rationally maximize profits. This too connects to Vollmer's approach to police reform. Vollmer explicitly compared the police department to a business, saying that the "modern police department is an up-to-date business institution conducting its affairs on a solid business basis, and to the fullest extent utilizing principles of the several sciences and gradually developing principles peculiar to police service."[20] This statement captures the spirit of rationalization that runs through both Weber's social scientific analysis and Vollmer's applied work as a bureaucratic entrepreneur.

GENERALIZATION VS. SPECIALIZATION IN THE MAKING OF MODERN POLICE DEPARTMENTS

As police departments were modernizing early in the twentieth century, they faced a pivotal question: To what extent should they be specialists as opposed to generalists? The specialist pathway would involve a predominant or exclusive focus on the violent crimes and property crimes typically considered to constitute antisocial conduct and to be the most serious. On the other hand, the generalist approach would entail focusing more broadly on a wider array of undesirable and proscribed behaviors, including things more associated with personal vices or immorality. In the language of the philosophy of law, the specialist approach reduces to the decision to concentrate efforts on offenses deemed *mala in se*: things considered to be wrong in and of themselves, such as violent crimes. Under the generalist approach, departments would cast a wider policing net to also include *mala prohibita* offenses: behaviors that are wrong because they are prohibited and prohibited because of the presumed harm they inflict on the collective welfare, the good of society, or the interests of the state.

The early twentieth century was a key period for considering this question, not just because of the Vollmer-led movement to modernize police departments but also because of bigger changes to the social and legal landscape. The law is constantly evolving, and the first decades of the 1900s included the enactment of many new laws that called for enforcement, either by police departments or, potentially, different government agencies. A leading example was the explosion in automobile traffic and the passage of a slew of traffic laws to regulate it. This period also saw the proliferation of laws targeting prostitution (notably including the Mann Act of 1910, discussed further in Chapter 7) and laws pertaining to drugs and alcohol (such as the Harrison Narcotics Tax Act of 1914 and the Volstead Act of 1919, discussed further in Chapter 3). Thus, at this pivotal historical juncture in the development of criminal justice, legal authorities faced the question of whether such things as traffic, prostitution, gambling, and intoxicating substances should be the province of police departments or of other, perhaps new, types of government agencies.

To be sure, police officers under Vollmer's command in both Berkeley and Los Angeles engaged in vice and traffic enforcement.[21] Vollmer, however, had reservations about police departments as generalists. He argued that "the suppression of vice" is closer to the appropriate purview of "sanitary and health inspections" than to the domain of law enforcement.[22] Regarding alcohol abuse, Vollmer commented, "I've never known a single case of alcoholism that was cured or curbed by a jail sentence. We spend huge sums of money to keep drunks locked up in our jails. We'd be wiser if we poured that money into research on the basic causes of alcoholism, so we could learn to prevent it, or at least to cure it."[23]

To Vollmer's mind, drugs, prostitution, gambling, and the like were fundamentally moral issues and police agencies should concentrate on more serious types of antisocial, *mala in se* offenses, not *mala prohibita* violations. He believed that vice enforcement tended to involve political considerations that policing violent and property crimes did not. Such issues were exactly the thing he wanted police departments to avoid, contending that entanglement in political controversies and enforcement in politically charged areas of the law threatened the independence and apoliticism he prized. Further, he feared that working in such areas as drugs, prostitution, and gambling created circumstances conducive to officers engaging in corruption and impeded the public perception of police professionalism and respectability he was working so hard to cultivate.[24]

Despite such reservations, the course of history found police departments largely moving into generalization, with responsibility for enforcing laws aimed at both *mala in se* and *mala prohibita* offenses. In part, this development exemplifies what historians and social scientists call path dependence: Decisions tend to follow the patterns of previous decisions or experiences, as people and institutions "depend" on the "paths" they are on. Police departments already existed (albeit to varying degrees of modernization and professionalization) and, more than any other established agencies, had the basic labor force and authority to do the work of enforcing a broad array of laws. Accordingly, it is unsurprising that new assignments and areas of responsibility would default to them, requiring their evolution as multitasking generalists. Further, in the areas of both traffic and vice enforcement, continued legal development saw laws grow more detailed, more comprehensive, and more punitive. With increasing numbers of people facing serious charges and penalties, enforcement called for the type of power and authority granted to police officers and few other government agents, including the authorization to use force and make arrests.

The development of modern police departments as generalists had significant implications for how policing and criminal justice more broadly would continue to evolve over the course of the twentieth century. These implications include both benefits and costs. From the perspective of citizens with problems to solve, one beneficial consequence was establishing police departments as the default go-to organizations for multifarious concerns and complaints related to lawbreaking and public order. And, from criminal justice authorities' perspective, wide-ranging areas of responsibility brought with them wide-ranging discretion and authority. As law enforcement generalists, police officers could operate with relatively few encumbrances, enforce a panoply of laws, and conduct wide-ranging investigations involving different types of allegations (e.g., organized crime investigations including multiple illegal activities).

The generalist orientation and its accompanying broad discretion and authority shaped the development of police organizations and policing practices. For the purposes of this book's car-window view of US criminal justice, of particular note is how the combination of traffic law enforcement and authority pertaining to other criminal laws paved the way for the "investigatory stop."[25] Investigatory stops involve officers pulling over vehicles to investigate people deemed suspicious, to probe for evidence of criminal activity, to check for outstanding warrants, and the like, rather than for road safety purposes. With the sweeping authority and discretion granted to modern generalist police, a vehicle stop becomes an opportunity for law enforcement officers to look for evidence of auto theft, assess drivers' suspiciousness, and check for drugs and weapons, leading to a variety of criminal charges.[26] As detailed in Chapter 6, investigatory stops have become both essential parts of contemporary police departments' enforcement practices and a major locus of racial disparities in criminal justice.

Although traffic enforcement authority represented a powerful resource for police agencies, traffic was also a demanding new responsibility. Police were also taking on other new tasks related to *mala prohibita* offenses in the early part of the twentieth century, but the exponential growth in the number of cars

on the road—and the exponential growth in an array of resulting problems—
engendered traffic's rapid ascent to a prominent place in policing. The police
academies that Vollmer championed soon came to dedicate significant chunks
of their instruction to traffic laws and enforcement tactics.[27] As more and more
Americans took to the road, departments tasked significant numbers of officers
with traffic duty, and enforcing traffic laws came to occupy a substantial share
of policing energy and resources.

This commitment to policing the roads helped the state respond to the
new risks and dangers resulting from the rapid influx of cars, including traffic
deaths, pedestrian injuries, and property damage. Traffic duties meant loads
of new work for law enforcement officers and lots of new arrests and (mostly
misdemeanor) charges associated with driving. Some evidence also indicates
that expanded traffic policing was associated with more policing in general; for
example, the legal historian Sarah Seo found that in the early years of automobility the Los Angeles Police Department made far more arrests not only for car-
related offenses but also for order-maintenance offenses such as panhandling,
public drunkenness, and disturbing the peace.[28]

However, from the perspective of people who contend that departments
should focus primarily (or exclusively) on *mala in se* offenses, adding traffic
responsibilities raises significant concerns related to police labor as a scarce
resource. Departments generally did not find themselves granted the resources
to hire as many new officers as they would want to effectively enforce traffic
laws at no cost to other enforcement activities. Thus, criticism in this vein
would point to the notion that dedicating officer time to traffic implies at least
some attenuation in the attention given to other, arguably more serious matters. For their part, many street-level officers and police department leadership
figures had at best mixed feelings about this massive new responsibility. It was
a major drain on their time and departmental resources and, in the eyes of
some, shifted departments' efforts away from "real" police work.[29]

Debates along these lines have persisted up to the present, with critics arguing that enforcement in such areas as traffic, vice, and order maintenance take
policing attention and resources away from other matters. Current iterations
of this argument sometimes invoke "clearance rates," pointing to the relatively
low percentage of crimes that law enforcement agencies are "clearing" by arresting, charging, and referring someone for prosecution. (Crimes can also be
"cleared by exceptional means," when law enforcement identifies and locates
an offender and gathers enough evidence to support a charge but some outside circumstance, such as death or the inability to extradite, impedes arrest
and prosecution.) According to the FBI's Uniform Crime Reporting Program,

clearance rates for many types of crime are not particularly high. In 2018, for example, FBI data show that only 45.5% of violent crimes and 17.6% of property crimes were cleared by arrest or exceptional means. Among violent crimes, law enforcement cleared 62.3% of murders, 52.5% of aggravated assaults, 33.4% of rapes, and 30.4% of robberies. Clearance rates for property crimes included 18.9% for larceny-theft, 13.9% for burglary, and 13.8% for motor vehicle theft. Critics of police departments as generalists sometimes point to such low clearance rates as evidence that criminal justice resources are being spread too thin and that insufficient investigative attention is being given to the *mala in se* offenses that present more manifest public safety concerns.

As traffic enforcement became a widespread police practice, it also became something of a public relations problem for law enforcement agencies. Suddenly, police efforts had shifted quite dramatically in focus, from interventions targeted overwhelmingly at people suspected of serious offenses and at disadvantaged, marginalized people such as vagrants and panhandlers, to pulling over "respectable" middle- and upper-class people driving their cars.[30] This led to significant backlash, especially when people perceived themselves as having been pulled over for the same things others were doing with impunity.[31] This too was a consequence that Vollmer had feared, as giving officers responsibility for traffic enforcement put them into situations in which their legitimacy and integrity were impugned in new ways. Noting the difficulties of the traffic enforcement role, Vollmer said that traffic police needed "the wisdom of Solomon, the courage of David, the strength of Sampson, the patience of Job, the leadership of Moses, the kindness of the Good Samaritan, the faith of Mary, the diplomacy of Lincoln, and the tolerance of Confucius."[32] The issues of public relations, trust in law enforcement, and people's perceptions of the criminal justice system as legitimate—or not—continued to arise throughout the next century of car-based policing.

THE TECHNOLOGY OF MODERNIZED LAW ENFORCEMENT

Modernizing police departments also emphasized new technological tools. With the rise of automobility, transportation was an obvious area for technological advancement. Here, too, August Vollmer and the Berkeley Police Department were national leaders. In 1905 Vollmer was the first police administrator to equip his entire force with bicycles.[33] Motorcycles and cars followed in 1912 and 1913, respectively.[34] By the end of 1914 every Berkeley officer had a Ford Model T patrol car, making Berkeley's "the first totally mobile patrol force in the country."[35]

The police car itself came to function as a marker of police efficiency, effectiveness, and distinction from preexisting, less professionalized models of police and private security forces, propelling Vollmer's vision of police as a professionalized crime control enterprise.[36] Adopting automobiles as new, highly capable law enforcement tools helped police present not just their equipment but also their departments as "well-oiled machines."[37]

In addition to new modes of transportation, late nineteenth- and early twentieth-century police forces had opportunities to embrace advancements in communication technology. In the mid-1800s the telegraph emerged as the first mode of electronic communication. Developed in the 1830s and 1840s, the telegraph used coded signals to send messages, most famously by means of Morse code. Samuel Morse's system of dots and dashes—or dits and dahs—became the international standard in the 1860s. To use the telegraph, senders would tap out messages, which were then transmitted over wires. A device on the receiver's end would automatically record the message, which could then be decoded.

Upon its widespread adoption, the telegraph became the first broadly available system allowing communication to travel faster than transportation. Previous communication technologies had generally relied on physical transportation of messages by horse, boat, or train. Some earlier systems had used signaling and coded messages, such as nautical semaphore systems using flags and signaling systems using fires; the telegraph took that general principle, integrated it with new electronic technologies, and systematized it. The result was a network that permitted nearly instantaneous communication of detailed messages.

The telegraph has subsequently been supplanted by telephone, fax, and internet communication, but it constituted the foundational breakthrough on which these subsequent technologies were built. And when it was first introduced and widely adopted, the telegraph revolutionized science, business, and other aspects of human affairs. With the first intercontinental communication between Europe and North America by transatlantic cable in 1858, we took a major leap forward in the globalization of information, culture, and economics.

Law enforcement was among the many enterprises that recognized the new technology's potential and took steps to capitalize on it. In 1840s England, after a suspected murderer boarded a London-bound train, local police wired ahead a notification with a description, allowing the suspect to be apprehended when he exited the train at London's Paddington Station. In turn, the arresting officers promptly informed the officials who had sent the notification of the arrest in a return message. With such examples to demonstrate the telegraph's value as a law enforcement tool, the UK's telegraph network quickly expanded from wires along railroad lines to include wires connecting local police offices to centralized police command at Scotland Yard.[38]

In US policing the telegraph similarly allowed for police headquarters to send out messages that officers could receive at local precincts throughout the city, and for those local stations to communicate with headquarters. Because using Morse code required specialized knowledge, early police applications included experimentation with the dial telegraph, which operators untrained in Morse code could use. Within a couple of decades of those first experiments in New York City in 1858, departments began requiring station keepers to learn and use Morse code because it was faster than the cumbersome dial telegraph.[39]

Even after embracing the relatively expedient Morse code, early uses of the telegraph in US policing were marked by several shortcomings. First, police agencies did not effectively implement the technology as a method for citizens to communicate with them. Second, law enforcement largely failed to exploit the telegraph's potential to facilitate interdepartmental communication and cooperation. Further developments proved necessary to begin breaking down the silos separating various police departments, including the formation of state police forces and extragovernmental organizations such as the International Association of Chiefs of Police, established in 1893.[40]

At the department level, a third shortcoming manifested in how police organizations developed telegraph networks and put the tool to work—and how they did not. Departments initially adopted the telegraph as a means of communicating between their central headquarters and local precincts; for many years there was no way to communicate with officers in the field using telegraphy. Departments would update officers on important matters at the beginning of their shifts, but once people were out on patrol, there was no way to use their new communication resource to alert patrolmen to emergencies or for officers to send in information or request help. This was in part an inherent limitation of the technology, which required running wires and installing equipment to allow communication to and from different locations. The infrastructural response to this issue was to implement box systems, with telegraph boxes scattered throughout the city for officers to use; it took police departments decades to embrace this approach.[41]

Moving into the late nineteenth and early twentieth centuries, modernizing police departments adopting Vollmer's vision of professionalized policing found their communication needs growing ever further. Forward-thinking leadership figures wanted to transcend the era of officers just walking the beat in favor of a systematized approach to crime control based on considered principles. The goals of efficiency and effectiveness in crime control required police departments to better organize and coordinate their activities. The adoption of box systems was a key step in this process. These systems began proliferating in the late 1800s, with local governments installing telegraphic boxes that allowed officers in the field to choose from a menu of several different messages to transmit back to their headquarters.[42]

The next major advancement in police communication technologies was the telephone. Alexander Graham Bell received a patent for the device in 1876, and police departments were beginning to put it into service around the same time that box systems were spreading in the country's cities. At first, departments used telephones similarly to early telegraph systems, to connect headquarters and local precincts. As a supplement to telegraphic box systems, the telephone also allowed for two-way communication and more detailed information; rather than just choosing a generic message to send, as they needed to with telegraph boxes, officers could send details such as descriptions of suspects and explanations of emergency situations. And telephones' utility was not limited to emergency response: They also helped centrally organized policing become more systematic and more effective through regular officer check-ins and quicker access to updated information. Telephones' greater communicative capacities made it much more feasible to institute comprehensive policing theories and strategies. With the greater flexibility and utility it provided, the telephone quickly supplanted the telegraph as the centerpiece of police organizations' electronic communication.

Recall systems were an important addition to telegraph and telephone boxes. Through flashing lights, bells, or horns on call boxes, recall systems allowed police command to signal to field officers that there was a message for them at the box. (The need for an auditory component atrophied as departments developed more sophisticated light systems.) August Vollmer's influence is apparent in this area, too; in 1906, one year after taking office, Vollmer introduced a signal-and-recall system in Berkeley, financed through a municipal bond of $25,000 (almost a quarter of a million in today's dollars).[43] These systems gave bureaucratic leaders something close to the same ability to communicate with officers in the field that they had to communicate with officers in the station house. Citizen call buttons were another significant update to box systems; these tools allowed members of the public to use the system to request police assistance.[44]

Police communication took a giant leap forward with the introduction of radio technology. For the first time, police departments could communicate without the limitations of a network dependent on physical wires. Wireless communication was particularly essential in the age of car-driving lawbreakers and motorized police forces. Although police officers driving cars could of course use call boxes, with the radio, patrol cars evolved from being tools of personal transportation and a means of chasing down and transporting suspects into mobile communication centers. This capacity lent patrol cars expanded functionality as rolling offshoots of the department itself, from which officers could stay in continuous contact with headquarters and, later, with other officers in the field.

US law enforcement first used wireless telegraphy in 1908, as a means to communicate with a New York City police boat, the *Patrol*. Wireless technology continued to be used primarily for communication with water-going vessels until World War I, and spread to other applications in the 1920s. The first radio station license for police use was issued in New York in 1920.[45]

These early uses of the radio were one-way: Headquarters would broadcast to patrol cars (or boats), where officers would listen on speakers. Much of the early development of police radio communication happened in Detroit; between 1921 and 1927 the Motor City became a national leader not just in automobile manufacturing but also in the radio dispatch of police automobiles. In 1923 the Detroit Police Department obtained a license to broadcast calls to their officers on local station KOP (provided that an "entertainment feature" accompany such broadcasts, a requirement that they satisfied by preceding their calls with a rendition of "Yankee Doodle").[46]

Detroit Police patrolman Kenneth R. Cox, who had studied engineering at Purdue University before joining the police force, played a crucial role in the department's early work in radio communication.[47] The department appointed Cox to lead their development of what we now recognize as the basic police radio system: using a dedicated frequency to communicate specifically and solely with police, first in their cars and later through personal radios that officers carried with them.[48] In 1928 the Detroit Police began regular one-way communication with patrol cars from W8FS, a new broadcasting station they established on Belle Isle.[49] Seeing the technology's benefits, other departments sought to follow suit—when they could afford to. According to one observer, four city police departments were using radio technology in 1931, "but by 1937 there were two thousand police agencies—including both local and state—utilizing radio."[50]

To best capitalize on the radio's potential, police needed two-way communication so that officers could send messages from their cars, not just passively receive information and instructions. Bayonne, New Jersey, introduced two-way radio technology in 1933, followed by Detroit a few months later and Boston in 1934; these early movers paved the way for the technology's adoption in police departments nationwide.[51] As the telephone call box had a few decades earlier, the two-way radio allowed officers to send in their own reports of emergencies and descriptions of suspects. Being wireless and car mounted brought the additional benefit of allowing communication from any place in radio range, even while on the move.

The radio and the patrol car complemented each other ideally. Together, the two were greater than the sum of their parts; each made the other far more useful than it was on its own. In a crisis situation, the police department's greatest strength is the ability of its officers to communicate with each other and to coordinate organized responses. Through coordinated, disciplined radio communication, officers can share the pertinent information with central dispatch, who can then implement a strategic response: planning intercept routes for police vehicles, setting up roadblocks, and so forth.

August Vollmer had recognized this from the earliest days of putting radios in police cars. Police car speed is certainly a relevant consideration, and it was clearly preferable to put officers in vehicles that could keep up with suspects' getaway cars. But, the decisive strategic factor is the speed at which the organization can transmit *information*. Suspects fleeing a scene almost always have a significant head start, and simply chasing after them rarely leads to a successful apprehension.[52] A radio call, however, is faster than any car. Electronic communication, and especially wireless radio communication, gave police a tool that allowed them to share information far faster than the speed of physical transportation. This capacity was crucial for implementing the kind of overarching crime control strategies and policing science that Vollmer stressed as essential to a modernized and professionalized police force and criminal justice system.

CALLING ALL CARS

In combination with extensive police automobility, the radio opened new doors for policing strategies and tactics. The car effectively collapsed physical distance, enabling law enforcement officers to cover more ground than was possible using prior means of transportation. Radio communication gave criminal justice authorities the additional capacity to coordinate and cooperate in responding to emergencies, apprehending suspects, and informing one another about their whereabouts and activities. The modern version of centrally orchestrated, administratively directed law enforcement activity arises directly from the ability of dispatchers to communicate with officers dispersed across their jurisdictions and from those officers' ability to communicate with their colleagues and their headquarters.

As time went on, cars and radio communication also came to figure centrally in responses to calls for service. Much of the direct contact between the public and the street-level bureaucrats of the criminal justice system originates not with proactive police patrol but with citizens reporting crimes or otherwise requesting action from law enforcement.[53] With the advent of the telephone, citizens gained a newfound ability to directly communicate requests to law enforcement, and the combination of automobility and radios enabled police to respond to these calls swiftly. From humble beginnings in the telegraph and call boxes, police communication technology evolved into modern 911 systems and centralized emergency dispatch. These developments culminated in the trends in criminal justice coordination, communication, and rapid response set in motion with the technological innovations of the late nineteenth and early twentieth centuries. In so doing, they reflect Vollmer's vision of police departments as effective and efficient enterprises, as well as contemporary police departments' status as multitasking generalists.

THREE

Fifths and the Fourth

Prohibition and Searches

n January 1920 Prohibition went into effect, bringing American culture, crime, and criminal justice to a historical crossroads. The national prohibition of alcohol was an unprecedented sociolegal experiment in banning a widespread and popular practice. Pushing alcohol onto the black market created the conditions that spawned the sophisticated, well-resourced criminal organizations with which law enforcement agencies would continue to contend long after the Eighteenth Amendment was repealed.

The illicit alcohol business ran through motor vehicles. Prohibition also marked the first time that US law enforcement agents were involved in a large-scale, systematic practice of searching for contraband. Together, these aspects of Prohibition-related lawbreaking and law enforcement raised unprecedented Fourth Amendment considerations. The Fourth Amendment protects the people against unreasonable searches and seizures; in the 1920s the Supreme Court was confronted with novel questions about how and to what extent Fourth Amendment protections limited law enforcement's methods for accessing and collecting evidence. In one landmark case, *Olmstead v. United States* (1928), authorities who were investigating Roy Olmstead's motorized Seattle bootlegging operation sought to use evidence gathered from warrantless wiretaps. Another, *Carroll v. United States* (1925), was the first vehicle stop case to come before the US Supreme Court; here, the Court addressed the extent to which the Fourth Amendment's protections against unreasonable search and seizure applied when officers wished to stop and search cars.

In both *Olmstead* and *Carroll* the Supreme Court granted considerable leeway to law enforcement. In *Olmstead* the Court held that no warrant was required to gather wiretap evidence so long as placing the wiretaps did not involve a physical trespass; this holding would remain controlling precedent for nearly four decades, until it was overturned in the 1967 case *Katz v. United States*. The *Carroll* decision established the automobile exception to search warrant requirements under the Fourth Amendment, holding that officers could search a vehicle without a warrant based on an assessment of probable cause. Unlike *Olmstead*, *Carroll* remains controlling precedent, having been affirmed and expanded in various ways in subsequent cases.

Prohibition was a watershed era in the history of US criminal justice. It helped define the modern relationship between law enforcement and the citizenry and staked out key legal standards regarding authorities' access to evidence in a modernized, motorized age. Moreover, many observers draw connections between the country's past experience with Prohibition and the ongoing war on drugs. Undoubtedly, there are significant differences between alcohol and the intoxicants that are the primary focus of contemporary drug enforcement efforts. The two enforcement enterprises' commonalities, however, merit consideration.

A CROSSROADS FOR CULTURE, CRIME, AND CRIMINAL JUSTICE

The historical intersection of emerging automobility and the federal outlawing of alcohol made the 1920s a pivotal decade in the evolution of criminal justice. Prohibition, however, was not a new idea when the Eighteenth Amendment was ratified in 1919. The United States had a long history of extensive and excessive alcohol use. The temperance movement garnered a significant following in the nineteenth century, with adherents pointing especially to the problems they associated with alcohol consumption. The drys, as they came to be known, saw alcohol as inherently destructive to people's morality, health, and mental stability. In their view, these individual-level consequences agglomerated and metastasized into collective social problems, such as joblessness, poverty, crime, mental illness, and violence, particularly violence against women and children. Accordingly, they foreswore even moderate drinking, arguing that alcohol is naturally addictive, and framed any indulgence as a gateway to heavy use and the associated destructive consequences.[1] Aside from the drys' claims to the moral elevation and societal betterment that Prohibition would create, their campaign had a darker side: roots in ethnic and racial prejudices and anti-immigrant sentiments and purported links between ethnic and racial minorities and the evils of alcohol.[2]

In the mid-1800s the temperance movement began to shift from primarily encouraging individuals to voluntarily abstain from alcohol use to pursuing a legal intervention: the prohibition of alcohol. After the turn of the century the Anti-Saloon League (ASL) emerged as a leader in the push to ban alcohol. Compared to its predecessors, the ASL was more organized and bureaucratized; in that regard, it paralleled the modernization and rationalization happening in police departments in Berkeley and elsewhere around the same time. The ASL is an excellent example of a single-issue special interest group. As such, it offered a model for other groups focused on law and policy on specific topics—such as abortion, guns, and the environment—that would arise later in the twentieth century. The ASL prioritized boosting elected officials who would vote for tougher liquor laws and provided "model legislation" for friendly politicians to propose in legislative bodies.[3] In the subsequent decades this approach would become increasingly popular with special interest groups looking to influence policy. The ASL also demonstrated facility with coalition building, allying early on with Protestant religious groups and later with the business community in the push for national prohibition.[4]

In 1913 the ASL threw its weight behind national prohibition by way of amending the US Constitution.[5] Corporations joined the effort, embracing the idea that Prohibition would make for a better, more disciplined labor force. World War I helped galvanize support, as Prohibitionists advanced the movement as a patriotic cause, helpful to the war effort and a way to push back against German beer manufacturers.[6] As its supporters emphasized, national prohibition through constitutional amendment would build on what to that point was a sustained series of successes in restricting access to alcohol through state-level prohibitions and "local option" laws that permitted counties and towns to forbid the sale of alcohol within their jurisdictions. The 1917 Senate debate over the proposed amendment included "reference . . . to the fact that twenty-six states had enacted state prohibition laws [and] that more than 60 per cent of our people and 80 per cent of the territory of the United States at that time were living under prohibition."[7]

Article V of the Constitution specifies the process by which the document can be amended. Congress can propose an amendment through a joint resolution passed by a two-thirds majority vote in each chamber, or two-thirds of the states' legislatures can vote to call a constitutional convention to propose an amendment. (So far, all twenty-seven amendments have been proposed through the congressional vote path.) For a proposed amendment to be ratified, it must be approved by the state legislatures of three-quarters of the states. Congress proposed the Eighteenth Amendment, which provided for the national prohibition of alcohol, on December 18, 1917. The proposed amendment would prohibit the manufacture, sale, transportation, import, or export of "intoxicating liquor." It took just over a year for the required three-quarters of the state legislatures to vote for ratification, which was achieved on January 16, 1919. Eventually, all but two of the then forty-eight states would sign on, with Connecticut and Rhode Island the only holdouts. In October 1919 Congress passed the Volstead Act to enforce the amendment, setting the alcohol content threshold for beverages that constituted "intoxicating liquor" at one-half of 1%. President Wilson vetoed the act, but Congress overrode his veto, setting the stage for the Volstead Act to take effect on January 17, 1920, a year after the amendment's ratification.

The drys' initial prognoses were optimistic. Having spent decades describing alcohol as the root of all evil, they were confident that Prohibition would bring about sweeping reductions in crime, poverty, and human suffering in all its many forms. But Prohibition's most diehard advocates never really got the chance to see what real Prohibition—meaning no alcohol being manufactured or sold—would have looked like or what the consequences would have been. The Volstead Act was violated widely from the outset. "Rumrunners" illegally imported alcohol from Canada and elsewhere, "moonshiners" made illegal whiskey, and "bootleggers" delivered illicit booze to retailers and consumers.[8] Americans across the socioeconomic spectrum imbibed illegally imported, manufactured, and distributed alcohol, at home and in private clubs and speakeasies.

As the frequency and flagrancy of Volstead Act violations suggest, many people were opposed to the new law. Obviously, people who wanted to drink alcohol openly and legally disliked Prohibition from the beginning. As the years went on and some of Prohibition's undesirable consequences became clear, more and more people began to see the law's drawbacks as outweighing its benefits.

Prohibition's impact was manifold. In the economic arena, the drys had prognosticated that Prohibition would bring about an economic boom, as more people would hold down jobs and escape poverty and thus have more resources available for consumer spending. Similarly, they predicted that improvements in the quality of life and neighborhoods' prosperity would be a boon to the real estate market. Businesspeople offering products that might function as substitutes for alcohol and bars also had high hopes for what Prohibition would mean for the bottom line in selling chewing gum, soft drinks, and theater tickets.[9]

Prohibition's economic effects, however, did not fulfill these rosy projections. Fewer people attended theaters, not more, and restaurants lost the considerable share of their profits that alcohol sales had composed. More directly, thousands of jobs were lost as distilleries, breweries, and drinking establishments closed and other occupations involved in the manufacture, distribution, and sale of alcohol disappeared.[10]

When the Great Depression struck in 1929, calls for repeal grew louder, with opponents arguing that repealing the amendment would create jobs and boost the economy as a whole.[11] And it wasn't just workers and private businesses hoping for a repeal-sized boost to their revenues; government wanted to get in on the action too. Prohibition slashed tax revenues, particularly by eliminating revenue from liquor taxes. In 1919 the federal government had collected close to $500 million from excise taxes on alcohol, to say nothing of excise taxes collected by state governments; projecting those figures forward suggested that billions in potential revenue had been sacrificed in pursuit of the goals of Prohibition.[12] Although people were still making and selling alcohol, Prohibition had pushed that activity into the black market and out of tax authorities' reach.

Of course, legal authorities' struggles during Prohibition were not limited to the sphere of taxation. The Volstead Act meant a sudden change in legal status for a major area of business and social life. Overnight, many activities that had been legal were suddenly illegal and subject to criminal penalties. Sociologists use the term *criminalization* to describe this type of process: making a particular activity, behavior, or even social status officially criminal and assigning criminal justice agencies to enforce those laws. Prohibition newly criminalized many people. That group included some people who had been previously distributing or selling alcohol and kept it up despite the ban. Others got into the black market business specifically. In this way, Prohibition itself contributed to "lawlessness" and criminality: By definition, making alcohol a black market good made it the province of criminal activity.

Much of this activity was small scale and decentralized, the world of backyard stills, bathtub gin, and homemade wine. Illegal liquor, however, also constituted an enormous new market for organized crime, especially in major cities. The booze trade brought criminal organizations a massive influx of profit and created intense new competition to provide alcohol to millions of thirsty Americans.

For all intents and purposes, Prohibition created modern organized crime in the United States. Gangs themselves were not new, but before Prohibition they were disorganized, small crews engaged primarily in extortion, gambling, and prostitution. Beginning in January 1920, however, legitimate enterprises shut down their operations in the manufacture, distribution, and sale of alcohol. Black market goods are organized crime's lifeblood; by banning a product as ubiquitous and popular as alcohol, Prohibition functionally ceded a massive market to underworld enterprises.[13] The country's experience with Prohibition demonstrated that demand for alcohol in America is what economists call inelastic: It does not respond directly or proportionally to factors such as price changes or inconveniences of purchase. Americans want booze, and they will buy it how they can get it; during Prohibition the market for alcohol remained robust, despite limitations in the available selection, questionable safety (especially in amateur-distilled liquor), increased costs, less convenience, and the potential risks of dealing with a criminal element.

With criminal organizations smuggling illegal liquor and attempting to hide its distribution from federal agents, the "iron law of prohibition" took effect.[14] This refers to the tendency in black markets for stronger intoxicants to push out their less potent alternatives; because less volume is needed to achieve the desired results, criminal operations can more easily move supplies undetected. Under Prohibition, rates of beer consumption dropped sharply, but consumption of wine and spirits actually increased.[15] Liquor's greater availability was a factor in the popularity of cocktails in Roaring Twenties speakeasies and in the popularization of American "cocktail culture" more broadly.[16] Later, with the war on drugs, the iron law of prohibition similarly explains the comparative profitability of powerful, concentrated substances such as heroin and cocaine for criminal enterprises.

Within a few years of the Volstead Act, criminal enterprises had constructed sophisticated organizations for rumrunning and bootlegging. Although their business was illegal, these organizations included many roles familiar to legitimate enterprises, including blue-collar staffs of truck drivers, distillers, and warehouse workers and white-collar workers such as lawyers and accountants. Bringing in money hand over fist, mob organizations needed to devise ways to launder their ill-gotten gains. These strategies including hiring bankers—or simply buying banks outright—who could assist in sending money overseas or investing it in real estate or legitimate businesses.

Providing illicit liquor to millions of Americans was big business, and criminal organizations evolved accordingly. They needed to attend to supply chain management and shipping logistics. There were pivotal relationships to manage with networks of suppliers and foreign exporters—as well as all the politicians, judges, and law enforcement officials on their payrolls. Shortly after police departments across the country took major steps toward Weberian rationalization and bureaucratization, criminal enterprises were following suit, building sophisticated organizational structures and prizing efficiency. Like their counterparts in the legitimate business world, they sought to best their competition and maximize profits, including through such strategies as vertical integration: controlling the supply of alcohol all the way from manufacture or importation to sale, at mob-owned speakeasies.

Of course, there was also violence: lots of it, and more as Prohibition wore

on. Turf wars and rivalries led to assaults, murders, and bombings; these problems were especially acute in major cities with thriving markets for alcohol, including New York and Chicago. The violence associated with the illegal alcohol
business came to be a leading source of popular disenchantment with Prohibition itself, as more and more people saw clashes between gangs and between
gangs and law enforcement as converting cities into war zones. In 1929, Chicago's infamous St. Valentine's Day Massacre proved a pivotal event. Members of
Al Capone's organization executed seven of their competitors, garnering newspaper headlines across the country and sparking a new wave of criticism of the
country's attempt to outlaw alcohol.

Indeed, enforcing Prohibition was never easy. Some of the challenges for
authorities involved activity that skirted the margins of legality, such as questionable pharmacies and dubious religious officials exploiting the Volstead
Act's exceptions for prescribed alcohol or wine used in religious ceremonies.[17]
Especially in dealing with large and profitable criminal organizations, law enforcement officers were also exposed to the kind of corrupting influences that
August Vollmer feared would follow from police taking responsibility for vice
enforcement. Indeed, although many resisted the temptation to take bribes,
many others did not, and mobsters across the country had local, state, and federal officials in their pockets. Again validating Vollmer's trepidation, awareness
of mobsters buying protection for themselves and their organizations damaged
criminal justice authorities' standing and legitimacy in the public mind.[18]

Fighting an increasingly unpopular—and ultimately quixotic—war against
alcohol placed law enforcement officers in an unenviable position. Many members of the public were unsupportive of their efforts, if not downright hostile;
this was especially the case in places where people perceived law enforcement
as picking on them or their communities, such as alleged moonshining areas.[19]
Moreover, officials who refused bribes faced pressure and backlash from elements within their own agencies or governments, either people on the take or
those simply sympathetic to bootleggers (after all, many of them were drinking
too).

Most dramatic and dangerous were conflicts between enforcement authorities and people involved in the illegal alcohol trade. Car chases and shootouts
became commonplace and produced something of an arms race between authorities and bootleggers. Arms themselves were part of this story, with criminal organizations adopting weapons such as the Thompson submachine gun.
Heavily armed gangsters killed each other, killed police, and killed and injured
innocent bystanders. The Prohibition-era surge of organized crime and gun
violence, notably including the use of fully automatic weapons, helped bring
about the first major piece of federal gun control legislation, the National Fire-

arms Act of 1934, which required registration and imposed excise taxes on certain categories of firearms, including machine guns, short-barreled rifles, and short-barreled shotguns.[20]

In the newly motorized world of the early twentieth century, automobiles were the name of the game. This was as true in bootlegging as it was anywhere, as criminal organizations used cars and trucks to transport illicit alcohol quickly and covertly. Bootleggers stood to benefit in particular from cars that looked ordinary—or "stock"—to an outside observer but had modified suspensions and powerful engines to evade pursuit from law enforcement. These cars' drivers also took to racing each other, and in 1947 a group met to agree on a set of rules for their races and formed the National Association for Stock Car Auto Racing—NASCAR.[21]

Bootleggers' and gangsters' use of faster cars and greater firepower reflected their embrace of technological development and interest in using technology to get a competitive advantage in the cat and mouse of Prohibition enforcement. Naturally, law enforcement wanted to do the same thing. In part, this included getting faster cars and better arsenals in an attempt to keep pace with moonshiners and bootleggers. Beyond such efforts, this period also saw criminal justice authorities developing new, powerful tools to help them deal with a new and unusually challenging law enforcement environment. Many potential witnesses were not cooperative—because of intimidation, bribery, distaste for Prohibition, or some combination of these factors—and accessing evidence was often difficult. Proving guilt beyond a reasonable doubt was a pronounced challenge when trying to prosecute sophisticated criminal organizations that had become savvy, careful, and good at covering their tracks.

As authorities looked to overcome such challenges, the Prohibition era provided the impetus for a new law enforcement tool that would come to be a centerpiece of criminal justice efforts related to organized crime (and many other types of offenses) throughout the twentieth century and into the twenty-first: wiretaps. Federal, state, and local officials began tapping phones and buildings, seeking to gather incriminating evidence on bootlegging and other crimes. Wiretaps were valuable resources for criminal justice authorities, presenting a novel way to gather information on alleged criminal activity. However, they also presented novel constitutional questions, especially with regard to the Fourth Amendment's prohibition of unreasonable search and seizure.

These issues came to the fore in the case of *Olmstead v. United States* (1928). Once an up-and-coming lieutenant in the Seattle Police Department, Roy Olmstead was alleged to have become one of the biggest bootleggers in the Pacific Northwest. Authorities believed that Olmstead, popularly known as "king of the rumrunners," led an expansive operation based on illegally importing alcohol from Canada and then distributing it using motor vehicles.[22] Seeking to gather evidence on Olmstead's activities, federal agents tapped his phones using devices in the basement of the building where Olmstead kept his office and in public locations near his home. The agents did not have a warrant to place the wiretaps, but there was also no clear evidence that they had broken the law in installing them, as they had not physically trespassed on Olmstead's residence or place of business. Using evidence gathered from the wiretaps, federal authorities convicted Olmstead (along with several others) of Volstead Act violations.

Olmstead, in turn, appealed his conviction, arguing that the wiretap evidence should not have been admissible because it was gathered in violation of his constitutional rights. (The "exclusionary rule" dictates that, with some exceptions, the government cannot use evidence obtained illegally or unconstitutionally in a criminal prosecution. *Weeks v. United States* [1914] established this rule for federal prosecutions, and *Mapp v. Ohio* [1961] extended it to state prosecutions.) Specifically, Olmstead argued that the wiretapping constituted an unreasonable search and seizure, a violation of his rights under the Fourth Amendment, and that recording his telephone conversations without his knowledge amounted to enlisting him unwittingly in self-incrimination, a violation of his rights under the Fifth Amendment.

The Supreme Court, however, did not agree with Olmstead's arguments. Writing for a 5 to 4 majority, Chief Justice Taft rejected Olmstead's Fourth Amendment claim. The Fourth Amendment refers to "the right of the people to be secure in their persons, houses, papers, and effects." Chief Justice Taft adhered to a narrow interpretation of this protection, holding that physical trespass or examination was necessary to constitute a search and seizure under the Fourth Amendment; listening in to a phone call from outside the boundaries of a private residence or office did not trigger the Fourth's limitations on search and seizure. Taft and the majority also rejected Olmstead's Fifth Amendment claim, holding that because federal agents did not induce or coerce his statements, he had not been "compelled in [a] criminal case to be a witness against himself," in the language of the Fifth.

The *Olmstead* decision would be binding precedent for almost forty years, until it was overturned in 1967's *Katz v. United States*. In *Katz* the Supreme Court held that government agents needed a warrant to bug a payphone, and Justice Harlan's concurrence established the reasonable expectation of privacy test—or *Katz* test—for determining whether government agents' actions constituted a search under the Fourth Amendment. In fact, the *Katz* Court held up Justice Brandeis's dissent in *Olmstead* as a key influence on their decision. In registering his disagreement with the majority's conclusion in *Olmstead*,

Brandeis argued that new technologies had given government far more invasive ways to monitor presumably private communications than were previously available and that meaningfully sustaining the Fourth Amendment required jurisprudence that recognized and responded to new means of surveillance as they came into being. In *Katz* a 7 to 1 majority of the Court agreed with Brandeis's line of thinking, rejecting the *Olmstead* majority's insistence that a Fourth Amendment violation required physical trespass or interaction with tangible property.

BOOTLEGGERS AND THE EMERGENCE OF VEHICLE SEARCHES

Automobility in the bootlegging business created another pivotal nexus of technology, criminal justice, and Bill of Rights protections. In transforming transportation, automobiles also transformed law. As a private means of conveyance on public thoroughfares, the new technology effectively exploded the classical public-private distinction in the Anglo-American legal tradition.[23] Privately owned cars were advertised—and used—in substantial part as rolling domiciles, containing personal effects, enabling family recreation, and facilitating private exchanges.[24] Yet ostensibly private car-based activities significantly implicated the general welfare and held particular interest for criminal justice authorities alarmed by criminal behavior involving cars.

This situation came to a head when the Volstead Act took effect in 1920. Among the novel challenges of enforcing Prohibition was the fact that, for the first time in US history, domestic law enforcement agents found themselves engaged in widespread and concerted searches for incriminating material, especially in the automobiles that moonshiners and bootleggers used to distribute illicit alcohol. As reflected in the *Olmstead* decision, classical understandings of the Fourth Amendment held it to apply to things in the private sphere. Private spaces, especially homes, required a warrant to search, and personal documents and other property typically held in such private spaces required a warrant to seize. These protections, however, generally did not extend to things outside the private sphere, in the public sphere. It was unclear how to think about cars under this general doctrine. Were they private spaces, like residences? Or were they fundamentally public, like streets or sidewalks? And, by extension, how should we understand the requirement (or lack thereof) for criminal justice authorities to obtain warrants before searching them?[25]

Prohibition was the first time in American history that there was widespread enforcement of a criminal law focused on contraband. Although the Eighteenth Amendment did not explicitly prohibit possessing alcohol, it did outlaw transporting it (along with manufacturing, selling, importing, and exporting it), and this historical juncture also marked the first widespread use of cars as a means of transporting contraband with speed and relative stealth. Previously, if authorities felt they needed to conduct a search, there was often more time to get a warrant, as getaways were harder without cars.[26] Automobiles offered a way to move illicit liquor relatively easily and covertly, as well as a means to quickly evade authorities and cross jurisdictional lines. Thus, under Prohibition, not only did law enforcement officers find themselves wanting to search far more private vehicles than ever before, but they also generally did not have time to secure warrants officially authorizing those searches before suspects could flee into another jurisdiction.

This context set the stage for the landmark Supreme Court decision in *Carroll v. United States* (1925), the first automobile search case to come before the high court. *Carroll*, like many matters before the Supreme Court, boiled down to deciding what words mean. In this case, this particularly meant interpreting the words of the Fourth Amendment.

Amendment IV

The right of the people to be secure in their persons, houses, papers, and effects, against unreasonable searches and seizures, shall not be violated, and no warrants shall issue, but upon probable cause, supported by oath or affirmation, and particularly describing the place to be searched, and the persons or things to be seized.

The Fourth Amendment provides a list of things protected from unreasonable searches and seizures. Should that list be understood to be comprehensive in and of itself, meaning only the specific things listed have the protection described, or are those items intended as examples, leading to a more capacious understanding of the amendment's protections? How should the Court respond to technological changes with new implications for individual liberties and the exercise of legal authority? When are searches of cars "unreasonable" for the purposes of the Fourth? Conversely, what level of intrusion into private vehicles should be considered "reasonable" without a search warrant? Most concretely, when (if ever) does the Fourth Amendment require law enforcement to obtain a warrant before searching a car?

Under the exclusionary rule established in *Weeks*, federal prosecutors could not use evidence obtained through unconstitutional searches in prosecutions for alleged Volstead Act violations. In *Carroll* the Supreme Court had to assess the constitutionality of vehicle searches and thus the admissibility of the evidence they produced. Their conclusions would also resonate more broadly, addressing the extent to which cars are public or private, under what conditions it is reasonable to search cars and seize property found there, and when (if ever) authorities should require warrants to inspect vehicles.

The facts of the case involved federal Prohibition agents who had been investigating a suspected bootlegger, George Carroll, as well as well as his associate, John Kiro, in Michigan. Working undercover, the federal agents arranged to buy three cases of whisky from Carroll and Kiro. Carroll and Kiro never came through with the illicit booze delivery, possibly because of suspicions of the buyers' affiliation with law enforcement. Two and a half months after the failed purchase, the federal agents (along with a state officer) spotted what they believed to be the Oldsmobile used by Carroll and Kiro near Ionia, Michigan, on the road from Detroit to Grand Rapids. The officers stopped and searched the car, without a search warrant, discovering sixty-eight quarts of whisky and gin hidden in the upholstery. Appealing his conviction for violating the National Prohibition Act, Carroll argued that the search violated the Fourth Amendment and thus that the liquor should be inadmissible evidence in his prosecution.

In his majority opinion in *Carroll*, Chief Justice Taft situated cars somewhere in the middle of the public-private distinction, finding them to be neither entirely private nor entirely public. Taft held that the government should recognize some "right to free passage without interruption or search" and that it is unacceptable for government agents to be authorized to stop every vehicle solely on the basis that a search *might* turn up contraband.[27] Along these same lines, he indicated that authorities must obtain warrants when feasible.

However, Taft argued, the requirement of obtaining a warrant before conducting a search is not practicable in situations where vehicles could quickly be moved out of the relevant jurisdiction. Noting the unique capacities of cars and the unique characteristics of roadside searches, Taft ultimately held that search and seizure without a warrant is acceptable under the Fourth Amendment if the "officer shall have *reasonable or probable cause for believing* that the automobile which he stops and seizes has contraband liquor therein which is being illegally transported."[28]

This was a transformation of the Court's Fourth Amendment doctrine. Previously, authorities were required to directly observe evidence of suspected lawbreaking to justify a warrantless search; under *Carroll* warrantless stops and seizures could be justified based on belief or suspicion. Reasoning that it is basically impossible for officers to directly observe evidence of alcohol being transported in a moving car, Taft posited that enforcement of the Volstead Act required allowing them to stop and search cars based on a less demanding standard: suspicion, rather than direct observation or knowledge.

The *Carroll* ruling established what became known as the automobile exception for search warrant requirements. This doctrine grants law enforcement officers broad discretion in deciding whom to pull over and assessing what constitutes probable cause for a search.[29] And it effectively introduced the vehicle stop as a new category of citizen-state interaction, a type of seizure below that of arrest, in which citizens are detained for the duration of the stop, giving officers time to determine whether probable cause for a search exists.

Solicitor General James Beck declared that alcohol's involvement in *Carroll* was "accidental." That is, the case was really about cars, which had "produced a more profound effect upon social conditions than any other invention of modern times."[30] This new technology, with its profound effects on economics, culture, politics, law—really every facet of social life—required the Court to reconsider old understandings of law enforcement's authority to conduct searches and seize people or property. This reflected a broader political and legal reorientation under Prohibition, a shifted vision of personal liberty and government authority that would shape both the exercise of legal power and citizens' experiences for decades to come.[31]

CONTEMPORARY VEHICLE SEARCHES

Carroll granted law enforcement officers the power to assess probable cause and on that basis to legally search vehicles without warrants. This constituted a revolution in police officers' discretionary authority. To have probable cause for a warrantless search, officers need to have knowledge of facts and circumstances that would lead a reasonable person to conclude that a crime is in progress or has been committed or that incriminating evidence is present. Vehicle searches without warrants are also permitted when drivers consent, which many do; overall, more than 90% of warrantless searches are conducted with individuals' consent.[32] Officers may also conduct warrantless searches that they believe are necessary for their safety, or under "plain view" doctrine, when incriminating evidence is openly visible.

In general, courts continue to hold that people do not have the same expectation of privacy in their cars as they do in their homes.[33] Several twenty-first-century Supreme Court decisions have further clarified relevant Fourth Amendment doctrine. In *Illinois v. Caballes* (2005) the Court held that a dog sniff of a vehicle during a traffic stop does not constitute a search and therefore does not require a warrant, consent, or a determination of probable cause for a search; rather, if the canine alerts to the presence of drugs, that alert constitutes probable cause justifying a physical search of the vehicle. However, in *Rodriguez v. United States* (2015) the Court held that, without reasonable suspicion, law enforcement officers may not unnecessarily extend a vehicle stop's duration to get a dog to the scene to conduct a sniff. This ruling demonstrated the Court's willingness to place some limitations on law enforcement's use of dog sniffs, namely, ruling it a Fourth Amendment violation to prolong vehicle stops for the sole purpose of waiting for a dog, absent a reasonable basis justifying the sniff.

United States v. Jones (2012) presented a test of the Fourth Amendment as applied to vehicles and developments in surveillance technologies. In this case, the FBI suspected Antoine Jones of narcotics trafficking. Wanting to track his movements, agents obtained a warrant to place a GPS tracking device on his car. The warrant gave the agents ten days to place the device and authorized them to do so within the District of Columbia. However, the agents installed the device one day after the ten-day window closed, and in Maryland, not DC. Based in part on information obtained from twenty-eight days' worth of GPS data, Jones was indicted and convicted of drug trafficking. Appealing his conviction, Jones argued that the data gathered outside the warrant's stipulations constituted a warrantless search in violation of his Fourth Amendment rights and thus should have been considered inadmissible in his prosecution.

Writing for a unanimous Court, Justice Scalia held that the government's actions did in fact constitute an unlawful search under the Fourth Amendment. In arguing their side of the case, the government contended that because the data in question pertained to Jones's movements on public thoroughfares, he had no "reasonable expectation of privacy," the *Katz* test standard. Writing for the Court, Justice Scalia found that contention to be irrelevant, saying that by installing the device, the government had trespassed Jones's personal property, the vehicle, his "effect," in the language of the Fourth. Thus, even under the most limited reading of the amendment, the government's actions constituted a search requiring a warrant, regardless of the outcome of an evaluation under the *Katz* test. By placing the device, the FBI had conducted a search, and by doing so outside the parameters of their warrant, they had violated the Fourth Amendment, rendering the GPS data inadmissible.

THE LEGACY OF FIFTHS AND THE FOURTH

Prohibition was an unprecedented venture in law, criminal justice, and, to a significant degree, social engineering. Consuming alcohol has long been a common practice in cultures around the globe, and drinking was particularly widespread in the early United States. Few government interventions of any kind anywhere have reached as broadly and deeply in attempting to change people's behaviors and remake society. In 1928 President Herbert Hoover described Prohibition as "a great social and economic experiment, noble in motive and far-reaching in purpose."[34] Reflecting this perspective, some came to refer to Prohibition as "the noble experiment." Other observers, perhaps less sanguine regarding Prohibition's nobility, called it "the most radical political and social experiment of our day."[35] Later historical analyses identifying the dry movement's foundations in nativism and prejudice call the Eighteenth Amendment's nobility further into question.

Although the drys were outwardly bullish about Prohibition's prospects, there was some evidence from the beginning that the experiment might not succeed. Previous efforts to ban alcohol had engendered creative legal evasions and outright hostility, including an 1855 riot in Portland, Maine, that caused the state to rescind its recently enacted prohibition law.[36] Despite such warning signs, the temperance movement aggressively pursued Prohibition on a national scale. And they sought not just to ban alcohol in federal law, but through amending the Constitution; this set the bar high for the movement to achieve their legal objective, but, once that bar was met, having changed the Constitution itself meant that Prohibition would be much harder to undo.

Once enacted, Prohibition was widely flaunted. The country's criminal justice system lacked the capacity to deal with the millions of people criminalized by the massive trade in illicit liquor. Law enforcement, prosecutors, courts, and corrections were all overburdened, and defendants faced long delays awaiting trial. This situation led to federal prosecutors increasingly relying on plea bargains to resolve charges and move people through the system, helping institutionalize plea deals as a ubiquitous aspect of the US criminal justice system.[37] Today, more than 90% of all criminal convictions result from plea bargains.

Prohibition also presented criminal justice authorities with the unprecedented challenge of battling the large, powerful criminal organizations that flourished by exploiting the lucrative black market for liquor. Federal and state governments were spending tens of millions of dollars on Prohibition enforcement and were losing hundreds of millions in potential revenues from liquor taxes. Decrying Prohibition's economic, fiscal, and criminal consequences, opponents began to organize and started making waves for repealing the Eighteenth Amendment in the 1920s, and the repeal movement intensified with the 1929 onset of the Great Depression.[38]

Ultimately, Congress proposed the Twenty-First Amendment repealing Prohibition in 1932. Passed by the required three-fourths of the state legislatures, the amendment was ratified on December 5, 1933. The ramifications of the "noble experiment," however, would reverberate for generations. Notably, the sophisticated organized crime outfits that arose under Prohibition continued to operate, creating a major new focus for criminal justice authorities. Although Prohibition's repeal cost them their most profitable product, they had established enduring infrastructure, knowledge, and tactics—not to mention considerable nest eggs of accumulated capital. With alcohol relegalized, they shifted their energies to other ventures, especially gambling and loan-sharking, as well as extortion, labor racketeering, and narcotics trafficking.[39]

The flourishing of organized crime under Prohibition—and law enforcement's efforts to disrupt these activities—also presaged paralleling phenomena that would rise to the fore a half-century later. Following President Nixon's declaration of "war on drugs" in 1971, the lucrative black market in drugs fueled the rise of powerful and violent international criminal organizations, echoing the mob's explosive growth after the Volstead Act. In contemporary debates about drug policy, as in last century's debates about alcohol policy, a core question is what fundamental approach the government should take: prohibition, in which outright bans are enforced with criminal sanctions, or legalization and regulation, in which substances are permitted but under certain rules and with taxes attached. After the country's largely disastrous experiment with alcohol prohibition, the United States adopted a legalization and regulation approach, with the various states designing and implementing their own rules regarding the production, distribution, and sale of alcohol. Some critics of the country's war on drugs argue for a similar shift in drug policy, in which some or all drugs would be decriminalized or legalized outright and a public health approach would be taken to issues of abuse and dependency. Others, however, point to differences in the substances' effects and addictive potential and maintain that criminalization is an essential tool for limiting drugs' proliferation and social impact.

Key Supreme Court decisions from the Prohibition era would also prove to have lasting influence on US law and daily life.[40] For the purposes of cars and criminal justice, *Carroll v. United States* (1925) was particularly impactful. The *Carroll* ruling established the automobile exception for search warrant requirements, effectively introducing the vehicle stop as a new category of citizen-state interaction and granting law enforcement officers sweeping discretion in deciding whom to pull over and assessing what constitutes probable cause for a search.[41] The resulting considerations around probable cause and consent to search formed a cornerstone of how we understand people's compliance with the law and deference to legal authorities.[42] Beyond midwifing modern Fourth Amendment doctrine, the *Carroll* precedent was also the background for the emergence of the vehicle stop as the primary setting of direct interactions between citizens and criminal justice authorities. As detailed in Chapter 6, vehicle stops would go on to become a major site of racial inequity and violence in police-citizen interactions.

FOUR

The Automotive Age of Majority

Youth, Driver's Licenses, and Legal Responsibility

Motor vehicles created unprecedented opportunities for personal mobility and, with that, new avenues to social mobility. These opportunities, however, were not open to everyone. Cars' cost was one major hurdle. Beyond this, governments soon began arriving at the idea that driving privileges should be restricted to only certain people. Driver licensing is a key example of how governments grant legal authorization—and assign legal accountability—to individuals. Pushes to require driver licensure foregrounded the danger that unqualified or incompetent motorists posed. Although automobiles offered the promise of newfound autonomy and independence for members of historically marginalized groups, including African Americans and women, these same marginalized groups often found themselves the target of prejudiced ideas about their safety as drivers. As states across the country adopted license requirements, another axis of social differentiation became a key consideration: age. Recognizing younger drivers' comparative riskiness behind the wheel, states sought to find an appropriate balance between granting teenagers the freedom of driving and limiting younger drivers' dangers to themselves and other road users.

These considerations relate to larger discussions about juveniles' appropriate treatment under the law and in the criminal justice system. Legal limitations on younger people's access to driving privileges and the broader history of the juvenile justice system are closely connected. Debates about who should be granted driver's licenses and with what stipulations constitute a crucial example of how governments grant legal authorization and assign legal accountability; similar debates characterize the emergence and development of a specialized domain of criminal justice tailored to young people's circumstances. After detailing the early history of juvenile justice in the United States, this chapter addresses several key court cases related to young people's treatment under the criminal law. These cases include *Kent v. United States* (1966) and *In re Gault* (1967), which offered new procedural protections for juvenile defendants; *Roper v. Simmons* (2005), which barred the death penalty for juvenile defendants; and *Miller v. Alabama* (2012) and *Jones v. Mississippi* (2021), which addressed lifetime imprisonment for juvenile defendants.

AUTOS AND AUTONOMY

Three fingers whiskey pleasures the drinkers
And moving does more than the same thing for me.
Willy he tells me that doers and thinkers
Say moving is the closest thing to being free.
            Billy Joe Shaver, "Willy the Wandering Gypsy and Me"

The advent of automobiles opened up a new world of mobility. It was now much easier for people to travel longer distances, more conveniently, without needing to stick to the schedules and limited routes of trains and boats. By eliminating or ameliorating many of the factors that impeded movement from place to place, cars ushered in an unprecedented era of comparatively unencumbered and autonomous physical mobility. In so doing, they helped to create new social and economic opportunities and to define the modern American vision of the independent, self-directed individual.[1]

From the outset, however, the freedom of physical and social mobility provided by cars was not available to everyone. Given cars' status as consumer goods, access to financial resources was a fundamental predictor of access to a private automobile. In the earliest years of automobility, cars were true luxury goods. Built largely by hand under a craft production model, each unit was custom manufactured and came at a cost that only wealthy buyers could afford. Pioneering auto executive Alfred P. Sloan referred to this early period as the "class market" in automobiles; only people of privileged class status could afford the first cars, which were produced in limited numbers through a labor-intensive process requiring skilled craftspeople.[2] (In 1906 future US president Woodrow Wilson, then president of Princeton University, stated that "automobilists are a picture of arrogance and wealth, with all its independence and carelessness.")[3] The way to extract maximum profits from the automobile business, Sloan argued, was to sell cars to people across the income spectrum, not just to the upper class. In 1908 Ford produced the first Model T; Sloan marked this year as the turning point from the "class market" to the "mass market," the transition to a period in which automobiles became attainable more broadly across the socioeconomic spectrum.[4]

Fordist mass production was undoubtedly a key factor in cars becoming attainable for a wider swath of Americans. However, even at the Model T's comparatively lower sticker price—$850 in 1908, down all the way to $360 by 1916—many people lacked the savings to buy a new car outright.[5] Thus, as historian Lendol Calder argues, the true beginning of the mass market dates not to the introduction of the Model T but to the rise of installment buying in the 1910s.[6] The movement of dealers, finance companies, and manufacturers themselves to allow buyers to purchase cars with monthly payments, rather than requiring lump-sum payments up front, made buying a car feasible even for households of modest means, and by the 1920s private car ownership had transitioned from a privilege of the wealthy to a middle-class norm.[7]

Different groups of Americans experienced the rise of mass-produced and mass-marketed automobiles differently. Denial of freedom of mobility is of course a foundational aspect of the African American experience. In the antebellum period Black people were forced to relocate to the United States and then forcibly confined in profoundly cruel and dehumanizing conditions of servitude.[8] After the Civil War formal and informal impediments to Black people's mobility persisted, with particular virulence in the Jim Crow South. Indeed, key moments in the ongoing struggle for civil rights involved limitations on access to transportation. These pivotal events include *Plessy v. Ferguson* (1896), in which the Supreme Court upheld racial segregation on railroads, establishing the separate but equal doctrine that they would later overturn in *Brown v. Board of Education* (1954), and the 1955–1956 Montgomery bus boycott protesting segregation on public transportation.[9]

Private automobiles offered the promise of escaping many of the restrictions on free movement and fair access to transportation that plagued African American history. Such luminaries as W. E. B. Du Bois and Booker T. Washington celebrated cars' potential for helping African Americans transcend racist laws and achieve upward social mobility.[10] Indeed, in light of the systematic oppression and marginalization of African Americans, car ownership offered them especially pronounced advantages in asserting the rights and privileges of citizenship and free movement.[11] Of course, the ability to purchase cars was not a panacea, as African American drivers faced—and continue to face— discrimination, vitriol, and violence from both members of the public and legal authorities. Private businesses refusing to serve Black customers, hostile law enforcement officers, and antagonistic locals made automobile travel often unwelcoming, humiliating, and dangerous.[12] Cars, though, offered unprece-dented opportunities for individual movement, and through that movement they constituted essential resources in the collective movement for racial equality and justice.[13]

Cars also offered the potential of new opportunities for women. The car cul-ture emerging in the early twentieth century did not spring forth fully formed. Rather, it built on preexisting culture, including dominant ideas and stereo-types about gender.[14] At the time, many (overwhelmingly male) writers, po-litical figures, and physicians framed women, especially upper-class women, as frail and requiring separation from the dirty and dangerous world outside the home. Exposure to the trials and tribulations of public life, this logic went, would overtax women's purported delicate constitutions and limited compe-tencies; thus, it was best for them to stay at home, protected.[15] Wealthy women had had access to horse-drawn private transportation for decades, but the au-tomobile offered new possibilities for women to claim the right to freedom of mobility and autonomous action.[16]

Across the country, women who could afford to avail themselves of cars' ca-pabilities did so, both as drivers and as passengers in chauffeured vehicles.[17] With more women purchasing and driving automobiles, manufacturers tar-geted some of their advertising directly to them, depicting cars and driving as instruments of self-direction and efficacy.[18] Adopting cars was a part of wom-en's push for greater representation in civil society and politics, and automo-biles themselves played a significant role in the suffrage movement.[19] Yet, like the larger struggle for gender equality, women's efforts to access the benefits of automobility met hostility and resistance, as women drivers continually fought social constructions of the motoring world as a masculine space.[20]

As cars and drivers continued to proliferate and diversify, questions of what role legal institutions should play in limiting their use came into sharper relief. The police power gave government the authority—indeed, the duty—to reg-ulate cars to promote safety and the general welfare. The exponential growth in collisions, injuries, and deaths in the first decades of automobility signaled clearly to governmental authorities that interventions were needed.[21] Early road safety campaigns focused on the novel dangers posed by automobiles' ca-pacity for speed. Indeed, in the earliest years of automobility, "speeding" did not carry its contemporary connotation of driving at speeds that exceed limits of good sense or the law; rather, speeding was an inherent characteristic of the car, a fundamental point of distinction from older, slower means of transpor-tation.[22] Creating traffic laws and enforcing them through police departments was one major aspect of the response to this issue; the push for driver education and certification programs was another.

With the automobile genie out of the bottle, authorities needed to act on the fly to develop frameworks for assessing and asserting drivers' legal responsibilities and liabilities. Colonel A. B. Barber, director of the US Chamber of Commerce's National Conference on Street and Highway Safety, spoke for many when he wrote in 1931 that the solution to the problem of injuries, fatalities, and property damage resulting from automobile crashes "is clear and unequivocal. It is restriction of the driving privilege to competent and capable drivers."[23] The process of imposing such restrictions, however, was diffused and ad hoc, yielding significant interjurisdictional differences in how to create and enforce regulations on drivers.

Driver licensing was one foundational measure to which all the states would come around—eventually. In 1903 Massachusetts and Missouri became the first states to pass driver's license laws, followed by New Hampshire and Vermont in 1905, New Jersey in 1906, and Connecticut in 1907.[24] To obtain these first licenses, however, drivers did not need to pass an exam; one obtained a license by applying for it and paying the fee, without the requirement to demonstrate knowledge of traffic laws or proficiency behind the wheel. Indeed, "controlling who should drive and under what conditions was less important than taxation in the early days of licensing."[25] As death and destruction from crashes continued to mount, however, governments shifted from license laws as an exercise of their power to tax and toward license and exam requirements as an exercise of their police power aiming to protect people and property.

In 1908 Rhode Island became the first state to require drivers to both obtain a license and pass an exam.[26] As other states slowly adopted license laws over the next several decades, Maryland (1910), New York (1924), the District of Columbia (1925), New Mexico (1927), Indiana (1929), North Carolina (1935), Ohio (1936), Maine (1937), Nevada (1941), and Wyoming (1947) followed Rhode Island's lead in instituting license laws that required would-be motorists to pass exams.[27] The rest of the states enacted initial license laws that did not require exams and then added exam requirements years or even decades later. Missouri, one of the first movers on driver licensing, was also one of the last to require drivers to pass exams, finally creating an exam requirement in 1952, nearly a half-century after they enacted their first licensing law.[28] Not until 1959, when South Dakota enacted an exam requirement, were drivers across the country required to pass examinations.[29]

States' licensure systems were created legislatively and managed administratively. Criminal justice agencies, however, were responsible for street-level enforcement of requirements that drivers bear governmental authorization. As described in Chapter 1, police departments found themselves with the demanding new assignment of monitoring the millions of automobiles traveling at ever greater speeds on the nation's streets and highways; through this assignment, they also assumed responsibility for trying to impose order and protect life, limb, and property. This was no mean feat. By 1931 automobile collisions were causing a million injuries and deaths per year.[30] Early returns on requiring driver examinations and licenses suggested that this regulatory intervention held promise for ameliorating this problem, with states that required their drivers to pass exams and driving tests seeing traffic fatalities grow more slowly than those that did not require such assessments of knowledge, acumen, and ability.[31]

Once licenses were legally required, checking drivers to ascertain their licensure status became part of law enforcement's responsibility with regard to automobiles. This phenomenon, in turn, suggests another key function that driver's licenses quickly assumed: as a primary form of official documentation. Driver's licenses became a valuable resource for government to keep track of people, catalog their basic characteristics, and confirm their identities. This resource, in turn, helped government more effectively exercise legal authority and social control over a large and growing national population.[32] At the beginning of the twentieth century, most of the main identification documents with which we are familiar today were limited in reach, or nonexistent altogether. Among the upper class, certifications of birth predated the Declaration of Independence, but until the twentieth century most births were unregistered, and not until the early 1930s did states across the country register at least 90% of births.[33] Passports had been issued throughout the nineteenth century but were relatively uncommon, and US citizens traveling abroad were not uniformly required to carry passports until 1952.[34] Following the 1935 creation of Social Security, Social Security numbers soon became the default federal identifier. Social Security cards, though, do not include pictures; as driver's licenses proliferated, they became the default all-purpose photo ID. Indeed, driver's licenses became so taken for granted and ingrained as the standard form of personal documentation that states began issuing "non-driver's licenses" or state IDs containing the same type of photograph and identifying information but without the certification of driving privileges.[35]

With examinations and driving tests in place as requirements for licensure, receipt of a driver's license indicated that, at least in theory, the state saw the licensed individual as an acceptably knowledgeable and proficient driver. More broadly, the granting of a license reflected the state officially categorizing the bearer as meeting certain standards of competence and responsibility. Unsurprisingly, given the marginalization of women and people of color with regard to freedom of mobility and accessing the full rights of citizenship, racism and sexism infused early debates about who should be considered fit to drive.

As laws mandating licenses to drive began taking effect in the early twentieth century, they met substantial resistance. Better-off White men, in particular, had long enjoyed the liberty to move about of their own volition and with minimal restrictions. Cars, it seemed to many, were an extension of this established liberty, and drivers had a natural, even God-given right to use their new machines as they saw fit, without governmental preclearance. Efforts to require such preclearance, in turn, constituted state overreach, or simply an unjustified new form of taxation.[36] (Given taxation's central role in early licensure programs, the latter perspective was not entirely unwarranted.)[37]

Race became a pivotal factor in shifting White male perceptions of driver's licenses, from an invasive and intrusive government intervention to an affirmation of personal liberty and a marker of the transition to adulthood.[38] Discourse about needing to eliminate the scourge of incompetent, dangerous drivers took on racist elements, with Black drivers (along with immigrants and other disfavored groups) held up as a menace behind the wheel.[39] Pseudoscientists depicted African Americans as impulsive and primitive, unsuited for the responsibilities of motoring.[40] In discussing the problems of inept and reckless driving and the resulting deaths and injuries, the popular press also focused disproportionately on collisions involving Black drivers. One prominent incident occurred in Atlanta, Georgia, in 1933, when White fire chief John Terrell was killed in a collision with a Black driver named Garfield Towers. Prosecutors charged Towers with murder for his alleged responsibility in the event, and local media coverage foregrounded Towers's race.[41] Popular and political outrage over the incident reinvigorated calls for Georgia to require licenses, culminating in the state's enactment of a licensing law in 1937 and an examination law in 1939.[42] At the national level, the movement of millions of African Americans from the South to northern cities during the Great Migration further amplified newfound Black mobility—of both the physical and social varieties—as a point of concern for White majorities in destination locales.[43] Altogether, these factors helped convince Whites that licenses and exams were an appropriate government intervention, both as a way to exclude these purportedly unqualified and reckless drivers and as a way to mark themselves as respectable and higher status.[44]

Women also faced disparagement of their aptitude and trustworthiness as safe drivers. Some alleged that women lacked the physical strength to handle automobiles, with one piece in *Outlook* magazine arguing that only one woman in a thousand was physically up to the task.[45] Men also attacked women's mental fitness for driving, contending that they were emotional rather than rational and prone to "hysteria" that made them hazards on the road.[46] In 1924, Fred A. Moss published an article in *Popular Science Monthly* detailing certain qualifications he believed an individual must meet to obtain legal driving privileges. For Professor Moss, these included having "normal arms, legs, feet, and at least one good eye," passing tests of eyesight and general intelligence, and being able to hear.[47] To these factors, Professor Moss added the novel requirement of an assessment of "emotional efficiency," a requirement that he contended disqualified many women. Picking up on this article, the *Washington Post* published their own account of Moss's findings under the headline "Scientific Tests Prove Men Best Auto Pilots."[48] Although efforts to deny women legal access to driving privileges would fail, sexist prejudices about their driving ability would persist.[49] These prejudices, of course, are not just ill-founded but opposite to reality. Statistics on moving violations and crashes consistently demonstrate that men, especially young men, are more dangerous drivers; the American Automobile Association formally recognized women's comparative competency behind the wheel all the way back in 1925.[50]

FREEDOM, SAFETY, AND RESPONSIBILITY
UNDER THE LAW: THE CASE OF DRIVING AGE

Opposition to women and people of color as motorists was based on prejudices, stereotypes, and pseudoscience. However, a more legitimate argument could be made for concern about extending driving privileges to another group: teenagers. As early as the 1920s, cars became "a social essential" for teens in the areas where automobility proliferated most rapidly.[51] With the automobile's continuing rise to predominance in the postwar era, cars increasingly became the means—and locations—of young people's social and romantic activities.[52] This expanded role in daily life gave new prominence to obtaining a driver's license as a rite of passage, a marker of the transition from the limitations of childhood to adulthood's freedom and independence. Indeed, Marshall McLuhan noted in 1964 that "American youth attributes much more importance to arriving at driver's-license age than at voting age."[53]

This crucial landmark of maturity and legal authorization provides an opportunity to consider how categorizations of individual responsibility under the law are created and changed. Discussions and debates about the age at which people should be eligible to obtain driver's licenses evoke larger considerations of the age of majority under the criminal law and how people younger than specified age cutoffs can and should be held legally liable for their actions.

Early on, these issues came to the fore through cars' role as a locus for "juvenile delinquency." A large share of early automobile thefts were instances of joyriding, in which mostly young people stole cars temporarily, not out of profit-seeking motives but as pleasure-seeking exercises, reflecting impetuousness, impulsiveness, or efforts to impress potential romantic partners.[54] In 1917, for instance, the chief of police in Detroit estimated that 90% of the city's auto thieves were joyriders, not calculating criminals.[55] The prevalence of this phenomenon raised important legal and criminal justice questions. Were different enforcement strategies called for to address this iteration of auto theft? And when teenaged joyriders were caught, should their punishments differ from those directed at "serious" auto thieves? The 1919 Dyer Act, discussed in Chapter 1, did not initially differentiate between these different types of violations; indeed, the federal government prosecuted numerous minors under the law. Ultimately, Congressman Leonidas Dyer, the bill's sponsor and namesake, called for the law to be repealed. As evidence of its unintended consequences, Dyer cited statistics on boys as young as 12 years old being incarcerated for Dyer Act violations and these offenders' significant representation among all juveniles incarcerated by the federal government.[56]

Related concerns about the appropriate legal approach to young people and cars recurred in the context of driver licensing. Under US law driving is a privilege, not a right; courts have confirmed that this gives government broad discretion to regulate driving and drivers to protect public safety and advance the general welfare as a valid exercise of the police power.[57] This authority extends to determinations that people below certain ages should not be considered ready for the responsibility of driving or that driving privileges should be more closely regulated for new drivers relative to their more established counterparts.

Early on, observers noted that young drivers might be comparatively dangerous, and a handful of states passed laws withholding driving privileges from people below certain age cutoffs before imposing general mandates that drivers be licensed.[58] The first driver's license laws did not specify a minimum age threshold; in 1909 Pennsylvania became the first state to treat younger drivers differently under its license law, specifying a separate license for people younger than 18.[59] In piecemeal fashion some other states adopted limited and provisional forms of licensure for younger drivers; more agrarian states, in which teens often worked on family farms, were more inclined to license drivers at earlier ages.[60]

In 1924 the federal government held the First National Conference on Street and Highway Safety, with future president Herbert Hoover, then secretary of commerce, acting as chairman. The conference's report included an address from President Coolidge, in which he described the meeting's purpose as "the devising of means and the making of recommendations toward the lessening of the numberless accidents which now kill and maim so many of our citizens."[61] Coolidge went on to argue that regulation of day-to-day traffic was the responsibility of the states, but that the federal government had an important role to play in guiding state and local governments such that the rules governing drivers and driving "may be wise and uniform."[62]

To advance this objective, the conference report provided recommendations on numerous statutory, administrative, and organizational matters related to automobiles and their drivers. This included a section on driver licensing, which suggested "that all States designate the minimum age limit, but that no person under sixteen years of age, and no person who cannot read English, should be permitted to operate, drive or direct a motor vehicle."[63] Building on their first national conference and subsequent work, the National Conference on Street and Highway Safety released a proposed Uniform Vehicle Code on August 20, 1926. The proposed code confirmed the 1924 recommendation of limiting operator's licenses to people age 16 or older and also indicated a minimum age of 18 for granting of chauffeur's licenses.[64] The conference also noted, however, that at the time of writing twelve states had no minimum age limit in place for operators. Of those with minimum age thresholds, eighteen set that threshold at the recommended 16 years old, while eight set it at 15 and six at 14, "with the remainder ranging from 12 years, in S. Car., to 18 years in Conn."[65]

With the federal government recommending 16 as the minimum age for driver licensure (and with labor laws setting 16 as the threshold for certain types of jobs), states began to converge on 16 as a default minimum driving age in the 1920s and 1930s.[66] Like the adoption of license and examination laws more generally, however, the creation of minimum licensure ages—and the federal government's desired uniformity in these standards—was slow and uneven. As injuries, deaths, and destruction resulting from automobile collisions continued to plague the country, various parties continued to rail against reckless and dangerous drivers, with young drivers singled out as one of the sources of problems on the roads. Such concerns led many states to adopt the earliest versions of what would evolve into the Graduated Driver Licensing (GDL) system: the creation of "junior operator" licenses, today called learner's permits, that authorized new drivers to gain experience behind the wheel with adult supervision before obtaining full licenses.[67]

However, young drivers continued to pose elevated risks on the road compared with their more experienced counterparts. A 1949 article in *Nation's Business*, a magazine published by the US Chamber of Commerce, posed the question, "Can We Afford Young Drivers?"[68] This piece flagged automobiles' deadly toll in American life, referencing "the murder on our highways" and citing over 32,000 lives lost to crashes in 1948, as well as a 24.3% increase in bodily injury rates and a 105.4% increase in property damage rates since 1941.

In turn, these costs to people and property translated to increases in insurance payouts, which themselves translated to higher premiums for policyholders. Younger drivers, the article noted, presented disproportionate collision risks, with almost 27% of fatal collisions in 1948 involving drivers between the ages of 18 and 25, despite these drivers constituting less than 20% of the total driver population. Altogether, these factors led to a 1948 change in insurers' general approach to policy rates. Previously, insurers had offered an A-1 rate to cars driven fewer than 7,500 miles annually and not driven by anyone younger than 25 and an A rate to private automobiles without thresholds for mileage or driver age. However, upon noting the elevated costs of claims for A rate cars, insurers made a change, subdividing the A tier into A-2 and A-3; now, households containing drivers under the age of 25 would need to pay the higher A-3 rate to compensate for the greater claims insurers saw coming from younger drivers.[69]

Concerns about new drivers' knowledge and abilities fueled calls for driver education programs and more rigorous driving examinations.[70] Given their financial stakes, it is unsurprising that insurance companies were among the parties pushing to institute driver's education in high schools. In an initiative reminiscent of the industry's early involvement in efforts to counteract motor vehicle theft (see Chapter 1), the Association of Casualty and Surety Companies (an insurers' trade group) began advocating for the institutionalization of driver's education in the mid-1930s.[71] These programs grew rapidly in the 1940s, with the number of school-based driver's education programs nearly doubling in 1948 alone. By 1949, 6,000 of the country's 26,000 high schools offered driving classes, and 464,000 of 1,697,000 eligible students were enrolled.[72]

These programs saw further growth in the 1950s and 1960s, facilitated by federal funding support and insurance companies' offers of lower rates for new drivers who completed driver's education.[73] However, initial safety returns from driver's education were not what its proponents had hoped or envisioned. Instead, there was little statistical evidence that completing driver's education reduced driving safety risks; increases in the numbers of drivers completing driver's education were associated with *higher* rates of moving violations and crashes involving young drivers.[74] Several factors seemed to contribute to this result. First, completing driver's education allowed young people to get full licenses earlier than they otherwise would have, putting more of them behind the wheel at younger ages and functionally giving them more time in the driver's seat during the highest-risk teen years. Completing driver's education may also have led young drivers to overestimate their driving capabilities, engendering riskier driving behaviors.[75]

With expanded driver's education counterintuitively appearing to lead to more fatal crashes involving teen drivers rather than fewer, enthusiasm—and federal funding—for these programs waned.[76] Fatal teen crashes remained an important problem, however. Over the later twentieth century, GDL programs came to constitute the primary mechanism by which states tried to reduce teens' involvement in motor vehicle crashes. GDL programs are based on progressing new drivers toward full licensure in distinct stages, requiring first a learner's permit, which allows driving under adult supervision, and then an intermediate or provisional license, which allows unsupervised driving under certain restrictions, and finally a full license. Based on research showing that young drivers bore especially elevated crash risk when driving at night and when carrying passengers, the National Highway Traffic Safety Administration proposed model GDL legislation for the states' consideration in 1977. Not until the 1990s, however, did states begin to adopt these measures; Florida was the first, in 1996.[77]

Today, all fifty states and the District of Columbia have GDL programs. Their details vary, but they typically include minimum ages for learner's permits, provisional licenses, and full licenses; requirements to hold the learner's permit for a certain period and accrue a certain number of supervised driving hours before obtaining the provisional license; and limitations on especially risky types of driving during the provisional stage, such as driving at night and carrying passengers.[78] Reviews of GDL programs' effects indicate that they reduce young drivers' rates of fatal collisions significantly, by between 8% and 14%.[79] Yet driving remains remarkably dangerous for teens; drivers between the ages of 16 and 19 are almost three times more likely than their older counterparts to be involved in a fatal crash, and motor vehicle collisions are the leading cause of death for American teens.[80]

YOUTH, MATURITY, AND LEGAL RESPONSIBILITY

The driver licensing context provides one example of how the assignment of legal privileges and legal accountability to adolescents evolved over time. Related dynamics characterized the historical evolution of young people's treatment under the criminal law. The development of the juvenile justice system illustrates how associated cultural and legal changes yielded contemporary understandings of how to appropriately conceptualize minors' legal responsibility and address their deviations from legal rules.

US legal institutions have grappled with questions about younger people's standing under the law since before the advent of automobility. In the colonial period, matters of juvenile deviance were largely left up to families. Criminal legal institutions were rudimentary during this time and were largely limited to adult systems of confinement and punishment. Accordingly, authorities did not typically differentiate between people of different ages in the application of formal sanctions. If the state did intervene in matters involving young people, the possible penalties were the same as those applied to adults, including whipping, time in the stocks, community expulsion, imprisonment, or execution.[81]

In the nineteenth century, growing attention to younger people's special circumstances and needs helped give rise to juvenile-focused "houses of refuge." Presuming children's problems to result from problems with parenting, these facilities sought to replicate the "ideal" Puritan family environment outside the home. This entailed creating a closely controlled environment in which paternalistic authority figures imposed order and commanded obedience through the harsh administration of discipline. If children's disorderliness and rule breaking stemmed from parents who were weak and failed to deliver appropriate discipline, houses of refuge would offer an atmosphere characterized by the firm and authoritative supervision presumed to be lacking in the home.[82]

In these early interventions the state demonstrated an increased willingness to intervene in the role of parents, or even take place of the family altogether, providing a surrogate—and allegedly superior—version of the conventional family setting. The results of houses of refuge, however, were not as favorable as their advocates had hoped, and many children were subjected to abusive and neglectful treatment. As the nineteenth century drew to a close, Progressive-era reformers sought to develop more humane, more rational, and more effective ways of handling human affairs across various social settings. Pushing for government to revisit its approaches to young people, reform advocates spurred the introduction of child labor laws and helped lay the foundation of the modern juvenile justice system.[83]

Progressive-era reformers in Chicago were appalled by the handling of children in the criminal justice system. The women activists based out of Jane Addams's Hull House had made improving children's lot in society one of their chief objectives, pushing for reforms in education, labor laws, and children's treatment under the criminal law. They decried the confinement of hundreds of children, mostly from poor and immigrant families, in the Cook County Jail. With the support of the Chicago Bar Association and religious organizations, progressives lobbied state legislators to create a specialized court for minors.[84]

Heeding their calls, the Illinois legislature passed the first juvenile court law, leading to the establishment of the first juvenile court in 1899, in Cook County. The new court drew its justification from the English legal doctrine of *parens patriae*, which provided the state with the power to take on the functional role of a parent, particularly in cases where parents are absent or deemed unable or unwilling to appropriately fulfill the parental role. Under the *parens patriae* doctrine the state can step in to act as the guardian or caretaker of children or other people who are determined to require the support and protection conventionally expected of parents.[85] In its report advocating for the juvenile court, a committee of the Chicago Bar Association espoused this form of government intervention.

> The fundamental idea . . . is that the State must step in and exercise guardianship over a child found under such adverse social or individual conditions as develop crime. . . . It proposes a plan whereby he may be treated, not as a criminal, or legally charged with a crime, but as a ward of the state, to receive practically the care, custody and discipline that are accorded the neglected and dependent child, and which, as the Act states, "shall approximate as nearly as may be that which should be given by its parents."[86]

The progressive reformers and their supporters argued that it was unjustified and counterproductive to functionally treat minors as identical to adults under the law. Instead, specialized measures should be put in place that would appropriately consider juveniles' distinct characteristics and design interventions accordingly. By this logic, measures tailored to the specifics of young people's cases could allow for juveniles to be "treated," even "cured," and thereby kept out of the adult system. The reformers contended that, in addition to being the more just approach, keeping young people out of adult jails and prisons would help them avoid adults' corrupting influence, which would otherwise further diminish their life prospects.[87]

Developments in cultural conceptions of childhood and adolescence helped push the early twentieth-century emergence of the minor as a new category of legal subject with special characteristics and demanding special considerations. In this pivotal era, legislative bodies, courts, and executive branch agencies entrenched the idea that juveniles were not wholly responsible for their actions, or least not responsible in the same way as adults. The US legal system, especially the criminal legal system, operates substantially based on assumptions that people are individually responsible for their actions and should be held individually accountable and punished when those actions constitute violations of law. Under the emerging conception of juveniles, however, these assumptions merited serious reconsideration in cases involving young people. When these people broke legal rules, rather than assuming that they acted as self-interested, atomized individuals, authorities should take into account their circumstances and the situations that led to the actions in question. Foregrounding factors such as socioeconomic status, neighborhood conditions, schools' quality, and family situations, the reformists fundamentally saw juveniles not as criminals in need of punishment but as vulnerable children in need of protection, moral guidance, and discipline. The juvenile

court was the legal institution to provide these things, through ordering interventions intended to guide wayward children.[88]

As juvenile courts spread throughout the country, they continued to justify
their interventions along these lines, arguing that ordering juveniles to spend
time in secure facilities was not punishment per se but rather a measure that
was corrective and restorative, not punitive, in nature.[89] As such, defendants in
juvenile proceedings lacked many of the constitutional protections provided
to their older counterparts in adult criminal proceedings. Observers, however,
noted that sentences of involuntary confinement resulting from juvenile proceedings bore a striking resemblance to the terms of incarceration resulting
from adult proceedings. And, through the practice of judicial waiver, juvenile
court judges could elect to transfer juvenile defendants to the adult system.[90]
Once transferred to the adult system, younger defendants lose the special considerations provided to minors in the juvenile courts and are generally subject
to the same types of punishments as older defendants.

Controversy about juveniles' treatment in the legal system reached the
US Supreme Court in the 1960s. The Warren Court, led by Chief Justice Earl
Warren, issued a series of impactful decisions related to civil rights and personal liberties, beginning with *Brown v. Board of Education* (1954). In addition
to landmark decisions related to due process protections for adults in the criminal justice system, such as *Gideon v. Wainwright* (1963) and *Miranda v. Arizona*
(1966), the Warren Court strengthened due process protections for juveniles
with their rulings in *Kent v. United States* (1966) and *In re Gault* (1967).[91] In *Kent*
the Court ruled that the judicial waiver process, by which juveniles could be
transferred into the adult system, needed to include certain due process protections to preserve juvenile defendants' constitutional rights. *Gault* reflected
a similar line of thinking, but with regard to juvenile court proceedings themselves. Holding that the Fourteenth Amendment's due process clause applies
not just to adult defendants but to juveniles as well, the *Gault* ruling extended
key constitutional protections to juvenile proceedings that could result in confinement. The newly guaranteed protections for juvenile defendants included
rights to notice of charges, assistance of counsel, and confrontation and cross-
examination of witnesses, as well as the Fifth Amendment privilege against
self-incrimination.[92]

After *Kent* and *Gault* judicial waivers and juvenile proceedings took on
more of the procedural characteristics of adult criminal proceedings. Prosecutors and courts, however, continued to confront questions about how to treat
minors accused of crimes, particularly serious violent crimes. With judicial
waivers resulting in many juvenile defendants being convicted in adult criminal court and sentenced to the same types of penalties as nonminors, some saw

incongruities between the stated purposes of the juvenile justice system and the realities of young people's treatment under the criminal law.

In the 2005 case *Roper v. Simmons* the Supreme Court issued an important qualification to the general practice of treating juvenile defendants the same as their older counterparts following transfer to the adult system. Hearing an appeal to a homicide conviction involving the use of a vehicle to transport a victim who was thrown off a bridge, the Court declared it a violation of the Eighth Amendment's prohibition of cruel and unusual punishment to impose the death penalty for crimes committed before the age of 18. This ruling overturned *Stanford v. Kentucky* (1989), in which the Court had upheld the constitutionality of capital punishment for people age 16 or older. *Roper v. Simmons* invalidated laws in many states that had permitted the execution of people younger than 18.[93] On the subject of lifetime imprisonment, the Court held in *Miller v. Alabama* (2012) that the mandatory imposition of life-without-parole sentences for juvenile defendants violated the Eighth Amendment's prohibition of cruel and unusual punishment. In *Jones v. Mississippi* (2021), however, a differently constituted Court held that trial courts need not reach a finding that a juvenile defendant is permanently incorrigible before imposing a sentence of lifetime imprisonment.

CARS, CRIMINAL JUSTICE, AND CREATING ACCOUNTABLE LEGAL SUBJECTS

In 1958 J. Stannard Baker, director of research and development at Northwestern University's Traffic Institute, wrote that "driver licensing cannot function separately from related activities of other governmental agencies."[94] Baker went on to note that, as the agencies assigned primary responsibility for street-level enforcement of licensure rules, police departments are prominently implicated in the requirement of licenses to drive.[95] Courts also play crucial roles in the system, by imposing penalties for license-related violations, providing administrative licensure authorities with information about license restrictions or suspensions resulting from their proceedings, and reviewing the constitutionality and legality of laws related to licenses and their revocation.[96]

The issue of driver licensing thus demonstrates the connections between lawmakers, agencies of the administrative state, and the criminal justice system. Legislative bodies created licensure laws, administrative license bureaus managed their implementation, and criminal justice authorities enforced the rules and enabled punishments for violators. As concerns about drivers' competence increased with cars' rapid proliferation, stereotypes and prejudices regarding race and gender influenced how laws were conceptualized, written, implemented, and enforced. Driver's licenses also became a primary site for grappling with questions about how the state should address questions of maturity, cognitive development, and at what ages to extend to people various legal rights, privileges, and obligations.

From the teenaged joyriders of the 1920s and 1930s, to midcentury debates about adolescents' legal responsibility and culpability, to the adjudication of juveniles' later car-based offenses and establishment of new common law doctrines, the automobile is a unifying thread running through the modern history of young people's status and treatment under the law. (Demonstrating long-standing concerns about young people's behavior in the vehicular context, the Lynds' famous study of *Middletown*, published in 1929, quotes a juvenile court judge stating that "the automobile has become a house of prostitution on wheels.")[97] Like many public policy conversations, the ongoing consideration of how best to grant teenagers rights and privileges—and assign them legal responsibilities—fundamentally involves questions of how to balance various values. Granting licenses at earlier ages advances the values of autonomy, independence, and self-direction for younger people; these values, however, exist in at least some tension with the value of public safety, particularly given younger drivers' comparatively elevated rates of moving violations and crashes. Organizing juvenile justice around principles of correction and restoration rather than punishment reflects compassion and sensitivity to minors' lack of input on the circumstances of their birth and upbringing, but the US criminal justice system's dominant values of retribution, deterrence, and just deserts stress individual accountability for criminal offenses and the appropriateness—indeed, the necessity—of punitive sanctions. These debates remain open in the twenty-first century, as lawmakers, courts, and citizens continue to engage with how to best balance oversight with liberty and protection with accountability.

FIVE

City Planning, Suburbanization, and Vehicle Patrol

Suburbanization was one of the most impactful social trends of the twentieth century. Cars, and the daily commuting they enabled, made suburban living newly feasible for millions of Americans. Families of color, however, were systematically excluded from opportunities to buy single-family suburban homes, a key factor in the racial disparities in wealth, health, education, and other areas that continue to plague American society. Further, the highways that facilitated more privileged people's suburban lifestyles were often built through neighborhoods of color. This pattern exacerbated residential racial segregation and concentrated disadvantage; the roads that carried better-off people and their tax dollars into suburban areas simultaneously cut off remaining urban residents from other parts of their metropolitan areas. With cars central to more and more Americans' social and economic lives, vehicle patrol emerged as the centerpiece of American policing. Squad cars changed the face of law enforcement, leading some observers to call for renewed commitments to the foot patrol and beat cops of earlier decades. However, the most influential version of these calls—Wilson and Kelling's "Broken Windows" article—led to its own profoundly negative consequences for police-community relations.

Several pivotal court cases shaped patterns of suburbanization, with important implications for criminal justice. These include *Buchanan v. Warley* (1917), in which the US Supreme Court invalidated statutes that explicitly imposed residential racial segregation, and *Corrigan et al. v. Buckley* (1926), in which the Court blessed private covenants with racially exclusionary terms.

Subsequent rulings in *Shelley v. Kraemer* (1948) and *Barrows v. Jackson* (1953) limited segregationists' ability to access courts to enforce racist private covenants; by that point, however, massive consequences for intergenerational wealth inequality were already baked in.

With both society and criminal justice increasingly car centered, the courts also continued to consider cases that addressed the balance between authorities' power and citizens' rights in vehicle stop situations. In *Brinegar v. United States* (1949) the Supreme Court notably reaffirmed the automobile exception established in *Carroll*. In so doing, it helped pave the way for the contemporary era of vehicle patrol and vehicle stops.

SUBURBANIZATION AND ITS DISCONTENTS

Historically, suburbs were poor, mostly populated by people who could not afford to live close to city centers. Before the Industrial Revolution, suburbs were dominated by tanneries, slaughterhouses, and other smelly, unsightly, and noxious industries.[1] This made them especially undesirable places to live. Outside the city walls of Paris, Montfaucon represented an even grislier feature of the suburban environment; from the medieval period up through the seventeenth century, an enormous gallows at Montfaucon suspended dozens of people sentenced to death by hanging, and "the remains of those drawn and quartered, beheaded, or otherwise executed in the city were suspended in chains."[2] The "crowd of skeletons swinging aloft, making mournful music with their chains at every blast of wind" constituted a stark reminder of the state's power over life and death and a dire warning of the penalties for running afoul of the law. Animals congregated at the site to scavenge the rotting corpses, whose stench sometimes reached the city itself.[3]

Industrialization provided the fundamental impetus for suburbs' transition to more desirable places to live. The rise of the factory system enabled greater separation between work and residence. Under the craft production model that predominated before the Industrial Revolution, skilled craftsmen lived near—or above—their shops with their extended families, acting as patriarchs overseeing a further extended "family" of employees and apprentices who lived with them.[4] Industrial production methods liberated factory owners from this sort of arrangement, allowing them to erect "both spatial and psychological barriers between themselves and their workers."[5]

In the nineteenth century changing economic and occupational arrangements made it possible for better-off people to move to suburban areas in greater numbers. Beyond the rise of industrialized production, this period also saw the development of transportation methods such as ferries, railroads, and the omnibus. These new ways of getting from place to place facilitated daily commuting, making it more feasible for people to live in outlying areas farther from their workplaces in more densely populated cities.[6] These developments presaged the private automobile's role in the development of modern suburbia.

Patterns in how people worked and where they lived changed over the course of the 1800s. Residents and developers in the Boston and New York metropolitan areas took significant steps toward contemporary suburbanization in the first half of the nineteenth century, and the suburbanization trend picked up in earnest in many major cities in the century's second half.[7] In 1849 one observer wrote that "nine-tenths of those whose rascalities have made Philadelphia so unjustly notorious live in the dens and shanties of the suburbs."[8] Over the next several decades, however, Philadelphia—like Buffalo, Cincinnati, Nashville, Chicago, San Francisco, and other large cities across the continent—saw many of its local elites moving to more spacious environs on the city's outskirts.[9]

In the twentieth century cars kicked suburbanization into overdrive. In the early days of the class market only wealthier Americans were able to access private automobiles, limiting the technology's capacity to broadly reshape the country's residential arrangements. The emergence of mass production and mass marketing helped larger shares of the public get behind the wheel; combined with significant investments in car-centered infrastructure, the increased share of American households with private cars made sweeping suburbanization possible. The Long Island Motor Parkway, completed in 1911, was the world's first road built exclusively for automobile use, and the American "road-building revolution" took hold in earnest in the 1920s.[10] This development of the infrastructure needed for automobile commuting enabled the 1920s boom in suburban housing development, with Los Angeles and Atlanta as leading models of the dispersed, low-density metropolitan form that arose in the era of automobility.[11] The National Automobile Chamber of Commerce reported that cars' proliferation caused an increase in home building of over 50% in 1922 alone.[12]

Automotive technology developed significantly in the interwar period, with manufacturers producing cars that were faster, more reliable, and more user-friendly than their predecessors. Together with the rapidly expanding and improving road network, these improvements allowed for cars to emerge as the go-to transportation technology. In turn, automobiles' rise to predominance among modes of transportation allowed urban planners and civil engineers to go all in on development projects that centered driving as the default—and preferred—way for people to move through space.[13]

The trend toward car-centered planning and building accelerated after World War II. "With the profitability, practicality, and political attractiveness

of car-centered activities well established, governments at all levels supple-
mented existing car-oriented transportation policies with new rules and
incentives governing land-use practices that redefined 'development' as 'car-
oriented development.'"[14] Building on the robust momentum established in
the first few decades of the twentieth century, the construction of the Interstate
Highway System cemented the automobile's privileged place in the US socioeconomic system.

Robert Moses's system of highways and bridges began reshaping the New
York metropolitan area in the 1930s. New ribbons of concrete connected Manhattan to Long Island and other outlying areas, enabling easier vehicle traffic for commuting and recreation. Moses's plan made these new arteries the
exclusive province of private autos, without provision for trains, subways,
or even buses, which were impeded by low overhead clearance on bridges.[15]
These decisions, of course, created inequities in how easily different groups of
people could move from place to place, with the better-off (disproportionately
White New Yorkers who could afford to purchase and maintain their own cars)
granted opportunities for mobility foreclosed to their less privileged counterparts. After World War II, with a massive influx of resources from the federal
government, Moses's power expanded, allowing him to build more of the car-
dedicated infrastructure that he prioritized over all else in his vision of how
to build the city. (Although Moses's focus on highways reshaped New York
and helped inspire car-centered urban planning and infrastructure projects
throughout the country, it is worth noting that Moses himself was skeptical of
the plan for a national highway system.)[16]

Moses's postwar road projects in New York included the Brooklyn-Queens
Expressway, the Cross Bronx Expressway, the Long Island Expressway, and the
Staten Island Expressway. Each of these massive public works undertakings
prioritized private cars above public transit and put the interests of better-off
people and vehicle commuters over those of less advantaged people.[17] The new
highways cut through established neighborhoods in Brooklyn, Queens, and
the Bronx. Moses aggressively used eminent domain to displace hundreds of
thousands of people living in the places he envisioned as the corridors for his
new commuter's paradise. And, once in place, the new highways functionally
isolated entire neighborhoods in the outer boroughs. People who could not
afford to move to the suburban developments prioritized in Moses's plan found
themselves largely cut off from the rest of the metropolis, as the new express-
ways bisected many of the subways, elevated train lines, and local streets and
sidewalks that had previously provided access to other parts of the city. The
highways produced isolation and immiseration in the neighborhoods they cut
through, contributing to poverty, segregation, and the rise of criminogenic

conditions. Areas adjoining interstates continue to be associated with higher rates of violent crime and property crime.[18]

Similar processes unfolded elsewhere in the country as other cities invested heavily in car-commuting infrastructure; Chicago's Dan Ryan Expressway, for instance, enclosed neighborhoods on the city's South Side, helping entrench poverty and racial segregation.[19] Decisions to route highways disproportionately through Black communities across the country displaced Black families, while those who remained in their neighborhoods but found themselves newly hemmed in were physically, symbolically, and psychologically isolated within their metropolitan areas.[20] And, in a pattern that reshaped entire metropolitan areas, highways became crucial mechanisms for moving better-off residents, tax bases, and other forms of capital away from city centers and toward urban peripheries, leading to the further concentration of disadvantage in increasingly segregated and socioeconomically marginalized urban neighborhoods.[21]

The Federal Housing Administration (FHA), created in 1934, offered people the opportunity to obtain mortgages with lower down payments and longer repayment periods than were previously available, making mortgages more accessible and driving down interest rates across the board.[22] As the FHA's influence continued to grow, the suburbanization trends of the interwar period expanded after World War II. Wanting to express the nation's appreciation for the soldiers, sailors, and airmen who had fought the Axis powers—and wanting to jump-start the economy in the transition to peacetime—Congress unanimously passed the Servicemen's Readjustment Act of 1944. Commonly known as the GI Bill, the law provided veterans opportunities to continue their educations and, most consequentially for suburbanization, guaranteed them access to home mortgages.[23] This program gave veterans the ability to purchase homes with no money down; in the immediate postwar years Uncle Sam helped 5 million returning service members get mortgages and buy houses.[24]

Many of these homes were located in the new housing developments that were proliferating on the margins of cities across the country. The federal government encouraged such projects, incentivizing developers to construct large blocks of single-family suburban houses.[25] One development in particular become synonymous with postwar suburban housing construction and the suburbanization of White middle-class life: Long Island's Levittown. Originally named Island Trees, the development was soon retitled to bear the surname of its developers. Levittown was a private housing development on a scale unprecedented in US history. Initially comprising 2,000 nearly identical houses, it grew to include more than 17,400 homes housing 82,000 residents.[26] Levittown was a symbolic center of the postwar baby boom as well as a significant material contributor to the demographic phenomenon; Levittown families had so many children that the development was nicknamed Fertility Valley and the Rabbit Hutch.[27]

Levitt and Sons had cut their teeth building residences for federal workers in the 1930s and during World War II, accumulating valuable experience in designing and implementing a mass-production approach to housing construction.[28] After the war they put this knowledge into full effect, carefully orchestrating an assembly-line-style system to build Levittown. The Levitts devised a 27-step plan for building each house. Starting from poured concrete slab foundations, specialized teams of workers went from site to site performing each construction stage in their preordained order. To increase efficiency and reduce costs, they used inexpensive standardized materials, took advantage of newly developed power tools, and did as much as possible to preassemble components of the houses off-site.[29] Using these methods, Levittown workers were able to complete forty houses per day.[30]

In developing this system for building single-family houses quickly, cheaply, and in great numbers, the Levitts functionally did for suburban residential developments what Henry Ford did for the automobile.[31] Taking primary control of the company in the postwar period, William J. Levitt became a prominent advocate of suburban living, and his Levittowns—first on Long Island and then in Pennsylvania and New Jersey—were iconic and influential models of how to churn out standardized homes rapidly enough to meet the surging demand for single-family residences.[32] Indeed, Levitt's successes in marshalling the efficiency advantages of standardized materials and assembly-line-style construction practices were so prominently reported and widely discussed that they inspired copycat builders across the country, from Boston to Los Angeles and from Houston to Chicago.[33]

In the 1950s and 1960s almost half of suburban housing was eligible for support from the FHA or the Veterans Administration.[34] Together with cheap mass-produced suburban houses, federal funding made it less expensive to purchase a new single-family home in the suburbs than to rent in the city.[35] By 1960 the number of Americans living in suburbs surpassed the number living in cities.[36] Over the coming decades most major cities actually lost residents, whereas tens of millions more would live in suburbs. The explosion of suburban developments composed of single-family houses in this period solidified suburbia as the default expectation for White middle-class life. At the same time, however, discrimination, redlining, and racially restrictive covenants closed such housing opportunities to people of color.[37] The country's experience with suburbanization demonstrates that residential racial segregation is not simply the result of preferences or people's decisions to self-sort by race. Rather, these patterns are the consequences of systematic racial exclusion on the part of both private sector and government actors.[38]

Discrimination by government agencies and private actors such as banks and homeowners' associations drove massive racial inequalities in housing access during suburbanization, creating patterns of residential segregation that continue to plague the country.[39] The FHA, created in 1934, negatively appraised houses in racially diverse areas and—until the Supreme Court's ruling in *Shelley v. Kraemer* (1948) forced their hand—expressed preferences for exclusionary zoning laws and recommended that deeds forbid reselling to Black home buyers.[40] Racial prejudice against African Americans led to back-lash from White neighbors when Black families attempted to integrate their neighborhoods, and ongoing discriminatory practices on the part of realtors presented systemic barriers to Black would-be home buyers.[41] Private lenders also took cues from the redlining practices embraced by the federal government's Home Owners' Loan Corporation and the FHA. As practiced by federal agencies, these policies systematically denied mortgage funds in neighborhoods with Black residents and in those postulated to possibly include Black residents in the future; in some cases this rendered entire cities ineligible for FHA-backed mortgages.[42]

In addition to serving as the model for the mass-produced suburban developments that soon swept across the country, Levittown also typified the racial discrimination and exclusion that characterized so many of them. The Levitt family themselves were early participants in "White flight," having left Brooklyn's Bedford-Stuyvesant neighborhood for Long Island upon the first Black family's arrival.[43] William Levitt demonstrated similar discrimination in the planning and management of Levittown. Contending that families of color would reduce White demand and drive down property values, Levitt decreed that "no dwelling shall be used or occupied except by members of the Caucasian race," and deeds to Levittown houses included covenants prohibiting owners from selling to nonwhites.[44]

These types of racially restrictive covenants date back to the 1800s but spread widely in the 1920s. In 1917's *Buchanan v. Warley*, the US Supreme Court held that a local ordinance barring African Americans from residing on majority-White blocks constituted a violation of the Fourteenth Amendment's due process clause. With such forms of residential exclusion by statute invalidated, private parties, such as developers and homeowners' associations, turned to racially restrictive terms in deeds and neighborhood bylaws to continue denying people of color opportunities to purchase homes.[45] After *Buchanan* these mechanisms of racial exclusion proliferated in cities and suburbs from coast to coast.[46]

Many local governments supported these measures, and state courts enforced them, ordering evictions of Black home buyers who were determined to have purchased houses in violation of exclusionary covenants. State courts also consistently upheld the constitutionality of racially restrictive covenants.[47] Despite government actors' involvement in the promulgation and enforcement of these rules, state courts deferred to their nominal status as terms imposed by private parties and thus outside the scope of the Fourteenth Amendment's mandate that states provide all people within their jurisdictions equal protection under the law. In 1926 the US Supreme Court similarly legitimized these rules, ruling in *Corrigan et al. v. Buckley* that private parties could establish covenants including racially exclusionary terms and that these agreements constituted legally enforceable contracts.[48]

After racially restrictive covenants survived judicial review at the Supreme Court in 1926, they continued to spread in communities across the country. In 1948's *Shelley v. Kraemer*, however, the Supreme Court returned to the matter, ultimately issuing a new decision that took a step back from *Corrigan v. Buckley*'s precedent. *Shelley v. Kraemer* involved an African American family who bought a St. Louis house in violation of a covenant the neighborhood had enacted in 1911 that prohibited people of African and Asian descent from buying homes in the area. Combining the case with a similar case coming out of Detroit, the US Supreme Court again considered the question of whether such racially restrictive covenants violated the Fourteenth Amendment. As in *Corrigan v. Buckley*, the Court held that, as private agreements, the covenants themselves did not constitute government action and thus did not trigger the Fourteenth's equal protection guarantee. Departing from their 1926 ruling, however, the Court held that state courts' enforcement of these covenants did constitute government action. Thus, private covenants that denied people access to housing opportunities on the basis of race were not illegal in and of themselves, but the Court declared them to be legally unenforceable, as judicial enforcement of such measures violated the equal protection clause.[49] Federal officials, including the leadership of the FHA, resented and resisted the *Shelley* ruling. The FHA came into compliance slowly and reluctantly over the next several years, and continued financing racially exclusionary housing developments until a 1962 executive order banned racial discrimination in federally supported housing programs.[50] Realtors' professional organizations and publications also continued to discourage selling homes in White areas to Black families.[51] Under the *Shelley* precedent a loophole had allowed private parties to sue people who sold houses in violation of racially restrictive covenants. In 1953's *Barrows v. Jackson* the US Supreme Court closed this loophole, ruling that state courts providing a venue for such suits consti-tuted a Fourteenth Amendment violation.[52] Although few new racially restric-tive covenants have been enacted subsequently, many preexisting covenants remained in place, albeit now lacking the force of law.[53] In recent years, however, multiple state legislatures have considered or passed bills providing homeown-ers ways to remove racially restrictive covenants from deeds.[54]

CRIMINAL JUSTICE AND THE AUTOMOBILE AGE

Cars and highways were essential elements in the suburbanization formula. The Levitts strategically located Levittown near three of Robert Moses's new parkways.[55] Similar patterns characterized suburbanization across the coun-try. Cars and highways facilitated suburban living. In turn, more people moving to suburbs meant more cars, more traffic, and more demands on road systems. This entrenched what transportation researcher Todd Litman calls the "cycle of automobile dependency": More people driving leads to car-centered infra-structure investments and development decisions, which then encourage (or require) more people to drive, propelling an ongoing, self-reinforcing circle of planning, building, and driving.[56] In the 1930s federal New Deal programs subsidized the construction of the Pennsylvania Turnpike, which offered a window into the high-speed, low-hassle car travel that limited-access high-ways enabled.[57]

Officially, the Federal-Aid Highway Act of 1956 launched the massive proj-ect of constructing the interstates that would reshape the American landscape, both physically and socially. Like the basic ingredients for the emerging car-centered world, however, the precursors to the Interstate Highway System began arriving decades earlier. Congress committed significant fiscal resources to road construction with the 1916 Federal Aid Road Act and the 1921 Federal Aid Highway Act; over the course of the 1920s the federal Bureau of Public Roads invested three-quarters of a billion dollars in road building and improvement, constructing or resurfacing more than 90,000 miles of highway.[58] The federal commitment to building and improving roads in the 1920s reflected the notion of connecting various parts of the country in a single, easily navigable network of vehicle routes, roads specifically designed to be interstate in nature.[59]

Trends toward suburbanization and automobile dependence advanced with more and more people buying cars. By 1951, 70% of US families had at least one car.[60] Eisenhower took office in 1953, and during his presidency Americans bought nearly 16,000 cars per day; by 1955 the number of registered automobiles reached 62.5 million.[61] Along with exploding numbers of privately owned cars, the country's experiences in the world wars of the early and mid-twentieth century furthered calls for highway development. During World War I, existing rail infrastructure proved insufficient to handle wartime shipping demands, and increased truck cargo deteriorated roads. The Federal Aid Highway Act of 1921 looked to address perceived shortcomings in the road system through granting highway construction funds to the states; these funds, in turn, supported the hiring of a quarter million construction workers.[62]

After World War II the federal government's highway-building program accelerated further. President Eisenhower's signing of the Federal-Aid Highway Act of 1956 pledged that the federal government would cover 90% of the construction expenses for interstate highways, allocated $25 billion in federal funds to the project, and created the Highway Trust Fund as an ongoing source of highway-building money.[63] The Bureau of Public Roads' plan for the system—officially named the General Locational of National System of Interstate Highways Including All Additional Routes at Urban Areas but commonly known as the Yellow Book—mapped out proposed routes for interstates across the country. This plan included not just the highways that would crisscross the country but also the local routes that would provide car-commuting arteries in the nation's metropolises.[64] This approach helped garner support from members of Congress, as it demonstrated how their constituents stood to benefit from the Interstate Highway System.[65] And, of course, prioritizing highways as car-commuter corridors in metropolitan areas functionally constituted a federal endorsement of suburbanization, as well as a commitment to dedicate major federal resources in support of the trend.[66]

By the 1950s observers had for decades noted the impact of automobility on criminal justice. In 1924, for instance, Arch Mandel of the Dayton Research Association wrote that "state lines have been eliminated by the automobile [and the] detection of criminals is becoming more and more a nation-wide task."[67] The thoroughgoing motorization of American society in the postwar era solidified the car and driver's status as "the basic police technology."[68] Fulfilling August Vollmer's vision of "motor-mounted policemen," departments across the country soon came to rely on car-driving police as a crucial law enforcement tool in an increasingly motorized society.[69] The conventional cop on the beat did not disappear altogether, but cruisers took on larger and larger shares of proactive patrol work and soon dominated in the area of rapid response.

As city and county police agencies evolved as generalists, responsible for enforcing a wide array of criminal laws and traffic ordinances, they created special-duty squads for dealing with such responsibilities as vice and traffic enforcement. The pronounced demands of policing cars and drivers also spurred the development of state police and highway patrol agencies. By the end of the 1930s nearly every state had a version of one of these centralized state-level law enforcement agencies, with traffic as their raison d'être and core responsibility.[70] Dissatisfied with the lack of communication and cooperation between different jurisdictions' local police departments, police reformer August Vollmer had advocated for state-level agencies that would unify municipal police departments and county sheriffs' offices under a single organization. In his vision these state police departments could functionally centralize policing within states' jurisdictions, facilitating the flow of information and providing more opportunities to enact systematic, coordinated crime control strategies.[71] However, Vollmer's vision of state police agencies as centralized command and control for the various subjurisdictions within their states did not come to pass. Rather, state police departments and highway patrol agencies emerged as independent entities with statewide jurisdiction—primarily including the enforcement of traffic laws—whereas city and county police agencies remained largely self-directing, operating in parallel and exercising jurisdiction in their local areas.[72]

Across jurisdictions, law enforcement agencies saw motorization as essential in the new age of automobility. Personal transportation, commerce, and culture were increasingly car based, and criminal activity followed suit. With more and more cars, a growing network of roads and highways, and populations spreading out from urban centers, "big city" problems increasingly came to smaller towns and rural areas. And cars themselves facilitated the commission of crimes crossing jurisdictional boundaries, making it less tenable for law enforcement authorities to rely on their old shoe-leather models of neighborhood beat patrol. Accordingly, between the 1930s and 1950s patrol cars almost entirely replaced conventional foot patrol, except in the most crowded northeastern cities.[73]

The proliferation of vehicle patrol was a sea change for American law enforcement. In addition to fundamentally reshaping the job for officers and citizens' experiences with the criminal justice system, the new wave of car-based policing sparked debates about how criminal justice should be organized, what core objectives it should pursue, and the best practices for advancing those goals.

Accountability and Transparency

Vehicle patrol and vehicle stops raised important new questions about individual liberties, the extent of legal authorities' power, and how constitutional protections should be applied to circumscribe exercises of authority, ensure accountability, and defend the rule of law. In their decision in *Carroll v. United States* (1925), the US Supreme Court granted law enforcement officers an unprecedented degree of discretionary authority to assess probable cause, and thus to decide whether a warrantless search was justified. With the *Carroll* holding in effect, stops, searches, and seizures on American streets and highways attracted contention and continued litigation. Some compared the heavy reliance on police discretion under the automobile exception for warrant requirements to the practices of totalitarian regimes, including Nazi Germany and Fascist Italy (recently defeated in World War II) and the authoritarian Soviet regime with which the nation contended in the ongoing Cold War.[74]

The American government and legal system pride themselves on their adherence to the rule of law. Under this principle the exercise of legal power is subject to limitations and constraints, as outlined in the Bill of Rights and elsewhere. The rule of law means that everyone is accountable under the law, even those invested with certain powers and responsibilities in government or the legal system. Although these systems entrust power to officials, the exercise of that power is not absolute, and its bearers are legally accountable. In short, no one is above the law.

The power of criminal justice authorities to act pursuant to their charge and within the scope of their jurisdiction does not inherently conflict with the rule of law. Rather, these officials' actions can become problematic when they occur—or appear to occur—outside the bounds of constitutionality or without appropriate regulation, oversight, and transparency.[75] The muscular discretionary authority provided to police officers in interactions with drivers presents the potential for problems in this area. Wide leeway to act based on training, experience, and personal judgment can open the door for exercises of legal power that are arbitrary, capricious, discriminatory, or otherwise out of sync with core constitutional protections related to due process and equal protection.

The Supreme Court wrestled with these questions in *Carroll*, ultimately holding that the practicalities and exigencies of effectively policing an increasingly car-centered social world required investing street-level officers with this elevated degree of discretionary authority. Similar questions—and similar facts—recurred when the Court agreed to hear *Brinegar v. United States* (1949). *Brinegar*'s circumstances strikingly paralleled *Carroll*'s. Like George Carroll, Virgil Brinegar was known to authorities for reputed involvement in the transportation of alcohol in violation of federal law. (The Volstead Act was of course no longer in effect in the 1940s; Brinegar was reputed to transport alcohol from Missouri, where its sale was legal, to Oklahoma, where it was not, in violation of the Liquor Enforcement Act of 1936.) Spotting Brinegar's vehicle westbound in Oklahoma near the Missouri border, federal investigators from the Alcohol Tax Unit pulled him over, based on their assessment of his reputation in this regard as well as their determination that the vehicle appeared to be weighted with cargo. At the scene of the stop, an investigator asked Brinegar, "How much liquor have you got in the car this time?" Brinegar said, "Not too much," and the officers searched the car, finding a case of alcohol in the front seat beneath a lap robe and twelve more in the trunk.[76]

Federal authorities charged Brinegar with transporting liquor in violation of the Liquor Enforcement Act and convicted him based primarily on the incriminating contraband resulting from the roadside search. Brinegar, in turn, appealed the conviction, arguing that the search had been conducted in violation of his Fourth Amendment rights and thus that the resulting evidence should have been ruled inadmissible. (Here, Brinegar attempted to invoke the exclusionary rule, the notion that if a search is unconstitutional or otherwise illegal, any evidence resulting from that search needs to be excluded from a subsequent prosecution. In *Weeks v. United States* [1914] the Supreme Court had established that the exclusionary rule applied in federal prosecutions; because Brinegar was charged under federal law, this was the precedent potentially at issue in his case. Through the process known as selective incorporation, the Supreme Court would extend the exclusionary rule to prosecutions under state law in *Mapp v. Ohio* [1961].)

The Supreme Court agrees to hear only a small fraction of the cases petitioners ask them to review. Typically, they prioritize cases that they believe involve unsettled statutory or constitutional questions; in theory, they are less inclined to hear appeals that involve straightforward application of established precedents, unless justices believe that those precedents should be overturned. In Brinegar's appeal of his conviction, the question before the Court appeared to involve the relatively straightforward application of the *Carroll* precedent, regarding whether reputational factors constituted probable cause to initiate a vehicle stop and subsequently a vehicle search without a warrant. With the case for probable cause in *Brinegar* so similar to the case for probable cause in *Carroll*, the principle of stare decisis would dictate that the Court should let the previous ruling stand and apply the *Carroll* holding to the instant case. The fact that the justices agreed to hear *Brinegar* suggested that they may have had concerns about the *Carroll* precedent.[77]

After considerable consternation and several changing votes, the majority ultimately decided to defer to *Carroll* and treat it as controlling precedent in *Brinegar*. In *Carroll*, the Taft Court established the automobile exception to warrant requirements as something of a compromise. Situating cars somewhere in the middle of the classical public-private distinction, the Court had provided criminal justice authorities with expanded powers that reflected the new realities of policing a motorized society, while also establishing the basic expectation that (in theory) law enforcement officers should not be permitted to stop any vehicle at any time for any reason. In *Brinegar*, a different group of justices declined to overturn this basic holding. Instead, they preserved the reliance on officers' judgment and deference to their expertise, suspicions, and suppositions in making determinations of probable cause. Justice Rutledge's majority opinion noted that "in dealing with probable cause . . . as the very name implies, we deal with probabilities. These are not technical; they are the factual and practical considerations of everyday life on which reasonable and prudent men, not legal technicians, act."[78] Accordingly, the Court endorsed relying on officers to assess whether "reasonable ground for belief of guilt" exists, providing the probable cause needed for a warrantless stop and search under *Carroll*. Justice Rutledge wrote that "long-prevailing standards seek to safeguard citizens from rash and unreasonable interferences with privacy and from unfounded charges of crime. They also seek to give fair leeway for enforcing the law in the community's protection."[79] Noting that the work of law enforcement often involves making decisions under conditions of uncertainty and ambiguity, Justice Rutledge argued that "room must be allowed for some mistakes on their part."[80] If, however, officers acted reasonably in drawing conclusions about probable cause, they should be considered within their remit and in compliance with Fourth Amendment protections. In *Brinegar*, the Court ultimately concluded, this standard was met, allowing the evidence used in the prosecution to stand under the Constitution.

Interaction, Familiarity, and Police-Community Relations

In addition to vehicle-based policing's implications for individual liberties and the rule of law, the replacement of the beat cop with the squad car changed the public face of criminal justice. In the conventional vision of foot patrol, officers would be known to local residents. According to one 1970s observer, such familiarity lent itself to "reassurance" as a function of police patrol: "the feeling of security and safety that a citizen experiences when he sees a police officer or police patrol car nearby."[81] Obviously, not all Americans feel reassured by police presence, and the likelihood of such reactions varies substantially across both social groups and specifics of circumstance. Part of our 1970s observer's proposal, however, was that a beat cop whom local residents recognize because of sustained community presence and interaction had a better shot of inducing feelings of reassurance than the comparatively unknown, anonymous officer cruising through the neighborhood in a squad car.[82]

Similar considerations have recurred throughout the history of car-based policing, deriving from the notion that the greater response speed and geographic coverage of vehicle patrol might come at the cost of losing some of the familiarity and trust that foot patrol better facilitates. All the way back at the origins of the modern, motorized US police department, influential police reformer August Vollmer had thoughts on both sides of the issue. Vollmer argued that officers should be intimately familiar with the neighborhoods where they worked, including "the character, occupation, and habits of every resident on his beat so that when inquiries are made concerning any person living within the boundaries of his beat he will be able to supply his commanding officer with correct information without delay."[83] Knowing the neighborhood's personalities and regular patterns of activity maximized the beat cop's effectiveness as the department's "eyes and ears" on the street.[84] At the same time, however, Vollmer famously advocated for "motor-mounted" police, a "roving police presence," to cover wide areas and more effectively deter crime.[85]

The costs and benefits of foot patrol relative to vehicle patrol were a crucial element in James Q. Wilson and George L. Kelling's remarkably consequential 1982 *Atlantic* article "Broken Windows," which laid the intellectual foundation for broken windows theory and precipitated a national—and international—revolution in criminal justice strategy and tactics. This article opened with a discussion of New Jersey's Safe and Clean Neighborhoods Program, which included shifting some officers' patrols out of black-and-whites and back onto the sidewalk. Such interventions, Wilson and Kelling argued, were crucial to changing neighborhood environments, engendering orderliness and strengthening mechanisms of informal social control. "In theory," they wrote, "an officer in a squad car can observe as much as an officer on foot; in theory, the former can talk to as many people as the latter. But the reality of police-citizen encounters is powerfully altered by the automobile. An officer on foot cannot separate himself from the street people; if he is approached, only his uniform and his personality can help him manage whatever is about to happen. . . . In a car, an officer is more likely to deal with street people by rolling down the window and looking at them. The door and the window exclude the approaching citizen; they are a barrier."[86]

Wilson and Kelling proposed that visible signals of social disorder, as observed in such things as broken windows in neighborhood buildings, increased the likelihood of more serious types of crime occurring. In a line of thinking paralleling arguments about marijuana as a gateway drug, they contended that minor crimes symbolizing disorder functioned as a "foot in the door" creating conditions conducive to the commission of more serious crimes. Broken windows theory posits that low-level offenses serve as a signal that the community is unwilling or unable to enforce norms. Such environments, in turn, make people more likely to commit crimes under the understanding that such behavior will be ignored or tolerated. On the other hand, people who are law-abiding or disinclined toward disorderliness are incentivized to leave the neighborhood if they are able, or to withdraw from social interaction if they are not.

This theory of crime causation implies particular prevention strategies. If low-level markers of urban disorder—graffiti, public drinking, literal broken windows—are believed to lead to criminal offending, then it logically follows that policing strategies should attempt to counteract these low-level offenses to reduce rates of more serious crime. Broken windows theory emphasizes that the norm of orderliness must be defended and suggests that police departments have a crucial role to play in that process. Premised on Wilson and Kelling's ideas, police departments across the country—indeed, around the world— embraced order-maintenance and quality-of-life policing strategies that emphasized proactive and aggressive enforcement of misdemeanor laws against offenses such as graffiti writing, loitering, public urination, public drinking, aggressive panhandling, turnstile jumping, and street-level prostitution. First in major cities and then in smaller cities and towns, broken windows theory produced a remarkable degree of consensus in policing circles that neglect of these types of offenses was a significant defect in historical approaches to urban policing.

Wilson and Kelling contended that increasing contact between the public and the police, including by shifting patrols out of cars and onto sidewalks, would deter crime and disrupt cycles of neighborhood decline. They argued that, in so doing, these strategies would help strengthen poor relationships between police and the communities they serve and would help fend off the type of antisocial conduct that leads to the most serious consequences for both victims and perpetrators. However, the outcomes of broken-windows-based policing strategies were not what Wilson and Kelling predicted. In New York City and other metropolitan areas across the country, stop-and-frisks, misdemeanor arrests, and heavy-handed order-maintenance crackdowns were concentrated overwhelmingly in poor and minority neighborhoods and directed more at people of color than at White people. Major increases in arrests and prosecutions widened the net of entanglement in the criminal justice system, causing many more people to cycle through arrest, detention, prosecution, and incarceration. Order-maintenance interventions also created many volatile confrontations between police and citizens. These confrontations, in turn, precipitated numerous high-profile killings of citizens that began with suspected misdemeanors, such as stealing Swisher Sweets (Michael Brown), selling "loosie" cigarettes (Eric Garner), or passing a bad twenty dollar bill (George Floyd).

Ultimately, the implementation of broken windows theory through policing strategies produced results that were in many ways the opposite of what its advocates had prognosticated. Rather than strengthen police-community relations, order-maintenance policing often weakened them further. Putting more officers on sidewalks and increasing their interactions with citizens may have put more of a human face on the police department relative to officers cruising by in squad cars. That face, though, turned out to be less reassuring and trusted than some envisioned[87] and more an emblem of intrusiveness, surveillance, and violence. Indeed, Kelling himself summarized his reaction to many police departments' implementation of broken windows theory with two words: "Oh, shit." In one interview Kelling said, "There's been a lot of things done in the name of Broken Windows that I regret." As he explained, "You're just asking for a whole lot of trouble. You don't just say one day, 'Go out and restore order.' You train officers, you develop guidelines. Any officer who really wants to do order maintenance has to be able to answer satisfactorily the question, 'Why do you decide to arrest one person who's urinating in public and not arrest [another]?' . . . And if you can't answer that question, if you just say 'Well, it's common sense,' you get very, very worried."[88]

In addition to the issues identified above, there is limited evidence that broken-windows-inspired policing works as advertised, in terms of reducing rates of more serious crime through cracking down on low-level offenses. Robert Sampson and Stephen Raudenbush concluded in 1999 "that the current fascination in policy circles . . . on cleaning up disorder through law enforcement techniques appears simplistic and largely misplaced, at least in terms of directly fighting crime."[89] Other observers have reached similar conclusions, flagging the lack of evidence for the effectiveness of order-maintenance policing as a way to limit serious crime and highlighting the approach's harmful consequences.[90]

COMMUNITIES, CITIZENS, AND COPS
IN A CAR-CENTERED SOCIETY

In 1964 Marshall McLuhan wrote that "the car has become the carapace, the protective and aggressive shell, of urban and suburban man."[91] These words vividly captured a new reality that had overtaken the US economy and culture in the preceding decades. Automobiles offered unprecedented levels of personal mobility, especially after massive governmental projects to build a network of roads, bridges, and highways catering to their use. These developments facilitated a profound shift in the country's residential patterns, as car commuting enabled millions of people to move to the suburbs.

Cars are fundamental to the story of American life in the twentieth and twenty-first centuries.[92] This story notably includes the trend toward suburbanization, which was propelled by cars becoming cheaper, faster, and more reliable and massive governmental investment in motor vehicle infrastructure. Lower-income people and people of color are more likely than other constituencies to rely on public transit systems, which the federal and state governments have systematically underfunded relative to car-focused projects.[93] These policy and fiscal decisions continue to make cars crucial resources. Meanwhile, people who cannot afford cars find themselves facing significant transportation-related barriers to opportunity and upward social mobility.

The predominant focus on facilitating car commuting, and automobile traffic more generally, demonstrated a prioritization of the needs and interests of the suburbanizing population. This population, of course, was not randomly selected or nationally representative. Suburbanization offered a mechanism for better-off Whites to move away from city centers and thus separate themselves from ethnic and racial minorities.[94] Limited-access highways catering to car commuters enabled the transition to a suburbanized society. White flight from cities to suburbs furthered residential racial segregation and concentrated disadvantage in urban neighborhoods. As sociologist Kevin Fox Gotham summarizes, "The mass suburbanization of Whites and the ghettoization of Blacks has been one of the most profound population shifts in the twentieth century."[95] This phenomenon, however, was not simply the result of comparatively advantaged people choosing to leave cities for the suburbs' single-family homes and backyards. Lenders, homeowners' associations, and legal institutions all provided opportunities to Whites and denied them to people of color. Thus, in addition to furthering the "cycle of automobile dependency,"[96] suburbanization and highway construction cemented race and class segregation and inequality, with profound consequences for American society and criminal justice.

In an increasingly motorized society, squad cars quickly emerged as the central tools of proactive police patrol and reactive rapid response. Following the *Carroll* decision's establishment of the automobile exception to warrant requirements, questions about police officers' exercise of discretionary authority in these interactions persisted. In 1949's *Brinegar v. United States*, however, the Supreme Court again endorsed the basic logic of the Court's holding in *Carroll*, confirming that responding officers' reasonable determinations of probable cause were constitutionally acceptable bases for stopping and searching vehicles without warrants. As vehicle stops became the primary way that citizens directly interacted with criminal justice authorities, *Brinegar* reaffirmed a core tenet of Fourth Amendment doctrine in the automobile age.

Altogether, the midcentury period saw federal, state, and local governments going all in on road and highway infrastructure, comparatively advantaged people moving to suburbs in ever greater numbers, and urban neighborhoods becoming increasingly disadvantaged and racially segregated. At the same time, policing shifted notably, away from the classical vision of the cop on the beat and toward car-centered policing strategies. In response to disorder, crime, and poor police-community relationships in urban centers, policing scholars and practitioners raised questions about the implications of car-based policing. Some highlighted the idea that separating officers from the community by putting them in patrol cars may have contributed to urban problems and that putting officers back on the sidewalk could facilitate relationships and communication between the people and the police. In turn, this could help counteract disorder and improve neighborhood environments. Most influential by far was Wilson and Kelling's article on "Broken Windows."[97] Broken windows theory spurred a nationwide overhaul of policing strategies, based on the notion that policing for order maintenance would strengthen local communities and ultimately reduce rates of more serious crime. These strategies' results, however, did not align with Wilson and Kelling's optimistic projections; instead, they further deteriorated trust in criminal justice authorities, fueled mass incarceration, engendered discrimination, and led to numerous violent deaths.

Dependence on cars in social life and policing not only reshaped the nature of mid-twentieth-century law enforcement; it also set the stage for the significant developments and heated controversies that came to characterize American criminal justice for the rest of that century and into the next. Cars, of course, continue to be central parts of most Americans' daily lives. The Census Bureau estimates that 86% of employed Americans rely on private motor vehicles for commuting.[98] Cars are similarly crucial means of transportation for other activities. In recent years, poverty has suburbanized, and more poor people now live in suburbs than in urban areas.[99] This development has further entrenched cars' necessity to people across the socioeconomic spectrum as well as vehicle stops' status as the most common setting for direct interactions between citizens and law enforcement officials. Chapter 6 turns attention to these interactions, addressing in detail the practice and the problems of contemporary car-based policing.

SIX

Discretion and Disparities in Car-Based Criminal Justice

Key issues of criminal justice fairness and equity arose in the automobile era. In many cases these issues hinge on the discretionary action that is definitional to the work of street-level bureaucrats. People working as street-level bureaucrats are required to respond to complicated, dynamic situations with limited direct oversight. This necessitates relying on one's training and experience to determine how to proceed. Because street-level bureaucrats are crucial gatekeepers in the distribution of benefits and the application of sanctions, their discretionary decision making has profound implications for people's lives. Police officers and 911 operators are key examples of street-level bureaucrats in the criminal justice system. These actors' discretionary actions are crucial factors in shaping people's experiences with—and perceptions of—criminal justice institutions.

Patterns in discretionary decision making that accumulate into systematic differences in different groups' experiences are injustices that violate constitutional protections. Emergency operators and vehicle patrol officers are pivotal actors in the reactive and proactive sides of contemporary car-based criminal justice. The people who answer 911 calls make crucial decisions about whether and to what extent criminal justice agencies will deploy reactive vehicular rapid response, affecting the distribution of both the supportive and the punitive aspects of government power. Vehicle patrol, on the other hand, has emerged as the predominant tool of proactive policing in the United States. Vehicle stops, accordingly, have emerged as the predominant form of direct interaction between members of the public and criminal justice authorities. The

Supreme Court's decisions in *Terry v. Ohio* (1968) and *Whren v. United States* (1996) give police officers wide latitude to stop and search vehicles and drivers they find suspicious. These stops are plagued by stark racial inequalities. Together, these facts make law enforcement officers' discretionary decisions about whom to pull over and how to handle vehicle stops a crucial site for understanding the pronounced disparities in different groups' experiences with the criminal justice system.

DISCRETION'S PIVOTAL ROLE IN CRIMINAL JUSTICE

In the summer of 1976 Warren Kelly was a young man of 25 or 26 years old. One morning, he was headed eastbound on Long Island's Southern State Parkway (one of Robert Moses's early New York highway projects) in a Toyota Corolla, a company car. He was driving against the primary direction of traffic; at that time of day, most Long Island drivers were headed westbound, toward jobs in the city, not eastbound, toward Long Island's residential areas. On the eastbound side traffic was flowing smoothly, with almost everyone exceeding the posted speed limit of 55 by at least 5 or 10 miles per hour. This group included Kelly, who recalls he was doing about 60 or a bit above, matching the general pace of the other cars on the uncongested stretch of highway. He was thus surprised to see the flashing red lights of a New York State Police cruiser in his rearview mirror; he did not think anything about his driving differentiated him from the other cars around him traveling at similar rates of speed. After he came to a stop on the shoulder and the trooper came to his window, Kelly relayed the same sentiment: "Why is it that you're pulling me over, when there's all these other people that are doing the same thing?" The trooper replied, "Sir, today is your day," implying, by Kelly's reckoning, "Tomorrow it will be someone else's turn."[1]

Mr. Kelly's experience provides an example of police discretion in action. In their day-to-day work of responding to the unpredictable and varied situations in which they find themselves, police officers are invested with authority to make decisions and act on them based on training, experience, and personal judgment. This type of discretion is a defining characteristic of what political scientist Michael Lipsky calls street-level bureaucrats: frontline government employees at "the agencies whose workers interact with and have wide discretion over the dispensation of benefits or the allocation of public sanctions."[2] Street-level bureaucrats are the people who do public-facing work for these agencies. In that capacity, they operate with limited direct oversight and considerable autonomy in allocating their time and energy, reading people, interpreting situations, and deciding how to try to resolve problems.

The category of street-level bureaucrats includes police and other law enforcement officers, other public-facing actors in the criminal justice system, public school teachers, social workers, public assistance agency employees, and so forth.[3] Workers in each of these roles are entrusted with making day-to-day decisions about providing members of the public with state-sponsored resources, such as SNAP benefits, mental health services, or responses to calls for police service, as well as imposing penalties, such as welfare fraud charges, school suspensions, or speeding tickets. As Lipsky's definition suggests, a hallmark of work as a street-level bureaucrat is the capacity to exercise discretion in making many of these calls: the ability to assess situations that arise and act accordingly based on one's best judgment. By necessity, these decisions are typically made without running questions up the chain of command, although their superiors can of course later hold street-level bureaucrats accountable for improper or illegal actions.[4] Given these workers' crucial role in shaping government responses to real-world situations, studies of street-level bureaucrats are a key element of research on policy implementation, assessing what actually happens on the ground when written laws and policies are put into action.

As Mr. Kelly learned firsthand on that summer day in 1976, police officers' discretion notably includes selecting whom to pull over, even if that means picking somewhat arbitrarily from among numerous people engaged in similar driving behaviors. As discussed further below, this experience relates to police officers' role as street-level bureaucrats tasked with imposing public sanctions (in Kelly's case, a traffic citation). Another group of street-level bureaucrats plays a notably consequential role in allocating policing resources as a public benefit, when people contact government agencies to request police response or other emergency services.

Every day, emergency service organizations in metropolitan areas across the country receive thousands of requests for various forms of assistance. According to the National Emergency Number Association, Americans call 911 about 240 million times a year.[5] The resources of police, fire departments, and emergency medical services are in high demand, and the dispatchers who work in 911 centers continually make decisions about how to respond to citizen requests. The implications of these decisions are hard to overstate; in many cases, choosing the appropriate course of action is literally a matter of life or death.

Operators who respond to citizens' requests for emergency services perform essential work at the boundary between the public and the organizations tasked with responding to their reports of emergencies requiring government intervention. Through their interactions with members of the public, these street-level bureaucrats make decisions about how emergency response resources will be distributed—or not—in response to public calls for service. In this sense they function as pivotal "gatekeepers," a term social scientists use to describe actors who control access to various types of resources, opportunities, and forms of social recognition.[6] Emergency call center operators mind the gate to governmental emergency response, making decisions about whether calls merit vehicular rapid response and, if so, making initial determinations of what kind of response is appropriate. In this crucial discretionary process, they need to delineate between emergencies and nonemergencies, between problems suited for emergency response and problems not suited for emergency response. If they determine that a response is appropriate, they also need to assess what form that response should take and how high a priority to give the incident. In making these decisions, emergency response operators frequently need to engage in forms of triage, in which they give more pressing matters preference over less urgent concerns in the allocation of response resources. Just as emergency rooms are not first come, first served, but instead attend to the most seriously ill and injured patients first, emergency response coordinators give first priority to issues that they conclude require immediate attention. This is a common theme in street-level bureaucracies; because demand for services regularly outstrips workers' supplies of time and energy, street-level bureaucrats have to make tough decisions about where to invest scarce resources.[7]

In their role as street-level bureaucrats at the forefront of emergency response services, 911 operators face a type of pressure that many frontline public service workers share. They need to navigate and negotiate the differing, and often conflicting, imperatives of responsiveness to citizens' needs and the limitations and priorities of police departments, fire departments, and emergency medical services, while also adhering to the requirements of law and policy. The realities of how government will respond, if at all, to citizens' calls for assistance hinge on how street-level bureaucrats interpret information they receive and their resulting discretionary actions. In the 911 context this means determining how much weight to give to different reports and deciding what to do about them. To guide this process, 911 operators deploy organizationally developed quasi-theories to make sense of often ambiguous citizen reports and translate them into coded categories that facilitate agency response.[8]

In addition, call takers face an often difficult task as they operate at the border between the concerned public and the officially detached, objective organs of the state. Complicating the bureaucratic roles and realities is the significant emotional labor necessary to maintain the even-keeled, cool demeanor expected of crisis-management organization representatives; when this carefully maintained relationship breaks down, the consequences can be disastrous.[9]

From the perspective of crime control and law enforcement, civilian reports are a crucial source of information. Police do not directly observe most crimes. Instead, they rely heavily on members of the public to inform them about potential crimes that have occurred or are in progress. Thus, beyond the high stakes for victims or other affected parties who call 911 to report emergencies, responding agencies themselves have a major interest in ensuring that civilian reports are received and handled properly. This makes efficiently processing information from civilian reports and effectively translating that information into official classification systems a crucial organizational function.[10]

Accordingly, frontline workers in emergency call centers play a pivotal and high-pressure role. Their organizations rely on them to record the civilian report information that provides the basis for most reactive law enforcement activity and to do so quickly and accurately, particularly when time is of the essence, as it often is in emergencies. As this characteristic of emergency situations suggests, 911 operators also have to reckon with the serious stakes involved in many of the calls they receive: a house is on fire, a robbery is in progress, someone is having a heart attack, someone has been stabbed—the list goes on and on. People who call 911 are often in the middle of the worst situations of their entire lives, and call takers have to assess their situations and determine the appropriate response. All the while, operators need to find a balance between the imperatives of responsiveness to citizens' needs and the limits of emergency services' resources and capabilities.

A variety of issues arise in rapid response to civilian calls. Fundamentally, communication failures between civilians and 911 operators can impede operators' ability to effectively receive and process information about the report. People calling 911 may be in states of panic or shock; they may have mental illnesses or be experiencing mental health crises; they may be drunk or high; they may be young children; they may speak a language that 911 operators do not. All these circumstances can make it difficult or impossible for call takers to understand reports and can thus hamper responses.

Whatever their precipitating circumstances, slow responses and nonresponses to civilian reports are an important issue, and one with particularly notable implications for police-community relations. Perceptions that emergency services deprioritize or ignore calls, especially calls from particular neighborhoods or constituencies, can erode civilians' trust in government and willingness to contact law enforcement when they have problems. In the song "911 Is a Joke," a single off Public Enemy's 1990 album *Fear of a Black Planet*, Flavor Flav captured this sentiment:

Now I dialed 911 a long time ago
Don't you see how late they're reactin'?
They only come and they come when they wanna
So get the morgue truck and embalm the goner.

. . .

A no-use number with no-use people
If your life is on the line then you're dead today.
Latecomers with the late-coming stretcher
That's a body bag in disguise y'all, I betcha.

. . .

So get up, get, get, get down
911 is a joke in yo' town.

Flavor Flav wrote this song after a friend of his was stabbed in a fight, suffering a collapsed lung. 911 was called, but it took about half an hour for an ambulance to respond. The stabbing victim went into a coma and died in the ambulance on the way to the hospital. Based on this experience, Flavor Flav concluded in the song, "I call a cab 'cause a cab will come quicker," suggesting his lack of faith in emergency response services and demonstrating his sense that people in his neighborhood cannot rely on local government to respond effectively to their reports of emergencies. And, of course, unwillingness to call 911 can derive from more than skepticism about responders' likelihood of helping; members of minority communities may justifiably believe that emergency response will pose an active danger to them. Denzel Curry encapsulated such sentiments in his 2022 song "John Wayne": "911, emergency will murder me the day I call 'em." For Curry, like many Black Americans, this threat is no abstraction; in 2014 his brother Treon Johnson died after being pepper-sprayed, Tased, and physically restrained by police responding to a call.[11]

From criminal justice authorities' perspective, people's mistrust of emergency responders and aversion to calling 911 are particularly problematic because of what they indicate about willingness to share information with law enforcement. Without civilian reports, many more crimes would escape police departments' notice. And when investigating crimes of which they are aware, police need people to be willing to share information and act as witnesses. When people view criminal justice authorities as unwilling or unable to help them in their times of need, they are less likely to engage in these forms of cooperation with police activities. This, in turn, makes it harder for police to apprehend and prosecute people who commit antisocial acts, threatening to create a vicious cycle: People perceive the police as uninterested in resolving problems in their neighborhoods, which makes them less likely to trust and work with police, which makes it harder for police to resolve problems in their neighborhoods. Furthermore, beliefs that police cannot or will not respond to serious criminal offending in certain neighborhoods may encourage people to take the law into their own hands and personally seek retribution for victimization incidents. Such tendencies foment more violence and more victimization and thus may further entrench the notion that the neighborhood is on its own when it comes to penalizing seriously harmful and antisocial behaviors.

Police officers themselves may also be unwilling or unable to respond to reports of emergencies because of their personal mental states or because they see a situation as too dangerous. As a recent incident in Detroit indicated, these circumstances can obtain even when a call for assistance comes not from a citizen but from another member of the police force.[12] In November 2019 Officer Rasheen McClain and his partner responded to a report of an armed home invasion in progress. At the scene Officer McClain led a four-officer team into the house to pursue the suspect. As the team entered the home's basement, the suspect opened fire, shooting McClain in the neck and striking his partner in the ankle. McClain's injury would prove fatal. As radio calls of "shots fired" and "officer down" went out, other officers in the area rushed to respond. Detroit Police sergeant Ronald Kidd, however, declined to follow his colleagues toward the scene of the incident to attempt to assist Officer McClain or apprehend the suspect. Instead, he opted to stay where he was a block away and take cover, and advised a newer officer working with him to do the same. After McClain died, Sergeant Kidd's inaction became the subject of significant criticism from local media and his own police chief, James Craig, who lamented that Kidd "sat in his scout car a block away while you could hear people screaming 'officer down' on the radio."[13] This incident also led to the resurfacing of previous issues in Sergeant Kidd's policing career. In 2014 the Detroit Police Department terminated him for cowardice after he failed to come to the assistance of his partner when a mentally ill man assaulted her in a detention facility; instead, video footage showed Kidd walking away from the scene.[14] Despite the department's determination that Kidd's actions constituted cowardice meriting termination, he was reinstated after sixty-eight days. After the 2019 incident Kidd's attorney defended his client's record of service as a Marine and police officer and said that an episode of post-traumatic stress disorder led to his failure to respond to the radio calls about Officer McClain's shooting. After a review of the incident, however, Sergeant Kidd was first suspended and then "compelled to retire," according to his attorney.[15]

Emergency services operators also need to make difficult decisions about how to allocate limited public resources. Emergency centers receive many requests for service and have to make tough calls about which most require immediate responses. The proliferation of cell phones has further complicated this issue. Today, four out of five 911 calls come from cell phones.[16] It is generally a good thing that it is now easier to contact emergency services than it was before most people carried a phone around in their pocket. However, the lowered barrier to contacting emergency services also means more calls coming in, more reports to sort through, and more hang-ups to call back. Emergency call centers have also had to make technological and organizational adjustments in their efforts to trace calls' origins, as locating cell phone users is significantly more complicated than identifying the location of a hardwired telephone.[17] Another problem has arisen in the era of smartphones and smartwatches. With many devices including an emergency call feature that requires only a tap or two to activate, 911 centers have seen spikes in the numbers of accidental calls they receive; each of these unintentional calls require a callback and sometimes a police response if operators are unable to reach callers.[18]

The ease of calling 911 on a mobile phone has also had significant implications for another issue in rapid response: escalation. This is the basic notion that relatively minor problems can become more serious situations as a result of police involvement. When police are called, something that began as a suspicion (perhaps unfounded) or an interpersonal squabble can turn highly contentious. This can create risks for responding officers, directly involved parties, and bystanders, and can lead to instances of violence, even death. Cell phones offer civilians more convenient and flexible means of contacting emergency services, but this enhanced connectivity also offers greater opportunity for escalating possible nonemergencies to perceived emergency status and potentially creating dangerous circumstances. Recently, high-profile instances of White people calling 911 to report unfounded or dubious claims about Black people have brought significant popular attention to this issue.

RAPID RESPONSE, VEHICLE PATROL, AND OVER- AND UNDERPOLICING

The sentiments expressed in Public Enemy's "911 Is a Joke" and the experiences of Black Americans who have been the subjects of unjustified 911 calls reflect a common theme in many Americans' relationships to the criminal justice system. Especially in the nation's poor and racial and ethnic minority communities, people often feel that they are both overpoliced *and* underpoliced. Perceptions of overpolicing reflect feelings of experiencing too much attention and too many intrusions from law enforcement in day-to-day life. Particularly since the advent of broken-windows-based policing tactics, many members of lower-

income and minority communities feel that they and people in their neighborhoods are too often stopped, questioned, and searched, too often arrested and
prosecuted for minor offenses, and too often injured or killed in interactions
with police officers responding to suspicions of low-level infractions. On the
other hand, many members of the same communities feel that their neighborhoods are actually *under*policed when it comes to serious and violent crime.
That is, when they call police to respond to situations in their neighborhoods,
they feel underserved, and they believe that criminal justice authorities are too
often either unable or unwilling to catch and prosecute people who commit
harmful acts.

Substantial statistical evidence supports such feelings. Controlling for estimates of crime participation rates, people of color, especially Black people,
are disproportionately likely to be stopped, questioned, and searched and to
experience uses of force.[19] Black and Latino people are also much more likely
to be arrested for misdemeanor offenses than White people.[20] Some of these
trends are due to greater police presence in poorer and minority neighborhoods; racial disparities, however, persist across different types of neighborhoods.[21] Numerous studies also indicate that clearance rates for serious violent
crimes, such as homicides, are lower in neighborhoods that are poorer and
home to more racial and ethnic minorities[22] and that murders involving victims of color are less likely to be solved than murders involving White victims.[23]
(The research on homicide clearance rates is not entirely consistent on these
matters, however.)[24] Due in part to these phenomena, people of color, and especially Black people, are less likely to trust the police and government in general
and more likely than White people to feel both underpoliced and overpoliced.[25]
Personal histories of involvement with the criminal justice system exacerbate
these racial differences.[26]

DISCRETION IN CAR-BASED POLICING

When he was stopped in the summer of 1976, Warren Kelly felt that the state
trooper's decision to pull him over was more or less random; indeed, the trooper's statement that today was his day seemed to confirm as much. This type
of decision making on officers' part, however, is central to car-based policing.
Indeed, discretion and judgment calls emerged right away as particularly crucial aspects of policing in the automotive age.[27] In the new era of traffic enforcement and vehicle stops, the law enforcement officer went from serving
primarily "as the protector of the people's lives and properties" to serving "as a
judge and jury upon many trivial matters on which he is expected to summar-
ily decide."[28] The mismatch between massive traffic volumes and police labor

and resources makes some degree of selective enforcement of traffic laws unavoidable. This situation also implies some inevitable conflict with members of the public who are unhappy to be chosen as targets for traffic enforcement.[29] As Kelly experienced firsthand, drivers may find it especially irritating if they are pulled over for driving behaviors that they perceive other drivers to also be engaged in.[30]

Traffic enforcement brought middle- and upper-class Americans into regular contact with the criminal justice system for the first time.[31] This was particularly the case in the automobile's early years, when only well-off people could afford cars. Thus, the automobile age entailed a certain element of universalization in exposure to policing: More Americans than ever found themselves involved in direct interactions with law enforcement officers, and comparatively privileged people found themselves in such interactions with far more regularity than they had before the automotive age.

In contemporary America, roadside vehicle stops are far and away the most prominent context in which citizens have direct contact with criminal justice authorities. US police pull over more than 20 million cars annually, and 80% of Americans' most recent direct interaction with a police officer occurred in the context of a vehicle stop.[32] Overall, well over half of all direct contact between civilians and law enforcement officers happens in vehicular contexts (usually vehicle stops, sometimes traffic collisions), and vehicle stops are a far more common reason than any other for people to have contact with police officers.[33]

Getting pulled over is not an equally distributed experience, however. Since *Carroll v. United States* (1925) established the vehicle stop under law, stark patterns of racial inequality have plagued the practice. Numerous studies have found that police disproportionately stop drivers of color, especially Black drivers, to varying degrees in jurisdictions across the country.[34] Drivers of color, especially Black drivers, are also more likely than their White counterparts to see vehicle stops as illegitimate and to perceive that police have treated them unjustly or improperly during roadside stops.[35] Nonwhite drivers are also significantly more likely than White drivers to receive citations.[36] Both experiences of vehicle stops and perceptions of being treated unfairly during these stops are associated with reduced likelihoods of proactively contacting police for help in the future.[37]

In their 2014 book *Pulled Over*, Charles Epp, Steven Maynard-Moody, and Donald Haider-Markel report the results of a landmark study of vehicle stops in the Kansas City metropolitan area. For this study, Epp and colleagues conducted an original survey of more than 2,300 drivers, as well as interviews with drivers. The authors found that Black drivers in their sample were about twice as likely as White drivers to be pulled over: 12% of White drivers were pulled over annually, compared with 24% of Black drivers. In addition to being stopped more frequently, African American drivers were also significantly more likely to experience intrusive, coercive, and punitive elements of vehicle stops (such as being searched, handcuffed, and aggressively interrogated) than were drivers from other racial and ethnic groups. Minority drivers, Epp and colleagues note, are also much more likely to view stops as unfair and to express general distrust of police.[38]

Beyond confirming that the general racial disparities established in previous research hold true in their sample, Epp and colleagues seek to explain the phenomena they observe. Addressing possible explanations for the pronounced racial disproportionality in vehicle stops, Epp and colleagues note some observers' tendency to ascribe the disparity to the actions of individual officers who act in explicitly racist or deliberately discriminatory ways. A similar tendency, they observe, also characterizes courts' approach to the issue. Courts, including the US Supreme Court, have typically framed the problem of racial disparities in vehicle stops—to the extent they have seen it as a legal problem at all—as one of discriminatory intent. In reviewing stops' constitutionality, the Court has ruled that if a stop is made *only* on the basis of race, that stop is illegal. However, the requirement of establishing such discriminatory intent makes it nearly impossible to challenge stops' constitutionality, because plaintiffs need to convince the court that a stop was motivated solely by the driver's race.[39] There are many, many legally acceptable reasons to initiate a vehicle stop; law enforcement officers have stated that state vehicle codes give them "hundreds" of such reasons (Florida), or "fifteen hundred reasons" (California).[40] So long as officers do not say that they pulled someone over based on their race, any one of these hundreds of legal reasons for stops will typically allow them to survive court challenges.[41]

In terms of drivers' perceptions of whether vehicle stops are fair and legitimate, Epp and colleagues address the related notion that people find vehicle stops problematic when they feel that officers were rude to them. Thus officers being polite should ensure that people see stops as justified. Epp and colleagues confirm that, unsurprisingly, people *prefer* when police are polite to them. They note, however, that politeness does not appear to be determinative in shaping drivers' overall perceptions of stops. Even unfailingly polite treatment from police does not change drivers' sense that some stops are illegitimate. And, conversely, drivers acknowledged that other stops are legitimate even when they feel that officers were less than entirely polite. For drivers of color in particular, the key issue in perceptions of stops is not whether officers did or did not comport themselves politely. Rather, people are particularly likely to see stops as illegitimate or discriminatory if they sense that a given stop is part of a pattern of unfair treatment, in which certain types of drivers are singled out for scrutiny and questioning.[42] For African American motorists, this reduces to the notion that one was pulled over for "DWB": Driving While Black.

Although some police officers may in fact harbor racial biases and resentments, Epp and colleagues stress that the overall differences that manifest in vehicle stop patterns are not attributable to the actions of discriminatory officers; instead, these disparities are the product of a systematic, institutionalized practice that is inherently unfair and discriminatory. Specifically, they contend "that a specific, well-entrenched, institutionalized practice of the *investigatory stop* is the main source of racial disparities in police stops and why the racial minorities subjected to these stops view them as deeply unfair even if carried out by a politely respectful officer."[43]

This argument hinges on differentiating between traffic safety stops and investigatory stops. A traffic safety stop is the type of thing that many people would think of as an ordinary police vehicle stop. As their name suggests, these stops are motivated by road safety concerns; officers engage in traffic safety stops to address dangerous or otherwise problematic driving behavior. Investigatory stops are different. As their name suggests, these stops are motivated by an interest in conducting a miniature roadside investigation: checking to see whether a driver has outstanding warrants, asking questions about where they have been and where they are going, probing for evidence that they are carrying drugs or guns, and the like. These types of stops are sometimes called *Terry* stops, a reference to the 1968 US Supreme Court decision in *Terry v. Ohio*, which confirmed the constitutionality of police officers stopping and temporarily detaining citizens about whom they have "reasonable suspicions" of criminal activity. *Terry* involved pedestrian stop-and-frisk; *Whren v. United States* (1996) formally extended similar discretionary power to officers in vehicle stops and confirmed that officers could use minor vehicle code violations as bases for stopping vehicles to conduct brief investigations. It is acceptable under the Fourth Amendment, the *Whren* Court held, for officers to initiate vehicle stops related to any violation of traffic law, even if the alleged violation is only a pretext to pull the vehicle over, question its occupants, and otherwise look for probable cause for more intrusive interventions, including full searches.

With first *Terry* and later *Whren* as their jurisprudential backbone, investigatory vehicle stops became a more prominent part of policing and the war on drugs in the 1980s and 1990s. Police leadership figures and professional organizations championed the tactic, and police departments across the country integrated it into officer training programs and made it a key element of their vehicle patrol practices. In alignment with the broken-windows-informed policing strategies sweeping the nation at the time, investigatory vehicle stops aimed to provide officers with as many opportunities as possible to check what people are up to and look for signs of wrongdoing, based on the notion that catching people with drugs, guns, or outstanding warrants is crucial to the kind of proactive policing that would allow law enforcement to intervene before more serious crimes occurred. Almost by definition, this means that most investigatory stops will not yield evidence of significant criminal activity. In the words of one member of the California Highway Patrol, "You've got to kiss a lot of frogs before you find a prince."[44] Indeed, the vast majority of people pulled over for investigatory stops are innocent of any wrongdoing, except perhaps minor violations of traffic laws or vehicle codes.

Police officers, of course, have limited time and energy. They cannot stop all drivers; instead, they make discretionary decisions about which drivers they find suspicious. This discretionary process, Epp and colleagues argue, is where patterns of racial disparity emerge. Building on research about stereotypes and implicit bias, they argue that unconscious beliefs and assumptions about Black people's relative likelihood of being involved in criminal activity shape decisions about whom to pull over.[45] Given the massive numbers of vehicle stops that American police officers initiate, even small differences in how officers view and act toward drivers of different races can aggregate to create major differences in drivers' experiences. Stereotypes of criminality among Black people, and especially among young Black men, are deeply entrenched in American society. As Frank Baumgartner and colleagues put it, "Crucially, even if for most officers these biases are slight, with only a small marginal likelihood of affecting their behavior, the cumulative effect could still be very great. That is, even if most officers are only slightly more likely to search a Black driver, on average Black drivers would experience many more searches than Whites."[46]

Epp and colleagues demonstrate that distinguishing between traffic safety stops and investigatory stops is crucial to understanding overall racial disparities in vehicle stops. Notably, their data show that traffic safety stops are racially equitable; their results indicate that police officers in the Kansas City area pull over drivers for traffic safety reasons based on observations of their driving behavior and that drivers' races are not significant factors in these types of stops. The overall Black-White disparity in vehicle stops results from the fact that Black drivers are 2.7 times more likely than White motorists to experience investigatory stops.[47] Investigatory stops are aimed at conducting roadside investigations, not at enforcing traffic laws. Black motorists' disproportionate exposure to this form of stop also means that they are disproportionately exposed to the intrusive and punitive elements that these stops tend to include: prolonged questioning, personal searches, vehicle searches, and so forth.[48]

Investigatory stops' inherent characteristics also largely explain Black drivers' comparatively greater sense that vehicle stops are illegitimate. Black drivers and White drivers view traffic stops similarly, as mostly legitimate. Drivers are more skeptical about investigatory stops; because Black drivers experience more of these stops, they tend to have more skeptical attitudes about vehicle stops overall. Over time, experiencing more investigatory stops makes Black drivers less trusting of police and more apprehensive about driving in certain areas.[49]

In total, Epp and colleagues find that Black drivers' far greater likelihood of being subjected to investigatory stops is the essential cause of their disparate experiences with being pulled over and the conclusions they draw from these experiences. It is worth reemphasizing that the authors stress that this phenomenon is not primarily attributable to intentionally discriminatory action on police officers' part. The problem does not fundamentally lie with motive or intent. Rather, the problem's source is in an institutionalized practice "and how this officially guided practice prompts officers to act on implicit stereotypes of who looks suspicious."[50] It is also worth noting that there is limited evidence that investigatory stops constitute an effective crime control intervention. These stops rarely result in recoveries of drugs or guns, and their tendency to produce distrust and dislike of police imperils the flow of information from members of the public on which law enforcement agencies rely to learn about crimes and to apprehend and successfully prosecute perpetrators.[51]

Furthermore, getting pulled over often has consequences far beyond being detained, questioned, and searched. As the killing of Philando Castile and similar incidents placed in stark relief, vehicle stops are not only the predominant form of direct citizen-police interaction. They are also a leading precursor of police uses of force, whether justified, unjustified, or in the large gray area in between. In 2015, for instance, almost one in three police shootings occurred in the course of vehicle stops.[52] Ostensibly routine vehicle stops are also common sites for other police uses of force, including dog bites. These incidents also demonstrate pronounced racial disparities. Since the time of slave patrols, legal authorities have used dogs as tools of racial terror and domination. Municipal police forces across the country created vehicle-based K-9 units during the civil rights era, a new weapon for disrupting protests and demonstrations and attacking their participants. Criminal justice authorities continue to use police dogs disproportionately against Black people, in both vehicle stops and other settings.[53]

PATTERNS, PRACTICES, AND OUTCOMES

As it is for all street-level bureaucrats, discretion is a hallmark of working in public-facing roles in the criminal justice system. People in these roles make consequential decisions about how public resources will be allocated—or not—and how to exercise legal authority and impose penalties. In this sense, they serve pivotal roles in mobilizing both the state's supportive resources and its punitive capacities.[54]

Emergency operators function as gatekeepers at the early stages of these processes. Their work entails interpreting and classifying citizens' claims for attention from state agencies, as well as citizens' efforts to mobilize the state's coercive power.[55] In drawing conclusions about citizens' calls and making preliminary determinations of what state response, if any, is appropriate, 911 operators use discretion to make crucial decisions about how the government should officially categorize information that flows to them from the public. To do so, they draw on occupational folk wisdom to craft official constructions of reported events. Emotion management and "facework" are crucial aspects of the process, as call takers strive to effectively obtain the information required for ascertaining proper government responses. If emergency services' responses to calls are seen as slow or ineffective, people may lose faith in agencies. On the other hand, particularly in the cell phone age, some people's use of 911 calls as a way to bring government's coercive power to bear on others has engendered significant concern and controversy. As the difficult issues surrounding 911 and emergency response indicate, many Americans, particularly Americans of color and those living in neighborhoods of concentrated disadvantage, feel simultaneously overpoliced and underpoliced. In the most basic sense this boils down to feeling that one's community is too tightly surveilled and aggressively policed for minor violations, but not allocated adequate or appropriate criminal justice resources to effectively counteract serious crime.

In our car-centric social world both police rapid response and police patrol revolve around vehicles. Since *Carroll v. United States* (1925), police officers have held substantial discretion related to stopping and searching vehicles. Throughout the history of vehicle stops, civil rights advocates have consistently raised allegations of racial profiling and racial biases in the practice. Indeed, contemporary statistics indicate that, to varying degrees in different areas, drivers of color, especially Black drivers, are more likely to be stopped and searched than are White drivers. Some argue that raising concerns about racial disparities in vehicle stops amounts to an attack on police or a claim that they act on the basis of explicit racial animus. The best research on the topic, however, as headlined by Epp and colleagues' *Pulled Over*, emphasizes that individual officers' motives or intentions are *not* the primary basis for the systematic patterns that numerous studies document in vehicle stops.[56] Instead, the practice of the investigatory stop itself explains the pronounced disparity in Black drivers' exposure to vehicle stops relative to White drivers, as well as the different effects these experiences have on motorists' beliefs and attitudes about police and government more broadly. Thus, trying to ferret out discriminatory intent on the part of individual officers is not just erroneous, but a distraction from the systematic interventions needed to effectively address systematic problems borne from systematic practices.

SEVEN

Interstate Crime

Federalism, Highways, and Criminal Justice

Federalism is a defining characteristic of US politics and government. In the American federalist system responsibility for criminal justice has conventionally fallen to the states. Over time, however, the federal government has come to play a larger and larger role in domestic law enforcement, prosecution, and punishment. This trend has been particularly notable in the last several decades. The broader historical push to get "tough on crime" included expanded federal activity in criminal justice initiatives, especially through the war on drugs.

As automobility (and other developments) made state borders less meaningful over time, interjurisdictional crime became more commonplace, paving the way for greater federal involvement in criminal justice. The "interstate crime" invoked in this chapter's title references crimes that transcend state boundaries as well as the fact that these activities often revolve around interstate highways. The federal government is uniquely situated to address crimes that involve activities in multiple states, including such things as drug distribution networks and human trafficking. Regarding the latter crime, pivotal early federal interventions came in the form of the Mann Act and its enforcement. More recently, federal authorities have taken new steps to coordinate and implement anti-human-trafficking initiatives. As a category of offense that relies heavily on automobile transportation and the interstate highway system, human trafficking presents a compelling case study of the criminal justice challenges that arise in an extensively motorized society.

FEDERALIST FOUNDATIONS

The United States has a federalist government. In a federalist system, certain powers and duties are afforded to a central government (in the US case this is the federal government, based in Washington, DC), and other powers and duties lie with regional or provincial governments (in the US case these are the governments of the various states). The basic federalist structure laid out in the US Constitution was designed to address and correct problems that arose under the Articles of Confederation, the agreement that functioned as the United States' first constitution. Virginia was the first of the original thirteen states to ratify the Articles of Confederation, in 1777, and the agreement finally reached the required unanimous approval of all thirteen original states when Maryland signed on in 1781.

The Articles of Confederation created a weak central government. The sole federal institution established in the articles was Congress. The articles did not provide for a president, or indeed any executive branch of the central government at all, just the ceremonial position of president of Congress. Nor did the articles establish a federal court system. Moreover, the Confederation Congress was feeble; the power to levy taxes was reserved for the states, leaving the central government largely powerless to finance itself, and Congress was unable to compel the states to abide by its decisions.

The Articles of Confederation formally reserved the ability to engage in diplomacy and international affairs for the central government. However, the articles did not provide a mechanism for the central government to protect this authority from encroachment by the state governments. Nor did the articles provide the central government with the power it needed to function effectively as a player on the world stage. For example, the Confederation Congress had the formal authority to ratify treaties and declare war, but it lacked the taxing authority required to muster military forces. Thus Congress could ask the states for money and soldiers but was unable to compel them to contribute resources to a national military.

The ineffectiveness of the central government under the Articles of Confederation quickly became plain. The young country was saddled with prodigious debts from the Revolutionary War, economic struggles, and significant civil unrest. The central government's limited powers also hampered Congress's ability to advance the national interest in dealings with foreign powers and their capacity to support and protect the growing population of White settlers on the Western frontier. These issues led to widespread recognition of the need for a new arrangement of government power.

In 1787 the Constitutional Convention met in Philadelphia to consider potential paths forward, including the basic question of whether to revise the Articles of Confederation or replace the articles altogether with a new foundational legal document. The Federalists, led by Alexander Hamilton and James Madison, argued vociferously for the creation of a much stronger federal government, including a powerful chief executive and a far more robust legislature. After extended debate and multiple compromises, the proposed constitution that emerged from the convention contained many of the attributes for which the Federalists had lobbied. To help secure the document's ratification, Hamilton, Madison, and John Jay wrote the Federalist Papers, a series of essays appearing in popular publications that explained the virtues they ascribed to the new, more powerful central government proposed in the Constitution and encouraging voters to support it. Ultimately, the Federalists' arguments—together with the indisputable problems the country was experiencing under the Articles of Confederation—proved persuasive. The Constitution reached the requisite number of state ratifications in 1788 and took effect as the new supreme law of the land in 1789. The Bill of Rights, which focused largely on protecting individual liberties from government encroachments, was ratified two years later, in 1791.

In numerous ways, the Constitution reflected the framers' intentional efforts to address the problematic shortcomings of the Articles of Confederation. Article I of the US Constitution laid out the powers of Congress, notably including the "power of the purse," that is, the authority to levy taxes and dictate federal expenditures. Article II laid out the president's authority, including control of the military and the pardon power. And Article III created the federal judiciary, including the Supreme Court. In Article VI the supremacy clause established a key basis of federal authority in the newly configured government, naming the Constitution and other federal laws as "the supreme law of the land." Thus, in the event of state constitutions or state laws conflicting with the US Constitution or other federal laws, federal laws take precedence. Article VI also mandated that executive, legislative, and judicial officers—whether federal or state-level—swear to support the US Constitution, further emphasizing the new document's status as the fundamental framework governing exercises of legal and governmental authority at both the state and federal levels.

Despite the great increase in the authority of the federal government under the Constitution compared with the Articles of Confederation, the various states retained significant power to govern within their borders. Indeed, the Tenth Amendment, the last in the Bill of Rights, made clear that the central government's powers were limited and that powers not expressly granted to the federal government should default to state governments: "The powers not delegated to the United States by the Constitution, nor prohibited by it to the states, are reserved to the states respectively, or to the people."

The balance between the powers and responsibilities of the states relative to the federal government has changed over time and is the basis of significant ongoing debate. The general historical trend has included some shifting of power away from state governments and toward the federal government. Agitation against this trend from various interest groups is sometimes framed as a defense of states' rights. The US Civil War constituted the most decisive fight about the division of power between the states and the federal government, when southern states seceded over fears that the federal government under President Lincoln would abolish slavery. The seceding states' choice to name their attempted breakaway government the Confederate States of America was not random. Rather, it reflected the secessionists' desire to return to a version of the weaker central government that had existed under the Articles of Confederation. Such an arrangement would give the states greater independence and autonomy to set laws and policies to their liking within their own territory— and thus allow states to maintain slavery, and White supremacy more broadly, against any perceived encroachments of the central government.

After the Civil War the federal government's power solidified further. Of particular note were the Reconstruction Amendments, the three amendments to the US Constitution ratified between 1865 and 1870, the five years following the war's conclusion. The Thirteenth Amendment abolished slavery and involuntary servitude, except for people convicted of crimes. The Fourteenth Amendment instituted birthright citizenship, required the states to provide due process protections, mandated that states provide people within their jurisdiction equal protection under the law, and forbade the states from passing or enforcing laws that would abridge citizens' "privileges or immunities." Last, the Fifteenth Amendment prohibited state governments, as well as the federal government, from denying or abridging citizens' right to vote "on account of race, color, or previous condition of servitude."

These measures compelled the states to provide some basic civil rights for people within their jurisdictions. Despite these constitutional requirements, however, states retained substantial authority to set their own laws and policies; indeed, under US federalism, regional governments are notably strong and influential compared with other countries using federalist systems. This level of autonomy results in significant interstate differences in law and law enforcement practices and corresponding differences in people's experiences with legal institutions. Many analyses, including this book, look to identify national trends. Given the major interstate variation in criminal justice policies and practices, however, such broad assessments can sometimes gloss over important differences between states.[1]

FEDERALISM AND CRIMINAL JUSTICE

For most of US history federal criminal jurisdiction has been quite limited, with the states holding primary authority and responsibility for enacting and enforcing criminal laws. In the country's early history the federal government's criminal jurisdiction was largely limited to crimes against the nation or against federal property. Day-to-day matters of public safety, individual victimization, and ordinary street crime were responsibilities of the states. Consequently, "there was virtually no overlap between federal and state offenses."[2]

The Constitution itself makes scarce mention of criminal law. It notes that Congress holds police power in federal enclaves and territories outside any state's jurisdiction, and it assigns to Congress authority pertaining to violations of international law and offenses against the nation itself: treason, counterfeiting, and piracy.[3] Early federal statutes dealing with criminal matters were similarly circumscribed. The Crimes Act of 1790, for instance, detailed offenses and punishments related to the federal criminal jurisdiction outlined in the Constitution and created new offenses related to the federal courts.[4] The 1810 Postal Act created new offenses related to interfering with the Postal Service, and the Federal Crimes Act of 1825 provided for prosecutions of crimes occurring on federal land based on the criminal laws of a surrounding state, even absent a directly applicable federal law.[5]

The Civil War and its aftermath brought about a shift in the balance of power between the federal government and the states, and with it a new vision of federal authorities' appropriate role in criminal justice matters.[6] A loosened interpretation of the commerce clause—the constitutional provision granting Congress the power to regulate commerce "among the several states"—allowed Congress to pass measures related to all manner of interstate activity, as well as "intrastate activity that could have a 'substantial effect' on interstate activity."[7] With the country urbanizing, industrializing, and modernizing in the late nineteenth and early twentieth centuries, Congress passed numerous laws aimed at addressing emerging issues, including new crime problems.

As Chapter 3 detailed, federal criminal justice activities took a major leap during Prohibition. Congress passed the Volstead Act, providing the mechanisms to enforce the Eighteenth Amendment; the Treasury Department's Bureau of Internal Revenue assumed primary enforcement responsibilities, with support from the Bureau of Investigation (and from state authorities), and federal prosecutors initiated tens of thousands of cases alleging Volstead Act vi-

olations every year.⁸ After the Twenty-First Amendment's ratification, Volstead
Act violations were no longer the subject of federal prosecutions, but federal
authorities remained active in areas such as organized crime, bank robberies,
and cases involving interstate issues.⁹

Cars were an important influence on the federal government's expanding
criminal justice footprint in the early and mid-twentieth century. Automobiles
offered fast and easy means of transportation, expanding criminal opportunities and facilitating various types of criminal offending. Conventional jurisdictional boundaries lost much of their meaning when people could far more
quickly cross city limits, county lines, and state borders, and when automobile-
supported crime could easily involve activities in multiple jurisdictions. August
Vollmer noted the lack of communication and cooperation between local law
enforcement agencies as a problem for effective crime control and argued for
concentrating policing authority in centralized agencies that could better
coordinate across the United States' large and varied geography. As automobility's implications for criminal justice continued to manifest, investing the
federal government with greater authority to conduct investigations, pursue
prosecutions, and help bridge divides between local and state jurisdictions
became increasingly appealing.

Outside of criminal justice, Congress also demonstrated growing interest
in bringing federal power to bear in the regulation of cars and driving more
broadly. Following the 1965 publication of Ralph Nader's book *Unsafe at Any
Speed*, which pilloried American automobile manufacturers for their products'
dangerousness, Congress held a series of hearings on highway safety. These
hearings led to laws requiring manufacturers to add safety measures such as
seatbelts to their cars, and also precipitated the creation of the United States
Department of Transportation in 1966.¹⁰ Also in 1966, Congress passed legislation that would culminate in the establishment of the National Highway Traffic
Safety Administration (NHTSA) in 1970. The NHTSA would become the leading
federal agency in addressing the problem of motor vehicle collisions, as well
as a regulatory body enforcing rules intended to counteract automobile theft.

The federal government's role in regulating behavior and investigating and
punishing crime continued to expand in the 1970s. Legal scholars and social
scientists note that trends over the last half-century demonstrate the "federalization" of criminal justice. This term refers to the enactment of numerous
federal criminal statutes and the expanded role of federal law enforcement, US
Attorneys (federal prosecutors), and federal courts in the investigation, prosecution, and punishment of crime in the late twentieth and early twenty-first
centuries In 1998 the American Bar Association Task Force on the Federalization of Criminal Law released a report finding that more than 40% of all federal

criminal statutes since the Civil War had been passed after 1970.[11] Laws passed in this period "include a series of omnibus crime bills addressing drugs, organized crime, and violence, and a stunning assortment of other crimes of every description, including carjacking, access to health clinics, child support recovery, veterans cemetery protection, telemarketing fraud, and an expansion of the scope of the Racketeer Influenced and Corrupt Organizations (RICO) statute."[12] (The RICO Act itself was enacted in 1970, giving federal authorities new power to investigate and prosecute organized crime activities.) By 2020 the US Code contained between 4,500 and 6,000 criminal provisions, plus at least 300,000 regulations backed by the possibility of criminal penalties.[13] Many of these federal laws are broad in scope, overlapping with other federal laws and with states' criminal codes.[14] Indeed, the dramatic expansion in the federal criminal code has made federal and state-level criminal law largely duplicative: Nearly all felonies are now potentially subject to prosecution by either state or federal authorities.[15]

The federalization trend is not just statutory. Federal law enforcement agencies and US Attorneys' offices have also taken on substantially increased roles in responding to forms of crime that have conventionally been the purview of state-level authorities, including drug crimes and violent crimes. Most criminal prosecutions still occur at the state level, with state prosecutors charging people with violations of state criminal laws, proceedings heard in state court systems, and convictions resulting in sentences of incarceration in local jails and state correctional facilities. However, federal prosecutions have expanded considerably. Between 1970 and 1980 federal prosecutors initiated about 50,000 criminal cases per year. That average grew significantly over subsequent years. Federal prosecutors filed an average of roughly 89,000 cases annually between 2007 and 2017.[16] In 2019 federal criminal filings were up to nearly 93,000, before dropping about 20% in 2020 due largely to COVID-19 restrictions.[17]

Federal convictions and incarceration have grown similarly. In 1980 the federal prison system held 24,252 incarcerated people, about the same number it had for the previous four decades. That number more than doubled by the end of the 1980s, to nearly 58,000, and more than doubled again in the 1990s, to roughly 136,000 in 1999. This explosive growth continued in the twenty-first century, reaching 217,000 in 2013, before beginning to decline.[18] Although state correctional systems collectively confine many more people than the federal system, the federal correctional system became the single largest prison system early in the twenty-first century, surpassing California's. In 2019 the Federal Bureau of Prisons held 171,000 people, beating out the current largest state prison system, Texas's, which held 154,000.[19]

Federal prosecutors' expanded activity also brought them into increased contact with state-level criminal justice authorities, including local prose-cutors. With most forms of serious crime now constituting violations of both state and federal laws, either level of government can potentially bring crimi-nal charges. In light of federalization, state and federal prosecutors more fre-quently need to work together to decide who will take a given case.[20] Federal authorities can have jurisdiction in any case where there is a nexus connecting the alleged criminal activity to federal law.[21]

In situations where both federal and state authorities have legitimate claims to regulate behavior and punish legal violations, one set of authorities or the other will typically prosecute any given case. However, it is also possi-ble for both state and federal authorities to prosecute the same offense, either concurrently or sequentially. The Fifth Amendment's double jeopardy clause prohibits the government from trying someone twice for the same offense. This means that it is typically unconstitutional for someone to be criminally charged for the same offense following an acquittal or a conviction. However, state and federal governments are considered separate "sovereigns" under US law. Thus, under the dual sovereignty doctrine, it is constitutional for both fed-eral and state authorities to bring separate charges against a defendant for the same offense, provided that the offense constitutes a violation of both federal law and the relevant state's law. (Relatedly, double jeopardy protections do not prohibit someone from facing both criminal charges and civil litigation con-nected to the same incident. The O. J. Simpson case famously demonstrated this: Although Simpson was acquitted of criminal murder charges, he was nev-ertheless found civilly liable for wrongful death.) In dual sovereignty situations either federal or state prosecutors will usually defer, allowing the other level of government to take the case, with the initially deferring government poten-tially circling back to bring their own charges if the first prosecution does not secure a conviction. Occasionally, however, both federal and state authorities may choose to file their own charges at the outset.

Prosecutors' offices are largely left to their own devices in deciding whether cases should be state or federal or both. This is one example of prosecutorial discretion: prosecutors' mostly unencumbered ability to make decisions about whether to bring charges and what kind of charges to bring. (Chapter 8 dis-cusses prosecutorial discretion in greater detail.) In situations where either federal or state authorities can legitimately pursue prosecutions, federal US Attorneys and state prosecutors can communicate and cooperate to decide on their preferred course of action.[22] Federalization research highlights a number of things that tend to give federal prosecutors comparative advantage relative to state prosecutors in the either-or situation, when only one government will pursue prosecution, at least initially. Usually (though not always), a number of features of federal prosecutions tend to make them more attractive than state prosecutions to authorities interested in securing convictions and severe punishments. The sources of federal advantage include greater ability to detain people before trial, more permissive rules about evidence admissibility, more advantageous rules of criminal procedure, typically longer prison sentences, and the prodigious resources and investigative capacities of the federal government relative to any one state.[23]

FEDERALISM AND THE WAR ON DRUGS

Increased attention to drugs and drug-related offenses has been a centerpiece of federalization. Today, about half of people incarcerated in federal prisons have a drug charge as their "controlling offense"—the criminal conviction leading to their incarceration, or the category of their most serious conviction if they were convicted of multiple offenses. By contrast, only about 15% of people incarcerated in state prison systems have a drug crime as their controlling offense.[24]

Congress's passage of the 1970 Comprehensive Drug Abuse Prevention and Control Act, also known as the Controlled Substances Act, marked the beginning of a new era of greater federal involvement in drug enforcement. The 1970 law created five different schedules for classifying drugs; Schedule I drugs would be the most strictly regulated and closely controlled, with levels of restriction decreasing down to the most lightly regulated category, Schedule V. The Controlled Substances Act specified that determining which schedule a given substance belonged to should be based on an assessment of three key factors: the drug's potential for abuse, its application in accepted medical uses, and its safety and potential for addiction. Schedule I drugs are those determined to have high abuse potential, to lack accepted medical applications, and to be unsafe to use with high addictive potential. The list of Schedule I drugs includes heroin, MDMA, psychedelics such as psilocybin, peyote, mescaline, and LSD, and cannabis.[25] Some other familiar recreational drugs are in Schedule II, because they have "some accepted medical use." This group includes cocaine, which can be used as an anesthetic; methamphetamine, which can be used to treat attention deficit disorders or in medically supervised weight loss programs; and various opioids prescribed as painkillers. The Controlled Substances Act does not regulate alcohol or tobacco products.

In 1971, one year after the passage of the Controlled Substances Act, President Nixon declared "war on drugs" on behalf of the federal government, particularly the executive branch. To help prosecute this war, the federal government created the Drug Enforcement Administration (DEA) in 1973, merging several other federal offices and departments into a new centralized agency within the Department of Justice. Assigned primary responsibility for enforcing the Controlled Substances Act, the DEA conducts drug investigations, gathers evidence for federal prosecutions of drug-related offenses, and works with other federal, state, and local criminal justice authorities.

Counteracting drug trafficking was a centerpiece of the federal government's newly aggressive stance. Drug trafficking, also known as drug distribution, is a category of criminal offending that includes the sale, transportation, or importation of illegal drugs. In federal law, 21 USC § 841 criminalizes manufacturing, distributing, or dispensing controlled substances, or possessing controlled substances with intent to distribute. Section 841 further specifies sentencing ranges for violations, including mandatory minimum and maximum sentences for various quantities of different controlled substances. Elsewhere in 21 USC, Section 846 criminalizes conspiring or attempting to engage in drug trafficking, with penalties matching those for distribution charges; Section 848 (the "Drug Kingpin Statute") provides severe penalties for running an organized crime operation involved in drug trafficking; and Section 856 (the "Crack House Statute") criminalizes maintaining a drug-involved premises. Section 1952 of 18 USC (the "Travel Act") criminalizes traveling, shipping, and using telecommunications in the service of drug trafficking.[26]

Nearly all the people convicted and imprisoned for federal drug crimes are convicted of trafficking violations; in 2012, 99.5% of people serving federal time for drug offenses were convicted of trafficking offenses, and about 97% of people convicted of federal drug offenses in 2020 were sentenced under trafficking laws.[27] Methamphetamine is the most common drug involved in federal drug cases, accounting for 45.7% of cases in 2020. Powder cocaine, crack cocaine, and heroin accounted for 16.5%, 7.4%, and 11.5%, respectively.[28]

In the automobile age, vehicles are pivotal parts of drug trafficking operations. Automobiles are key means by which controlled substances are illegally imported, and highways constitute the primary network by which drugs are transported throughout the United States. Car-based activities also extend to retail drug sales, with street-level dealers driving to meet customers and deliver product.[29] Federal authorities have national jurisdiction to take on investigations and prosecutions involving international activities or activities occurring in multiple US states. This makes the DEA and other federal law enforcement agencies the tip of the spear in addressing importation, interstate transportation, and large drug conspiracies.

Given motor vehicles' importance to drug trafficking enterprises, vehicle stops and searches are key tools in the war on drugs. Federal authorities' use of this tactic to catch drug traffickers evokes the vehicle searches for illegal liquor that were at issue in *Carroll v. United States* (1925) and *Brinegar v. United States* (1949), suggesting the tactical similarities of enforcing bans of different types of substances in an automobile-centered society. This, of course, is only one of numerous parallels between Prohibition and the war on drugs.

Federal prosecutions for drug offenses exploded under federalization and the war on drugs, "rising approximately 300% in the stretch from 1980 to 1990 and another 45% from 1990 to 2000."[30] As they did during Prohibition, federal agents involved in the war on drugs have focused significant attention on organized trafficking networks. In both enforcement contexts, however, federal agents have also pursued smaller investigations and prosecutions. In the drug war this includes federal intervention in numerous cases that would have conventionally been the purview of state or local law enforcement agencies, and US Attorneys' offices actively prosecute low-level drug sales.[31] In fact, federal law criminalizes even the possession of controlled substances: 21 USC § 844 specifies a one-year maximum sentence for the misdemeanor of simple possession and provides for elevating the offense to a felony and imposing longer sentences for people with previous drug convictions.[32] (Simple possession of intoxicating liquor was not technically illegal under the Volstead Act.)

With new laws giving federal authorities broad authority concerning drug crimes (as well as other types of crime), a key question arises for federal prosecutors: Given the multitude of drug cases in which they could potentially bring charges, how do they decide which ones to prosecute? Particularly in light of the conviction-supporting resources that federal authorities can bring to bear and the generally stricter penalties available in federal prosecutions compared with state prosecutions, a federal prosecutor's decision to take a case is consequential. Based on interviews with prosecutors, defense attorneys, judges, and federal law enforcement agents, criminologist Mona Lynch identified several types of drug cases that are particularly attractive to federal prosecutors: cases in which federal mandatory minimum sentences or sentence enhancements are implicated; cases involving people believed to be involved with gang activity or gun crimes; and cases involving people who prosecutors believe might be useful as informants to help them build other, potentially bigger cases.[33] Lynch's data also suggest that prosecutors' decisions about which cases to take are a pivotal stage in producing racial, ethnic, and class-based disparities in criminal justice outcomes. Namely, the concentration of federal enforcement in lower-income and minority neighborhoods leads to the concentration of arrests and prosecutions in these neighborhoods and thus the overrepresentation of poorer people and people of color among those charged with federal drug crimes. These patterns can lend themselves to self-fulfilling prophecy effects.[34] That is, if authorities concentrate their activities in certain areas, they will tend to make more arrests and secure more convictions in those areas, which can then serve as retroactive justification for the targeted enforcement or encourage them to double down on such strategies. Creating more criminal records in these neighborhoods also leads to more severe penalties for affected people: Drug crime statutes specify longer sentences for people with previous drug felony convictions. Multiple convictions can also trigger other federal criminal statutes, such as the Armed Career Criminal Act.

INTERJURISDICTIONAL CRIME

How government should address crimes that cross jurisdictional boundaries has long been a point of consideration in the United States. In 1894's *State v. Hall*, for instance, the North Carolina Supreme Court heard the appeal of two North Carolina residents convicted of shooting and killing a man while they stood in North Carolina but the victim stood across the state line, in Tennessee. The defendants were convicted under North Carolina law, but the court vacated that conviction, ruling that Tennessee had sole jurisdiction to charge a crime in the case.

When cars came on the scene in the early twentieth century, it soon became clear that they had pronounced implications for federalism, interstate crime, and a largely localized criminal justice system. In 1924, for example, Arch Mandel of the Dayton Research Association wrote that "state lines have been eliminated by the automobile. Detection of criminals is becoming more and more a nation-wide task."[35] Improvements in automotive technology and development of the country's system of roads and highways further compounded automobility's consequences for coordinating criminal justice across state jurisdictions.[36]

Local law enforcement agencies often found themselves at a loss when trying to address criminal offending that transcended their jurisdiction. This led to calls for the federal government to take on a larger role in helping to coordinate systematic criminal justice responses and in responding directly to interjurisdictional crime. As noted in Chapter 1, the 1919 Dyer Act was a landmark step toward the federalization of criminal justice. The Dyer Act made interstate trafficking in stolen vehicles a federal crime.[37] The Department of Justice's Bureau of Investigation (later renamed the Federal Bureau of Investigation) took on primary responsibility for enforcing the new law. The bureau's activity in this area was crucial to its early development. Dyer Act violations offered jurisdictional hooks that permitted federal authorities to lead investigations of high-profile criminals, and the tools and resources developed to help pursue Dyer Act cases served as a foundation for the bureau's continued growth and expanded activity throughout the twentieth century.

Another pivotal instance of federal involvement in criminal justice addressed an issue that we would today call human trafficking. Although authorities previously used laws against vagrancy and nightwalking to arrest and punish sex workers, laws specifically targeting prostitution were not a prominent part of American criminal justice until the early twentieth century. Prostitution became an area of focus for the Progressive movement, with activists pushing for targeted anti-prostitution statutes and helping get brothels and red-light districts across the country shut down.[38] Growing concern about prostitution as a social problem intersected and overlapped with rapidly disseminating beliefs that many sex workers were being tricked or coerced into working at brothels, or even drugged, abducted, and forced into sexual slavery.[39] The popular discourse around this topic keyed on notions that these young women constituted "White slaves" and that their victimizers were "White slavers."[40]

The federal government jumped into this issue with both feet when Congress passed the White Slave Traffic Act of 1910, better known as the Mann Act. Demonstrating the hyperbolic thinking and overheated rhetoric that had come to characterize the White slavery topic—to say nothing of the blatant racism— the bill's sponsor, Congressman James R. Mann, said in comments to Congress that "the white-slave traffic, while not so extensive, is much more horrible than any black-slave traffic ever was in the history of the world."[41] Mann's colleague, Representative Coy of Indiana, echoed this appalling and absurd position, saying White slavery was "a thousand times worse and more degrading in its consequences and effects upon humanity than any species of human slavery that ever existed in this country."[42] The bill passed both houses of Congress with strong support, and President Taft signed it into law on June 25, 1910.[43] Invoking Congress's power to regulate interstate commerce under the Constitution's commerce clause, the Mann Act federally criminalized transporting a "woman or girl" across state lines or national borders for purposes of "prostitution or debauchery, or for any other immoral purpose."[44] The act similarly penalized transporting or assisting transporting women or girls based on a defendant's *intent* to enlist them to engage in prostitution "or to engage in any other immoral practice."[45]

The Mann Act was a landmark piece of legislation in the rise of federal law enforcement, including the history of the FBI. The incipient agency, created in nascent form in 1908, had only thirty-five investigators in 1910, with operations circumscribed almost entirely to Washington, DC. The Mann Act dramatically expanded their jurisdiction, leading to a major increase in their numbers and reach, with field offices established first in Baltimore and soon around the country.[46] By 1912 enforcement of the Mann Act constituted the bulk of the bureau's workload.[47] Early prosecutions often focused on transportation via railroads. As cars came to predominate among modes of transportation, patterns in Mann Act prosecutions changed accordingly.

The Mann Act's language was extremely broad. The law's use of the phrase *immoral purpose* allowed it to be applied to a wide array of situations. And indeed, federal investigators and prosecutors used the law to go after people for a variety of disfavored or stigmatized sexual activities, including consensual sex outside marriage. In *Caminetti v. United States* (1917), the US Supreme Court upheld F. Drew Caminetti's Mann Act conviction. Caminetti, a married man, had traveled from Sacramento, California, to Reno, Nevada, with another woman, Lola Norris, as well as his friend Maury Diggs and Diggs's mistress, Marsha Warrington. A federal court jury convicted Caminetti of transporting Norris for immoral purposes, and the judge sentenced him to eighteen months in prison and ordered him to pay a $1,500 fine.[48] The Supreme Court upheld Caminetti's conviction on appeal. Writing for a five-justice majority, Justice Day held that the conduct at issue fell within the plain meaning of "immoral purpose," the language used in the law.[49] (Not until *Lawrence v. Texas* [2003] would the Supreme Court rule that laws prohibiting private sexual activities between consenting adults are unconstitutional.)

The broad authority that the Mann Act granted to federal investigators and prosecutors also lent itself to misuse and abuse. J. Edgar Hoover used the law to advance his vision of what a moral America should look like. These efforts included organizing high-profile raids and pushing Mann Act investigations of prominent public citizens, for example, Errol Flynn and Charlie Chaplin.[50] The politics of sex, crime, and race were particularly pronounced in the case of Jack Johnson. Johnson became the first Black heavyweight boxing champion in 1908. In 1910, Johnson defended his title, defeating the White former champion Jim Jeffries in a match that both Jeffries and the White press framed as a contest to reassert White supremacy in the ring.[51] As Johnson attracted White vitriol and outrage, federal prosecutors seized an opportunity to use the Mann Act to prosecute him for having sex with a White woman. After trying and failing to pull together one prosecution in 1912, they succeeded in 1913, when an all-White jury convicted Johnson of transporting Belle Schreiber across state lines for prostitution and "other immoral purposes." On appeal, the appellate court threw out the prostitution charge but upheld the immoral purpose conviction, ruling that transporting Schreiber for the purposes of sex was itself sufficient to trigger penalization under this part of the Mann Act.[52]

HUMAN TRAFFICKING AS A CONTEMPORARY
CRIMINAL JUSTICE ISSUE

The Mann Act represented an aggressive intervention from the federal government to address what we now call human trafficking. (This was the theoretical objective of the Mann Act, at least; in practice, it was also widely used for other ends, including as an instrument for enforcing certain visions of morality and targeting individuals and groups for surveillance, investigation, and punishment.)[53] Today, human trafficking remains a prominent topic of national and international attention and concern. The United Nations Office on Drugs and Crime defines human trafficking as "the recruitment, transportation, transfer, harboring, or receipt of people through force, fraud or deception, with the aim of exploiting them for profit."[54] Thus *human trafficking* is an umbrella term encompassing a variety of activities involving one party manipulating, coercing, or otherwise forcing a person or people to do things. Most commonly, human trafficking involves sexual exploitation, in which trafficking victims are tricked or forced into performing sex work, or labor trafficking, in which traffickers manipulate or coerce victims into slavery, involuntary servitude, or otherwise illegal labor conditions. These types of exploitation have long social histories and have been subject to various forms of legal regulation and criminal justice interventions. Twenty-first century policymakers have increasingly agreed that it is appropriate to treat the various types of exploitation that can constitute human trafficking as different iterations of the same fundamental thing and to address this overarching category of victimization through criminal justice interventions.[55]

The 2000 Trafficking Victims Protection Act headlines the US federal government's response to human trafficking as a crime problem. The act "defined human trafficking as a crime that involves the recruitment and exploitation of individuals by means of force, fraud, or coercion for the purposes of commercial sex, labor, or services."[56] Subsequently, all the states have passed their own laws against human trafficking.[57] In addition to conducting their own investigations and pursuing their own prosecutions, federal authorities have also made concerted efforts to nationally coordinate responses through information-sharing and collaborative enforcement activities, with an eye particularly toward facilitating effective enforcement in an arena commonly involving interjurisdictional issues. Lawmakers, law enforcement officials, researchers, nongovernmental organizations, and concerned citizens have dedicated considerable time and energy to understanding how human trafficking occurs, especially via the country's interstate system, and to disrupting these activities.[58] The connection between highways and federal efforts to address human trafficking is particularly plain in two statutes enacted in 2018. The No Human Trafficking on Our Roads Act permanently banned anyone convicted of using a commercial vehicle to facilitate a human trafficking felony from holding a commercial driver's license, and the Combating Human Trafficking in Commercial Vehicles Act required the Department of Transportation to take a number of aggressive steps intended to help prevent and catch human trafficking activity on the nation's roads.[59]

Despite these efforts, counteracting human trafficking is a difficult task for criminal justice authorities in the United States, as it is elsewhere. Numerous problems impede human trafficking enforcement. Despite federal efforts to alleviate them, jurisdictional issues remain a hurdle. Human trafficking frequently involves transporting people from one place to another (using force, fraud, or deception). Automobiles facilitate transporting trafficking victims quickly and covertly, and the interstate highway system makes it relatively simple to move victims between states or across the country. Enforcement, therefore, often requires authorities in different jurisdictions to communicate and cooperate with each other. This coordination can be inefficient, cumbersome, and sometimes even contentious. When it is unclear who should take on investigation of a multijurisdictional case, diffusion of responsibility is also a possibility.

Other issues further complicate criminal justice responses to human trafficking. Human trafficking is typically less visible than the felonies, misdemeanors, and traffic violations on which police predominantly focus, rendering it more elusive as an enforcement topic.[60] Law enforcement officers may not see human trafficking as an issue in their local areas or may not recognize it as a crime within the scope of their authority.[61] Indeed, even if confronted with an instance of human trafficking, police may not recognize it for what it is.[62]

And police being able to recognize human trafficking situations when they see them is particularly crucial because human trafficking victims are unlikely to report their victimization to law enforcement. Victims hesitate to talk to police for a variety of reasons. They may depend—or believe they depend—on their relationships with the people exploiting them, or they may fear retaliation from their exploiters. In many cases victims are traumatized, incapacitated, or otherwise unable to report.[63] Others are unsure whether they want to leave the exploitative situation, owing to uncertainty about whether whatever alternative situation they might find themselves in would be any better.[64] Many victims fear or distrust the police, particularly if they have histories of negative interactions with law enforcement. People in this situation may believe that police will not be able to help them; indeed, the things trafficking victims often want—services, support, or simply to be seen and heard—are things that the criminal justice system is not generally well equipped to provide.[65] Further, victims may believe that they themselves might face legal liability or other harmful consequences as a result of reporting their victimization.[66]

Such fears are not unfounded. Some trafficking victims are arrested, either as a way to "get them into the system" and help facilitate their access to supportive services, or potentially as a precursor to entering prostitution court or facing criminal charges.[67] Law enforcement officers themselves acknowledge that victims are sometimes viewed—and charged—as prostitutes.[68]

These types of issues lead to a broader set of concerns about sex trafficking crackdowns. These cases are often complicated, and lines between voluntary sex work and human trafficking may not be entirely clear. Proponents of sex trafficking crackdowns frame these interventions as a way to protect women and prevent their exploitation. Many women's rights activists and sex worker advocates decry this formulation, alleging that these efforts in fact penalize women and create new vulnerabilities. These issues surfaced prominently in the debate around and reaction to the enactment of FOSTA-SESTA in 2018. (SESTA is the Stop Enabling Sex Traffickers Act, and FOSTA is the Fight Online Sex Trafficking Act.) Expressly motivated by Congress's interest in counteracting sex trafficking, and especially the trafficking of children, FOSTA-SESTA holds online publishers legally responsible for prostitution ads posted on their platforms. The law's critics, however, contend that its burdens have fallen primarily on consensual sex workers, exposing them to risks by removing their ability to vet clients and control their own working conditions through arranging encounters online, while doing little to nothing to reduce rates of trafficking.[69]

POWER AND PRIORITIES IN CRIMINAL JUSTICE

A federalist system is characterized by the division of powers, rights, and responsibilities between the central government and regional governments. In the United States, federalism considerations are central to questions of regulation and governance. These issues arise prominently in the evolving balance between federal and state roles in criminal justice.

States have traditionally held primary authority to set criminal justice policies and coordinate law enforcement and prosecution within their boundaries. Today, state prosecutions continue to constitute the large majority of all criminal prosecutions. This convention has shifted over time, however. In the twentieth century Congress began to take a more proactive stance concerning criminal laws. This evolving position included particular attention to crimes involving interstate activities, as the federal legislative branch passed laws pertaining to moving both ill-gotten property and people across state lines in the Dyer Act and the Mann Act, respectively. Motor vehicles are central to the story of both of these major pieces of federal criminal legislation. Stolen cars were the Dyer Act's raison d'être, and automobiles were at the center of many Mann Act investigations and prosecutions.[70] Federal authority to enforce these two acts provided the jurisdiction and resource allocation that propelled the FBI from a small federal subagency into the powerful, far-reaching law enforcement organization that we recognize today.

Moving forward in the twentieth century, federal law enforcement agencies and courts continued to deal with crimes that occurred on federal land, crimes involving activities in multiple states, or crimes that were specifically violations of federal laws, such as the Volstead Act under Prohibition, federal gun laws, or federal immigration offenses. Since the 1970s, however, Congress has greatly expanded the federal criminal code, meaning that most felonies can be investigated and prosecuted by either state or federal authorities (or both). The last half-century's federalization in criminal justice has seen federal law enforcement agencies, prosecutors, and courts playing greatly expanded roles in criminal justice. This notably includes a central role for federal criminal justice authorities in the war on drugs.

During Prohibition federal agents played a leading role in enforcing the Volstead Act. Today, federal criminal justice authorities play a similar leading role in drug enforcement. Statutory bases for this activity include federal laws addressing interstate drug trafficking, with the investigation, prosecution, and punishment of trafficking operations that cross state lines falling under federal jurisdiction. However, federal authorities are also involved in the investigation of low-level drug crimes and other offenses that have historically been under state and local authorities' purview. Initiatives to detect and catch the transportation of drugs on the nation's highways are a centerpiece of the war on drugs, notably paralleling the prominence of vehicle stops and searches in pursuit of illicit alcohol during Prohibition.

First through 1910's Mann Act and more recently through other legislation, the federal government has also invested significant energy in counteracting human trafficking, particularly sex trafficking. Recent conversations around this issue highlight the complex and often controversial nature of designing government interventions related to sex work, gender inequality, and exploitation. Indeed, laws such as FOSTA-SESTA offer an important context for reflections on how the criminal justice system handles sex work and human rights and for consideration of the approach's effectiveness in advancing—or hindering   individual liberties and the general welfare.

In drug trafficking, human trafficking, and a host of other areas, the fed-

eral government's expanded footprint in criminal legislation and law enforcement shows no signs of shrinking. Critics of federalization, however, note that
this trend has come with significant costs—including major expenditures on
federal investigations and prosecutions, a massively expanded federal prison
population, an eroded boundary between federal and state jurisdictions, and
a shift in power away from elected local prosecutors and toward appointed US
Attorneys—without evidence of appreciable public safety benefits.[71]

EIGHT

MADD Prosecutors?

Drunk Driving and Prosecutorial Discretion

Drunk driving's treatment under the criminal law underwent a remarkable transformation in the late twentieth century. Historically, somewhat forgiving drunk driving laws had been laxly enforced and violations were lightly sanctioned. Today, following an impactful series of reforms, stricter laws are enforced more strenuously and violators face stiff penalties. Moral entrepreneurs are crucial to this story. In the late 1970s and 1980s organizations such as Remove Intoxicated Drivers and Mothers Against Drunk Driving played pivotal roles in shifting public perceptions of drinking and driving and also achieved major successes in changing drunk driving laws and their enforcement.

One of the notable consequences of the changed social and legal perspective on drunk driving was the growth of laws and prosecutions pertaining to situations in which intoxicated drivers cause fatalities. These types of cases offer a revealing context for exploring prosecutorial discretion, a hallmark feature of US criminal justice. Prosecutors' broad leeway to decide whom to prosecute and what specific charges to bring manifests in their determinations of what criminal charges are appropriate when impaired drivers cause death. As in other types of cases, prosecutors' decisions here are highly consequential for defendants and victims' families. In the aggregate, these decisions constitute significant influences on the overall character of the criminal justice system.

DRIVING, DRINKING, AND DANGEROUSNESS

Cars are a highly individualized mode of transportation. "Unlike the airplane, the railroad, or mass transit, [driving] is not in the care of highly trained, paid, and certified personnel. The automobile is available as an accessory to the gamut of our moods, our arenas of living, and our daytime and nighttime tasks and adventures."[1] Private automobiles are available to their owners at any time, for whatever purpose that owner sees fit. Cars are also remarkably dangerous among modes of transportation. Motor vehicle collisions are responsible for about 95% of all transportation fatalities in the United States.[2] Most of these fatalities involve drivers or passengers in motor vehicles, but cars endanger other users of streets and sidewalks as well; in 2018 and 2019, about 17% of motor vehicle fatalities were pedestrians and another 2–3% were bicyclists.[3] Of course, automobiles' overwhelming predominance among sources of transportation fatalities owes significantly to their general predominance among modes of transportation. Automobiles, however, are also far more dangerous per mile traveled than other ways of getting from place to place. In 2019 there were .45 passenger deaths for every 100 million miles traveled in passenger vehicles, compared with .05 deaths for buses, .005 for passenger trains, and .0004 for airlines.[4]

Automobiles' versatility and the freedom of individual movement they offer are among their most attractive characteristics as modes of transportation. However, driving also puts motor vehicles' destructive power under the control of a single individual, and drivers have wide leeway to choose when, where, and how to drive. Drivers' mistakes are costly, dangerous, and often deadly, for both their vehicles' occupants and others. Together, these qualities make driving a weighty ethical and legal responsibility.

As described in Chapter 4, early pushes to require driver licensure and examinations reflected efforts to limit driving privileges to people deemed competent. The issue of driver safety, however, does not stop after someone successfully completes a driver's exam and obtains a license. Every time someone gets behind the wheel, their decisions and actions have significant implications for the health and safety of themselves, any passengers they carry, and the people and property they encounter on the road.

Driving's risks become particularly acute when alcohol is involved. Drinking affects judgment, impairs motor function, and slows reaction times, all paramount requirements for safe driving.[5] From the outset of the automobile age, observers noted the public safety risk that intoxicated drivers presented, and various states and local jurisdictions enacted laws banning drunk driving.[6] The first scientific report on how drinking affected drivers of "motorized wagons" appeared in 1904.[7] By 1912, the *Automobile Journal* reported on prohibitions of intoxicated driving in New Jersey, New York, and Pennsylvania, as well as a similar measure under consideration in West Virginia.[8] This same journal issue described a bill in the Massachusetts legislature that would provide for between a month's and a year's imprisonment and permanent license revocation for those caught driving while intoxicated, strengthening a 1909 Massachusetts law that had provided for up to six months' imprisonment and a fine of up to $200 for these offenses.[9] New York, an early mover on traffic law in general, was notably aggressive with respect to drunk driving, becoming one of the first states to make driving while intoxicated a felony and to provide mechanisms for offending drivers to lose their licenses.[10]

However, enforcement of early bans on driving while intoxicated was spotty, and penalties for those caught breaking these laws were often minor. Of initial responses to the issue in New York City, a judge wrote in 1912, "It is ridiculous that a man should be able to drive a car in the streets of Manhattan Borough, at least, while intoxicated, and escape with a fine of $25."[11] With alcohol a central feature of American social life and a transportation system increasingly reliant on private automobiles, drinking and driving emerged as a significant social problem. In 1938 the American Medical Association (AMA) and the National Safety Council (NSC) engaged in a joint initiative to investigate automobile crashes and alcohol's role therein. Emerging from this effort was a 1939 AMA report, on which the NSC signed off, that identified excessive drinking as the leading cause of the "slaughter" on the roads.[12] To combat the problem, the committee issued recommendations for charging and prosecution based on different blood alcohol contents (BACs): No one should be prosecuted for driving under the influence (DUI) with a BAC below .05%, and a BAC above .15% should lead to a DUI prosecution. In the wide range of BACs between .05% and .15%, however, the committee suggested prosecution only if physical and circumstantial evidence provided "definite confirmation of such influence."[13] This report was pivotal: Both the established BAC thresholds and the general notion of giving authorities discretion about whether to charge and prosecute drivers in the broad "middle range" of BAC proved to be enduring influences on state legislatures that were crafting drunk driving laws and on police departments' enforcement—or nonenforcement—practices.[14]

Despite repeated alarms about the dangers of driving while intoxicated and recommendations for more strenuous government interventions, drinking and driving remained a common practice, and one to which, in many people's eyes, the criminal justice system demonstrated a disappointing degree of indifference.[15] A series of changes beginning in the mid-1960s reflected an emerging consensus around the notion that drinking and driving was a serious social problem that demanded tighter regulation and vigorous enforcement interventions. The 1966 establishment of the Department of Transportation marked the federal government's interest in centrally coordinating regulation of transportation, particularly cars and drivers. One of the department's first initiatives was creating federal standards regarding drinking and driving and pressuring states to adopt corresponding changes to their laws, including lowering legal BAC maximums from .15% to .10% and testing BACs for all drivers involved in fatal collisions.[16]

Within the Department of Transportation, the National Traffic Safety Agency (later renamed the National Highway Traffic Safety Administration [NHTSA]) took a leading role in efforts to reduce death and destruction on American roadways. In 1968 they released a report on drunk driving holding alcohol responsible for 800,000 crashes and 25,000 fatalities per year.[17] The *1968 Alcohol and Highway Safety Report* contained a number of suggestions for reducing rates of drunk driving and thus ameliorating the associated "tragic . . . loss in life, limb and property damage."[18] The federal government expanded its efforts related to drunk driving following the 1968 report. Between 1969 and 1976 the Alcohol Safety Action Projects under the NHTSA funded thirty-five programs in local jurisdictions. These programs provided federal funds to support training law enforcement officers in catching intoxicated drivers through such practices as sobriety checkpoints.[19]

The federal government's promulgation of preferred standards and support of local drunk driving countermeasures did not have the major impact that its proponents had hoped. Although federal interventions led to significant increases in DUI arrests—even doubling them in certain Alcohol Safety Action Projects sites—it was unclear whether these interventions had reduced alcohol-involved crashes or associated mortality.[20] Facing low likelihoods of being caught, Americans continued to drink and drive by the millions in the 1970s, and alcohol continued to be a contributing factor in tens of thousands of crashes and fatalities. As federal enthusiasm for committing resources to the problem dwindled, however, a new set of players came onto the scene, sparking a moral entrepreneurship campaign that would dramatically reshape both public perceptions of drunk driving and legal responses to the behavior.

MORAL ENTREPRENEURS STEP IN

Joseph Gusfield describes the shift in public perceptions of drinking and driving that began in the mid-1960s as constituting a new "moral drama" around the issue, with those who drive after drinking framed as villains.[21] As a matter of basic terminology, Gusfield notes the transition in newspaper stories away from the label of "drinking-driver" to the now familiar "drunk driver."[22] This changed depiction reflects a consolidation around the idea that drinking and driving is a source of consequential social disorder and an immoral thing to do, and the corresponding view that serious criminal sanctions are an appropriate social response to the behavior. Indeed, under this changed construction, the driver impaired by alcohol is a more serious offender than a sober driver who breaks traffic laws; drinking and driving makes one a "menace," even a "killer-drunk."[23]

The moral entrepreneurship campaign around drunk driving distilled these changing sentiments and used them in the service of a far-reaching effort to change relevant policies and how they were enforced. Renowned American sociologist Howard Becker coined the term *moral entrepreneur* in his 1963 book *Outsiders: Studies in the Sociology of Deviance*: "Rules are the products of someone's initiative and we can think of the people who exhibit such enterprise as *moral entrepreneurs*."[24] In conventional usage, an entrepreneur is someone who starts a business. In Becker's formulation, a moral entrepreneur is someone who demonstrates similar initiative and commitment in the effort to address something in the social world that they see as profoundly wrong or a weighty problem they believe is not receiving its due attention. As moral entrepreneurs, *rule creators* endeavor to change rules, especially legal rules. "The existing rules do not satisfy him because there is some evil which profoundly disturbs him. He feels that nothing can be right in the world until rules are made to correct it."[25] Becker identifies activists for the abolition of slavery, proponents of criminalizing marijuana, and the temperance movement as examples of consequential moral entrepreneurs. When rule creators—or, in their prototypical form, "crusading reformers"—succeed, "we often find that a new set of enforcement agencies and officials is established."[26] These *rule enforcers* are responsible for applying the new sets of rules that result from successful campaigns of rule creation, but may not share rule creators' passion for the rules themselves.[27]

In prototypical rule creator fashion, drunk driving moral entrepreneurs took on the mantle of crusading reformers, seeking to alter what they saw as an unconscionable state of affairs surrounding drinking, driving, and death on America's roads in the late 1970s and early 1980s. They were not alone in this opinion. In 1981, for instance, Douglas Besharov, who had recently served as the first director of the US National Center on Child Abuse and Neglect, memorably depicted a "night in the cooler" as the relatively minimal deprivation of liberty faced by a prototypical drunken driver.[28] In 1982 an article in *Newsweek* magazine called driving while intoxicated a "socially accepted form of murder."[29] That was also the year in which the NHTSA began estimating the number of alcohol-related fatalities on the nation's roads; for 1982 they estimated 26,172 such deaths.[30]

Specific events, however, sparked the genesis of the two most important groups in the drunk driving moral entrepreneurship campaign: Remove Intoxicated Drivers (RID), founded by Doris Aiken in New York in 1978, and Mothers Against Drunk Driving (MADD, originally named Mothers Against Drunk Drivers), founded by Candy Lightner in California in 1980. In the case of RID, Aiken was driven to action after learning of a Schenectady, New York, incident in which a drunk driver killed two local teenagers.[31] For Lightner, the precipitating incident was as close to home as it gets: Her influential work as a moral entrepreneur began when a drunk driver struck and killed her 13-year-old daughter, Cari Lightner. The details of the Lightner case brought the relative laxity of drunk driving rules and enforcement into sharp relief: Police had arrested the driver, Clarence William Busch, for driving while intoxicated (DWI) on four previous occasions, leading to a total of only forty-eight hours in jail time. Busch's most recent arrest came just two days before he hit Cari.[32]

RID's early tactics included tracking specific DWI cases and pressuring prosecutors, legislators, judges, and the Department of Motor Vehicles to aggressively pursue drunk driving offenses and impose serious penalties on those who committed them. Plea bargaining in DWI cases was a particular point of emphasis for RID, with Aiken and others in the organization arguing that prosecutors who accepted guilty pleas in exchange for reduced sentences effectively let drunk drivers off the hook.[33] Their campaign of pressuring prosecutors included writing district attorneys directly, noting that RID was following DWI cases and expected alleged drunk drivers to face significant punishments.[34] These letters implied that, should prosecutors act in ways that failed to meet RID's vision of appropriate levels of punitiveness, RID would publicize their perceived leniency; especially because most district attorneys are elected, and thus directly accountable to local voters, the threat of such publicity can be an effective cudgel. In the classic mode of Becker's rule creators, RID framed their efforts to influence public officials as a humanitarian enterprise, aiming to protect the innocent and enhance public safety through counteracting the scourge of impaired driving. Pushing prosecutors to throw the book at drunk drivers was necessary, they contended, because the lack of significant jail time—or any jail time whatsoever—in many DWI cases failed to disrupt patterns of repeat offending and functionally signaled that drinking and driving was acceptable behavior.[35]

Within five years RID had chapters in thirty states.[36] The organization achieved particularly notable success in rule creation in Aiken's home state of New York. In 1980 and 1981 RID's pressure campaign led to the passage of thirteen New York laws strengthening drunk driving policies and enforcement practices. These measures included allocating funds to buy breathalyzers and pay police overtime, revoking repeat DWI offenders' licenses, and, true to Aiken's vision, limiting prosecutors' ability to reduce sentences through offering plea bargains in impaired driving cases.[37]

RID was a pivotal early actor, but Lightner's MADD would prove even more influential. Lightner was tenacious, as exemplified by her commitment to show up at California governor Jerry Brown's office every day until she secured his commitment to create a drunk driving task force.[38] Lightner also proved a gifted public advocate for the cause, making provocative and compelling appearances on popular television programs such as *60 Minutes*, the *Today* show, and *Donahue*.[39]

MADD grew even faster than RID had, reaching more than 300 chapters in its first five years.[40] The fledgling organization soon became one of the best known and most favorably viewed nonprofits in the country, securing high-profile celebrity endorsements and a prominent place in the public imagination.[41] Like RID, MADD also secured several notable victories in changing state-level rules and enforcement practices, including a lower legal BAC and provisions related to roadside BAC testing in Maryland and several measures leading to harsher drunk driving penalties in California.[42]

Both organizations' legal and political impact reached a zenith in their impact on the federal government in the 1980s. On April 14, 1982, the anti-drunk-driving coalition achieved a landmark victory. On that day President Reagan gave an address in the White House Rose Garden decrying drunk driving as an epidemic and announcing the establishment of a Presidential Commission on Drunk Driving.[43] Also in 1982, Congress passed and Reagan signed the first major federal statute addressing drinking and driving. The law provided tens of millions of dollars in federal support for highway construction for states that agreed to criminalize per se driving with a .10% or higher BAC, to provide for license revocations, to require that repeat DWI offenders go to jail or perform community service, and to commit to more aggressively pursue drunk driving charges.[44] In 1984 the federal Minimum Legal Drinking Age law used the same highway funding incentive to pressure all the states to raise their legal drinking ages to 21 (at that time, more than half the states permitted drinking at age 18 or 19).[45]

Both of these landmark pieces of federal legislation were effective, helping to drive a flurry of legislative activity in the states in the 1980s and into the 1990s. By 1984 all states that had previously permitted a higher legal BAC had lowered their maximum legal BACs to .10%, and by 1988 all fifty states had set their minimum legal drinking age at 21.[46] The dozens of laws that state legislatures passed in this period included several of the federal government's specified priorities, such as making it illegal per se for people to drive with BACs above certain thresholds and providing for license revocations before DUI convictions, as well as imposing zero tolerance BAC limits for motorists younger than 21.[47] Newly aggressive drunk driving policies and enforcement measures received some pushback. For instance, sobriety checkpoints—"or, less euphemistically, the drunk driving roadblock"—garnered criticism for their potential unconstitutionality under the Fourth Amendment and questionable effectiveness.[48] Nevertheless, in the late 1980s drunk driving charges were the most commonly prosecuted crimes in the country.[49] (By 2019 drunk driving arrests had fallen behind arrests on drug charges, but arrests of adults for drunk driving remained more frequent than arrests for any one type of property or violent crime.)[50]

The moral entrepreneurship campaign and resulting rule creation also had an appreciable impact on drunk driving behavior and its often tragic results. Roadside driver surveys indicated substantial reductions in rates of impaired driving between the 1970s and 1990s. Researchers conducted three similar national surveys in 1973, 1986, and 1996, stopping drivers between 10 pm and 3 am on Friday and Saturday evenings and screening their BACs. In the 1973 survey 36% of drivers had positive BACs; in 1996 the percentage was less than half the 1973 number, with only 17% of drivers having positive BACs.[51] By 1992 annual drunk driving fatalities were below 15,000, down from the 26,172 recorded in 1982, the first year the NHTSA began making estimates.[52] In the past decade, annual drunk driving fatalities numbered between just under 10,000 to just under 11,000, a pronounced decrease since 1982, and the rate of drunk driving fatalities per 100,000 Americans decreased about 65% between 1982 and 2018.[53]

The moral crusade against drunk driving and associated legal changes transformed the behavior's treatment in the criminal justice system, with stricter enforcement, harsher penalties, and far more prosecutions than in previous decades. Depending on jurisdiction and the nature of the offense, drunk driving charges can be categorized as DUI (driving under the influence) or DWI (driving while intoxicated or driving while impaired). Most states also provide for more serious aggravated DUI or DWI charges based on exacerbating factors such as a BAC far above the legal limit of .08%, especially risky driving behavior, or resulting harms to people or property. As in other contexts of criminal offending, prosecutors decide when to bring these charges and what specific charges to bring. The concept of prosecutorial discretion denotes their empowerment to make these highly consequential decisions based on their own judgment and priorities, with few regulations and minimal oversight.

PROSECUTORIAL DISCRETION

Something was fishy in the case of John Yates. After being caught by a federal inspector with undersized red grouper, Yates instructed a member of his crew to throw the offending fish overboard. Yates was subsequently convicted under 18 U.S.C. §1519, a federal law providing for imprisonment of up to twenty years to punish destruction of evidence.

Yates appealed his conviction up to the US Supreme Court. At oral argument in *Yates v. United States* (2015), Justice Antonin Scalia asked what kind of "mad prosecutor" would seek a 20-year prison sentence in response to these sorts of allegations. Justice Scalia's comment highlights a crucial theme in American criminal justice: the power of prosecutors, who have nearly unfettered discretion in choosing which defendants to prosecute, how many charges to file against a given defendant, and what specific charges to bring.

Prosecutors' broad authority to decide whom to charge and how aggressively to pursue particular cases gives them an unmatched degree of influence over case outcomes.[54] Courts have repeatedly affirmed this degree of authority and only rarely find against prosecutors in cases of alleged misconduct.[55] (Indeed, the wide discretion granted to prosecutors itself complicates efforts to specify what sorts of behaviors constitute misconduct and to detect such violations when they occur.)[56] Decisions about whether to file charges at all are especially pivotal, and rest entirely in prosecutors' offices. "In deciding whether to file a case in the court, the prosecutor is free to use any standard between 'probable cause,' the standard required for the police to make an arrest, and beyond a reasonable doubt."[57] Prosecutors' offices set their own standards on this issue and can proceed with prosecutions based on evidence that falls substantially below the threshold of demonstrating defendants' culpability beyond any reasonable doubt. Prosecutors' capacity to make calls about whether to prosecute and what to charge—or whether to dismiss charges—becomes particularly problematic if decisions on these matters are arbitrary or biased. These processes transpire largely behind closed doors, with minimal oversight, and research on the subject is somewhat limited. Available data, however, suggest that there may be systematic differences in how prosecutors approach different types of cases. Statistics indicate that prosecutors are more likely to pursue prosecutions of nonwhite defendants, especially Black defendants.[58] There is also evidence that factors such as race, ethnicity, and gender influence prosecutors' decisions about whether to pursue charges that bring mandatory minimum sentences or sentence enhancement rules into play, or whether to request "downward departures" from otherwise applicable sentencing guidelines.[59]

In 1940 US Supreme Court justice Robert Jackson wrote that "the prosecutor has more control over life, liberty, and reputation than any other person in America."[60] Since that time, prosecutorial discretion has grown even more consequential with the introduction of tighter sentencing guidelines and mandatory minimum sentence laws. By more closely specifying what types of sentences must be imposed for various categories of convictions, these measures reduce judges' and juries' influence on sentencing outcomes. By extension, they functionally move discretion upstream in the criminal legal process, away from courts and toward prosecutors' offices. When judges and juries have less input on sentencing decisions, prosecutors' determinations of what charges to file become more significant, with charging decisions themselves bearing greater implications for what sentences will look like in the event of conviction.[61] In 1940 Justice Jackson called the ability to make charging decisions "the most dangerous power of the prosecutor"; that power's danger has only expanded subsequently, and it remains "virtually unreviewable."[62] Overlapping provisions in criminal codes further concentrate power in prosecutors' offices: "Most states' legislatures, by creating too many policy choices, have effectively abdicated public policy-making to the prosecutor since it is the prosecutor, and not the legislature, that has the final decision in determining which public policy, if any, is breached by an individual's conduct."[63]

Prosecutors' power to make these decisions is what underlies plea bargaining. In a plea bargain, a defendant agrees to plead guilty, forfeiting the right to a jury trial guaranteed by the Sixth Amendment, in exchange for the prosecutor's promise to go easy on them. This commonly includes dropping one or more other charges that the defendant faces or charging them with a less serious type of offense.[64] This "distinctively American practice," in the words of law and society scholar Mary Vogel, is historically long-standing.[65] However, it has become an increasingly central part of the criminal legal process over US history. Today, the vast majority of criminal convictions result from guilty pleas, not from the conventional vision of a courtroom trial; at least nine out of ten convictions result from plea-bargaining processes.[66] In 2012 Supreme Court justice Anthony Kennedy summarized, "Plea bargaining . . . is not some adjunct to the criminal justice system; it is the criminal justice system."[67]

PROSECUTORIAL DISCRETION IN DRUNK DRIVING AND DWI FATALITY CASES

The application of criminal penalties in specific cases depends fundamentally on the statutes that legislatures pass, which specify offenses and provide sentencing guidelines. In practice, however, what happens to individual defendants results directly from what prosecutors decide to do in their cases.

Anti-drunk-driving moral entrepreneurs had their own ideas about what sorts of criminal penalties should be applied in these cases and achieved significant success in bringing both popular opinion and relevant laws into closer concordance with their position. In addition to their focus on changing formal rules, these crusaders recognized the importance of shaping the discretionary action of legal authorities such as police and prosecutors. After all, these actors are responsible for putting written rules into action, and their enforcement of drunk driving laws and prosecution of those who violate them were crucial to a movement that did not just want to change the law on the books, but to fundamentally alter the calculus around drinkers' decisions whether to drive. In RID, Doris Aiken understood well prosecutors' pivotal role in ensuring that people caught driving drunk faced significant penalties; accordingly, she dedicated substantial energy to pressuring prosecutors to charge and convict intoxicated drivers and not to offer plea bargains that would allow DWI offenders to receive shorter sentences or avoid jail time altogether.[68]

Putting aside some statutory limitations—such as the DWI plea-bargaining guidelines that RID successfully pushed for in New York[69]—prosecutors have substantial leeway to decide how to proceed when considering charges related to drinking and driving. A study of prosecutors' decisions about whether to dismiss or prosecute drunk driving cases in the Houston, Texas, area suggests that people are more likely to be prosecuted for drunk driving offenses when they submit to breathalyzers and when their BACs are higher.[70] These researchers found that these factors might contribute to racial, ethnic, and age disparities in patterns of prosecutorial decision making because Black motorists were more likely than White motorists to submit to breathalyzers and because Latino drivers and older drivers were likely to have comparatively elevated BACs.[71]

Beyond routine DUI and DWI cases, prosecutorial discretion is notably implicated in the thousands of cases every year in which fatalities are connected to impaired driving. Criminal legal activity in this space has expanded considerably as a consequence of the changed social and legal framing of drunk driving that emerged in the later twentieth century. This increased activity has included changes to both written laws and prosecutors' discretionary actions with respect to charging decisions.

Overall, drunk driving laws were laxly enforced up until the 1970s. When prosecutors elected to prosecute drunk drivers who caused fatalities, they relied on traditional homicide statutes.[72] Traditional homicide statutes take different forms in different jurisdictions. However, the states are consistent in defining murder as killing with "malice aforethought." First-degree murder refers to killings that are both intentional and premeditated, or deliberately planned.

Second-degree murder refers to incidents in which defendants intended to kill in the moment but did not plan to kill in advance. Nearly all states also have felony murder laws. These statutes permit prosecutors to charge defendants with murder when someone dies during the commission of another violent felony or, in a few states, during the commission of any other felony at all.[73]

Manslaughter charges, on the other hand, pertain to killings without malice aforethought. Manslaughter offenses include voluntary manslaughter, which refers to a killing that is intentional but occurs amid mitigating circumstances, such as strong provocation or a defendant's diminished capacity. The more familiar manslaughter charge is involuntary manslaughter, in which a defendant causes someone's death through reckless behavior. Rather than involuntary manslaughter charges, defendants can also face the lesser charge of criminally negligent homicide for behavior causing death that was negligent but not reckless, with recklessness triggering greater culpability than negligence under the criminal law.[74]

When using traditional homicide statutes to prosecute fatalities caused by intoxicated or otherwise reckless drivers, prosecutors would most commonly bring manslaughter charges. In 1911, for instance, the Nebraska Supreme Court upheld a motorist's conviction of manslaughter charges for careless driving leading to a death.[75] Prosecutors rarely charged drunk drivers who caused deaths with murder.[76] Indeed, following a surge in these types of cases in the early years of automobility, they dropped off considerably during the midcentury period: "Some states which had previously established a vehicular murder doctrine stopped using it altogether, and, aside from those arising in [Alabama, Georgia, Tennessee, and Texas], only a handful of vehicular murder cases appeared at all."[77] In the late 1960s courts in Arizona, Kansas, and Ohio "specifically rejected the vehicular murder doctrine, and some commentators thought the doctrine was virtually dead."[78]

Later in the twentieth century, however, the social and legal construction of drunk driving as a social problem changed dramatically.[79] Amid the moral entrepreneurs' crusade against drunk driving, the issue attained a much more prominent place in the minds of the public and policymakers. DWI fatalities were at the center of this conversation. In response, state legislatures passed laws pertaining to intoxicated driving in general and DWI fatalities specifically, and prosecutors demonstrated increased interest in bringing homicide charges against drunk drivers who caused deaths, including murder charges.[80]

Laws pertaining specifically to motorists causing death due to intoxication or recklessness are not entirely new. For instance, in 1919 Nebraska enacted a statute criminalizing reckless driving that resulted in death or that seriously "maim[ed] or disfigured any person," with prison sentences of one to ten years and fines of $200 to $500 for violations.[81] In 1935 the Nebraska legislature amended this law to specifically address intoxicated drivers who caused fatalities.[82] Utah passed a similar law in 1957, creating the crime of automobile homicide, which applied to situations in which drivers who had been drinking caused death by driving recklessly, negligently, or carelessly; like the Nebraska law, the Utah statute carried a penalty of one to ten years in prison.[83] By the early 1960s states that had either enacted statutes pertaining specifically to motor vehicle homicide or amended their manslaughter statutes to include direct references to automobiles included Alaska, Arizona, California, Kentucky, Maryland, and Rhode Island.[84] Illinois, Indiana, Maine, and South Carolina used reckless homicide statutes to prosecute these offenses, which permitted convictions when drivers' conduct demonstrated "reckless disregard for the safety of others."[85] In 1967 Ohio enacted a law pertaining to "first degree homicide by vehicle," which included deaths caused by driving under the influence, as well as those caused by reckless driving and drag racing.[86] Ohio replaced this offense with aggravated vehicular homicide in 1974 and further amended the statute in 1983 to clarify how findings of intoxication would affect sentencing for convictions.[87]

The 1983 amendment to Ohio law was part of a broader trend. Legal changes in this period pertaining specifically to drunk driving fatalities prominently included new statutes that specifically targeted the crime of intoxicated driving leading to death.[88] For instance, in 1992 Michigan created a new felony providing for up to fifteen years in prison for motorists with BACs of .10% or higher who caused death.[89] States also amended existing laws to foreground drinking as a basis for legal culpability in deadly traffic collisions; the emphasis on intoxication in Ohio's 1983 amendment to their vehicular homicide statutes exemplifies this sort of change.[90]

Following the surge of legislative activity in the 1980s and 1990s, nearly all states now have specific vehicular homicide statutes, although their details vary somewhat from state to state. Jurisdictions have different laws specifying conditions and penalties for charges of aggravated vehicular homicide, vehicular homicide, vehicular manslaughter, and so on. In general, the label *vehicular homicide* refers to offenses in which a driver kills someone due to intoxication or recklessness. Crimes categorized under this label "overwhelmingly . . . involve substance abuse and reckless driving."[91] Although sober drivers who cause death through recklessness may face vehicular homicide charges, these statutes are most often used to prosecute drunk driving fatalities.

New or revised vehicular homicide laws that foregrounded drinking as a contributor to legal culpability in traffic deaths reflected heightened awareness of drunk driving as a problem and public outrage directed toward its perpetrators, especially when they caused injuries and deaths. They also helped prosecutors avoid the pitfalls that occasionally characterized prosecutions of DWI fatalities under traditional homicide statutes, particularly murder statutes. Statutes criminalizing murder and voluntary manslaughter include an element of intent. Sometimes, juries considered intoxication a form of diminished capacity mitigating the intent necessary for a conviction of murder or voluntary manslaughter.[92] This issue arose in Wisconsin in 1922, when the first court upheld a vehicular murder conviction. In that case, the defendant did not attempt to invoke impairment as a defense against murder charges, but the court indicated that intoxication could in fact alleviate his culpability if it was "such a degree of drunkenness as robbed the defendant of his powers of volition."[93] This suggests the logic that a certain level of intoxication could raise questions about whether the court should consider a defendant's actions truly intentional. Vehicular homicide statutes aimed to invalidate any such arguments by specifically identifying intoxication as a source of legal culpability, not a potential release from such culpability.

Particularly given the pronounced dependence on automobiles that emerged in the mid-twentieth century—and generally laxer attitudes toward drinking and driving—some juries also demonstrated uncertainty about whether they should consider cars to be instruments of killing the way they would think about more conventional weapons such as guns and knives.[94] Vehicular homicide statutes addressed this issue as well, by specifying driving as the context to which the law applied and automobiles as the means of killing.

Today, state laws pertaining to intoxicated drivers who cause deaths specify a wide range of sentences. In Oklahoma motorists convicted of these offenses face at most one year in prison.[95] Sentencing ranges increase from there. In Maryland, for instance, zero to five years in prison are on the table; in Mississippi, five to twenty-five years; in Nebraska, one to fifty years; in Alaska, one to ninety-nine years; and in North Dakota, zero years to life.[96]

Contemporary prosecutors have a range of options when deciding what to charge, if anything, when impaired drivers are involved in crashes that cause fatalities. Depending on the facts of the case and their own judgment, they can choose to charge defendants under traditional homicide statutes. Such actions can include murder charges, particularly if prosecutors believe that the driving behavior that led to death was of an especially egregious or heinous nature. In New York, for instance, prosecutors can seek murder charges against drivers in DWI fatality cases under a provision in state law that specifies killing "under circumstances evincing a depraved indifference to human life" as a form of second-degree murder.[97] Other states demonstrate similar tendencies. For example, courts in Michigan have affirmed that, when intoxicated drivers cause death, prosecutors can seek second-degree murder charges—and the longer prison sentences these charges entail—rather than applying statutes written specifically to address DWI fatalities.[98] Washington courts have affirmed prosecutors' right to pursue first-degree murder charges rather than vehicular homicide charges when a defendant's conduct reflects "extreme indifference to human life" and thus establishes the mens rea required for a conviction of first-degree murder.[99] Courts in California and Tennessee have reached analogous conclusions, with Tennessee going so far as to declare the act of drunk driving itself as *malum in se* and thus a basis for a finding of criminal intent in support of a murder charge.[100] Under California law DUI homicide "has evolved into a de facto strict liability crime."[101] This means that a defendant "who drives under the influence and causes a death may be charged solely with murder at the whim of prosecutorial discretion."[102] By contrast, a California defendant who, while intoxicated, "kills by any means other than a vehicle has the real and distinct hope and possibility of escaping with no more than a manslaughter conviction. This strange twist of law leads to the inescapable conclusion that the 'drunk' who shoots and kills a pedestrian is in a potentially far superior legal position than the 'drunk' who runs over and kills a pedestrian."[103] Moreover, prosecutors in several states can use felony murder statutes to prosecute drunk driving vehicular homicides as murders, even first-degree murders, based on the principle that the homicides occurred in the context of another felony being committed.[104]

Prosecutors file murder charges against drivers in DWI fatalities to signal social opprobrium and to seek the most serious penalties they can. In many jurisdictions second-degree murder convictions carry the possibility of life in prison. Based on their assessment of the case and the specifics of their states' statutes, prosecutors can also decide to charge intoxicated drivers who cause death with other traditional homicide crimes, including manslaughter or criminally negligent homicide. Since the near-universalization of vehicular homicide statutes, most prosecutors can also elect to file these charges. Sentencing ranges for vehicular homicide offenses vary considerably, as noted above. Depending on the state, convictions on these charges can involve longer or shorter sentences than traditional manslaughter convictions. Sentences for vehicular homicide are typically shorter than those for murder and longer than those for criminally negligent homicide.

Many factors are relevant to prosecutors' decisions about what to charge in DWI fatality cases.[105] One group of factors relates to their assessment of the defendant's degree of culpability: Does the defendant's legal responsibility in the case rise to the level of a murder charge? A vehicular homicide charge? A criminally negligent homicide charge? Or perhaps no charge at all? Points of consideration include things like the objective dangerousness of the defendant's behavior: Did the defendant drive 80 miles per hour through a crowded school zone, or did their driving appear to demonstrate general adherence to traffic laws? Further, is there evidence that the defendant was aware, or should have been aware, of the risks of driving and disregarded those risks?[106] These considerations are highly relevant to charging decisions: If the defendant demonstrated disregard for human life, this can constitute the recklessness needed to support a charge of vehicular homicide or involuntary manslaughter. If the behavior went beyond this and demonstrated complete indifference to others' lives, this may rise to the level of the malice aforethought needed for a murder conviction.[107]

Prosecutors in these cases also need to think about what outcome from the case is most appropriate and desirable.[108] Given the available evidence, what penalty best fits the crime? Further, what outcome should be sought to incapacitate or deter this defendant and to generally deter the sanctioned behavior among others? Potential considerations here include the extent of death and destruction resulting from the defendant's actions, the preferences of the victim's or victims' families and other stakeholders, the defendant's relevant criminal and substance abuse history, and the defendant's actions after the incident, including whether the defendant accepts responsibility and demonstrates remorse.[109] Prosecutors also have a pronounced interest in obtaining convictions and avoiding acquittals; this interest may encourage them to lean toward vehicular homicide charges, which are written specifically to address DWI fatality cases, and away from more general homicide charges, which might be harder to prove beyond a reasonable doubt.[110]

CAUSES AND CONSEQUENCES
OF CHANGES IN CRIMINAL JUSTICE

Motorists are not legally compelled to drive as well as they possibly can at all times. Driving exams and licensure programs aim to restrict driving privileges to those deemed to meet a general threshold of driving competence. After satisfying these baseline requirements, drivers are largely entrusted to take the responsibility of driving seriously and to drive as attentively and safely as they are able.

Laws pertaining to drunk driving reflect policymakers' determination that certain levels of alcohol intoxication impart a degree of impairment that makes drivers an unacceptable danger to people and property. "It is possible that an 'impaired' driver might still be driving more skillfully and with better control than a good number of unimpaired drivers and, in any event, above the minimum objective standard [of competent driving]. In a sense, the drunk-driving laws superimpose a relative standard of competency over an objective standard."[111] Recent regulations concerning phone use and other forms of distracted driving reflect a broadening of legal attention to conditions and behaviors that impede motorists from driving as well as they are able. Drinking, however, occupies an elevated position among potential contributors to drivers' dangerousness on the road. Accordingly, law enforcement agencies commit significant resources to enforcing drunk driving laws, and lawmakers specify serious penalties for violations.

This was not always the case. Perceptions of drunk driving as a problem began shifting in the 1960s,[112] and a highly effective campaign of moral entrepreneurship in the late 1970s and 1980s helped bring about a transformed social and legal framing of the issue. Remove Intoxicated Drivers (RID), Mothers Against Drunk Driving (MADD), and other moral entrepreneurs played a pivotal role in bolstering the country's drunk driving laws.[113] These changes included strengthened rules and enforcement related to the behavior itself and new laws and prosecution strategies directed specifically at intoxicated drivers who caused deaths. The country's experience in this domain is a compelling demonstration of how interest groups' activities can bring about changes in the criminal law and criminal justice practices.

Legal processes depend on written laws but also on how those laws are implemented. The US criminal legal system empowers multiple actors to make discretionary decisions with major implications for the experiences of suspects, arrestees, and defendants. This list includes police officers, judges, and—particularly notably—prosecutors. Whether prosecutors decide to file charges, what charges they select, and what terms they are willing to offer in plea bargains are all hugely consequential in shaping case outcomes.

Before states enacted specific vehicular homicide statutes, prosecutors largely relied on traditional homicide statutes to file charges for deaths resulting from drunk driving.[114] When they brought these cases, they would usually charge motorists with manslaughter, and only rarely pursue murder charges. With greater social concern about drunk drivers and their social impact, prosecutors found themselves with a reinvigorated mandate to pursue DWI fatality cases and an array of charges to consider when making charging decisions. Contemporary prosecutors can choose between vehicular homicide statutes and traditional homicide statutes when determining what to do in DWI fatality cases. These decisions about the implementation of the criminal law reflect fundamental issues related to the assignment of legal responsibility and culpability and the dynamic relationship between structure and agency in driving the character and outcome of criminal justice processes.

NINE

Roadblocks

Collateral Consequences and Driving Privileges

Legally speaking, driving is a privilege, not a right. Numerous state laws provide for the temporary or permanent restriction of that privilege for various reasons. Many of these laws constitute examples of collateral consequences—things that happen to people as a result of criminal convictions beyond their official sentences from criminal proceedings. To varying degrees across different jurisdictions, collateral consequences touch virtually all aspects of social life, including work, family, and housing. They also implicate the driving privileges that, for many people, enable participation in society and the economy.

Legal restrictions on driving privileges include license suspensions, which may be imposed for specified periods or indefinitely. Indefinite suspensions last until the suspended driver meets some condition, often payment of money they owe to the state resulting from fines, fees, restitution orders, and the like; collectively, such liabilities are known as legal financial obligations.[1] Some types of charges can also result in permanent license revocation.

Historically, authorities temporarily or permanently limited driving privileges primarily for reasons related to driving, under the basic logic that public safety concerns justified removing motorists deemed unacceptably hazardous from the roads. In the late twentieth and early twenty-first centuries, however, there was a notable shift away from this stance and toward the use of license suspensions as consequences for non-driving-related offenses or for failure to pay fines and fees. For example, more than 90% of suspensions in New Jersey between 2004 and 2018 resulted from something unrelated to driving, most commonly failure to pay a fine.[2] These measures reflect government's acknowledgment of driving privileges' value and policymakers' willingness to use the loss of driving privileges as leverage to enforce compliance. In the past several years, though, numerous states have begun to see these policies as counterproductive or self-defeating and changed their laws to limit license suspensions and facilitate reinstatements.

BEYOND FORMAL PUNISHMENTS

When one thinks about the legal consequences of being convicted of a crime, the first things that come to mind are typically the criminal penalties to which defendants are formally sentenced after conviction. These penalties include periods of incarceration in jail or prison, probation, orders to pay fines and fees, community service obligations, and various combinations of these things.

The fallout of a criminal conviction, however, often extends far beyond these familiar penalties. The term *collateral consequences* refers to the additional disadvantages and disabilities that result from conviction but are not part of the formal sentence handed down in criminal proceedings. The collateral consequences of convictions are multifarious. Depending on jurisdiction and charge, people convicted of crimes may become ineligible for public assistance and housing assistance programs, be barred from holding certain jobs or occupational licenses, or lose the right to vote.[3] These are civil penalties, not criminal ones; collateral consequence statutes are separate from criminal sentencing statutes and impose civil disabilities without the same procedural due process protections that apply in criminal proceedings.

These sorts of provisions are not altogether novel. Indeed, Europe has a long historical tradition of civil death. Under these European provisions, people convicted of serious crimes would functionally cease to be legal subjects in several significant ways, including "the permanent loss of the right to vote, to enter into contracts, and to inherit or bequeath property."[4] In the United States, however, collateral consequences have become much more extensive and far-reaching over the last several decades.[5] Many collateral consequence laws apply to both felonies and misdemeanors, and the disabilities imposed can last for the rest of people's lives. Outside the formal laws imposing collateral consequences, people convicted of crimes also face numerous informal collateral consequences. These informal consequences are not officially matters of federal, state, or local law but still happen to people as a result of criminal convictions.[6] General stigma against people who have been convicted of crimes is historically long-standing, but has escalated amid the proliferation of "tough on crime" policies since the 1970s.[7] This stigma prominently manifests in multiple informal collateral consequences. For instance, employers may decline to hire candidates with criminal records, even if no law prevents the candidate from holding the position. Similarly, private landlords may decline to rent to people with criminal records, compounding housing difficulties resulting from formal collateral consequences. Informal collateral consequences also include various spillover effects for people other than the criminal record holder. Partners, children, and other stakeholders frequently feel the effects of stigma and disabilities resulting from arrests and convictions, particularly when those disabilities generate financial trouble, housing instability, and difficulty accessing supportive resources.[8]

Sociologist Bruce Western memorably described incarceration as "a key life event that triggers a cumulative spiral of disadvantage."[9] Formal and informal collateral consequences are a key mechanism driving and sustaining these downward spirals.[10] Over the last four decades states have enacted a host of statutes requiring organizations to conduct criminal background checks on applicants whom they are considering for jobs or other opportunities.[11] People with criminal records thus face greater barriers when seeking employment.[12] And those who can find work are typically limited to the secondary labor market: low-paying, unstable positions with scarce opportunities for advancement and few or no fringe benefits. It is also harder for people with records to find a place to live, particularly one that is affordable and desirable. People with records are frequently ineligible for public housing support. Many private landlords will not rent to them, and those who will are often exploitative: Knowing that these renters' options on the housing market are limited, unscrupulous landlords charge above-market rates for substandard housing. A criminal record is a powerful "negative credential" that makes it harder to access all kinds of resources and opportunities.[13] Perhaps ironically, this effect also includes impediments to accessing educational and training opportunities that could help people accrue positive credentials and potentially help them achieve greater stability and avoid involvement in crime.

For these reasons, in many cases the criminal penalties imposed at the time of conviction pale in long-term significance relative to the collateral consequences that conviction triggers. Formal and informal collateral consequences have far-reaching implications for people's ability to meaningfully participate in social life for years, decades, or forever. Yet these consequences often fly below the public's radar. Criminal justice researcher Jeremy Travis labeled collateral consequences "invisible punishment."[14] Travis notes that these forms of punishment are invisible in several ways: They transpire largely out of the public eye, are excluded from discourse and debates about criminal sentencing, and are established outside the usual process of enacting criminal law.[15]

Historically, defendants were often unaware of what collateral consequences they would face as a result of pleading guilty, with defense attorneys sometimes failing to explain these civil penalties, or even not knowing themselves. In recent years awareness of collateral consequences has grown, and defendants and their counsel are savvier about the implications of accepting a plea bargain. Prosecutors, for their part, also demonstrate familiarity with collateral consequences, and considerations of the civil outcomes associated with different categories of convictions influence discretionary prosecutorial decisions about filing charges and offering deals.[16]

DRIVING PRIVILEGES ON THE LINE

Restrictions on driving privileges constitute one notable category of collateral consequences. Driver's licenses—and the official validation of driving privileges they represent—are a form of property distributed and controlled by the government.[17] Like many other government-backed certifications and resources distributed to individuals, driver's licenses are valuable. Indeed, in most areas of the United States a driver's license is borderline essential. Without driving privileges—and access to an automobile to use them—people are functionally unable to access many opportunities for education, employment, and participation in politics and civil society. Among available modes of transportation, private automobiles offer notable convenience and versatility. Their status as personal pieces of technology is central to their desirable qualities.[18] As personal technologies, however, automobiles are also dependent on individual drivers. Traffic safety depends on motorists driving capably and responsibly. Driver's licensure and exam requirements aim to ensure a certain baseline of competency in motor vehicle operation. Accordingly, limiting licenses to those deemed competent—and withholding them from others—allows government to pursue its legitimate interest in advancing health, safety, and the general welfare.

Early legal discourse emphasized that "the use of motor vehicles on the public highways was a privilege that was 'derived wholly from the state.'"[19] But the state giveth and the state taketh away. Driving was a privilege that the state could revoke for certain reasons. Historically, those reasons were generally understood to be specific to driving itself, with losing your license temporarily or permanently a consequence of driving-related offenses that signaled you were incompetent or dangerous behind the wheel. This line of thinking has long appeared in conversations around issuing and retracting driver's licenses. In 1931, for instance, A. B. Barber, director of the US Chamber of Commerce's National Conference on Street and Highway Safety, wrote that driving is a privilege that the states should reserve for "competent and capable drivers." This means that states should require licenses. "Furthermore, it means the suspension or revocation of a license after it is issued if the privilege of driving that is granted by the state is abused, or a person in the actual operation of his vehicle demonstrates that he is unfitted and unqualified to drive with safety to himself and others."[20]

Protecting public safety is often the putative justification for collateral consequence statutes that impose civil disabilities on people who have been convicted of certain crimes. Legislative discourse might focus on the need to ban people with certain types of criminal records from working in particular settings, to protect children or other vulnerable parties.[21] Private sector actors similarly argue that excluding people with criminal histories is an important prophylactic measure to insulate themselves from legal risk.[22] Similar protective motivations are the ostensible justification for driver's license suspension laws. Conventionally, these measures are presented as a mechanism through which governments exercise their police powers, advancing public safety by withholding driving privileges from motorists who have been adjudged unacceptably dangerous behind the wheel. There is still a general public perception that limitations on driving privileges are safety oriented, aiming to limit risks to the general public from people assessed to be dangerous behind the wheel. Into the 1970s, restricting driving privileges continued to be understood as a government intervention justified more or less entirely by the state's authority and responsibility to protect life, limb, and property on streets and highways.[23]

However, the way these penalties are used today diverges significantly from conventional road safety justifications. Before the 1980s state laws overwhelmingly imposed license suspensions as a consequence for driving-related offenses.[24] Since that time, though, the pattern has changed substantially, with states enacting a bevy of laws that restrict driving privileges as a consequence for other types of legal violations.[25] License suspensions proliferated accordingly, with restrictions imposed for non-driving-safety reasons at levels far above historical norms. This reflects authorities' use of license suspensions as a broader criminal justice tool. This type of phenomenon can also be observed in other arenas of collateral consequences. In occupational licensure, for instance, restrictions originally proposed with the justification of keeping people who might be dangerous to children out of positions where they might have contact with children ended up affecting much broader groups of jobs and offense records.[26]

1992 was a pivotal year for the contemporary restriction of driving privileges as a collateral consequence for non-driving-safety offenses. In that year the federal government enacted an impactful statute related to drug crime and driver's license suspensions. The Drug Offender's Driving Privileges Suspension Act "require[d] states either to suspend the driver's licenses of drug offenders or actively *refuse* to do so," either by imposing license suspensions of at least six months on everyone convicted of a drug offense or by explicitly declining to impose these collateral consequences through legislative resolutions or letters from governors.[27] To pressure states to choose one path or the other, Congress used the same approach as they had in the key 1980s drunk driving statutes discussed in Chapter 8. If states neither imposed the specified suspensions nor explicitly declined to do so, they would lose federal highway dollars: 5% of their federal highway funds if they did not comply by 1994, rising to 10% if they did not comply by 1996.[28]

In the subsequent years numerous states adopted so-called "use [drugs] and lose [your license]" laws, suspending licenses for people convicted of drug offenses, including distribution and simple possession.[29] By 2000 at least eighteen states and the District of Columbia had enacted laws imposing these consequences on adult offenders, and at least another eleven states enacted use-and-lose laws that applied to juvenile offenders.[30] One observer estimated that these statutes affected more than a million motorists' driving privileges between 1991 and 2004.[31]

More recently, multiple states have taken advantage of the opt-out provision in federal law related to suspending licenses for people convicted of drug crimes. However, as of 2022, twenty-four states continue to restrict driving privileges as a collateral consequence for drug convictions.[32] Nineteen of these states restrict driving privileges for drug offenses that have nothing to do with driving. The other five target the consequence at offenses that somehow connect to cars, for example, a possession or trafficking conviction involving a vehicle.[33] All these statutes are separate from laws that restrict driving privileges as a consequence for driving under the influence of drugs (or alcohol).

Driving privilege restrictions have also emerged as a prominent tactic for enforcing child support orders. In 1988 the federal Family Support Act encouraged states to suspend licenses as a consequence of failure to pay child support.[34] Initially, the federal government again used the possibility of losing federal funding as leverage to encourage state legislation that aligned with federal priorities; several years later, the Personal Responsibility and Work Opportunity Reconciliation Act of 1996 mandated that states establish policies permitting these license suspensions.[35] "To avoid burdening state court systems, this act encouraged the use of administrative procedures."[36] Such administrative processes are typically faster and easier for states than court proceedings, further encouraging the states to embrace the threat of license suspensions as a way to pressure people to meet their legal child support obligations and as a way to punish people who failed to meet these obligations. By 1997 all fifty states authorized license suspensions for failure to pay child support.[37] Many states applied this tool aggressively; Indiana, for instance, suspended 8,099 licenses for failure to pay child support in 2010 alone.[38]

Despite growing awareness of their deleterious implications for affected parties' financial self-sufficiency and ability to participate in social life, license suspensions and revocations continue to be widespread and impactful collateral consequences. Courts have upheld these laws' constitutionality, even when statutes suspend or revoke driving privileges for offenses unconnected to cars or driving.[39] In November 2021 the National Inventory of Collateral Consequences of Conviction listed 2,421 statutes and regulations that impose formal collateral consequences related to driving and noncommercial motor vehicles.[40] Many of these provisions apply to non-driving-related offenses. Indeed, laws in all fifty states provide for driver's license suspensions for at least some infractions unrelated to driving. In Indiana, researchers estimated in 2016 that 420,000 Hoosiers had active license suspensions; most of these suspensions were for non-driving-related reasons, and more than half were for failure to pay traffic fines.[41] A 2020 study of North Carolina found that 1,225,000 people had active driver's license suspensions for failing to appear in court or failure to pay fines. This amounted to 15% of the state's 8.25 million licensed adult drivers, with Black and Latino motorists greatly overrepresented among drivers with suspended licenses relative to their overall shares of the licensed driver population.[42]

Numerous offenses can trigger these civil penalties. In Wisconsin, suspensions have resulted from curfew violations and disorderly conduct convictions, and in Florida, for truancy.[43] As of 2015, Vermont law provided for license suspensions for seventy-four different non-traffic-related offenses.[44] Today, it is especially common for states to suspend driver's licenses when people fail to pay legal financial obligations (LFOs), that is, the court debt that people accumulate from nonpayment of fines, fees, and other costs related to traffic violations or criminal convictions.[45] These suspensions are not imposed as criminal penalties for whatever violation led to the fine, fees, or court costs in question. Rather, taking licenses when people fail to pay LFOs is intended to encourage people—if not coerce them—to pay financial penalties the state has imposed. As such, these collateral consequences have little to no justification as traffic safety interventions. Indeed, they are not connected to driving behavior in any meaningful way.

Different states have different policies related to suspending licenses for unpaid LFOs. Many suspend licenses for unpaid fines and fees related to traffic violations or for surcharges connected to traffic cases. Numerous other states

suspend licenses for failure to pay LFOs in non-traffic-related criminal matters.[46] Altogether, these laws have caused tens of millions of Americans to lose
legal driving privileges. In 2017, for instance, 1.8 million Texans and nearly 1
million Virginians had active suspensions for unpaid LFOs, and "over 4 million Californians, representing 17 percent of the state's adult population, [had]
licenses suspended for failure to appear/pay in traffic cases."[47] In Vermont and
Wisconsin, as in many other states, well over half of license suspensions in 2017
were for failure to pay LFOs.[48]

LFOs can be expensive. Particularly when people face LFOs in multiple
cases, it is easy for their debt to the government to reach thousands of dollars.
Sometimes, nonpayment of LFOs results from people forgetting or outright
refusing to pay these debts. Money owed, however, routinely exceeds people's
ability to pay. Millions of Americans, and not just those living below the poverty line, live paycheck to paycheck, without the savings to cover such unexpected expenses.[49]

Consider, for instance, the results of the Federal Reserve's *Report on the Economic Well-Being of U.S. Households in 2018*.[50] The Federal Reserve conducted a
survey of the American people that included a question of how their household
would handle a hypothetical "small, unexpected expense" of $400.[51] Sixty-one
percent of adults said that they had the means to cover such an expense using
what the researchers categorized as "cash or its equivalent": money on hand,
available savings, or a credit card that they could pay off at the next statement.
The other 39% of adults, however, said they did not have a spare $400 available
and would have to try to do something else to cover the expense: add it to a
credit card balance, borrow it from a friend or relative, sell something, use a
payday loan, or the like.[52] And 12% of respondents reported that they absolutely
could not cover an unexpected $400 expense by any method.[53] These results il-
lustrate how ill-equipped tens of millions of Americans are to handle unantic-
ipated expenses; nearly 40% of adults said that they would have to make some
kind of immediate sacrifice or take on a different type of indebtedness to come
up with $400 or that they couldn't come up with $400 at all. Especially given the
disproportionate rate at which socioeconomically disadvantaged people are
exposed to law enforcement and subject to criminal charges and prosecution,
it is easy to understand why so many people end up facing license suspensions
as a result of LFOs. For many people across the country, paying off hundreds or
thousands of dollars in court debt is extremely difficult, if not impossible.

Other non-driving-related violations also routinely impose driving restrictions. Typically, people with open warrants related to any type of criminal charge cannot obtain or renew driver's licenses,[54] and laws in many states
impose driver's license suspensions for people convicted of non-car-related

crimes.[55] These restrictions of driving privileges are not based on concerns related to traffic safety; instead, they use the value of a driver's license as leverage
to pressure people to pay fines and fees to the state and to induce compliance
more generally. In addition to providing state governments with a powerful
tool for compelling people to pay LFOs that they have accrued in separate proceedings, license suspension programs can also be significant revenue generators themselves through fees charged for license reinstatement. For example,
in fiscal year 2015 Indiana pulled in nearly $10 million in license reinstatement
fees.[56] This was significantly less than the $17.7 million the state had projected
they would receive that year, and tens of millions of dollars in unpaid license
fees remained outstanding.[57] Numerous barriers impede suspended drivers'
ability to pay reinstatement fees. Many of these people are already indebted
to the government—indeed, in Indiana, like many states, this is the primary
reason people's licenses are suspended in the first place. Motorists may also
need to come up with the money to obtain car insurance, a requirement for
license reinstatement. Further, license suspensions themselves commonly
cause financial strain, including introducing new challenges to securing or
maintaining paid employment. Thus, although states may garner appreciable
sums through reinstatement fees, extracting this money is sometimes akin to
drawing the proverbial blood from a stone.[58] As the Indiana government reckoned with the low rate at which they were collecting on license reinstatement
fees, they chose to increase fees in an attempt to increase revenue generated
from this source. Taking effect in 2015, the fee for recovering a license after a
first suspension increased from $150 to $250; for a second suspension, from
$225 to $500; and for a third or subsequent suspension, $300 to $1,000. These
constituted fee increases of 67%, 122%, and 233%, respectively.[59]

Of course, states also still suspend licenses based on road safety considerations. In some jurisdictions, however, only a small minority of license suspensions result from the safety concerns commonly presumed to underlie
these restrictions. For example, a team of researchers analyzing suspensions
in New Jersey between 2004 and 2018 found that more than 90% resulted from
something unrelated to driving, most commonly failure to pay a fine.[60] Another review of New Jersey data found that less than 6% of license suspensions
resulted solely from considerations related to driving and that the majority of
suspended drivers had zero points on their licenses for traffic violations.[61] We
often think of DUI offenses as a primary reason that people lose their licenses,
but this study found that only 3% of New Jersey suspensions resulted from DUI
convictions.[62]

CHARACTERISTICS AND CONSEQUENCES
OF LICENSE SUSPENSIONS

Like other collateral consequences of conviction, losing legal driving privileges has significant implications for people's lives. First, losing your driver's license means losing work opportunities. This is generally true because of the United States' car-reliant transportation infrastructure. Most Americans use cars to get to work.[63] In the large swaths of the country without meaningful public transportation options, cars may be the only feasible means of commuting. Further, even if one is able to get to work without a car, many employers require a valid driver's license as a condition of employment. (This, of course, is particularly applicable to the significant share of American jobs that include driving as a work responsibility.)[64] For these reasons, experiencing a license suspension or revocation can cost a person their job even if they are able to get to work without driving. A New Jersey study found that close to half of people whose licenses were suspended lost their jobs. Nearly half of those people were unable to find a different job during the suspension, and, among those that did, the new job paid less for more than eight in ten workers.[65]

Altogether, these issues mean that having one's driver's license suspended has major implications for financial well-being and economic self-sufficiency, both for drivers themselves and their personal networks. This prominently includes considerations related to employment and housing stability. Many of these consequences are particularly acute when licenses are suspended for unpaid LFOs. Unlike a specified term of suspension imposed as a direct penalty for a legal violation, suspensions resulting from failure to pay tend to be indefinite, lasting as long as it takes for people to come up with the money to pay their legal debts. Suspensions for unpaid LFOs are also more likely to be total suspensions of driving privileges, without the possibility of accessing a restricted license that may be available for other types of suspensions.[66]

Beyond this, license suspensions also open people up to other legal problems, including new criminal charges. Largely because cars are so essential, most people continue to drive despite legal restrictions. One recent report estimated that three-quarters of people faced with suspensions drive on suspended licenses.[67] As a result, hundreds of thousands of motorists face these charges every year. In recent years authorities in North Carolina alone have filed 160,000 charges annually for violating legal restrictions of driving privileges.[68] Violations of license suspensions are significant charges, leading to new LFOs and possibly incarceration. Like a technical violation of the conditions of probation or parole, charges for driving on a suspended license are independent of whatever reason led to the initial suspension; thus, a person who drives on a license that was suspended because they could not afford to pay court debt faces the same procedure and possible penalties as someone who drives on a license that was suspended because of dangerous behavior behind the wheel.[69]

Outside of costs to people who face suspensions and to others whom those suspensions directly affect, the practice of suspending licenses for non-driving-related reasons also has appreciable broader implications. In economic terms, millions of people being unemployed or underemployed because of restriction of their driving privileges impedes economic productivity. In fiscal terms, this means increased demand for public assistance programs. The costs to government of processing all these cases is also significant. All major elements of the criminal justice system are involved, including police, prosecutors, courts, and corrections, and representatives of each of these groups need to invest their limited time and resources in dealing with the large workflow connected to license suspensions and suspension violations. Just on the policing side, the Washington State Patrol estimates that every arrest for a suspended license violation requires a commitment of about nine hours of officer time.[70] In terms of corrections resources, a recent study of five Texas counties found that between 6% and 20% of people entering jails were admitted for license offenses.[71] Obviously, there are straightforward tax and budgeting considerations here, as there are in any context of public policy design and implementation, but the opportunity cost dimension bears emphasizing. That is, every hour of time that a law enforcement officer, public defender, prosecutor, judge, or jail official spends dealing with a license suspension issue is an hour they are not spending on something else.[72]

States also expend resources defending their license suspension policies when people sue over them. Often focusing on cases in which suspended drivers allege they were willing to pay but could not afford to, these lawsuits contend that states' license suspension and revocation laws violate constitutional protections related to procedural due process and equal protection.[73]

Despite such contentions, courts have generally upheld the constitutionality of statutes that impose driver's license suspensions and revocations for non-driving offenses and for failure to pay LFOs. In 1971's *Bell v. Burson* the Supreme Court ruled that certain procedural due process protections apply to driver's licenses. However, states are not necessarily required to provide "actual notice" when suspending a motorist's license; rather, "notice that is 'reasonably calculated' to reach affected parties" may suffice.[74] In more recent cases lower federal courts have evinced some openness to arguments that suspending the licenses of people who cannot afford to pay LFOs may violate equal protection and due process protections.[75]

Recently, state legislators and governors have demonstrated their own interest in reconsidering laws related to license suspensions. This has included some states rolling back policies that imposed suspensions for drug convictions and other nondriving offenses. Many states and municipalities have also introduced relicensing programs intended to help people get their licenses reinstated and strengthened procedural protections for drivers facing possible suspensions.[76]

Numerous states are also considering and enacting legislation to curtail the suspension of licenses for failure to pay LFOs. Missouri recently reinstated licenses that had been suspended because of nonpayment of legal debt.[77] In 2017 the California State Legislature passed AB 103, which eliminated the state's prior practice of imposing license suspensions on drivers who failed to pay traffic fines. A 2020 California appeals court ruling that limited suspensions for failure to appear in traffic cases resulted in license reinstatements for more than 400,000 Californians.[78] Vermont and Washington, for their part, have abolished suspensions for criminal offenses unrelated to driving, but have retained policies authorizing suspensions for failure to pay LFOs resulting from traffic cases.[79]

The Collateral Consequences Resource Center reported that in 2019 six other states repealed statutes that had required license suspensions or revocations for nondriving offenses or unpaid LFOs.[80] Florida, Mississippi, and New York changed laws that had mandated losing one's driver's license for nondriving offenses, and Montana and Virginia removed requirements that people lose their licenses for unpaid court costs. New Jersey, on the other hand, repealed multiple laws that caused people to lose their licenses for both nondriving offenses and unpaid LFOs. Also in 2019, Minnesota enacted a new measure authorizing local jurisdictions to implement programs supporting driver's license reinstatements.[81]

Indiana is among the most recent states to reconsider its stance toward driver's license suspensions. On April 20, 2021, Governor Eric Holcomb signed House Bill 1199 into law. Becoming Public Law 1199, the measure addressed Indiana's most common misdemeanor charge: driving with a suspended license and a prior conviction.[82] In 2019, 330,000 Hoosiers had suspended licenses.[83] Most of these suspensions were for financial reasons, including unpaid LFOs or failure to maintain car insurance.[84] Addressing the issue was a priority for the Holcomb administration and HB 1199 garnered the support of a broad coalition, including some strange bedfellows. The measure's advocates included Republicans, Democrats, prosecutors, public defenders, judges, the Indiana Department of Corrections, the Indiana Bureau of Motor Vehicles, and members of the insurance industry.[85]

The new Indiana law does not change policies with regard to criminal suspensions or licenses that have been suspended for traffic safety reasons.[86] Instead, it focuses on licenses that are suspended because of failure to pay. The policy overhaul includes eliminating suspensions for failure to appear in court and allows motorists to pause suspensions for nonpayment of LFOs by obtaining car insurance.[87] The law also provides new avenues to reinstatement for motorists whose licenses have been suspended due to failure to pay court debt or child support or failure to maintain insurance, "allowing their driver's license to be reinstated if they provide proof of future financial responsibility and agree to a payment plan."[88]

The law's advocates recognized how financial struggles, license suspensions, and unemployment can combine to create downward spirals of debt and poverty and aimed to undo some of the legal provisions contributing to those spirals. The Indiana Department of Corrections expressed particular concerns about how people newly released from prison are vulnerable to these types of cycles. Writing in support of the bill, a spokesperson noted, "Many offenders are ineligible to obtain a valid driver's license due to fees that have accrued either prior or during incarceration. Suspensions for infractions among the offender population [are] common, and this bill will assist incarcerated individuals as they re-enter the community."[89] To advance that objective, the measure offers temporary waivers of reinstatement fees for people who have completed sentences for nonviolent convictions and are actively undertaking job training or holding down a job. These waivers can become permanent and licenses fully reinstated for those who are able to keep steady employment for three years without a new suspension.[90] Applauding the legislature for passing a bill that aligned with his priorities, Governor Holcomb said that "possessing a valid driver's license is nearly essential for Hoosiers to remain employed in today's workforce, and the suspensions have a bigger impact on low-income populations, rural residents, and ex-offenders. Allowing Hoosiers the opportunity to get back on the road safely and lawfully by introducing productive reforms helps individuals and employers, in addition to freeing up government and public safety resources."[91]

THE CONTINUING COSTS OF CRIMINAL JUSTICE INVOLVEMENT

For many people charged with crimes, the impact of formal sentences pales in comparison to the long-term consequences of being convicted, or even just arrested. The collateral consequences of criminal justice involvement are broad and multifarious. Depending on jurisdiction and charge, nearly every aspect of life can be affected by a criminal conviction, including work, housing, family, and participation in politics and civil society.

In our car-dependent social world, driver's license suspensions are among the most impactful of collateral consequences. Conventionally understood, denying, suspending, or revoking driving privileges was a road safety tool, designed to protect the public's well-being by keeping reckless, dangerous, and incompetent drivers off the streets and highways. Over recent decades, however, driver's license suspensions and revocations became a popular option for penalizing various nondriving offenses, as well as a consequence for failure to pay LFOs.

Such limitations of driving privileges exemplify how involvement in the criminal justice system begets broader civil disabilities. Suspended driver's licenses for outstanding legal debt starkly demonstrate how initial charges and convictions can cascade into increasingly debilitating penalties and restrictions.[92] Millions of Americans have experienced license suspensions for nonpayment of legal debt.[93] In most of the country a driver's license is a functional necessity for earning an income, compounding the complications of being subject to these restrictions. Thus, the case of driver's license suspensions and revocations distills key parts of broader controversies about the collateral consequences of criminal justice involvement.

Joshua Page and Joe Soss recently described the revenue-generation dimensions of contemporary criminal justice as amounting to predation. The "predatory dimensions of criminal justice," these authors argue, entail governments and private contractors extracting billions of dollars from the citizenry, particularly from disadvantaged and marginalized groups.[94] Wresting fines and fees from the citizenry is a central element of this resource extraction. The threat of losing driving privileges is a significant source of leverage that the state can bring to bear to compel compliance with LFOs. Especially because many motorists whose licenses are suspended feel that they have no choice but to continue driving despite the legal suspension of that privilege, license suspension laws also become the source of further criminal justice entanglement and the accumulation of additional legal debt.

Noting these measures' deleterious—and perhaps self-defeating—implications for people's financial solvency and prospects for self-sufficiency, policymakers have recently demonstrated comparatively elevated interest in reconsidering restrictions to driving privileges, especially when these restrictions result from things unrelated to driving. A number of states have changed their laws to reduce the extent of license suspensions and revocations and to facilitate people's efforts to regain legal driving privileges following a suspension. Indeed, at a historical juncture when collateral consequences are generally as widespread and impactful as they have ever been, these reforms represent a noteworthy trend. Nevertheless, these policies remain widespread; all states still have laws in place leading to license suspensions for non-driving-related reasons, many of which provide for licenses to be suspended indefinitely.

Criminal records impose a host of disabilities, touching nearly every aspect of life, from getting a job, to accessing public programs, to parental rights.[95] Driver's license suspensions and revocations, though consequential in their own right, are only one iteration of this often hidden but enormously consequential dimension of American criminal justice. And, as Chapter 10 goes on consider, driving privileges are only one of the ways that contemporary criminal justice policies have entangled cars, money, and social control.

TEN

Civil Asset Forfeiture and
the Limits of the Criminal Law

Civil asset forfeiture laws permit government to seize and keep property that authorities determine to be in some way connected to crime, even if the property's owner is never convicted of a crime, or even charged with one. Asset forfeiture is closely related to this book's car-window view of criminal justice because forfeiture actions routinely involve automobiles: Contemporary forfeiture actions typically originate with vehicle stops, and cars themselves are frequent forfeiture targets.[1]

Civil forfeiture itself is not a new phenomenon. Nineteenth-century cases such as *The Palmyra* (1827), *United States v. Brig Malek Adhel* (1844), and *Dobbins' Distillery v. United States* (1877) upheld authorities' power to seize and keep property connected to illegal activity, even if the property's legal owner was uninvolved in the lawbreaking. Cases such as *Goldsmith-Grant Co. v. United States* (1921) and *Van Oster v. Kansas* (1926) upheld similar forfeitures of cars, bringing the doctrine into the automobile age.

Civil forfeiture expanded dramatically in the late twentieth and early twenty-first centuries as the federal government and various states passed numerous forfeiture laws and greatly expanded their use of this technique. Forfeiture has emerged as a particularly prominent tactic in the war on drugs. In recent years the federal government alone has garnered billions of dollars annually in proceeds from asset forfeitures; some years' federal forfeiture totals exceed the total value of property lost to burglaries nationally in the same year. Some court rulings have suggested possible limits on governments' use of civil forfeiture (see *Austin v. United States* [1993], *United States v. Bajakajian* [1998], and *Timbs v. Indiana* [2019]). However, the courts have generally upheld the practice's constitutionality (see *Calero-Toledo v. Pearson Yacht Leasing Co.* [1974] and *Bennis v. Michigan* [1996]), and it remains an important, if controversial, part of contemporary criminal justice.

POLICING PROPERTY

Civil asset forfeiture laws permit law enforcement agencies to seize private property based on probable cause to believe that the property is tainted by a connection to lawbreaking. These are legal actions against the *property itself*; the implicated property serves as the defendant, and criminal charges against property owners are not required.[2] (This results in facially bizarre case captions such as *United States v. $38,005 in United States Currency, United States v. One Pearl Necklace, United States v. One Parcel of Property Located at 508 Depot Street, United States v. One 1987 Mercedes 560 SEL*, and *United States v. Approximately 64,695 Pounds of Shark Fins*.)[3]

Property can be connected to illegal activity and thus subject to civil forfeiture in several ways. The property itself might be contraband, that is, something that it is illegal to import, export, or possess. Forfeited property may also be ill-gotten proceeds: cash or items of value garnered as profits from criminal enterprises. Last, government can move to forfeit property that is an instrumentality: property that is used or intended to be used in any way related to illegal activity.[4] As the deputy chief of the Justice Department's Criminal Division, Asset Forfeiture and Money Laundering Section, Office of Policy Training, summarized in 2012, asset forfeiture "is the taking of property derived from a crime, involved in a crime, or which makes a crime easier to commit or harder to detect."[5] Civil asset forfeiture actions commonly implicate homes, cash, and—notably for our purposes—cars. If law enforcement officers determine that there is probable cause to believe that a car has any connection to a crime, federal and state statutes authorize them to seize it. Simply possessing large amounts of cash can be considered suspicious and grounds for seizure under civil forfeiture laws. In December 2021, for instance, police seized approximately $107,000 from a woman at Dallas's Love Field Airport after a police dog alerted them to her bag. The bag contained only blankets and two envelopes containing the cash, and the woman was not arrested or charged with a crime, but police indicated that they intended to confiscate the money through civil forfeiture. A Facebook post celebrating the seizure depicted K-9 Officer Ballentine with the seized cash and proclaimed, "We need to get him some treats!"[6]

Recent years have seen a notable surge in civil asset forfeiture activity. By the 1990s states and the federal government had enacted hundreds of statutes authorizing civil forfeitures.[7] At the federal level, US Attorney General Richard Thornburgh said in 1989 that "it's now possible for a drug dealer to serve time in a forfeiture-financed prison after being arrested by agents driving a forfeiture-provided automobile while working in a forfeiture-funded sting operation."[8] These forfeiture laws are written broadly, providing criminal justice authorities with sweeping discretion to seize and confiscate property with even tenuous connections to crime. Routine traffic stops, for example, might result in seizure of "suspicious" cash, and vehicles implicated in any way in criminal offending can be seized and forfeited. At least fourteen federal agencies engage in property forfeiture actions, and others assist with managing and selling confiscated property.[9]

"Forfeiture" refers to the government acting to keep an asset after law enforcement has initially seized it. As the name suggests, civil asset forfeitures are civil legal actions: Prosecutors file these actions separately from any criminal charges the property owner may or may not face, and the civil forfeiture process is independent of any criminal proceedings. Indeed, civil asset forfeiture has emerged as a consequential form of criminal justice action operating largely in separation from the conventional criminal process; in 80% of contemporary civil asset forfeitures, affected property owners are never criminally charged.[10] Authorities can also use *administrative* forfeiture to keep property if no one contests a seizure; because most forfeiture actions go uncontested, most federal forfeiture actions are technically administrative forfeitures.[11]

These laws are distinct from laws providing for *criminal* asset forfeiture. Federal and state authorities can initiate criminal asset forfeiture as part of broader criminal proceedings.[12] Like other criminal actions, criminal asset forfeitures are legal actions against people. For the seizing authority to forfeit property under criminal forfeiture law, the defendant must be convicted of a criminal offense connected to the property in question.[13] In the criminal context, forfeiture occurs after the government obtains a sentence, whereas in civil forfeiture there is no need for a criminal charge or conviction for the government to obtain property. Criminal forfeiture is generally less controversial than civil or administrative forfeiture.

THE HISTORY OF ASSET FORFEITURE

US law has long provided for asset forfeiture. In some ways, the framers and early lawmakers limited the practice relative to their forebears in the Anglo-American legal tradition. Distinguishing the new nation's laws from the broader forfeiture authorization provided by the laws of England, "the Constitution [forbade] forfeiture of estate as a punishment for treason 'except during

the Life of the Person attainted,' . . . and the First Congress also abolished forfeiture of estate as a punishment for felons."[14] However, the same First Congress "passed laws subjecting ships and cargos involved in customs offenses to
forfeiture,"[15] and "other early statutes also provided for the forfeiture of pirate
ships."[16] Further, the First Congress used the word *forfeit* to refer to the levying
of a fine,[17] perhaps suggesting some degree of perceived equivalence between
requirements to pay financial penalties as direct consequences for legal violations and measures authorizing the government to take property associated
with legal violations.

Foundational figures in American law followed the English tradition of permitting forfeiture under customs and maritime law.[18] In the maritime context,
courts upheld forfeitures of property involved in illegal activity, even if the
property owner was not implicated in the relevant crimes. In *United States v.
The Cargo of the Brig Malek Adhel* (1844), for example, the Supreme Court upheld
the confiscation of a vessel—the brig in question, the *Malek Adhel*—which was
determined to have been involved in "piratical aggression," despite the ship-
owners' lack of culpability in the piracy. "The innocence of the owner has been
fully established," Justice Story noted, writing for the Court.[19] The target of
the forfeiture action, however, was the ship, not the owners. In Justice Story's
words, "The vessel which commits the aggression is treated as the offender, as
the guilty instrument or thing to which the forfeiture attaches, without any reference whatsoever to the character or conduct of the owner."[20] This decision
paralleled a previous ruling in *The Palmyra* (1827). In this case, the Court similarly upheld the forfeiture of a ship involved in piracy, despite the lack of any
finding of legal culpability on the part of its owners or crew; legal scholar Deborah Challener identifies the *Palmyra* decision as the juncture when "the guilty
property fiction was implanted in American jurisprudence."[21]

Moving forward, lawmakers continued to enact and authorities continued
to enforce statutes providing for forfeitures in several contexts besides activities
on the high seas. During the Civil War, Congress passed the Confiscation Acts,
which authorized the seizure and forfeiture of property of Confederates whom
the government was unable to prosecute directly.[22] This was a major development in forfeiture law, establishing the principle of using forfeiture actions as
a way to impose punishments on individuals without needing to observe all
the procedural due process protections that the Constitution requires for legal
actions against persons.[23]

The Supreme Court decided *Dobbins' Distillery v. United States* in 1877. This
ruling upheld the seizure and forfeiture of a distillery and connected property based on tax fraud perpetrated by the lessee of the distillery, regardless of
whether the distillery's owner and lessor had any involvement in the lessee's

cooking of the books. For the Court, Justice Clifford wrote, "Nothing can be plainer in legal decision than the proposition that the offence therein defined is attached primarily to the distillery, and the real and personal property used in connection with the same, without any regard whatsoever to the personal misconduct or responsibility of the owner."[24]

Forfeiture actions—and legal challenges to them—continued into the twentieth century. The outcomes were similar. In another case connected to alcohol and taxation, the Supreme Court decided *J. W. Goldsmith, Jr.-Grant Company v. United States* in 1921. This case involved a challenge to the seizure and forfeiture of a taxi: "a Hudson automobile of the appraised value of $800."[25] The owner, the Grant Company, had sold the vehicle to J. G. Thompson, a taxi driver, while "retaining the title for unpaid purchase money," making the Grant Company the vehicle's legal owner until Thompson paid off the debt and received the title. Thompson went on to use the automobile to transport liquor in violation of federal tax laws without the Grant Company's knowledge or consent. Challenging the forfeiture, the Grant Company contended that the confiscation of the car, despite the company's lack of involvement in the criminal activity, constituted a violation of the Fifth Amendment, which prohibits the deprivation of property interests (as well as life and liberty interests) without due process of law. The Court, however, disagreed. As they had held previously and would continue to hold subsequently, the "guilt" of the property was sufficient to uphold its legal forfeiture, regardless of the owners' noninvolvement in the offending behavior.[26]

During Prohibition, authorities also used forfeiture laws to seize and confiscate property connected to activities banned by the Volstead Act, notably including cars used in transporting illegal liquor.[27] The guilty property doctrine underlying the courts' support for other forfeiture actions manifested in these cases as well. One court colorfully depicted a car used in bootlegging as an "inanimate 'outlaw.'"[28] In another criminal justice prelude to the war on drugs, Prohibition agents used forfeiture laws to disrupt bootlegging activities and cut into illicit organizations' profits by confiscating cars, as well as cash, distilling equipment, and other property connected to bootlegging schemes.[29] In *Van Oster v. Kansas* (1926), the Supreme Court blessed confiscation of a vehicle used in the illegal transport of liquor even though the vehicle's owner was not a party to the violation. Echoing prior cases, the *Van Oster* Court upheld the forfeiture of a car that a Kansas woman had lent to someone else, who then used it to move liquor.[30]

The law of Prohibition authorized forfeiture of "any receptacle or container" used to move alcohol in violation of the Volstead Act.[31] Legal authorities used this provision to test the extent to which the Fourth Amendment limited their power to search motor vehicles. If using a car to transport illegal liquor auto-matically triggered the vehicle's forfeiture to the government, they reasoned, an inspection by government agents that turned up alcohol could not legally have been a search; because the car was carrying alcohol, it was not actually the defendant's property but the government's.[32] After Prohibition, forfeiture went on to play a major role in government's subsequent major effort to control intoxicating substances through criminal laws and criminal sanctions: the war on drugs.

CONTEMPORARY CIVIL ASSET FORFEITURE

The historical roots of asset forfeiture trace back centuries, and these measures have been used in the United States since colonial times.[33] For most of that history, however, authorities applied civil asset forfeiture policies relatively sparingly and selectively. That paradigm shifted in the last half-century. Asset forfeiture has expanded greatly since the 1970s. The practice's use as a weapon in the war on drugs is the centerpiece of this historic growth.

A series of federal statutes laid the foundation for authorities' more exten-sive use of civil and administrative forfeiture. The Comprehensive Drug Abuse Prevention and Control Act of 1970 empowered federal agents to confiscate drug-related contraband and instrumentalities of drug trafficking.[34] Subse-quently, President Nixon declared "all-out, global war on the drug menace."[35] The legislative branch, in turn, expanded from the initial focus on contraband and instrumentalities, authorizing the forfeiture of cash and other monetary proceeds from drug trafficking in 1978 and providing for forfeiture of impli-cated real property in 1984.[36] Two years later, they went a step further, enabling confiscation of property of equal value to forfeitable property that authorities were unable to seize.[37] In 1998 legal scholars Eric Blumenson and Eva Nilsen noted that forfeiture laws "continue to be billed as the weapon of choice in the Drug War," citing the "Director of the Department of Justice's forfeiture unit testi[mony] to a congressional subcommittee that '[a]sset forfeiture can be to modern law enforcement what air power is to modern warfare.'"[38]

The Comprehensive Crime Control Act of 1984 was particularly consequen-tial in establishing civil asset forfeiture as a powerful and far-reaching tool of contemporary criminal justice in the war on drugs and beyond. In addition to authorizing the forfeiture of real property connected to criminal activity, this measure established the Department of Justice's Assets Forfeiture Fund.[39] This fund collected the proceeds of federal asset forfeitures and earmarked them as resources to be dedicated to law enforcement activities. The Comprehensive Crime Control Act of 1984 also established the equitable sharing program. Equitable sharing is intended to incentivize state-level authorities to aggressively pursue forfeiture actions. It does so by enabling state-level criminal justice authorities to convey forfeited assets to the federal fund and subsequently to receive typically 80% of the value back from the federal government, a greater percentage of the proceeds than many state laws allow seizing agencies to retain.[40] "Seized funds are subject to relatively little oversight and can be used for, among other things, payments for law enforcement equipment, weapons, salaries and overtime, training, expenses for travel, informant reward money, and detention facilities."[41] The equitable sharing program also facilitates federal-state cooperation in this area by authorizing state-level authorities to collaborate on federal investigations and to receive proceeds from federal asset forfeitures.[42] Federal authorities, for their part, also benefit by receiving a cut of the assets that state and local law enforcement confiscate.[43]

Civil asset forfeiture gives law enforcement a powerful tool for counteracting organized drug trafficking. Seizing assets allegedly connected to criminal activity can disrupt ongoing illicit enterprises and eat into their profits. In 1974 the Supreme Court gave their blessing to using forfeiture in this way with their decision in *Calero-Toledo v. Pearson Yacht Leasing Co.* Echoing earlier matters before the Court in *Dobbins' Distillery*, *Palmyra*, and *Malek Adhel*, *Calero-Toledo* involved a leasing company challenging the forfeiture of one of their yachts, which had been seized and confiscated after its lessees used it to transport illegal drugs without the company's knowledge.[44] As they had in preceding cases, the Court upheld the forfeiture, despite the property owner's noninvolvement, and emphasized that such confiscations serve to disrupt criminal profits, impede ongoing criminal activities, and discourage owners from allowing others who may break the law to possess their property.[45]

The Comprehensive Crime Control Act of 1984, associated changes to state laws, and the resulting ballooning of forfeiture actions had transformational impact. In 1985 the Department of Justice's Asset Forfeiture Fund collected a comparatively modest $27 million.[46] The next year, that figure more than tripled, to $93.7 million.[47] By 1993 the number had grown more than twentyfold since 1985, to $556 million.[48] The growth did not stop there. By 2012 the figure had septupled from 1993, with federal authorities alone garnering almost $4.2 billion in proceeds from forfeitures.[49] Over the next five years, federal proceeds from asset forfeitures nearly doubled again; in 2017 more than $8.2 billion flowed into the Asset Forfeiture Fund, leaving aside the money collected under state forfeiture laws.[50]

Between 2000 and 2019 state and federal authorities combined forfeited at least $68.8 billion in assets (due to missing data from multiple states, the true total is some unknown amount higher than this).[51] In some years the value of cash and other property seized through forfeiture exceeded the FBI's estimates of property lost to burglaries. In 2014, for example, the FBI estimated that burglary victims suffered $3.9 billion in property losses, while state and federal governments forfeited well over $5 billion in cash and other property.[52] In 2015 the disparity was even greater: Burglaries cost victims an estimated $3.6 billion, whereas forfeitures totaled well over $6 billion.[53] Many of these forfeitures resulted from drug enforcement activity. In 2000 a senator estimated that 98% of forfeitures arose from drug cases.[54] Studies have also found that the focus on forfeiture in the war on drugs shaped policing strategies and arrest rates.[55]

Beyond the war on drugs, authorities have used forfeiture actions to target and penalize other disfavored behaviors. In 1999, for example, New York City under Mayor Rudolph Giuliani moved aggressively to counteract drunk driving by authorizing the confiscation of motorists' cars after a first drunk driving offense. This measure went a step further than previous state laws in New York and elsewhere that provided for the forfeiture of vehicles as a consequence for repeated drunk driving violations.[56] Civil forfeiture is also a valuable tool for federal authorities working to counteract white-collar crime and provide restitution to its victims.[57]

The explosion in authorities' use of civil asset forfeiture led to calls for reform. Congress began holding hearings on the issue in 1996 and passed a significant bill in 2000.[58] The Civil Asset Forfeiture Reform Act (CAFRA) aimed to standardize civil forfeiture practices.[59] The bill that emerged after negotiations in Congress did not alter the fundaments of civil forfeiture law.[60] It did, however, address a number of identified issues.[61] Among other reforms, CAFRA located the burden of proof in civil forfeiture cases with the government, but adopted a preponderance of the evidence standard of proof, rather than the higher clear and convincing standard that some advocates sought.[62] CAFRA also provided for people in some circumstances to mount "innocent owner" defenses to civil forfeitures and to retain property up to the point of a final outcome to forfeiture proceedings if deprivation of the property in question would constitute a "substantial hardship" (this provision generally excludes currency).[63] Further, the legislation dictated that a "substantial connection" must exist between the relevant crime and the forfeited property and encouraged authorities to use criminal forfeiture, with its greater procedural protections, rather than civil forfeiture.[64]

Beyond establishing more uniformity in civil forfeiture processes and establishing some new procedural protections for its targets, CAFRA strengthened legal authorities' hand in civil forfeitures in several ways. These changes included specifying that it is illegal to evade forfeiture by removing or destroying property, expanding government access to information from grand juries in forfeiture cases, permitting the confiscation of "fungible property" without the requirement to connect it to criminal activity in all civil forfeiture cases, and giving the government five years after learning of an offense or two years after learning of property's implication, whichever is longer, to file forfeiture actions.[65] Consequentially, CAFRA "authorizes the civil forfeiture of the proceeds of any offense defined as 'specified unlawful activity' in 18 U.S.C. § 1956(c)(7)."[66] This "effectively gives the government the authority to seek the forfeiture of the proceeds of virtually all serious federal crimes, and a number of state and foreign crimes as well."[67] CAFRA also permits the government to confiscate property without presentation and evaluation of evidence if the forfeiture is uncontested, as about 80% of civil forfeitures—and 88% of federal forfeitures—are.[68] When federal forfeitures are uncontested, they are technically administrative forfeitures, not civil forfeitures.[69] (Many forfeitures go uncontested because people do not have the resources to fight the government's forfeiture action. Even for parties that could afford a fight, the expense of pursuing a legal challenge often outweighs the value of the forfeited property; about $500 worth of property is at stake in the median forfeiture action.)[70] Additionally, CAFRA empowered law enforcement agencies to keep 100% of the proceeds from forfeiture actions.[71]

As the statistics above indicate, authorities have continued to use civil forfeiture extensively and to great effect in the years since CAFRA's enactment.[72] A number of factors are at play here. First, most civil forfeitures are uncontested, functionally mooting some of CAFRA's expanded procedural protections. Although CAFRA shifted the burden of proof in establishing property's forfeitability to the government, the preponderance of the evidence standard has proven quite easy to meet.[73] Similarly, although CAFRA established preponderance of the evidence, rather than probable cause, as the standard of proof in civil forfeiture cases, probable cause may still be the standard by which property is seized, and potentially kept by the government if the forfeiture is uncontested, making the forfeiture an administrative action.[74] And, although CAFRA provided for affirmative defenses based on owners' innocence, the burden of proof in establishing such innocence falls on owners.[75] As of 2017, thirty-one states shared the federal government's preponderance of the evidence standard to justify civil forfeitures.[76] Seventeen states imposed a higher standard, while Massachusetts and North Dakota still permitted forfeiture based only on probable cause.[77]

CIVIL FORFEITURE AND DUE PROCESS

Civil asset forfeitures are technically legal actions against property, not people. (Legally, this is known as an *in rem* action, from the Latin meaning "against a thing," whereas criminal proceedings are *in personam*, "against the person.")[78] Key constitutional provisions related to due process provide protections for people, not property, and greater protections obtain in criminal proceedings than in civil matters. Accordingly, many of the procedural protections extended to criminal defendants do not apply to civil forfeiture actions.

Generally, property owners facing potential civil forfeitures do not have the right to have attorneys provided for them if they cannot afford to hire private representation. The right to publicly provided counsel first established in *Gideon v. Wainwright* (1963) applies to criminal defendants; like involvement in other civil legal matters, civil forfeiture proceedings generally do not trigger this protection. CAFRA did establish certain specific contexts entitling indigent parties to have counsel appointed for them in civil forfeiture proceedings, namely, if they already have a public defender in a linked criminal case or if they stand to lose their primary residence as a result of the forfeiture.[79] However, most property owners need to be able to hire their own counsel if they want representation to challenge a civil forfeiture. Attorneys' services in these cases often cost more than a thousand dollars.[80]

The presumption of innocence, a cornerstone of the US criminal legal system, does not apply to civil asset forfeiture cases in the same way that it applies to criminal proceedings. Law enforcement can seize property based only on probable cause, a low standard of proof that is exceedingly easy to meet. Property owners, on the other hand, need to navigate complex bureaucratic systems and expend considerable time and energy to contest confiscation of their property. In forty states property owners hold the burden of proof in such challenges.[81]

After property is seized under the probable cause standard of proof, the government continues to enjoy a lower standard of proof than the beyond a reasonable doubt standard familiar from criminal proceedings. Under the preponderance of the evidence standard, a court needs to believe only that the property is *more likely than not* forfeitable for a government confiscation to stand. This is a far lower bar to meet than the evidence of guilt beyond any reasonable doubt required for a criminal conviction. The preponderance of the evidence standard is also easier to satisfy than the clear and convincing evidence standard used in some other civil contexts.

CONCERNS AND CONTROVERSIES

In 1974 the Supreme Court noted that "contemporary federal and state forfeiture statutes reach virtually any type of property that might be used in the conduct of a criminal enterprise."[82] Since the 1970s federal and state authorities have used forfeiture in far more sweeping and aggressive fashion than ever before in US history. This proliferation of forfeiture as a criminal justice tool has had serious consequences and engendered serious debate.

Supporters of civil asset forfeiture defend it as a valuable asset for debilitating organized criminal activity, reducing profits for both individuals and criminal organizations, and ideally discouraging them from offending altogether.[83] Forfeiture's proponents also point to its potential for social benefit. For instance, the forfeiture of a residence used as a location of illegal drug sales can remove a public health and safety hazard from a neighborhood.[84] Forfeited assets can also be returned to victims; CAFRA authorized broader use of forfeited funds for victim restitution, and the Department of Justice has returned billions of dollars to criminal fraud victims through its Victim Asset Recovery Program.[85]

Critics of civil asset forfeiture, though, voice multiple concerns about the practice. Civil forfeiture raises fundamental constitutional questions about property rights, the extent of due process protections, and the legitimate powers of criminal justice authorities. Whereas supporters of the practice argue for its deterrent value and its importance as a tool for disrupting organized crime, critics allege that it amounts to legalized theft and an unconstitutional violation of citizens' property interests and constitutional rights.[86] Particularly given the limited due process protections available to forfeiture targets, critics contend that forfeiture is too often used as a mechanism for filling government's coffers at the citizenry's expense. Asset forfeiture is a lightning rod for criticism of law enforcement and prosecution strategies that allegedly amount to "policing for profit" in contemporary criminal justice, especially the war on drugs.[87] This line of criticism of asset forfeiture connects to critiques of "predatory" revenue-generating practices in criminal justice more broadly.[88]

Many of these critiques foreground contentions that pursuit of forfeiture proceeds shapes police departments' priorities and enforcement practices. As legal scholar David Pimentel summarizes, "This practice has been criticized as creating a conflict of interest, arguably encouraging a law enforcement strategy of targeting assets rather than stopping crime."[89] At times, law enforcement officials have openly acknowledged such effects. In New York, for instance, Police Commissioner Patrick Murphy admitted that the NYPD had a financial incentive to deploy aggressive enforcement tactics on southbound I-95, where they had better chances of seizing money intended for illegal drug transactions, rather than on northbound I-95, where they were more likely to recover the drugs themselves. "After all," Commissioner Murphy summarized, "seized cash will end up forfeited to the police department, while seized drugs can only be destroyed."[90]

Only seven states and the District of Columbia do not use forfeiture proceeds for law enforcement purposes (Indiana and Missouri direct all forfeiture proceeds to public education).[91] In the rest of the country law enforcement agencies retain between half and all of forfeiture proceeds.[92] Police departments are generally authorized to spend forfeiture proceeds in whatever way they see fit. The general idea is that these resources should be reinvested into law enforcement and used to purchase equipment, fund investigations, and so forth. Other uses of forfeiture proceeds, however, have attracted attention and criticism: "Some examples include a tanning salon, a margarita machine, illegal drugs, and prostitutes. Forfeiture money has been used to pay off a prosecutor's student loans, to hire a clown named Sparkles, buy a popcorn machine, CeeLo Green concert tickets, and gold plated whistles. Forfeiture money has even been used to fund political campaigns."[93]

In addition, evidence indicates that state and local law enforcement authorities subject to more restrictive state forfeiture laws disproportionately use— and benefit from—the federal equitable sharing program.[94] Equitable sharing allows state-level law enforcement agencies to get around their states' forfeiture laws and take advantage of more permissive (and lucrative) federal forfeiture policies.[95] Due to these issues, asset forfeiture has also attracted criticism as a problematic context of federalization in criminal justice, with federal agencies and federal law exerting unwarranted influence on day-to-day criminal justice policies and practices.[96]

Observers of civil asset forfeiture have further argued that law enforcement agencies have come to *depend* on the revenue the practice yields.[97] In some periods, various federal prosecutors' offices have reported confiscating assets equal to—or far exceeding—their own operating budgets.[98] Based on a survey of hundreds of law enforcement leaders, criminal justice scholar John Worrall reported in 2001 that many agencies did, in fact, rely on forfeiture proceeds, not just as a piece of their budgets, but as a necessary funding source.[99] Administrators at large police agencies reported particularly high levels of budgetary dependence on forfeitures; more than 45% of these respondents either agreed or strongly agreed with the statement "Civil forfeiture is necessary as a budgetary supplement," whereas only a third disagreed or strongly disagreed.[100]

Law enforcement officials have also signaled their awareness—and prioritization—of forfeiture's financial benefits in other ways. A 1993 Justice Department report encouraged law enforcement to consider whether they stood to garner greater forfeiture proceeds from targeting fewer major drug traffickers or greater numbers of smaller dealers.[101] A Justice executive suggested that law enforcement should "forfeit, forfeit, forfeit. Get money, get money, get money."[102] The Bureau of Alcohol, Tobacco, Firearms, and Explosives (ATF) sought to obtain gear bearing the unofficial motto "Always Think Forfeiture."[103] Qualitative research has similarly concluded that law enforcement supervisors are highly sensitive to the budgetary boon that forfeitures can provide and weigh potential remuneration from forfeitures as a significant factor in deciding which cases to prioritize and how to allocate limited departmental resources.[104]

When property owners are facing criminal charges, forfeiture can also shape plea-bargaining processes. Criminal defendants with forfeitable assets may offer to give up valuable property in exchange for lesser charges or more lenient sentencing recommendations, suggesting that "plea bargaining with forfeitures allows criminals to buy off prosecutors, with cash, in return for lighter sentences, and that the financial incentives are so strong that it may be unreasonable to expect law enforcement to resist such temptations."[105] Courts have upheld deals involving charge reductions in exchange for forfeitures of currency and other assets.[106] Authorities sometimes offer forfeiture waivers to property owners who are distressed and lack representation, strongly pressuring them to forfeit assets in exchange for promises that giving up their property will allow them to avoid criminal charges or other negative legal consequences, such as the loss of parental rights.[107] In these settings "the absence of procedural safeguards makes it exceedingly easy for law enforcement to confiscate property even when the property is not legally subject to forfeiture."[108]

In addition to flagging lower-income people's greater vulnerability to forfeiture actions, critics have highlighted civil asset forfeiture's unequal racial impact. People of color, particularly African Americans, are more likely to be pulled over, searched, arrested, and have their property seized under these laws, making civil asset forfeiture in substantial part a method by which legal authorities disproportionately penalize African Americans and other minorities relative to their White counterparts.[109] In Oklahoma, a three-quarters White state, almost two-thirds of cash seizures implicate property owners of color.[110] Investigations in Pittsburgh and Orlando found that 77% and 90%, respectively, of those cities' forfeiture actions involved minorities.[111] Department of Justice investigations in Baltimore, Maryland; Ferguson, Missouri; and elsewhere have uncovered large and systematic racial disparities in how police departments target enforcement efforts, including revenue-generating tactics.[112]

CONTEMPORARY COURT CASES

Despite controversy and challenges, judges have generally held that civil asset forfeiture is permissible under the Constitution.[113] A series of cases in the early 1990s suggested the possibility of a more restrictive judicial stance on civil forfeiture, with the Supreme Court invalidating several forfeiture actions. Notably, in *Austin v. United States* (1993) the Court indicated that forfeiture actions included a dimension of punishment and that Eighth Amendment protections against excessive fines should therefore apply in these cases.[114]

In 1996, however, the Supreme Court again endorsed broad forfeiture powers in *Bennis v. Michigan*. Citing—and doubling down on—the long line of forfeiture cases dating back to the early nineteenth century, the *Bennis* Court upheld the constitutionality of confiscating a 1977 Pontiac owned jointly by John and Tina Bennis.[115] The civil forfeiture resulted from John Bennis's arrest after police observed him and a prostitute engaged in a sex act in the car. Tina Bennis had no knowledge of—let alone support for or involvement in—the criminal activity. Challenging the forfeiture, Tina Bennis contended that the forfeiture violated her due process rights under the Fourteenth Amendment. Her suit emphasized that she had no culpability in the violation of Michigan indecency law for which police arrested her husband and added that she had supplied the bulk of the car's $600 purchase price.[116] Nevertheless, because Mr. Bennis had used the car with her consent, not stolen it, the Court held that the forfeiture was legitimate under established law.[117]

By contrast, in *United States v. Bajakajian* (1998) the Supreme Court struck down a federal criminal forfeiture that they determined to be "grossly disproportional"; this was the first time the Court used the Eighth Amendment's excessive fines clause to overturn a forfeiture.[118] Delivering the opinion of the Court, Justice Clarence Thomas indicated that the forfeiture in *Bajakajian* was punitive in nature, making this financial penalty subject to the excessive fines clause. Thomas's majority opinion, however, also noted that "traditional in rem forfeitures were thus not considered punishment against the individual for an offense. Because they were viewed as non-punitive, such forfeitures traditionally were considered to occupy a place outside the domain of the Excessive Fines Clause."[119] The forfeiture at issue in *Bajakajian* was a criminal, *in personam* action; the majority identified this action as involving an element of punitiveness, but, especially with the Court's invocation of the traditional view of civil forfeitures, it was unclear how to square the *Bajakajian* holding with *Austin*'s holding that *in rem* actions often involve punitiveness, making the Eighth Amendment's proscription of excessive fines applicable to these cases.[120] In short, "did the Court intend the [*Bajakajian*] test to be used for in rem forfeitures [as well]?"[121] Further, what exactly was that test? The Court held that the forfeiture in *Bajakajian* reached the level of "grossly disproportionate," but it "did not provide guidance on what magnitudes would qualify as grossly disproportionate [in future cases]."[122]

The Supreme Court recently returned to the issue in *Timbs v. Indiana* (2019). Like many civil asset forfeiture cases, *Timbs* involved cars and drugs; the state of Indiana forfeited Tyson Timbs's Land Rover after he used the vehicle to transport heroin, which he then sold to a police informant.[123] The vehicle's purchase price was $42,058.38.[124] Timbs argued that, because the property's value far surpassed the maximum possible fine for the drug charge to which he pleaded guilty, its forfeiture violated the Eighth Amendment prohibition of excessive fines.[125]

When *Timbs* reached the Supreme Court, the fundamental question for the justices was whether the Eighth Amendment's excessive fines clause was incorporated against the states, that is, whether this component of the Eighth Amendment proscribes certain actions on the part of state governments—in this case, the government of Indiana—or only imposed limitations on the federal government. Citing the Court's previous decision in *Bajakajian*, the justices unanimously agreed that the excessive fines clause was incorporated against the states and that civil forfeitures could potentially violate this protection. Ultimately, this ruling led to the forfeiture of Timbs's vehicle being overturned as unconstitutional.[126]

In *Bajakajian*, the Court indicated that criminal forfeitures were subject to the excessive fines clause. CAFRA extended excessiveness protections to federal civil forfeitures generally and codified the "grossly disproportional" standard.[127] These Eighth Amendment protections apply to forfeiture actions determined to contain punitive elements. In *Timbs*, the Court suggested that the civil forfeiture of the Land Rover was at least partly punitive and that the *Bajakajian* gross disproportionality standard may apply. On remand the lower courts ultimately reached this conclusion and held the forfeiture unconstitutional.

For the purposes of constitutional law, *Timbs*'s most significant consequence was the incorporation of the excessive fines clause against the states. (*Bajakajian*, by contrast, had dealt with a federal case involving the Bank Secrecy Act of 1970.) However, the ruling also attracted significant attention for its potential to significantly alter the legal landscape of civil asset forfeiture. It is difficult to say with certainty what *Timbs* will mean for asset forfeiture in the states; it is still early, and the available data are limited. Relevant legal and institutional factors, though, suggest that *Timbs*'s impact will be modest. Many forfeiture actions are simply not subject to excessive fines review, and most of the forfeitures that could be challenged on these grounds will not be appealed, if they are contested at all.[128] A limited impact for *Timbs* would track with *Bajakajian*'s minor impact on federal forfeitures; retired Assistant U.S. Attorney and forfeiture expert Stefan Cassella counted only three times in the fourteen years following the *Bajakajian* ruling that courts determined forfeiture actions to be excessive under the gross disproportionality standard.[129]

PROPERTY'S GUILT AND GOVERNMENT'S POWER

> If a bull gores a man or woman to death, the bull must be stoned to death, and its meat must not be eaten. But the owner of the bull will not be held responsible.
>   —Exodus 21:28 (NIV)

Laws authorizing the forfeiture of property connected to illegal activity have a long history. The epigraph quotes a relevant Bible verse that has appeared in judicial opinions in forfeiture cases. This verse offers a Judeo-Christian fundament for the notion that guilty property—in this example, an animal—can be forfeited independent of any wrongdoing or culpability on the part of its owner. Indeed, in this example, the bull's owner not only loses their interest in the animal itself, but also the capacity to benefit from its death by consuming its edible portions. The ancient Greeks and the Anglo-Saxons also provided for legal forfeiture of property used in criminal acts.[130] The practice made its way into the English legal tradition, and ultimately the American as well. In recent decades, civil and administrative asset forfeiture have seen greatly expanded use under the contemporary set of policies that emerged during the war on drugs. Today, a multitude of state and federal laws authorize authorities to confiscate cars, cash, and other property that they suspect to be somehow connected to criminal activity.

Courts have largely upheld these forfeiture actions as constitutionally acceptable, drawing fundamentally on the idea that actions against guilty property are a legal category separate and apart from proceedings *in personam*.[131] Yet, as Justice Thomas noted in a 2017 statement on the Supreme Court's denial of certiorari in *Leonard v. Texas*, "Modern civil forfeiture statutes are plainly designed, at least in part, to punish the owner of the property used for criminal purposes."[132] This framing paralleled the Court's holding in *Austin v. United States* that forfeiture actions contain an inherent punitive element.[133] Justice Thomas's comments in the certiorari denial also evoked concerns he had raised in his concurrence in *Bennis v. Michigan*, where he wrote that "improperly used, forfeiture could become more like a roulette wheel employed to raise revenue from innocent but hapless owners whose property is unforeseeably misused, or a tool wielded to punish those who associate with criminals, than a component of a system of justice."[134]

Justice Thomas, of course, is not the only person to raise concerns about legal authorities' use of civil asset forfeiture. A long line of critical commentary on the issue presents a laundry list of concerns, including how forfeiture shapes law enforcement incentives and priorities, the shortcomings of procedural due process protections for property owners targeted for forfeitures, and the disproportionate impact of forfeiture actions on different racial and socioeconomic segments of the population.[135] However, law enforcement, prosecutors, and other stakeholders continue to defend civil forfeiture as a crucial tool for counteracting criminal activity through undercutting profits and disrupting ongoing illicit enterprises. Altogether, civil asset forfeiture is a compelling case for considering the limits of what the criminal justice system can do and to whom it can do it.

ELEVEN

Watching the Wheels

Following their introduction in the United States, traffic cameras emerged as another issue involving cars, criminal justice, money, and significant controversy. Automated traffic enforcement using speed cameras and red-light cameras first spread abroad in the 1960s and 1970s and began appearing in the United States in the 1980s and 1990s. Since then, adoption has seen fits and starts; cities such as Washington, DC, and Chicago have embraced extensive automated enforcement systems, while some states have banned or closely circumscribed the technology's use.

Much of the discourse around automated enforcement reduces to a debate over whether these tools primarily serve their stated purpose of advancing road safety through encouraging safer driving, or instead function primarily as tools for generating revenue for governments and the private companies that install and maintain the systems. Several studies have found that automated enforcement produces significant public safety returns. Other analyses have questioned the devices' public safety benefits, or at least whether the systems are implemented in ways that focus on road safety rather than revenue generation. Some automated enforcement advocates have highlighted these systems' potential to reduce the disparities in police vehicle stops highlighted in Chapter 6. However, others have found that, as implemented, automated enforcement systems themselves tend to disproportionately target motorists in neighborhoods of color. For their part, privacy advocates have contended that automated enforcement systems implicate the Fourth Amendment, particularly in light of *Carpenter v. United States* (2018), which suggested a right to privacy with regard to individual movements.

THE ARRIVAL OF AUTOMATED ENFORCEMENT

Massachusetts pioneered the use of photography to capture images of moving vehicles and assess their speed in 1909.[1] In this rudimentary traffic camera system, officers would compare two photographs taken sequentially to estimate traveling speeds and cite speeders. New York's "photo-traffic cameras" of the 1950s improved on this system by cutting out some of the human element; this early version of automated speed enforcement incorporated devices that could calculate speeds on their own, without requiring officers to compare photographs.[2]

Modern traffic camera systems originated in Europe. In 1958 Dutch rally driver Maurice Gatsonides invented a new speed-measuring device, the Gatsometer, and founded the company of the same name. In the same year, Gatsometer sold their first speed-measurement systems in the Netherlands, and they began marketing a red-light camera in 1965.[3] Gatsometer began exporting products in the 1960s, and by the 1970s numerous European countries were using traffic cameras.[4] Modern automated speed enforcement first appeared in the United States in Galveston County, Texas, in 1986.[5] In late 1985 and early 1986, New York City ran a trial of a red-light camera at the intersection of Third Avenue and 86th Street.[6] Based on these and other early tests, the New York state legislature authorized the installation of fifty red-light cameras at New York City intersections.[7] Subsequently, red-light cameras spread to other jurisdictions, with more than twenty municipalities authorizing automated red-light enforcement systems by the late 1990s.[8]

The term *automated enforcement* refers to systems that use cameras to detect and sanction moving violations.[9] Contemporary speed cameras use radar to calculate vehicle speed and issue tickets when vehicles are recorded exceeding speed limits by specified amounts. Red-light cameras are installed at intersections with electronic traffic signals (also known as signalized intersections); the images they capture are used to issue citations when vehicles pass through intersections in violation of signs and signals.

As of July 2021, about 350 local governments in 22 states and the District of Columbia used red-light cameras. More than 150 local governments across 16 states and Washington, DC, used speed cameras.[10] Multiple jurisdictions, though, have banned red-light cameras, speed cameras, or both; Maine, Mississippi, New Hampshire, South Carolina, Texas, and West Virginia all disallow both types of automated enforcement.[11] Generally, governments contract with private companies to install camera systems and manage their day-to-day operations in exchange for a cut of the revenue they generate. In 2021, Verra Mobility (formerly American Traffic Solutions), the largest operator of traffic cameras in the United States, bought Redflex Traffic Systems, the second-largest operator in the United States and their onetime rival.[12] This acquisition enabled Verra to "elevate its already dominant position to the status of near monopoly in the red light camera and speed camera market."[13] As of August 2021, the expanded company operated nearly 6,000 cameras in jurisdictions across the country, with hundreds more planned for installation in Georgia, New York, and Washington.[14] In the second quarter of 2021, Verra netted $4 million, returning to profitability after losing millions earlier in the COVID-19 pandemic.[15]

MAKING DOLLARS OR MAKING SENSE

Various points of contention have surfaced as jurisdictions across the United States have considered and implemented automated enforcement. In many of these conversations the fundamental issue is a debate over automated enforcement's true motivation or purpose: public safety or money. That is, do local governments implement these systems primarily for their perceived benefits for road safety or because of their capacity for generating revenue?

Arguments that traffic cameras are more about revenue generation than public safety cite the significant amounts of money that these systems can yield. Tickets for photo-enforced traffic violations range in cost. In the mid-2000s a red-light camera ticket cost a Washington, DC, motorist $75.[16] In Cleveland in 2011 automated enforcement citations could cost $100 or more.[17] A 2015 Centers for Disease Control and Prevention report cited automated enforcement citations ranging from $40 to $300 in various states.[18] These fines add up. Washington, DC, started using red-light cameras in 1999. By the beginning of 2005 photo enforcement at just a few dozen traffic lights in the district resulted in more than half a million tickets and almost $30 million in fines.[19] The city added speed cameras in 2001. By the beginning of 2005 the city's speed camera system had resulted in over 1.2 million citations and almost $70 million in collected fines.[20] Chicago contracted with Redflex Traffic Systems to introduce red-light cameras in 2003 and soon built the country's most extensive automated red-light enforcement system.[21] Over the next decade-plus, Chicago drivers paid over $400 million in fines resulting from Redflex camera enforcement, netting the company $120 million.[22] In 2013 the city added speed cameras, creating a new revenue stream.[23]

Public officials are sensitive to the budgetary boon that traffic enforcement cameras can provide. For instance, when the city of Cleveland was considering red-light cameras, Mayor Jane Campbell specifically invoked the proposition as a way to resolve the city's yawning budget deficit, estimating that install-ing the cameras would net $6.5 million in proceeds in the first year alone.[24] Cleveland city council members, for their part, shared the mayor's awareness of cameras' fiscal implications, if not her enthusiasm for the plan. Like ordinary Ohioans facing the prospect of citations and fines from the new technology, members of the city council raised concerns, questioning whether the cameras would primarily serve to advance public safety, or to fill the city's coffers. Coun-cilman Joe Cimperman opined, "Maybe we should worry about real economic development rather than nickel and diming commuters."[25]

Camera placement has also been a point of contention in debates about whether this technology's implementation places first priority on road safety or revenue generation. In Washington, DC, some cameras' placement on road-ways known more for speeding than for accidents drew criticism. In 2004, for instance, speed cameras caught almost 60,000 speeders on MacArthur Boule-vard NW, despite no recorded speed-related collisions on that stretch of road since the 1990s.[26] Discussing the notion that authorities might choose to place cameras in locations that would serve as remunerative speed traps rather than in places where they would do the most to advance public safety, an American Automobile Association spokesperson noted, "It's important [to know] whether this is a 'gotcha' game for greenbacks or whether we're doing this for safety. And I don't think we know."[27] DC police, on the other hand, said that neighborhood concerns, not just crashes and fatalities, informed where they placed speed cameras.[28] Similarly, in 2009 the Washington State Department of Transporta-tion contracted with American Traffic Solutions (now known as Verra Mobility) to deploy a system of photo radar vans in highway work zones. The department explained this arrangement as necessary to protect worker safety, despite no instances of motorists killing road workers in the preceding seven years.[29] In Chicago, a *Tribune* investigation found that close to 40% of red-light cameras were placed at intersections without significant crash problems.[30]

Some critiques of cameras' revenue-generation function focus especially on the proceeds this technology produces not just for government, but for com-panies. Typically, local governments sign contracts with private businesses, which are then responsible for camera systems' installation and upkeep. Fees for these services vary. In the mid-2000s three-quarters of Toledo's camera fines went to their cameras' vendor.[31] Around the same time, St. Louis's vendor got one-third of their tickets' value.[32]

When private contractors collect fees for each citation they issue, they have a clear incentive to maximize citations. This fundamental profit motive factor is grounds for concern about potential misalignment between the interests of camera contractors and the interests of the citizenry. Notable scandals have placed contractors' financial motivations in especially stark relief. Prosecutors have obtained multiple convictions related to corruption in traffic camera contracting, with camera company executives, political figures, and lobbyists implicated in various scandals.[33] Just one company, Redflex Traffic Systems, has been investigated for offering politicians bribes in exchange for contracts in numerous states, including Arizona, California, Colorado, Florida, Georgia, Illinois, Massachusetts, Missouri, New Jersey, New Mexico, Ohio, Tennessee, Virginia, and Washington.[34] Other scandals have involved a Texas judge who signed an illegal contract with American Traffic Solutions and a Washington, DC, police officer sentenced to a year in prison for embezzling $178,611 from the district's camera program.[35] Redflex was implicated in especially high-profile bribery cases in Columbus, Cincinnati, and Chicago.[36] The $2 million Chicago bribery scandal resulted in a ten-year federal prison sentence for John Bills. The onetime second in command at the Chicago Department of Transportation, Bills was convicted of bribery, conspiracy, extortion, and fraud for his role in securing contracts for Redflex.[37] Following the prosecution of Bills and a lobbyist, as well as the cooperation and eventual guilty plea of Redflex CEO Karen Finley, the company itself secured a nonprosecution agreement with the US Department of Justice, agreeing to pay $100,000 in restitution to Columbus and additional money in restitution and compensatory damages to Chicago.[38] Redflex ultimately agreed to pay Chicago $20 million to settle the city's civil suit against the company.[39] Traffic camera companies have also sued governments to challenge laws that they contend inappropriately impede their ability to enter into contracts to provide automated enforcement services.[40]

Nevertheless, many governmental actors maintain interest in traffic enforcement cameras. Despite high-profile scandals and ongoing investigations in Chicago and its suburbs, Lori Lightfoot's new mayoral administration remained sanguine about the technology itself and its potential to encourage safer driving.[41] New federal support for traffic cameras—and camera companies—arrived in 2021. A provision of the Infrastructure Investment and Jobs Act permits states to use federal infrastructure funds to establish traffic camera systems in work zones and school zones.[42] Given contractors' predominance in this arena, a significant share of federal funds allocated to such programs will go to private entities.

Although critics of automated enforcement can point to the significant revenue that these systems generate, the technology's supporters also have evidence of its public safety benefits. Multiple studies have suggested that automated enforcement systems advance road safety.

Several reports indicate that speed cameras discourage speeding violations.

A few years after Washington, DC, established their speed camera system, police reported that only about 3% of motorists were speeding in covered areas, compared to about one in four motorists in the same areas before the cameras' installation.[43] A review of the automated speed enforcement system in nearby Montgomery County, Maryland, found that cameras were associated with a 10% reduction in average driving speeds and a pronounced reduction of 59% in vehicles' likelihood of exceeding speed limits by more than 10 miles per hour at camera locations. These researchers concluded that speed cameras reduced the likelihood that collisions would cause fatalities or incapacitating injuries by almost 40%.[44] A 2005 review of fourteen relevant studies conducted in various countries found that, in all fourteen studies, speed cameras were associated with reductions in crashes and casualties.[45] The size of reductions varied greatly, however; across different studies, declines in crashes ranged from 5% to 69%, declines in injuries from 12% to 65%, and declines in fatalities from 17% to 71%. Overall, these authors called for more and higher-quality data on speed cameras' outcomes.[46]

Scottsdale, Arizona, implemented the first program of fixed speed cameras on a major freeway in 2006. Studies found that, during the nine-month demonstration period, speeding declined, as did all types of crashes except for rear-end collisions, and that speeding increased again after the initial pilot program concluded.[47] Charlotte, North Carolina, began a three-year speed camera pilot program in 2004, focused on busy urban arterials. Results here indicated that collisions dropped by about 10% on roads where cameras were introduced and that cameras were associated with reductions in driving speeds.[48]

Other evidence points to safety benefits for automated red-light enforcement. Advocates point especially to studies indicating that red-light cameras reduce the rates at which people run red lights, thus cutting down on the hazardous T-bones and other serious crashes that result from failure to heed traffic signals.[49] A study of Philadelphia intersections, for example, found that adding red-light cameras decreased red-light running by 96%.[50] A review of Oxnard, California, concluded that, relative to comparison cities that did not install red-light camera systems, Oxnard's system reduced total crashes at signalized intersections by 7%, crashes causing injuries by 29%, T-bone crashes by almost a third, and T-bone crashes causing injury by over two-thirds.[51] Fairfax, Virginia, began using automated red-light enforcement in 1997; a year later, red-light violations had dropped by 40% across both intersections with cameras and those without cameras.[52] At the national level, a 2011 study compared large cities that adopted red-light camera systems with those that did not. These researchers found that, controlling for relevant factors, cities that added red-light cameras saw 24% fewer fatal crashes caused by red-light running than they would have in the absence of red-light cameras and a 17% reduction in all fatal crashes at intersections with traffic signals.[53] The most comprehensive assessment of red-light cameras and crashes is a 2020 review of forty-one analyses across thirty-eight studies, mostly focused on the United States and Australia.[54] These authors found that, overall, red-light cameras were associated with a 20% reduction in crashes causing injuries, a 24% reduction in T-bone collisions, and a 29% reduction in T-bone collisions causing injury. Yet red-light cameras were also associated with a 19% increase in rear-end collisions. Due in part to the offsetting effect of the increase in rear-end collisions, these authors were unable to ascertain red-light cameras' effects on total crashes.[55] A 2020 study focused on Texas similarly concluded that red-light cameras changed the types of crashes occurring at intersections, but did not appear to reduce total crash numbers.[56]

These studies are not the only reports to complicate—or outright disavow—the idea that cameras reduce crashes. In the District of Columbia, for instance, police reported reductions in speed-related collisions and fatalities after they installed speed cameras in the early 2000s.[57] Others contended that this correlation did not imply causation, and noted that numerous factors and idiosyncrasies contribute to the incidence of traffic fatalities.[58] A 2005 *Washington Post* study also questioned the safety benefits of the district's red-light camera program; there, data indicated that in the first six years of the city's red-light camera program, crashes—including especially dangerous T-bone impacts—rose significantly, as did resulting injuries and deaths.[59] Although crashes and casualties increased throughout the city, the increases at intersections with cameras were comparable to or greater than the increases at intersections without cameras.[60] These results generated critiques that the cameras served more of a revenue-generation purpose than a public-safety purpose. The findings also fueled continued calls to reconsider whether cameras were located at the intersections where they could, in principle, best engender safer driving.[61]

As indicated above, there is also some evidence that red-light cameras increase rear-end collisions at intersections with camera-monitored traffic signals. For instance, a *Chicago Tribune* investigation found that red-light cameras increased rear-end collisions that caused injuries by 22%.[62] A study of Charlotte, North Carolina's red-light camera program found evidence of increases at many intersections in both rear-end collisions and sideswipes, the latter presumably resulting from efforts to avoid rear-end crashes.[63] Many road safety advocates dismiss concerns about these types of crashes as a red herring and contend that some increase in instances of property damage or comparatively minor injuries is more than acceptable as a tradeoff for reducing rates of the often disastrous—and deadly—collisions that result from red-light running. The *Tribune* investigation found that red-light cameras decreased T-bone collisions by 15%; this constitutes a significant reduction in these highly dangerous crashes, but also notably less than the 47% reduction in these collisions that Mayor Rahm Emanuel's administration had previously claimed.[64] According to traffic engineering experts that *Tribune* reporters interviewed, the 47% figure was derived from flawed data and the city's analysis failed to account for other factors influencing crash rates.[65] Another *Tribune* report found that many suburban jurisdictions failed to adhere to requirements to report information on crashes and that crashes had increased at a quarter of the suburban intersections with red-light cameras for which data were available.[66] A Minnesota study using driving simulations similarly concluded that automated speed enforcement systems alone did not appear to significantly increase motorists' attentiveness in work zones.[67]

AUTOMATING TRAFFIC DUTY

Conversations about cameras and policing resources and priorities also invoke the idea that, at least in theory, automated traffic enforcement frees up law enforcement officers from traffic duty and thus gives them more time to focus on other things. Additionally, because automated enforcement tickets are commonly processed outside of conventional criminal proceedings, issuing citations through automated enforcement can help reduce caseloads in overburdened court systems and allow prosecutors to dedicate more time to other types of cases, including violent crimes.[68] This procedural distinction also saves police officers' time by removing obligations to appear in traffic court.[69] Accordingly, hours that officers would otherwise have spent on providing traffic testimony can be allocated to other things.

On the other hand, from the law enforcement perspective, less officer time dedicated to traffic duty also translates into fewer opportunities to conduct investigatory stops. As detailed in previous chapters, investigatory stops are a central component of contemporary car-based policing practice. Cutting down on officer-initiated vehicle stops reduces opportunities for officers to conduct miniature roadside investigations, check for outstanding arrest warrants, and potentially catch other crimes in progress. It is also worth noting that automated enforcement takes away some of the discretion that police officers conventionally exercise in traffic enforcement. Traffic cameras cannot make judgment calls.

Further, some, including some law enforcement officers, feel that camera-based enforcement systems are less effective at changing individuals' patterns of driving behavior than conventional vehicle stops. This line of thinking suggests that the possibility of receiving a ticket in the mail is less psychologically impactful than the possibility of being pulled over by a uniformed officer, and that the experience of being pulled over and interacting directly with an officer may do more to deter illegal driving behavior in the future. These ideas manifested, for example, in a 2016 report on camera enforcement in work zones commissioned by the Minnesota Department of Transportation.[70] The researchers surveyed law enforcement officers and road workers and found that these stakeholders perceived automated speed enforcement to be the least effective of six methods for getting people to drive more slowly in work zones. On the other hand, respondents saw traditional officer-initiated traffic enforcement as the most effective of the six methods for encouraging both short- and long-term speed reductions in work zones.[71]

Legal historian William Mercer has framed traffic camera contracts as a significant issue for government sovereignty.[72] Governments enter into contracts with private companies to install and maintain camera systems. Some of these contracts also authorize private entities to issue citations to citizens. The cameras themselves take on a role conventionally reserved for law enforcement officers. For these reasons, Mercer argues that contracting with businesses to provide traffic camera systems equates to delegating a share of government's police powers to private entities.[73] This functionally transfers law enforcement powers to private entities' leadership and staff.[74] Legal challenges to traffic camera systems have raised similar concerns, alleging that municipalities granting private entities the authority to levy and collect fines creates new types of legal processes that may be impermissible under state law.[75]

CAMERAS, COPS, AND CITIZENS

Perspectives on what automated enforcement augurs for police-community relations vary. On the one hand, when motorists receive a ticket in the mail rather than experiencing an in-person vehicle stop, the possibility of escalation and violence that characterizes roadside interactions is absent. Concerns about inequities and uses of force in vehicle stops have led some to call for removing police from traffic duty altogether and shifting responsibility for enforcing the rules of the road to alternatives such as camera systems or civilian agents.[76]

On the other side of the ledger, it is conceivable that getting a ticket in the mail might seem less legitimate than receiving a citation from a uniformed officer. Particularly to the extent that citizens are aware of the profits—and scandals—associated with automated enforcement systems, affected people might perceive receiving a citation from a camera more like a cash grab than a valid exercise of legal authority. Such reactions may be particularly acute if people realize that substantial portions of the revenue from camera tickets are going to private companies, not government.

As on many issues, the American people are not in total agreement on the desirability of automated enforcement. Several studies have found that majorities of drivers reported favorable opinions of traffic cameras.[77] Automated enforcement's opponents, however, have voiced vigorous complaints and formed groups dedicated to pushing back on governments' use of the technology.[78]

On what automated enforcement means for race and equality, there are again varying perspectives. As documented in this book and elsewhere, social scientific studies and law enforcement statistics clearly indicate disparities in the rates at which officers pull over different categories of motorists. Racial and ethnic disparities in stops are especially stark. Drivers of color, particularly Black drivers, are more likely than their White counterparts to be pulled over and to experience other consequences that can result from vehicle stops, including searches, property seizures, and arrests.[79]

Noting these disparities, some have extolled the virtues of automated enforcement to reduce racial biases and inequities in car-based policing.[80] Traffic cameras do not take drivers' race into account (indeed, in many cases, they do not capture images of drivers at all). Thus, more automated enforcement has the potential to reduce racial disparities in the policing of cars and drivers. Such reductions would equate to fairer enforcement of traffic laws and potentially help ameliorate racial disparities in searches, arrests, and uses of force resulting from vehicle stops.

However, other evidence suggests that patterns in how traffic cameras are currently deployed may produce their own inequities. A traffic camera does not know the race of the motorist whose vehicle it photographs. It also has no control over whose vehicles pass through its area of coverage. But decisions about where to place cameras have the potential to systematically shape different groups of motorists' exposure to automated enforcement systems. Especially given the high levels of residential racial segregation in the United States, different camera placements can ensnare very different populations of drivers.

A recent case study of Washington, DC's camera system highlighted such issues. The district relies heavily on automated traffic enforcement. In 2016, 96% of nearly a million citations for moving violations and 97% of close to $115 million in associated fines originated with cameras.[81] These penalties, however, were disproportionately distributed across the city. Although crashes per capita are "remarkably similar" across neighborhoods with different racial makeups, motorists in predominantly Black areas were cited at double the average rate, and motorists in predominantly White areas were cited at one-eighth the average rate.[82]

Examining a different city with a robust automated enforcement system, another recent report emphasized the disproportionate debt from tickets that Black Chicagoans face. As of 2018, of the city's ten ZIP codes with the highest per-adult ticket debt, eight ZIP codes were majority Black.[83] The disproportionate accumulation of debt in neighborhoods where more people struggle to pay tickets, accordingly, leads to disproportionate rates of related financial hardships, including bankruptcy filings.[84] Between 2015 and 2019 Chicago's automated enforcement system ticketed households in predominantly Black and Latino neighborhoods at about twice the rate of households in White neighborhoods. In 2020 the disparity between Black neighborhoods and White neighborhoods increased to 3 to 1.[85]

LEGAL AND CONSTITUTIONAL QUESTIONS

Others have raised more technical questions about cameras' legality. Cleveland, for instance, faced criticism that the municipal ordinance authorizing their red-light camera system violated the Ohio Constitution by treating moving violations as civil offenses, whereas the state's laws treat them as criminal offenses.[86]

With regard to fundamental constitutional matters, cameras' critics have raised concerns about equal protection and due process. Equal protection is potentially implicated in differences in motorists' disparate exposure to sanctions depending on whether they encounter traffic cameras on their routes.[87] When automated enforcement ordinances hold car owners responsible even if they were not driving at the time a violation is recorded, they may also run afoul of equal protection by exposing individual owners to legal liabilities from which automobile manufacturers and retailers are shielded.[88]

In the area of due process, it is relevant to note that, when tickets from cameras are categorized as civil infractions, governments need to meet only the preponderance of the evidence standard to prove a violation.[89] Conventional officer-issued citations and criminal traffic cases, on the other hand, impose upon government the much more stringent beyond a reasonable doubt standard of proof. Further, tickets that camera systems issue arrive in the mail complete with a presumption of culpability; should they wish to contest a citation, motorists typically hold the burden of proof in convincing the court that they should not be held legally responsible for the alleged violation the camera recorded. This inverts the US criminal legal system's conventional presumption of innocence.[90] With the photographic record accepted as prima facie evidence of culpability, officers are also relieved of the conventional obligation to offer testimony to support moving violation charges.[91]

Both general criticism and legal challenges to specific citations have foregrounded these concerns, as well as the related issue of ascertaining not just the vehicle, but whether the vehicle's owner was in fact behind the wheel when the alleged violation occurred. Traffic camera systems generally photograph vehicles and their license plates, not drivers.[92] Litigation, including cases in Louisiana and Missouri, has highlighted traffic cameras' failure to capture drivers' faces as a potential due process violation.[93]

Courts have rejected numerous lawsuits raising these sorts of legal and constitutional issues. Upon the first use of photography-based speed enforcement in Massachusetts in 1909, the new technology promptly faced a legal challenge alleging that the camera system was unreliable and that evidence derived from it should not be considered probative of legal culpability. In 1910, however, the Massachusetts Supreme Judicial Court rejected this challenge, upholding this first iteration of a traffic camera system as an acceptable means of ascertaining moving violations and a legitimate basis for imposing sanctions on drivers.[94] Considering contemporary automated enforcement ordinances in Cleveland and Chicago, federal courts have rejected challenges involving equal protection, due process, and excessive fines claims.[95] The United States District Courts for the Districts of Maryland and Oregon have dismissed constitutional claims for want of federal jurisdiction, and the Ninth Circuit affirmed the Oregon dismissal in 2005.[96] In 2008's *Mendenhall v. Akron* the Ohio Supreme Court upheld municipalities' authority under the Ohio Constitution to enact automated enforcement ordinances.

Other state courts have shown greater willingness to overturn automated enforcement ordinances than federal courts typically have. In 2007's *State v. Kuhlman* the Minnesota Supreme Court struck down Minneapolis's red-light camera law, holding that it violated Minnesota state law and that it denied defendants the constitutionally protected presumption of innocence.[97] In 2015 the Missouri Supreme Court similarly struck down St. Louis's red-light camera law, holding that it placed an unconstitutional burden on vehicle owners to prove they were not behind the wheel if someone else was driving when their vehicle was involved in a violation captured on camera.[98] At the same time, the Missouri Supreme Court also invalidated a red-light camera program in St. Peters and a speed camera law in Moline Acres. The court did not, however, hold that automated enforcement systems were necessarily illegal. Noting this fact, a spokesperson for American Traffic Solutions, which had operated St. Louis's red-light camera system, stated, "We look forward to working with communities throughout Missouri to restart their safety programs in full compliance with the direction provided in the multiple opinions issued today."[99] Although St. Louis initially indicated their interest in reinstating their camera program under a new ordinance that complied with the court's ruling, by June 2017 only one Missouri jurisdiction, Hannibal, was using red-light cameras, down from about thirty jurisdictions in 2011.[100]

BIG BROTHER'S NEW TOYS?

A general line of criticism directed at automated enforcement systems depicts traffic cameras as insidious components of an expanding surveillance state, and one that endangers or outright invades individuals' privacy rights. Such critiques sometimes explicitly invoke Big Brother of George Orwell's *Nineteen Eighty-Four*.[101]

Others see these concerns as overwrought. The behaviors that traffic cameras focus on—namely, speeding and running red lights—are, of course, against the law. Automated enforcement's proponents contend that new means of detecting and sanctioning these violations do not necessarily constitute appreciable impositions on citizens' privacy interests. When it comes to constitutional protections, particularly under the Fourth Amendment, the automobile exception to warrant requirements established in *Carroll v. United States* (1925) is also a relevant consideration. The same reasoning that underlies the Supreme Court's authorization of officers to conduct warrantless vehicle searches based on probable cause could extend to automated traffic enforcement systems.[102] Further, because license plates are clearly visible on cars' exteriors, they might be excluded from Fourth Amendment search protections under plain view doctrine.[103]

There is also some tension between considerations with regard to due process and those related to privacy. That is, whereas privacy advocates have voiced concerns about traffic cameras photographing drivers and passengers, cameras that capture only vehicles and license plates, *not* drivers, complicate efforts to ascertain who was driving a vehicle at the time a camera recorded a violation.[104]

New technological developments have engendered some elevated privacy concerns related to cars and cameras. Of particular note are automated license plate readers (ALPRs). ALPRs are specialized cameras that automatically record images of every license plate that enters their field of view, along with details on when and where the image was recorded.[105] Information that ALPRs record can be automatically checked against various databases, allowing the system to alert police if a license plate that is associated with a missing person, open warrant, or stolen car or that authorities have otherwise flagged as a vehicle of interest pops up.[106] Some states' hot lists of vehicles of interest include vehicles connected to drivers with suspended, revoked, or restricted licenses.[107] In their mobile version, ALPRs can be mounted on vehicles, creating a rolling surveillance device that automatically captures the plate of every vehicle it comes across. Outside of law enforcement, this utility has found purchase in the private sector. For instance, some vehicle repossession companies that can afford the cameras and the service's fees have adopted ALPRs, allowing them to scan streets and parking lots looking for any car with an outstanding repossession order.[108]

Criminal justice authorities greatly value ALPRs as powerful law enforcement tools.[109] However, this technology's capacity to collect extensive data about individuals and their movements has led legal observers to raise serious concerns about its constitutionality under the Fourth Amendment.[110] In *Carpenter v. United States* (2018) the US Supreme Court ruled that government agents must obtain a warrant to access location data held by cellular service providers. In her legal scholarship on the topic, Stephanie Foster argues that the *Carpenter* decision clearly signals a right to privacy with regard to individual movements.[111] Accordingly, she contends that government agents should be required to obtain warrants to query databases produced by ALPRs just as *Carpenter* dictated they must to access cell providers' records of individuals' movements. Although acceptance of ALPRs within law enforcement agencies is high, officials are aware of the scrutiny that the technology has attracted. This leads to significant reluctance on law enforcement's part to participate in research on the topic, even when that research is commissioned by a government agency.[112]

AUTOMATION DEBATES AND THE FUTURE OF CRIMINAL JUSTICE

Using photography to enforce the rules of the road is almost as old as the policing of cars itself, with Massachusetts creating an early forerunner of today's traffic camera systems in 1909.[113] Radar technology became available in the 1940s[114] and subsequently emerged as the technological foundation for contemporary speed camera systems. These speed cameras and red-light cameras saw widespread adoption in the late twentieth and early twenty-first centuries, spreading first in Europe and other countries and somewhat later in the United States. In the US context, the technology's adoption has been characterized by controversies and fits and starts. Critics have raised numerous concerns about privacy and potential constitutional issues, along with fundamental questions about the extent to which automated enforcement serves revenue-generation interests relative to public safety interests. Perceptions that automated enforcement systems are overly intrusive or function primarily to extract money from the citizenry have led multiple jurisdictions to ban or restrict traffic cameras; this group notably includes Texas, the state where the first modern automated speed enforcement system in the United States appeared in 1986.[115]

Debate and litigation surrounding the tools that legal authorities use to gather information about people driving on public roads have continued. On one side of the conversation, some argue that automation helps get police officers out of traffic enforcement, potentially mitigating some of the problems addressed in Chapter 6 and freeing up criminal justice authorities to focus on more serious types of criminal offending. On the other side, critics allege that these technologies further entrench a surveillance state and specifically note automated enforcement's disproportionate impact on communities of color. Thus, discourse about information technology's appropriate role in law enforcement does not exist in isolation, but connects to fundamental questions about equity, fairness, and the very idea of justice itself.

Critiques of governmental use of private contractors to run camera systems and issue citations evoke broader conversations about privatization in other aspects of government.[116] Privatization trends have accelerated in recent decades, touching everything from public assistance,[117] to toll roads[118] and parking meters,[119] to criminal justice domains such as incarceration.[120] In both the broader debate and the camera-specific conversation, the effects of contractors' profit motives are a central concern. The most profitable approach for businesses may not be the approach that is most in the public interest. Traffic camera companies that earn money on every citation they issue have a clear-cut incentive to issue as many tickets as they can. The idea of traffic cameras as revenue generators sits poorly with many, particularly when proceeds go not only to government, but also to private businesses. Automated enforcement has furthered the accumulation of personal debt and caused bankruptcies, while significant questions remain about traffic cameras' contribution to safer streets and highways. Especially when combined with recent innovations such as automated license plate readers, traffic cameras arguably blur the line between general surveillance and enforcement of specific criminal laws, again bringing privacy concerns to the fore. Altogether, discussions about the virtues and vices of automated enforcement involve crucial considerations about what kind of criminal justice system we have—and want to have—as we move deeper into the twenty-first century.

TWELVE

Monitoring Mobility

The ability to track people's movements is one of the most powerful tools available to contemporary criminal justice authorities. As technological capacities enabling location tracking expanded in the late twentieth and early twenty-first centuries, these tools came to play larger and larger roles in multiple facets of criminal justice, from crime detection, to police investigation, to prosecution, to punishment. Automobility enabled historically unprecedented freedom of individual movement. One can view location tracking as a direct response to that freedom of movement, a way for authorities to keep tabs on citizens in an era of automobility. As in the case of automated traffic enforcement discussed in Chapter 11, authorities' adoption of these new tools has attracted significant controversy and seen challenges in court.

This chapter first addresses the development and implementation of human-worn location tracking devices, before shifting focus to the GPS and cell phone tracking that is especially prominent in our car-dependent social world. Several Supreme Court decisions have placed limitations on police and prosecutors' use of information derived from these sources, including rulings requiring warrants for monitoring vehicles' movements via GPS trackers (*United States v. Jones* [2012]) and for obtaining information about individuals' movements from their cellular service providers (*Carpenter v. United States* [2018]). The *Jones* and *Carpenter* rulings changed course from the previous cases *United States v. Knotts* (1983) and *United States v. Karo* (1984), in which the Court had held that authorities generally did not require warrants to track movements on public thoroughfares.

Despite recent Supreme Court rulings imposing warrant requirements for authorities to access certain types of location data, other modes of gathering such data continue to raise Fourth Amendment questions. These include bulk purchases of location information from third-party companies and geofence warrants that provide authorities access to location information about entire groups of people whose cell phones were in particular areas at particular times. These techniques indicate the ongoing questions about privacy, individual liberties, and state power that continue to characterize twenty-first-century criminal justice.

TRACKING BODIES

Today, much of the hardware that legal authorities use to track individuals' movements relies on Global Positioning System (GPS) tracking. This is a newer innovation in the field of electronic monitoring (EM), following in the footsteps of its older cousin, radio frequency (RF) tracking. Familiar to many through popular discussion of house arrest, RF tracking was the brainchild of Ralph Schwitzgebel, a Harvard scientist who in 1964 invented a wearable device that used a screen to track a person's location (within 400 meters) via radio waves. Jack Love, a New Mexico state judge, originally conceptualized the use of an RF tracking bracelet to track people convicted of crimes in 1977, borrowing the idea from an *Amazing Spider-Man* newspaper comic strip. Love coordinated with a computer salesman named Michael Goss, who created a corporation called National Incarceration Monitor and Control Services. Goss's company began manufacturing the necessary hardware in 1983, and Judge Love tested the device himself, wearing a tracking bracelet for three weeks. He handed down the first sentence requiring an individual to wear an RF tracking device later that year.[1]

Radio frequency EM enjoyed considerable popularity in the years immediately following its introduction. However, it soon lost cachet with policymakers and public officials who were increasingly favoring incarceration and investing resources in prison construction.[2] With the introduction of GPS tracking, though, EM experienced a dramatic resurgence in popularity in the mid- to late 1990s. GPS tracking operates on the same general principle as RF tracking, in that people are required to wear an anklet that tracks their movements, allowing supervising agencies to enforce restrictions on their whereabouts. But, because it uses a satellite network, GPS offers greater functionality than RF tracking devices. GPS tracking can keep tabs on people's locations anywhere in the world, twenty-four hours a day, seven days a week, and can automatically generate comprehensive chronological records of devices' location on the planet.[3] The Department of Defense began developing the GPS system in the 1970s, and the last satellite needed to create the full modern GPS system was launched in 1993.[4]

Robert Martinez, a Florida politician turned businessman, played a central role in the development of body-worn GPS trackers as a criminal justice tool. Martinez started his major political career as the officially nonpartisan mayor of Tampa, Florida, serving from 1979 to 1986, until resigning to run for governor of that state as a Republican. After winning the 1986 gubernatorial election, he served one term before losing his reelection campaign. Following this defeat, President George H. W. Bush appointed Martinez director of the Office of National Drug Control Policy (or "drug czar"). He remained in this position until the end of Bush's single term as president.[5]

So, in 1993, Martinez found himself out of a job. He returned home and founded Pro Tech Monitoring in Tampa, Florida. Transitioning from the public to the private sector, he established a new beachhead in corrections commerce. Using connections made while holding national-level office, he assembled a team of eight aerospace engineers, drawn largely from the staff of the Department of Defense and with expertise in that organization's Global Positioning System.[6] Together, they set about creating the foundational elements of the modern system of tracking people using GPS.

Although founder, president, and a chief investor, Martinez reported to the press that he "len[t] the clout of his name to help market the company," whereas others handled the nuts and bolts.[7] Indeed, after the organization of the company, Martinez served primarily as a prominent pitchman. In interviews with reporters, he championed the new powers of surveillance associated with GPS tracking as far beyond those of its predecessor, RF tracking, which could tell supervising agencies only whether a monitored person was at home.[8] He opined that satellite tracking was a "milestone for our criminal justice system" and stressed Pro Tech Monitoring's status as the industry leader, the primary patent holder on the cutting edge of developments in the field.[9]

Like other major developments in information and communication technology—such as the internet itself[10] and geographic information systems[11]—GPS has strong military roots. The technology was originally designed for martial applications and continues to run on a network of Department of Defense satellites. Martinez directly invoked this military legacy in his efforts to sell the new technology, describing how his surveillance product utilized the "battlefield-proven" Global Positioning System to keep a watchful eye on people.[12]

With Martinez as the company's public face, chief operating officer and engineer Hoyt Layson Jr. assumed responsibility for managing the day-to-day business.[13] After a period of research and development, in 1996 Layson began filing a patent per year, each with Pro Tech Monitoring as the assignee. First, in 1996, he filed the patent for the physical tracking apparatus to be attached to a person's ankle;[14] next, in 1997, he and colleagues filed the patent for a tamper detection system, designed to discourage people from attempting to remove or disable their tracking anklets.[15] Then, in 1998, he filed a patent for the conceptual design of the passive (versus active) monitoring system.[16] Each patent was granted about two years after it was filed.

While Layson was overseeing development of the requisite hardware and software for human GPS tracking, Martinez brought his son Alan Martinez on board to act as another principal in the company and its marketing chief. Alan Martinez had a clear vision of the market for GPS tracking. Speaking to the American Probation and Parole Association Conference in early March 1996, he described a criminal justice system with 3.8 million individuals subject to community supervision, only about 1.5% of whom were being electronically monitored. Alan Martinez foresaw a pivotal role for Pro Tech Monitoring in changing this state of affairs. He described a business plan in which Pro Tech would "aggressively pursue the existing house arrest market." Further, he correctly predicted a dramatic increase in rates of electronic monitoring, and envisioned his company controlling a commanding share of the resultant profits.[17]

This type of candid language about an underexploited market niche helps situate the rise of GPS tracking within criminologist Nils Christie's discussion of crime control as an industry.[18] Christie identified a "crossover point" in 1977, after which more was spent on private security than on public law enforcement organizations. Since that time, expenditures on private security and employment in the for-profit security industry have grown steadily.[19] Christie also describes a "technological push" that had significant effects on the corrections field in the early 1990s. As more and more people became subject to lengthier, more intensive periods of observation and control after incarceration (parole) and as an alternative to incarceration (probation), private industry stepped in to provide the technological means.[20]

Writing in the early 1990s, Christie focused on the use of RF monitoring in house arrest, along with the growing market in drug testing. Later events in the development of GPS tracking, however, parallel his observations on the earlier stages of EM. He noted how EM technologies were marketed in trade publications such as *Corrections Today*, in advertisements that stressed the efficiency, automaticity, and comprehensiveness of electronically enhanced monitoring techniques.[21] The practice of marketing GPS tracking technology at meetings for professionals in parole and probation was noted above; correctional administrators were also some of the first to be treated to demonstrations of the original working prototypes, in May 1996.[22] Additionally, like RF tracking, GPS EM received early attention in the corrections trade press.[23] Moreover, coverage in industrial publications was not limited to corrections-specific audiences. During its earliest stages, the general technology news site *Newsbytes* (which later became part of *The Washington Post*'s "Technology News" section) reported on the emerging business, as did the leading aerospace magazine *Aviation Week and Space Technology.*[24]

This spree of press releases and direct marketing capped three and a half years of research and design and an untold investment of time, energy, and social capital in planning, networking, and deal making. In the first days of January 1997, a few months after developing prototypes and filing the patent for the first human GPS tracking device, Pro Tech Monitoring secured a contract with the Florida Department of Corrections (FDOC). This five-year agreement, for which Pro Tech was the only bidder, guaranteed them $340,000 in payments in the first year.[25] For company president Bob Martinez, this was just the latest development in a close relationship with the FDOC; during his four years as governor, he oversaw the addition of 30,000 beds to the state's prison system.[26]

Noteworthy parallels in conceptualization and rhetoric between the private company and the criminal justice organization characterized the FDOC's adoption of Pro Tech's GPS tracking system. Alan Martinez coined the term *orbiting warden* as a tagline for their new product, using the evocative phrase in the press releases, trade shows, and professional meetings where he marketed the technology.[27] When the FDOC issued statements in 1996 indicating interest in GPS tracking technology—and specifically, GPS tracking technology supplied by Pro Tech Monitoring—they used the same language, describing the system as one of "orbiting wardens."[28]

Furthermore, Bob Martinez helped shape implementation of the technology and set the stage for the development of GPS tracking in the direction it has taken. In early comments about the business, Martinez justified Pro Tech's emphasis on criminal justice applications by referring to the "unfortunate amount of crime and the problems with pedophiles and domestic violence." In accordance with this conceptualization, the first applications of Pro Tech's proprietary GPS tracking technology in Florida and Lackawanna County, Pennsylvania, did indeed focus on people convicted of sex crimes[29] and, to a lesser extent, individuals convicted of domestic violence.[30]

GPS monitoring has widely diffused since its 1997 introduction in Florida. Following in Pro Tech's footsteps, other companies, including Advanced Business Sciences and later BI Incorporated, developed their own versions of

GPS tracking equipment.[31] Similarly, other states moved to adopt the Florida model, as a flurry of legislative activity created GPS tracking programs all over the country. Bob Martinez and Pro Tech recognized that authorities could have numerous applications for GPS tracking, and jurisdictions have experimented with using the technology in various contexts. Early adoptions, though, overwhelmingly deployed human GPS tracking as an intervention for people convicted of sex crimes. By 2009, forty-six states and the federal government used GPS tracking for people convicted of some categories of sex offenses.[32]

Although most people convicted of sexual offenses are required by law to submit to some form of supervisory monitoring while on probation or parole,[33] the specifics of GPS tracking policies vary substantially from state to state. Most states require GPS tracking only for people categorized as high risk after release from incarceration. Methods for this classification vary as well; in many states, conviction of a crime against a child automatically qualifies someone as high risk. Other states use the technique to supervise probation and parole for people convicted of a broader range of offenses.[34] A particularly stringent policy is the requirement of GPS monitoring beyond the periods of official supervision under probation or parole, sometimes for life. Florida led the way here as well, with the 2005 passage of the Jessica Lunsford Act. This law, enacted by the Florida legislature in response to the abduction, rape, and murder of a 9-year-old girl by a registered sex offender, required that any person convicted of sexual crimes involving a child under age 12 remain on lifetime GPS surveillance, at his or her own expense.[35] Other states, including Wisconsin and North Carolina, have enacted similar laws. People subjected to lifetime monitoring statutes have challenged them under the Fourth Amendment, with mixed results.[36] In *Grady v. North Carolina* (2015), the US Supreme Court held that the requirement to wear a GPS tracker under the North Carolina law constituted a search under the Fourth Amendment.[37]

It is also important to note that, although GPS trackers offer greater functionality for supervising agencies, RF tracking for house arrest is still very much a part of the US criminal justice system. Indeed, electronic home monitoring has become more common, with more than 125,000 people on electronically tracked house arrest in recent years.[38] The expanded use of EM for pretrial supervision and as a condition of probation or parole has attracted scholarly attention as a significant component of mass supervision in the criminal justice system.[39]

TRACKING VEHICLES

Location-tracking systems offer criminal justice authorities a valuable resource for obtaining and recording information about where criminal suspects and persons of interest travel in automobiles. Like the first human-worn location-tracking devices, early vehicle tracking devices, called beepers or bird dogs, used radio technology.[40] These devices give off electronic pulses that authorities can monitor. When following vehicles of interest, officers use variations in the radio signal's strength to assess relative proximity.[41] As this description suggests, these devices require active attention from officers to be useful for location tracking. On their own, they simply produce a signal that authorities can pick up; they do not create logs of targets' movements.[42] RF beepers' range is limited, particularly in areas with more radio interference, and their accuracy and reliability are less than ideal.[43] If pursuing officers get too far from the beeper, they can lose the signal altogether.[44]

As in the human-tracking world, the advent of GPS technology was a major step forward from RF tracking. Instead of just facilitating tailing vehicles of interest, GPS trackers create chronological records of everywhere a vehicle goes. This information reveals far more about what someone has been up to. And, because GPS tracking does not require active monitoring, the farther-reaching and more revealing picture of daily activities that this technology provides is available at a fraction of the worker-hours required to continuously monitor RF vehicle trackers.

When the GPS system became fully operational, GPS vehicle trackers were rapidly adopted in the business world as an effective way for trucking companies, taxicab companies, and so forth to monitor and coordinate their fleets.[45] Companies also moved to integrate GPS into vehicles for roadside assistance and theft recovery purposes.[46] On the consumer side, GPS became a staple of driving navigation, first through dedicated GPS hardware and vehicles' integrated navigation systems and subsequently through smartphone apps.

As used by criminal justice authorities, different versions of GPS tracking devices provide different levels of functionality. Passive devices do not have a transmitter; they log movement information in onboard memory for later retrieval. For passive body-worn anklets, information about movements is downloaded and sent to supervisory agencies when people sentenced to GPS tracking charge the units. When passive GPS trackers are affixed to vehicles, authorities need to recover the unit to download location information. Active systems, on the other hand, track movements in real time, transmitting location information at set intervals. Like other hardware, GPS tracking devices have become smaller and cheaper. In the early 2000s the devices cost $1,000 or more and were roughly the size of paperback books.[47] In 2021 online retailers offered devices a fraction of that size (albeit with limited battery life) starting at around $20, with additional monthly fees for service subscriptions. GPS chips themselves are now the size of postage stamps.[48] An officer can attach a magnetic GPS tracker in a discreet location beneath a vehicle in just a few seconds. With battery size and capacity as a consistent hurdle for engineers seeking to shrink GPS vehicle trackers, some agencies, including the FBI, have opted for devices that connect to target automobiles' electrical systems.[49] This relieves the necessity of removing devices to recharge their batteries.[50]

Law enforcement agencies have used GPS vehicle trackers to track suspects' movements in investigations of robberies, illegal marijuana grows, home invasions, abductions, drug sales, and terrorism.[51] Like GPS tracking anklets, GPS vehicle trackers can also be used to detect and sanction sex offenders' violations of legal restrictions on their movements.[52] Law enforcement has also turned the power of GPS tracking against their own; a New Jersey police department used GPS tracking of patrol cars to substantiate allegations of officers filing false reports about their on-duty activities.[53]

GPS vehicle trackers have played pivotal roles in multiple high-profile investigations. In 1999, for instance, police in Washington State suspected William Bradley Jackson of killing his missing 9-year-old daughter, Valiree. In the course of their investigation, police temporarily impounded Jackson's car and truck and—with warrants but without Jackson's knowledge—attached GPS trackers to the vehicles. About three weeks after Valiree went missing, one of the GPS devices recorded Jackson visiting a remote location off an unmarked logging road. Upon visiting the site, police found Valiree's body buried in a shallow grave. The GPS tracker led to the evidence that prosecutors used to convict Jackson of murder.[54] Jackson appealed his conviction, arguing that police lacked probable cause for the GPS tracking warrant. Reviewing the case, the Washington Supreme Court confirmed that legal authorities require warrants to attach GPS trackers to private automobiles, but rejected Jackson's claim that police lacked valid probable cause to obtain warrants in his case.[55] And, in the highly publicized Scott Peterson case, California prosecutors used GPS tracking to establish "a pattern of a criminal returning to a crime scene."[56]

TRACKING CELL PHONES

Today, authorities do not necessarily need to attach a tracking device to a person or a vehicle to obtain location information. Most Americans carry devices that can accomplish this objective around with them in their pockets.

Any cell phone can be a means of obtaining location data via cell-site location information. This method involves assessing a phone's location by measuring "the strength, angle, and timing of the caller's signal" at multiple cell towers, while also accounting for relevant characteristics of the local cellular network.[57] As cell towers have proliferated and technology has advanced, cell-site location information has become much more precise.[58] Modern cell phones also contain chips that enable GPS tracking.[59] Authorities can recover GPS location information from various apps that record these data.

Criminal justice authorities began obtaining information about cell phones' location and using it to support prosecutions as early as 1998.[60] As with GPS vehicle trackers, authorities have used location information derived from cell phones to support numerous cases, including investigations of drug trafficking, robbery, and murder, as well as for broader surveillance focused on areas of interest or concern to legal authorities.[61] Cell-site simulators, commonly called Stringrays, provide law enforcement with particularly extensive information. Imitating cell towers, these devices "directly capture texts, numbers of outgoing calls, emails, serial numbers, identification, GPS location, actual contents of conversation, and other raw and detailed information from unsuspecting phones and track the location of targets and non-targets in apartments, cars, buses, and on streets through mapping software. They can even make the tracked device send texts and make calls."[62] Several federal courts have ruled that government's use of cell-site simulators constitutes a search under the Fourth Amendment, and thus requires a warrant, but the Supreme Court has not yet weighed in.[63]

LOCATION TRACKING AND THE CONSTITUTION

The Fourth Amendment's protection against unreasonable searches and seizures is the fundamental constitutional provision at issue in location-tracking cases. Several key US Supreme Court precedents underlie twenty-first-century rulings that deal directly with legal authorities' use of location-tracking technologies.

Katz v. United States (1967) is a crucial decision in this area. As discussed in Chapter 3, *Katz* overturned the Court's previous holding in *Olmstead v. United States* (1928) that government agents needed to have engaged in physical trespass to conduct what would be considered a search under the Fourth Amendment. In *Katz*, the Court rejected this logic, ruling that FBI agents had conducted a search by placing a listening device on the exterior of a phone booth, even though they had not physically entered the phone booth to do so. Thus a warrant was required for the evidence gathering in question. Justice Harlan's concurrence with the majority opinion established a two-part test for determining whether something government agents did constituted a search: (1) Did the affected party demonstrate a subjective expectation of privacy? And, if yes, (2) is that an expectation that society is prepared to accept as reasonable? This reasonable expectation of privacy test, or *Katz* test, has served as bedrock for much subsequent Fourth Amendment jurisprudence.[64]

United States v. Knotts (1983) was the first Supreme Court case dealing specifically with tracking devices. *Knotts* involved an investigation of methamphetamine manufacturing, in which Minnesota police arranged for the placement of a radio transmitter, or beeper, inside a five-gallon container of chloroform sold to a suspect. Aided by a helicopter carrying a radio receiver, authorities tracked the container to a Wisconsin cabin. Officers proceeded to surveil the cabin for three days and obtain and execute a search warrant. Inside, they found a drug manufacturing laboratory and enough chemicals to produce 14 pounds of pure amphetamine. Prosecutors used evidence from the search to charge Knotts and two codefendants with federal drug offenses. Challenging his conviction for conspiracy to manufacture controlled substances, Knotts contended that officers needed a warrant not only for the search, but also to track the container's movement. Without a warrant for the location tracking, Knotts argued, evidence resulting from law enforcement's monitoring of the beeper should have been excluded from the criminal proceedings.[65]

In *Knotts* the Supreme Court needed to decide whether electronically tracking the container's movement without a warrant violated Fourth Amendment protections. Applying the *Katz* test, the Court held that no warrant was required, reversing the holding of the Eighth Circuit Court of Appeals. For the high court, Justice Rehnquist wrote, "A person traveling in an automobile on public thoroughfares has no reasonable expectation of privacy in his movements from one place to another."[66] Citing previous cases in which the Court had identified a reduced expectation of privacy when traveling in automobiles, the Court reasoned that, because one's movements on public roads are generally subject to visual observation by anyone, using an electronic device to collect information that authorities could otherwise have obtained through warrantless visual surveillance does not necessitate a warrant.[67]

The year after the *Knotts* ruling, the Supreme Court issued another decision related to electronic location tracking. Like *Knotts*, *United States v. Karo* (1984) involved the movement of chemicals suspected to be related to drug trafficking; in *Karo* the chemical in question was 50 gallons of ether. An informant advised a Drug Enforcement Administration (DEA) agent that smugglers had imported clothing infused with cocaine and that Karo and co-conspirators intended to purchase the ether from the informant and use it to extract the controlled substance from the clothing. Working with the informant, DEA agents placed a can with an RF tracker in the shipment for Karo. With the aid of the beeper, DEA agents tracked the can as it moved in succession to three different houses, two different storage lockers, and then two more houses. Finally, agents confirmed that the beeper was inside the last house and used this information to support a search warrant affidavit. With the warrant, they searched the house, seizing cocaine and making arrests.[68]

Considering Karo's Fourth Amendment claims, the Court reached several conclusions. First, installing the beeper with the informant's consent did not require a warrant. Second, per *Knotts*, monitoring the beeper while the truck carrying it traversed public thoroughfares did not constitute a Fourth Amendment violation. However, the Court held that electronic tracking devices *do* potentially run afoul of the Fourth when they provide information about private spaces that government agents could not have obtained from external observation outside the home's curtilage. Thus, monitoring electronic devices inside spaces protected from search generally does require a warrant.[69] The Court reached a similar conclusion in *Kyllo v. United States* (2001), where they held that government agents need a warrant to use thermal imaging technology to provide information about activities transpiring inside a home.

Like the thermal imaging at issue in *Kyllo*, as GPS came into wide use, it was a new technology that expanded on previous tools' surveillance power. Relative to RF tracking devices, GPS devices allow authorities to gather more comprehensive and intrusive information regarding people's whereabouts.[70] Early in the twenty-first century state courts split on whether authorities required a warrant to conduct GPS-based surveillance. Courts in New York, Oregon, and Washington State ruled that warrants were required, whereas courts in California and Nevada held that they were not.[71] Several federal courts, including the Courts of Appeals for the Seventh and Ninth Circuits, upheld warrantless GPS tracking of vehicles in the late twentieth and early twenty-first centuries.[72] These courts, however, did not materially engage with the question of how GPS's greater capacities relative to earlier forms of location-tracking technology might alter the Fourth Amendment calculus when considering government's use of GPS tracking.[73]

In 2010 a federal circuit court held for the first time that installing and monitoring an electronic location-tracking device constituted a search under the Fourth Amendment, and thus required a warrant. In *United States v. Maynard* (2010), the Court of Appeals for the District of Columbia ruled that monitoring a vehicle's movements outside the parameters of a warrant constituted a Fourth Amendment violation. To reach this conclusion, the DC Circuit applied a "mosaic theory" of the Fourth Amendment, which "asserts that individually meaningless pieces of information, when aggregated, combine to create a revealing 'mosaic,' which is far more intrusive than any one piece of information."[74] GPS trackers offer detailed information regarding patterns of movement and behavior, potentially over long periods of surveillance, making this mode of evidence gathering particularly effective for generating useful pieces to assemble into illuminating mosaics.[75] The DC Circuit noted this in their ruling in *Maynard*.[76]

When *Maynard* reached the US Supreme Court, it was known as *United States v. Jones*; Antoine Jones was Maynard's co-defendant in the original criminal case, and the tracked vehicle was registered to Jones's wife, giving Jones standing to challenge the tracker's placement.[77] In their ruling, the Court affirmed that government agents seeking to gain information about a vehicle's movements must act within the parameters of a legally executed warrant. Argument in the case hearkened back to the challenges raised nearly 100 years earlier in *Carroll v. United States* (1925), connoting how the classical legal distinction between private and public spaces begins to lose coherence in an era of automobility. Defending the actions of officers who had collected data about Jones's vehicle's whereabouts using a GPS device attached outside the specifications of a warrant, the government invoked *Knotts*, arguing that Jones had no reasonable expectation of privacy when moving about on public thoroughfares.

Notably, Justice Scalia's majority opinion for a unanimous Court did not actually hinge on a reasonable expectation of privacy test. Instead, Scalia based his reasoning on a narrower interpretation of the Fourth Amendment. Focusing on the installation of the tracking device itself, Scalia stated that Jones's vehicle clearly constituted his personal property—one of his "effects," for the purposes of the Fourth—and that government agents had violated his Fourth Amendment rights by trespassing upon it to place the tracker.[78] Although Justice Scalia's majority opinion did not apply the *Katz* test, five justices writing in concurrence with Justice Scalia's opinion suggested that the Court should have applied the *Katz* test in *Jones* and that government's use of the GPS tracker outside the specifications of the warrant did violate a reasonable expectation of privacy.[79]

Until *Jones*, a line of precedent since *Knotts* relied on the idea that motorists lacked a reasonable expectation of privacy when traversing public thoroughfares.[80] Thus, information about their movements on the streets and highways lacked warrant protections under the Fourth Amendment. The *Jones* ruling diverged from these precedents in effect, although the majority opinion did not depend on a reasonable expectation of privacy assessment or the particular nature and extent of information about people's activities to which GPS technology provides access. Sensitivity to the sweeping information access made possible by twenty-first-century technologies played a bigger role in *Riley v. California* (2014). In this case the Supreme Court held that government agents generally must obtain a warrant to search the cell phone of someone who has been arrested. Writing for a unanimous Court, Chief Justice Roberts noted that cell phones are "now such a pervasive and insistent part of daily life that the proverbial visitor from Mars might conclude they were an important feature of human anatomy."[81] Chief Justice Roberts went on to argue that not only is the inspection of digital information stored on a cell phone a search, but, given the nature and extent of information that phones contain, a search of a cell phone is actually *more* intrusive than a search of a home, that space long considered to be most private and most protected from government intrusion in Fourth Amendment jurisprudence.[82]

Carpenter v. United States (2018) brought together issues raised in *Jones* and *Riley*. In this case the Supreme Court held that government agents generally need a warrant to access cellular service providers' records of customer location data. Chief Justice Roberts again wrote for the majority (this time, only a five-justice majority, with Justices Breyer, Ginsburg, Kagan, and Sotomayor joining Roberts). For that majority, Roberts wrote, "We decline to grant the state unrestricted access to a wireless carrier's database of physical location information."[83] Citing both *Jones* and *Riley*, the chief justice noted that technological advancements had greatly enhanced government's ability to document people's private affairs and argued that the Court's Fourth Amendment jurisprudence must attend to these developments. Thus, *Carpenter* reckoned directly with the revealing information about people's lives that digital data sources provide. In Carpenter's case, numerous connections to his carrier's network over 127 days yielded nearly 13,000 data points pertaining to his phone's location.[84]

By seeking location records held by a business, in *Carpenter* the government sought protection from Fourth Amendment warrant requirements through the third-party doctrine. Under this doctrine, Fourth Amendment jurisprudence has conventionally exempted warrant requirements for information that individuals transfer to third parties.[85] Obtaining location information in this way also allowed government agents to avoid the physical trespass upon a person's effects that keyed Justice Scalia's majority opinion in *Jones*. The majority, however, rejected the argument that individuals forfeit their privacy interests by using cell phones, which, as Chief Justice Roberts previously noted in *Riley*, have become largely indispensable for participating in contemporary society.

The *Carpenter* ruling was not all-encompassing. The holding specifically addressed cell-site location data and did not directly weigh in on GPS data derived from cell phones. *Carpenter* also dealt specifically with historical information about where a phone *had been*; it left whether *real-time* monitoring of cell phones' locations constitutes a search under the Fourth Amendment an open question.[86]

After *Carpenter* several federal agencies employed a workaround that involved purchasing marketing data which included location data collected from apps on people's cell phones.[87] Because this technique involves buying data from a third party rather than obtaining location information directly from a cell service provider, some government lawyers have determined that such warrantless data collection is constitutionally acceptable. Concerns about the IRS Criminal Investigation division's use of such data led Senators Elizabeth Warren and Ron Wyden to request a review of this practice; in February 2021, the Inspector General for Tax Administration issued a letter suggesting that, under *Carpenter*, government's purchase and use of location information from marketing companies may in fact require a warrant.[88]

In recent years reverse location searches have also seen greatly expanded use in the criminal justice system. These searches involve law enforcement requesting information about all mobile devices that were operational in a particular area at a particular time. In a reverse location search, law enforcement officials are seeking information about a pool of people, from which they might derive suspects, rather than trying to ascertain information about specific people's movements. In *Carpenter*, the Supreme Court did not specify whether their ruling applied to "tower dumps," in which authorities request location information for all mobile devices that linked to particular cell towers at certain times.[89]

There are also unanswered Fourth Amendment questions about geofence warrants. These information-gathering efforts are much broader than tower dumps; after a geofence warrant is approved, "companies conduct sweeping searches of their location databases and provide a list of cell phones and affiliated users found at or near a specific area during a given timeframe."[90] Criminal justice authorities can procure additional information about individuals—including information about their locations outside the original specified time—via follow-up requests.[91] Despite concerns about geofence warrants functioning as new iterations of the general warrants that the Fourth Amendment was designed to protect against, numerous states and the federal government have adopted the practice. Technology companies have received tens of thousands of geofence warrants. Google receives the most, and appears to disclose user information in most cases.[92]

SURVEILLANCE AND PRIVACY IN CONTEMPORARY CRIMINAL JUSTICE

Location tracking is a powerful criminal justice tool. Authorities use location-tracking technologies to investigate crime and monitor individuals of interest. These technologies are also an important element in broader data collection and analysis programs. Their development, sale, and use has attracted attention as a notable aspect of what Stephen Graham calls the security-industrial complex.[93] They also raise notable concerns related to citizens' privacy interests and the Fourth Amendment prohibition of unreasonable search and seizure.

For many years federal courts held that location-tracking devices did not necessarily require warrants, particularly when the information derived from them related to movements in public.[94] It is also relevant that these cases typically involve automobiles, which are subject to relaxed Fourth Amendment protections under *Carroll v. United States* (1925).[95] It was thus possible to argue that, as a new tool providing functionally similar information, GPS tracking should similarly be exempted from warrant requirements. GPS, however, provides more data and more precise data than previous technologies. GPS tracking systems also create an independent record of devices' locations over time, rather than requiring officers to actively monitor and physically follow tracking devices.

In *United States v. Jones* (2012) the US Supreme Court held that authorities require a (valid) warrant to install and monitor GPS trackers. The *Jones* decision was a crucial precedent for subsequent rulings in cases such as *Riley v. California* (2014), in which the Court held that police must obtain a warrant to search an arrested person's cell phone, and *Carpenter v. United States* (2018), in which the Court held that the government generally needs a warrant to collect records of location data about cell phone companies' customers. However, multiple legal questions related to location tracking and other forms of government surveillance remain unsettled. As federal, state, and local law enforcement agencies, prosecutors' offices, and departments of correction continually move to adopt data-intensive techniques for gathering and analyzing evidence and intelligence, they are all but certain to continue testing constitutional limitations.

Legal authorities' use of location tracking is a key element in the broader rise of big data policing. Big data policing involves analyzing large amounts of data drawn from various sources to predict patterns of crime, inform policing strategies, support investigations, and assess law enforcement's performance.[96] As part of a big data law enforcement approach, authorities can combine location-tracking data with data from other sources, including crime reports, traffic management systems, and maps containing addresses for businesses, residences, and other points of interest.[97] Thus, beyond creating simple chronological records of suspects' comings and goings, law enforcement agencies can easily generate more sophisticated analyses of activities and relationships to people and places. These techniques, in turn, raise further questions about balancing government's interest in collecting information about the populace and citizens' privacy interests.

CONCLUSION

Objects in Mirror Are Closer
than They Appear

2020 was an eventful year for US criminal justice. Two happenings were especially consequential. Most directly related to criminal justice was Minneapolis Police Department officer Derek Chauvin's murder of George Floyd on May 25, 2020. More broadly, the COVID-19 pandemic massively disrupted social life, with specific implications for criminal justice, driving, and public safety. The ramifications of the Floyd murder and COVID-19 illustrate how key events can change the problems that governments face, bring new attention to long-standing issues, and create the potential for structural reforms. At the same time, the observable outcomes in both cases demonstrate the intractability of certain patterns of social behavior and the enormous difficulty of fundamentally reorganizing deeply entrenched institutional arrangements.

The Floyd murder increased awareness of the Movement for Black Lives and spurred protests against racism in the criminal legal system and police violence. In connection with this book's focus, some of these demonstrations intentionally blocked traffic on roadways. Recognizing automobiles' importance to basic social functioning, organizers impeded traffic flow as a tactic to demonstrate the seriousness of their convictions and elevate the cause of criminal justice reform.

Yet, this push for change also engendered backlash from opponents. Police forces across the country responded to protests militaristically, using violence and mass arrests. Failures in police preparedness, training, and communication often escalated situations, rather than defusing tensions.[1] In many jurisdictions the backlash to protests included legislation intended to undermine public demonstrations. Numerous state legislatures passed laws broadening police power in dealing with demonstrations, as well as strengthening existing penalties and introducing new penalties for protest-related activities.[2] Some of these new statutes specifically targeted protest activity involving traffic obstruction. Moreover, Republican lawmakers in Florida, Iowa, and Oklahoma passed measures protecting motorists who strike protestors with their vehicles from legal liability.[3]

In a sense, these developments recall early twentieth-century contestation over who was authorized to use the streets and in what ways. When protesters impeded automobile traffic to try to advance their agenda, countervailing forces responded in turn. Cracking down on street protests reaffirmed motorists' century-old legal prerogative among street users. Extending legal indemnity to drivers who hit protestors constitutes an especially stark statement from lawmakers about which activities on streets are valued and which are not. As in many aspects of American criminal justice, consequential action in this domain played out on streets and highways. Cars and drivers served as pivotal figures in both embodied, ground-level action and the surrounding legal and political discourse.

In certain quarters of that legal and political discourse, "defund the police" became a rallying cry. Some activists' goals for defunding included the elimination of existing law enforcement agencies and their replacement with alternative agencies employing different tools to address problems and support communities. For many others, "defund" did not mean abolishing police altogether, but rather reconsidering levels of investment in police departments relative to other public-facing agencies. This notion also connects to themes discussed in this book. Police departments evolved as generalists, tasked with responding to a wide array of problems and situations. The assignment of traffic duty to police was a particularly notable development, and one that fundamentally shaped US policing and police departments in the twentieth and twenty-first centuries. Many of those interested in the prospect of defunding police imagine a reconfiguration of public services that would move police departments in the direction of specialists focused on violent crime and other serious offenses, while shifting responsibility for other types of issues to different officials. Advocates argue that this sort of transition would reduce conflicts and violent incidents between citizens and police. In theory, a move toward specialized police departments focused on serious crime might also bolster clearance rates for these offenses. Effects in both categories could help improve police-community relations battered by decades of antagonism. Notably, some calls for reconsidering police departments' role in governance focused specifically on traffic enforcement, arguing that shifting traffic responsibilities away from police would do a great deal to reduce racial disparities and incidents of police violence.[4]

Despite the phrase's prominence in public discourse, however, a major transition toward defunding the police and shifting budgetary resources to service-oriented agencies never materialized. Initially, several cities did move money around in their budgets, but a year later many had largely returned to their old funding status quo.[5] At the federal level, the Biden administration has committed to major increases in law enforcement spending, with the express purpose of getting more officers on the street.[6] Yet, although the budget-focused aspect of the recent criminal justice reform movement did not come to realization, jurisdictions across the country have demonstrated some willingness to consider reforms aimed at ameliorating problems in policing. Such reforms include deploying nonpolice personnel as first responders to certain types of 911 calls and embedding mental health professionals and trained social workers in police departments.[7]

George Floyd's murder and the associated demonstrations and activism focused specifically on the criminal justice system, with noteworthy implications for public perceptions of criminal justice and some consequences for the system itself. Of course, 2020 also saw the onset of the COVID-19 pandemic, a more broadly disruptive and impactful event. The pandemic's many significant effects included several in the domains of driving, public safety, and criminal justice.

As quarantining and remote work peaked in 2020, Americans traveled more than 430 billion vehicle miles fewer than they had in 2019, a reduction of over 13%.[8] Despite this decreased driving, however, the National Highway Traffic Safety Administration (NHTSA) reported that traffic fatalities *increased* more than 7.5% over the same period, from 36,096 in 2019 to 38,824 in 2020.[9] Early 2021 estimates indicate an even bigger spike: a 10.5% increase to 42,195 deaths, the largest annual percentage increase that the NHTSA has recorded since they began keeping these statistics.[10] The overall increases include greater numbers of deaths across a variety of crash types and contexts. Pedestrian fatalities in motor vehicle collisions saw among the largest percentage increases, growing 17% between the first half of 2020 and the first half of 2021.[11] The NHTSA largely attributes the increased fatalities to increases in dangerous—and illegal—driving behaviors, including speeding, driving while intoxicated, and not wearing seatbelts.[12]

COVID's effects reached other areas of crime and criminal justice as well. According to police statistics, key categories of violent crime increased significantly in 2020 relative to 2019. A study of thirty-four cities found a 30% increase in homicide rates, an 8% increase in firearm assaults, and a 6% increase in aggravated assaults.[13] Official rates of domestic violence increased by just over 8% in the wake of stay-at-home orders.[14] Conversely, most categories of property crimes fell between 2019 and 2020, including a 16% reduction in larceny rates and a 24% reduction in residential burglary rates, but motor vehicle theft rates increased by 13%.[15] Robberies (thefts involving force or its threat) dropped over 9% in 2020 compared with 2019.[16] Recorded drug offenses, meanwhile, fell by the same 30% that homicides increased.[17]

These trends indicate how events that disrupt daily life can shape both patterns of criminal behavior and law enforcement activities. Notably, opportunities for residential burglaries decrease when more people are at home, and crimes such as robbery and larceny, which often target businesses, are harder to commit when many businesses are closed.[18] Conversely, the economic and psychological strain that the pandemic inflicted appeared to drive spikes in violence. In domestic contexts, these factors combined with stay-at-home orders may have created circumstances conducive to violent victimization; more neighbors at home may also have contributed to increased reporting of domestic violence incidents.[19] Drug offenses are typically victimless crimes that come to authorities' attention through law enforcement activities. Stay-at-home orders may have curtailed opportunities for the street-level drug transactions that are particularly susceptible to police detection. The stark decrease in recorded drug crimes, though, likely also reflects changes in police activities and priorities during this period.[20]

Broadly speaking, the observed effects of the COVID-19 pandemic on crime statistics show how crisis situations can affect people's behavior. These trends also illustrate how important law enforcement priorities and practices are for our understanding of crime's occurrence, especially when it comes to things such as drug offenses. Some of the observed effects relate closely to the auto-centric character of our society and criminal justice system. Reduced rates of driving may have created more opportunities for motor vehicle theft, which spiked in 2020. Even though fewer cars were on the road, vehicular fatalities increased, apparently reflecting increases in risky and illegal behavior behind the wheel. As government orders, employer closures, and concerns about spreading or contracting COVID-19 kept more people at home, domestic violence reports increased as well; to some degree, this trend likely reflects how restrictions on personal movement created conditions conducive to victimization and limited potential victims' ability to remove themselves from these situations.

Freedom of mobility was the automobile's greatest initial appeal, and in most parts of the contemporary United States freedom of mobility depends on access to a car. Public policy decisions, private sector activities, and the interrelationship between business interests and governmental action have made the United States into a uniquely automobile-dependent place. Cars' centrality to daily life has also lent them outsized importance in American law enforcement. Much of what we recognize as modern criminal justice institutions—indeed, much of what we recognize as modern American society—developed from the advent of automobility. Today, the organization of daily life and our primary mechanisms of formal social control revolve around cars. As the chapters above describe, examining the criminal justice system from the car-window perspective facilitates insights into how the criminal law and law enforcement organizations change, both gradually and slowly. Car-related contexts also offer revealing examples of discretion's crucial role in the administration of criminal justice, how governments allocate legal privileges and legal accountability, and the penalties that governments impose for legal violations. The prominence of vehicle stops, vehicle searches and seizures, and surveillance of vehicular travel highlight key debates related to privacy, due process protections, and criminal justice activities as sources of revenue generation. In concert with these considerations, the marked inequalities that characterize the past and present of autocentric US criminal justice raise crucial questions about discrimination and fairness.

The long-term impact of current dynamics in American criminal justice remains to be seen. The possibility of significant changes to policing features prominently in imagining how criminal justice might look different in years to come. Crime and policing are resurgent in popular and political discourse. Heightened awareness of racial inequalities in criminal justice contact and allegations of police brutality spurred many to call for reform. These calls, however, met with resistance. Post-2020 crime rate increases and associated media coverage further undermined enthusiasm for shifting resources away from conventional policing and toward alternative interventions. At this juncture, incremental changes to police organizations and practices in specific jurisdictions seem more probable than fundamental reconfigurations of law enforcement and punishment systems.

As noted above, some recent calls for police reform have proposed removing traffic duty from conventional police departments' list of responsibilities. Relocating traffic duty to other officials or to automated enforcement systems could help address the problems with vehicle patrol that Wilson and Kelling identified in their influential 1982 article on broken windows theory.[21] The theory itself appears to be fundamentally flawed, and the way it was implemented in jurisdictions throughout the country did profound damage to communities and their relationships with police. Nevertheless, the authors may have had a point

in contending that car-based policing does no favors for police-community relations. Beyond the alienation from the public that Wilson and Kelling highlighted, vehicle stops have emerged as prominent sites where racial inequities
manifest and instances of police violence occur. New technological capacities
and greater awareness of the problems with vehicle stops could open doors to
significant changes in this area of enforcement. As yet, though, only the few
jurisdictions that have most aggressively embraced automated traffic enforcement show significant momentum toward implementing such changes. Moreover, the controversies surrounding automated enforcement programs could
imperil their prospects for widespread adoption.

The future of American incarceration is also unclear. Mass incarceration
is the defining feature of US criminal justice in the late twentieth and early
twenty-first centuries. As many readers are likely aware, for decades the United
States has enjoyed the dubious distinction of leading the globe in both the rate
at which it incarcerates its citizens and the raw number of people it incarcerates. In recent years, however, incarceration rates have leveled off, and even
declined somewhat (although US incarceration rates remain far above our international counterparts' and our own historical norms). Court orders requiring corrections systems to reduce overcrowding explain some of the decline.
There is also growing sensitivity to incarceration's high fiscal costs, especially
as health care expenses increase for an aging prison population. So-called
"smart on crime" policy initiatives emphasize the potential for budgetary savings in limiting the use of incarceration for people deemed low public safety
risks.

Here too, recent events are relevant. COVID-19 had pronounced implications for incarcerated people. Like other communicable illnesses, the virus
spreads easily among confined populations. COVID-19 infections and associated deaths hit incarcerated people much harder than their free-world counterparts.[22] These infections, of course, also implicate correctional staff; many
corrections employees also contracted the virus and served as vectors between
incarcerated populations and free-world populations. Better understandings
of jails' and prisons' implications for public health—as well as public budgets—
suggest the potential for further steps toward reining in the US criminal justice
system's incarceration numbers. Bringing the United States close to international norms or its own historic incarceration rates, though, would require a
major realignment of criminal justice priorities and sentencing practices. At
present, there is limited evidence to indicate that such a shift is in the offing.

In the area of surveillance, the ongoing evolution and proliferation of technology all but guarantee continued increases in legal authorities' ability to
monitor the population and document their activities. This includes all the

ways of tracking driving behavior and vehicle movements described in this book. It also includes the continued development and implementation of other tools, such as facial recognition technology, algorithm-driven predictive policing, and wide-net methods of monitoring online activities. Partnerships with private companies further expand criminal justice agencies' information-gathering power. Amazon, for instance, provides over 2,000 police departments access to footage from the company's Ring video doorbells; in the first half of 2022, the company gave such footage to police without owners' consent at least eleven times.[23]

Constitutional protections, especially the Fourth Amendment, are the primary bulwark against government surveillance. These protections' realization depends on the courts. Over the decades, the US Supreme Court has often leaned toward deference to law enforcement, including on surveillance issues. In several key decisions, however, the Court has also demonstrated willingness to limit authorities' power to gather certain types of information without a warrant. Relatively recent rulings such as *Jones* (2012) and *Carpenter* (2018) exemplify such willingness. Especially given the subsequent changes in the Court's personnel, it is uncertain how similar cases will fare in terms to come. Regardless, the reactive nature of lawsuits alleging constitutional violations and the prolonged nature of such litigation mean that the courts are always playing catch-up when it comes to constitutionally questionable surveillance practices. This phenomenon is likely to worsen as the pace of technological innovation accelerates.

Technological innovation is also what originally set us on the course to our autocentric society and criminal justice system. The automobile's rise to predominance engendered sweeping changes to our law, our government, our economy, and our daily lives. Quite literally, cars got us to where we are.

Here too, there is the potential for change. The exigent circumstances of the COVID-19 pandemic spurred new thinking about the possibility of remote work in many occupations. Even after formal restrictions on in-person work relaxed, many organizations continued to permit—or require—employees to work remotely part- or full-time, reducing commuting's place in many people's daily routines. Better public transit systems, improved cycling infrastructure, and an embrace of higher-density housing can all help reduce the country's dependence on cars. Easing congestion through these measures could, in turn, reduce cars' prominence as a public safety issue and traffic duty's prominence as a component of the criminal justice system. Such trends might precipitate adjustments to law enforcement priorities and reallocations of criminal justice resources, but fundamental alterations to the car-centered system do not appear to be imminent.

Automobiles opened new frontiers of mobility, independence, and personal freedom. Automobility also had sweeping consequences for public health, equality of opportunity, and the environment. The story of modern American criminal justice is also in large part a story of the car. The criminal law and criminal justice institutions evolved in response to automobility's profound impact on society. In turn, many of the key issues and controversies that characterize American criminal justice manifest in how the system handles cars and drivers. Internal combustion is slowly giving way to electric power, and autonomous vehicle technology may someday take at least some driving responsibilities out of human hands. The deep interconnection between cars and criminal justice, however, doesn't seem to be going anywhere.

ACKNOWLEDGMENTS

This book grew out of a criminal justice course I designed at Purdue University. Thanks to Shawn Bauldry for suggesting the idea of turning the class into a book. I am indebted to David McElhattan and Shaun Ossei-Owusu for feedback on Chapters 9 and 10, respectively. Marcela Maxfield and the rest of the team at Stanford University Press managed the publication process expertly, including the recruitment of two exceptional anonymous reviewers. I am also grateful to these reviewers, whose comments helped me strengthen the manuscript considerably. Allison McKay read both the book proposal and the complete manuscript and offered suggestions on clarity and flow, while also encouraging me to stay on track and focused throughout the writing process. She is the motor that made the whole thing go.

NOTES

Introduction

1. McKenzie (2015).
2. See Flink (1988) and Heitmann (2018).
3. Shill (2020, 502).
4. Calder (1999); Farber (2002); Olney (1989, 1991); Reyes and Headworth (2022).
5. See Caro (1974).
6. Jackson (1985).
7. Shill (2020).
8. *Merriam-Webster, s.v.* automobility, https://www.merriam-webster.com/dictionary/automobility (2021).
9. Burnham (1961); Seiler (2008, 4–5); Wells (2012, 300).
10. Sheller and Urry (2000); Urry (2000; 2004).
11. Seiler (2008, 5).
12. Manning (2003, 109).
13. Cressey (1974).
14. Baumgartner et al. (2018); Epp et al. (2014).
15. See Seo (2019).
16. Epp et al. (2014).
17. See Lipsky (2010).
18. See Clemens et al. (2014, 4).
19. Thanks to an anonymous reviewer for suggesting this phrasing.

Chapter 1

1. Flink (1988, 22).
2. Flink (1988, 23).
3. Frank's victory, albeit historic, was as the first of two finishers from among six entrants (Elias 1995, 17).

4. Flink (1988, 25).

5. Seiler (2008, 36).

6. Seo (2019, 76).

7. Heitmann (2018, 76).

8. Wells (2012, 13, 18).

9. Heitmann (2018, 77).

10. Wells (2012).

11. American Automobile Association (2021).

12. Holmes (1901, 319).

13. Heitmann (2018, 77).

14. Holmes (1901, 319).

15. Holmes (1901, 326).

16. Lichtenstein (1993; 1996); Mancini (1996).

17. C. H. Davis (1914, 242).

18. McAfee (1990); Wilmot (1914).

19. Kling (2013). See also Cronon (1991).

20. Norton (2008, 135).

21. Kling (2013).

22. Norton (2007).

23. Wells (2012).

24. Norton (2007).

25. Seo (2019, 22).

26. Seo (2019, 22).

27. Norton (2008, 27).

28. Norton (2008, 44).

29. Norton (2007, 337).

30. Norton (2007).

31. Norton (2007, 342).

32. Norton (2007, 352–53).

33. Simpson (2021).

34. Shill (2020).

35. A. Schmitt (2020, 66).

36. A. Schmitt (2020, 67).

37. Norton (2008, 49).

38. Norton (2008, 48).

39. Wells (2012, 13–15).

40. Seo (2019, 23).

41. Norton (2008, 52).

42. Michigan Department of Transportation (2015); Norton (2008, 52).

43. Norton (2008, 54).

44. Norton (2008, 59–60).

45. Norton (2008, 49)

46. Norton (2008, 54).

47. Heitmann and Morales (2014, 13).

48. Post (2006, 125).

49. Mandel (1924, 192–93).

50. Heitmann and Morales (2014, 13).

51. Jenkins and Butterworth (2019); Wagner (2021).

52. Finley and Drew (2021).

53. Heitmann and Morales (2014, 7).

54. Heitmann and Morales (2014).

55. Heitmann and Morales (2014).

56. Heitmann and Morales (2014, 12).

57. Ford (2005).

58. Hegman (1972).

59. Heitmann and Morales (2014,14).

60. See Kagan (2001).

61. Heitmann and Morales (2014).

62. Heitmann and Morales (2014, 10).

63. Heitmann and Morales (2014, 10).

64. Heitmann and Morales (2014, 10).

65. Heitmann and Morales (2014, 10).

66. Heitmann and Morales (2014, 11).

67. Heitmann and Morales (2014, 11).

68. Heitmann and Morales (2014, 25).

69. Heitmann and Morales (2014, 26).

70. Heitmann and Morales (2014, 22).

71. Heitmann and Morales (2014, 22).

72. Although the Dyer Act was a government intervention, the insurance companies that had led early efforts to control auto theft played a significant role here as well: They influenced the drafting of the bill, lobbied for Congress to pass it, and pushed for strenuous enforcement after it became law (Heitmann and Morales 2014, 22–23).

73. Federal Bureau of Investigation (2019).

74. Federal Bureau of Investigation (2019).

75. Federal Bureau of Investigation (2019); Langum (1994).

76. Federal Bureau of Investigation (2019).

77. A. Martin (2020).

78. Federal Bureau of Investigation (2019); A. Martin (2020).

79. Henry Ford Museum, Clyde Barrow to Henry Ford Praising the Ford V-8 Car, April 10, 1934, https://www.thehenryford.org/collections-and-research/digital-collections/artifact/281082/#slide=gs-211855.

80. Federal Bureau of Investigation (2021).

81. Heitmann and Morales (2014, 31).

82. Federal Bureau of Investigation (2019).

83. Vehicle Identification Number Requirements, 73 Fed. Reg. (April 30, 2008), 23368.

84. Vehicle Identification Number Requirements, 23,368.

85. Vehicle Identification Number Requirements, 23,368.

86. Vehicle Identification Number Requirements, 23,368.

87. Federal Motor Vehicle Theft Prevention Standard, 67 Fed. Reg. (June 26, 2002), 43076.

88. US Department of Justice (2020).

89. US Department of Justice (2020).

90. National Auto Auction Association (2017).

91. National Auto Auction Association (2017).

92. National Auto Auction Association (2017).

93. Federal Bureau of Investigation (2019).

94. Cressey (1974, 213).

95. See Seo (2019).

Chapter 2

1. Manning (2003, 109).

2. McShane (1994, 22).

3. Go (2020, 1196).

4. Go (2020); Seo (2019).

5. Oliver (2017).

6. Oliver (2017, 162); Seo (2019, 64).

7. Seo (2019, 64).

8. Go (2020).

9. Seo (2019, 107).

10. Oliver (2017, 234–36).

11. See Oliver (2017, 216, 249).

12. Seo (2019, 68).

13. *United States v. Scheffer*, 303.

14. Oliver (2017, 162).

15. Oliver (2017, 148).

16. M. Weber (1978, 8).

17. Douglass (2016); M. Weber (2003).

18. For an overview of Weber's analysis of bureaucracy, see M. Weber (1978, 956–1005).

19. *Merriam-Webster, s.v.* nepotism, https://www.merriam-webster.com/dictionary/automobility (2021).

20. Seo (2019, 68).

21. Oliver (2017).

22. Seo (2019, 72).

23. Oliver (2017, 219).

24. Oliver (2017, 157); Seo (2019, 72–73).

25. See Epp et al. (2014).

26. Seo (2019, 110).

27. Seo (2019, 87).

28. Seo (2019, 112).

29. See Seo (2019, ch. 2).

30. Cressey (1974).

31. Seo (2019, 82).

32. Seo (2019, 84).

33. Oliver (2017, 177). Berkeley was not the first place where police used bicycles; the New York Police Department had experimented with bicycle patrol as early as 1885. Before implementing the department-wide policy in Berkeley, Vollmer himself tested the technology by conducting his own patrol on a bicycle. Mockery of his trial run from the public and local media did not dissuade him from the idea (Oliver 2017, 177).

34. Seo (2019, 68).

35. Oliver (2017, 260).

36. Seo (2019, 108).

37. Seo (2019, 108–9).

38. Leonard (1938, 1–2).

39. Leonard (1938, 2–3).

40. Leonard (1938, 2).

41. Leonard (1938, ch. 1).

42. Leonard (1938, ch. 1).

43. Seo (2019, 66).

44. Leonard (1938, ch. 1).

45. Leonard (1938, 22).

46. Poli (1942, 194).

47. Leonard (1938, 35).

48. Poli (1942, 195).

49. Van Wagenen (2017).

50. Poli (1942, 194).

51. Dobson (2001); Manning (1992, 25).

52. Seo (2019, 98–99).

53. Manning (1988). See also Lipsky (2010) and Maynard-Moody and Musheno (2003).

Chapter 3

1. Levine and Reinarman (1991, 462).

2. M. A. Lerner (2007, ch. 4).

3. Levine and Reinarman (1991, 462).

4. Levine and Reinarman (1991, 463).

5. Levine and Reinarman (1991, 463).

6. M. A. Lerner (2007, 30–33).

7. National Commission on Law Observance and Enforcement (1931, 9–10).

8. See Nelson (1995).

9. M. A. Lerner (2007, ch. 2).

10. M. A. Lerner (2007, ch. 2).

11. Levine and Reinarman (1991).

12. M. A. Lerner (2007, 271).

13. Demleitner (1994).

14. Levine and Reinarman (1991, 466–67).

15. Levine and Reinarman (1991, 467).

16. Levine and Reinarman (1991, 467).

17. M. A. Lerner (2007, 121).

18. M. A. Lerner (2007, ch. 3).

19. Nelson (1995, ch. 10).

20. Leff and Leff (1981).

21. Billock (2017).

22. Post (2006, 139).

23. Seo (2019).

24. Flink (1988).

25. Seo (2019).

26. It also appears that suspects on horseback could often escape from any intended search; legal historian Sarah Seo notes that "there are no reported cases involving a search of a horse-riding suspect" (Seo 2019, 117).

27. Seo (2019, 136).

28. Quoted in Seo (2019, 137–38); emphasis in original.

29. Seo (2019, 138–39).

30. Quoted in Seo (2019, 124).

31. Post (2006).

32. Sommers and Bohns (2019, 1966).

33. Seo (2013, 1034–35).

34. "'A Noble Experiment' Held Distorted Phrase," *New York Times*, October 21, 1964.

35. Post (2006, 12).

36. M. J. Barker (2014).

37. M. A. Lerner (2007, 87–90).

38. M. A. Lerner (2007).

39. Albanese (2014).

40. Post (2006).

41. Seo (2019, 138–39).

42. See Sommers and Bohns (2019) and Tyler (2006).

Chapter 4

1. Feldman (2001).

2. Farber (2002, 63).

3. T. Lewis (1997, 31).

4. In the mid-1920s, Sloan argued, the "mass-class" market appeared, with a more diverse range of models offering cheaper options for less well-off buyers and more expensive models for the better resourced. This was fundamental to Sloan's vision for how General Motors could outcompete Ford, epitomized by GM advertising promoting "a car for every purse and purpose" (Farber 2002, 63–64).

5. Calder (1999, 186).

6. Calder (1999, 186).

7. Calder (1999, 203).

8. Sorin (2020).

9. Sorin (2020).

10. Sorin (2020, ch. 3).

11. Sorin (2020).

12. Archer (2020, 1263–64).

13. Archer (2020, 1263); Sorin (2020).

14. Scharff (1991). See also Ridgeway (2011).

15. Scharff (1991, ch. 1).

16. Scharff (1991).

17. Scharff (1991).

18. Seiler (2008, 61–62).

19. Scharff (1991, 85).

20. Scharff (1991); Seiler (2008, ch. 2).

21. Norton (2008).

22. Norton (2008, 31).

23. Barber (1931, 14).

24. Federal Highway Administration (1997).

25. Baker (1958, 54).

26. Federal Highway Administration (1997).

27. Federal Highway Administration (1997).

28. Federal Highway Administration (1997).

29. Federal Highway Administration (1997).

30. Barber (1931).

31. Barber (1931, 14).

32. Rule et al. (1983).

33. Rule et al. (1983, 224).

34. Rule et al. (1983, 225).

35. Rule et al. (1983, 225).

36. Adair (2019).

37. See Baker (1958, 54).

38. Adair (2019, 575).

39. Seiler (2008, 109).

40. Adair (2019, 581).

41. Adair (2019, 582–83).

42. Adair (2019); Federal Highway Administration (1997).

43. Adair (2019, 571).

44. Adair (2019).

45. McShane (1994, 158).

46. McShane (1994, ch. 8); Scharff (1991); Seiler (2008, ch. 2).

47. Moss (1924, 67).

48. Adair (2019, 580).

49. McShane (1994, 158); Scharff (1991).

50. Flink (1988, 163).

51. Flink (1988, 159).

52. Flink (1988, 160–62).

53. McLuhan (1966, 194).

54. Heitmann and Morales (2014, 23).

55. Heitmann and Morales (2014, 25).

56. Heitmann and Morales (2014, 26).

57. Reich (1964, 740).

58. Hamilton (2014, 1032–33).

59. Hamilton (2014, 1033).

60. Hamilton (2014, 1033).

61. National Conference on Street and Highway Safety (1924, 5). Strikingly similar language continues to characterize federal officials' statements on these issues; for instance, in September 2021 US National Transportation Safety Board chair Jennifer Homendy remarked to the Governors Highway Safety Association conference that "the carnage on our roads has to stop. You know it, and I know it" (Krisher 2021). In 2020 vehicle miles traveled decreased by over 430 billion compared with 2019 due to the COVID-19 pandemic (National Highway Traffic Safety Administration 2021). Road deaths, however, increased substantially; the NHTSA recorded 38,824 road deaths in 2020—the highest total since 2007—and the National Safety Council estimated that 42,060 people died in motor vehicle crashes in 2020, with the 24% increase between 2019 and 2020 the largest in almost a century (Domonoske 2021; National Highway Traffic Safety Administration 2021, 2022).

62. National Conference on Street and Highway Safety (1924, 5).

63. National Conference on Street and Highway Safety (1924, 17).

64. National Conference on Street and Highway Safety (1926, 47).

65. National Conference on Street and Highway Safety (1926, 60).

66. Baker (1958); Hamilton (2014, 1033–34).

67. Hamilton (2014, 1034).

68. Bartlett (1949).

69. Bartlett (1949).

70. See, for example, Kearney (1948).

71. Bartlett (1949).

72. Bartlett (1949).

73. Hamilton (2014, 1036).

74. Hamilton (2014, 1036).

75. Hamilton (2014, 1036).

76. Hamilton (2014, 1036–37).

77. Hamilton (2014, 1037–38).

78. Centers for Disease Control and Prevention (2016).

79. Bock and McGrath (2011).

80. Centers for Disease Control and Prevention (2016).

81. Ferdinand (1989); S. J. Fox (1970).

82. Ferdinand (1989); S. J. Fox (1970).

83. Ferdinand (1989); S. J. Fox (1970).

84. Tanenhaus (2004).

85. Zimring (2005, 5–6).

86. Quoted in Whitlatch (1967, 1240).

87. Tanenhaus (2004).

88. Tanenhaus (2004).

89. Tanenhaus (2004).
90. Zimring (2005).
91. Pagnanelli (2007).
92. Zimring (2005, 54–55).
93. Myers (2006).
94. Baker (1958, 59).
95. Baker (1958, 59–60).
96. Baker (1958, 60–61).
97. Lynd and Lynd (1929, 114).

Chapter 5

1. Wells (2012, 9).
2. Jager (2004, 184).
3. Jager (2004, 182–84). See also Foucault (1979).
4. Bottles (1987, 7); Jager (2004, 86).
5. Bottles (1987, 7).
6. Jackson (1985, ch. 2).
7. Jackson (1985, ch. 2).
8. Jackson (1985, 17).
9. Jackson (1985, 25).
10. Flink (1988); Jackson (1985, 166).
11. Flink (1988, 144–47).
12. Seo (2019, 107).
13. Wells (2012). See also Shill (2020).
14. Wells (2012, xxxii).
15. T. Lewis (1997, 45).
16. T. Lewis (1997, 45).
17. See Caro (1974).
18. Kim and Hipp (2018; 2022); McCutcheon (2021); McCutcheon et al. (2016).
19. Austen (2018, 46).
20. Archer (2020; 2021); Rose and Mohl (2012).
21. Archer (2020); Darden et al. (1987); Jackson (1985); Ware (2021, 102–3); W. J. Wilson (1987).
22. Jackson (1985, 204–5).
23. T. Lewis (1997, 74).
24. T. Lewis (1997, 74).
25. T. Lewis (1997, 74).
26. Jackson (1985, 235).
27. Jackson (1985, 235).
28. Jackson (1985, 234).
29. Jackson (1985, 234–35); T. Lewis (1997, 76).
30. T. Lewis (1997, 76).
31. T. Lewis (1997, 75–76).
32. T. Lewis (1997, 77).
33. Jackson (1985, 237–38).

34. Jackson (1985, 215).
35. Massey and Denton (1993, 53).
36. T. Lewis (1997, 71).
37. Jackson (1985, ch. 13); Massey and Denton (1993); Rothstein (2017).
38. Gotham (2014).
39. Massey and Denton (1993); Rothstein (2017).
40. Jackson (1985, 208–14); Rothstein (2017, 83–84).
41. Massey and Denton (1993, 49–51).
42. Jackson (1985, 217); Massey and Denton (1993, 51–55); Ware (2021).
43. T. Lewis (1997, 78).
44. T. Lewis (1997, 78).
45. Rothstein (2017, 78).
46. Rothstein (2017, 79–81).
47. Rothstein (2017, 82).
48. Rothstein (2017, 82); Ware (2021, 96). The same year, in *Village of Euclid v. Ambler Realty Company*, the Supreme Court permitted a workaround to their decision in *Buchanan* (1917), which had prohibited explicitly racial zoning ordinances. In the 1926 ruling, the Court gave their blessing to zoning schemes that permitted only single-family houses in certain neighborhoods and barred apartment buildings. Although not explicitly racial in their language, these zoning measures were motivated by desires to exclude poorer families and families of color and were racially discriminatory in effect (Rothstein 2017, 52–53).
49. Rothstein (2017, 86).
50. Rothstein (2017, 88).
51. Ware (2021, 98).
52. Rothstein (2017, 90).
53. Rothstein (2017, 90–91).
54. Haigh (2021).
55. T. Lewis (1997, 81).
56. Litman (2011, 12).
57. T. Lewis (1997, ch. 3).
58. T. Lewis (1997, 18, 20). At this time, the Bureau of Public Roads was operated under the authority of the Department of Agriculture. The Department of Transportation Act of 1966 created the Department of Transportation as a cabinet-level department and established the Federal Highway Administration as a division within it. The newly formed division took over the Bureau of Public Roads' functions in 1967 (Association of Centers for the Study of Congress 2021).
59. T. Lewis (1997, 18).
60. Seo (2019, 179).
61. T. Lewis (1997, 104–5).
62. Heitmann (2018, 79).
63. T. Lewis (1997, 121–22).
64. J. Weber (2017).
65. T. Lewis (1997, 120–21).
66. Archer (2020; 2021).

67. Mandel (1924, 193).

68. Manning (2003, 109).

69. Seo (2019).

70. Seo (2019, 78).

71. Seo (2019, 76–77).

72. Seo (2019, 78).

73. Seo (2019, 109).

74. Seo (2019, 160).

75. Seo (2019).

76. Seo (2019, 163–64).

77. Seo (2019, 164).

78. *Brinegar v. United States*, 175.

79. *Brinegar v. United States*, 176.

80. *Brinegar v. United States*, 176.

81. Bahn (1974, 340).

82. Bahn (1974).

83. Seo (2019, 105).

84. Seo (2019, 106).

85. Seo (2019, 105).

86. J. Q. Wilson and Kelling (1982).

87. Bahn (1974).

88. Childress (2016).

89. Sampson and Raudenbush (1999, 638).

90. See, for example, Bell (2016), Harcourt (2001), Harcourt and Ludwig (2006), and Hinkle and Weisburd (2008).

91. McLuhan (1966, 200).

92. See Flink (1988) and Heitmann (2018).

93. Archer (2020, 1290; 2021, 2141–45).

94. Bottles (1987); Jackson (1985); T. Lewis (1997).

95. Gotham (2014, 1).

96. Litman (2011, 12).

97. J. Q. Wilson and Kelling (1982).

98. McKenzie (2015).

99. Kneebone and Berube (2013).

Chapter 6

1. Thanks to Brian Kelly for originally relaying this anecdote and to Warren Kelly for providing the details and granting me permission to use his story here. Warren Kelly also recalled another incident a few years later, in 1986, in which the reason he was stopped was less mysterious. Pulled over driving a 1977 Oldsmobile Cutlass, the officer approached his window and asked, "Do you know how fast you were going?" "Sixty-five?" Warren ventured. "Ninety-four," the officer corrected.

2. Lipsky (2010, xi).

3. Headworth (2021); Lipsky (2010); Maynard-Moody and Musheno (2003); Moskos (2008); Riccucci (2005); Watkins-Hayes (2009).

4. Moskos (2008, 112–13).

5. National Emergency Number Association (2021).

6. See, for example, Broadhead and Rist (1976), Headworth and Ríos (2021), and Rivera (2015).

7. Lipsky (2010). See also Headworth and Ríos (2021).

8. Gilsinan (1989, 339).

9. K. Tracy and Tracy (1998); S. Tracy and Tracy (1998).

10. Manning (1988, 21–22).

11. Coleman (2016); "Hialeah Police Investigating Death of Man Shot with Taser After Alleged Dog Beatings," NBC Miami, March 4, 2014, https://www.nbcmiami .com/news/local/hialeah-police-investigating-death-of-man-shot-with-taser -after-alleged-dog-beatings/73478/.

12. Dupnack (2019); Hunter (2019).

13. Hunter (2019).

14. Dupnack (2019).

15. Hunter (2019).

16. National Emergency Number Association (2021).

17. Paoletti (2012); Sanders (2006).

18. See, for example, Baldeck (2021).

19. Baumgartner et al. (2017); Epp et al. (2014); Ferrandino (2015); A. Gelman et al. (2007); Levchak (2021); Rojek et al. (2012). For more on police stops, see the Stanford Open Policing Project (https://openpolicing.stanford.edu/).

20. Ferrandino (2015); Kohler-Hausmann (2018, 51–52); Shoub et al. (2020); Stevenson and Mayson (2018, 759).

21. Kohler-Hausmann (2018, 53); A. Gelman et al. (2007).

22. Lundman and Myers (2012); Magee et al. (2020); Petersen (2017); Puckett and Lundman (2003).

23. Litwin and Xu (2007); Magee et al. (2020); Xu (2008).

24. See, for example, LoFaso (2020), Ousey and Lee (2010), and Roberts (2007).

25. See Bell (2016) and Campeau et al. (2021).

26. Lerman and Weaver (2014); R. J. Miller and Stuart (2017).

27. Seo (2019, 90–91).

28. Quoted in Seo (2019, 93).

29. Seo (2019, 92).

30. See also Seo (2019, 82).

31. Cressey (1974).

32. Baumgartner et al. (2021, 864).

33. Baumgartner et al. (2018, 5).

34. Baumgartner et al. (2018); Bejarano (2001); Epp et al. (2014); Gaines (2004); Lundman and Kaufman (2003); Missouri Attorney General's Office (2021); Pierson et al. (2020).

35. Engel (2005); Lundman and Kaufman (2003).

36. Engel and Calnon (2004, 71); W. R. Smith et al. (2003).

37. Chenane et al. (2020).

38. Epp et al. (2014).

39. Epp et al. (2014, 6–7).

40. Baumgartner et al. (2018, 8).

41. Epp et al. (2014, 7).

42. Epp et al. (2014).

43. Epp et al. (2014, 7).

44. Quoted in Baumgartner et al. (2017, 25–26).

45. Epp et al. (2014).

46. Baumgartner et al. (2017, 26).

47. Epp et al. (2014, 64).

48. Epp et al. (2014).

49. Epp et al. (2014, ch. 7).

50. Epp et al. (2014, xv).

51. Baumgartner et al. (2018); Epp et al. (2014); Policing Project (2018).

52. Seo (2019, 266).

53. R. Martin et al. (2020); VanSickle and Stephens (2020).

54. On the "many hands of the state," see Morgan and Orloff (2017).

55. See also Headworth (2019) and Headworth and Ríos (2021).

56. Epp et al. (2014).

Chapter 7

1. Examples of studies foregrounding state-level phenomena include V. Barker (2009), Lynch (2009), Page (2011), and Perkinson (2010).

2. Quoted in Divine (2020, 165).

3. Divine (2020, 165); L. L. Miller (2008, 30–31).

4. Divine (2020, 165).

5. Bhagat (2011); L. L. Miller (2008, 31).

6. Divine (2020, 166).

7. Divine (2020, 166–67). See also L. L. Miller (2008, 35).

8. Federal Bureau of Investigation (2020); Rubin (1934, 497).

9. L. L. Miller and Eisenstein (2005, 244).

10. B. H. Lerner (2011, 60).

11. L. L. Miller and Eisenstein (2005, 242).

12. L. L. Miller and Eisenstein (2005, 242).

13. Divine (2020, 167).

14. Barkow (2011, 524).

15. Divine (2020, 167).

16. Slobogin (2020, 944), citing Menell and Vacca (2020).

17. United States Courts (2019; 2020).

18. Federal Bureau of Prisons (2021).

19. Sawyer and Wagner (2019); Sentencing Project (2020).

20. L. L. Miller and Eisenstein (2005).

21. See Lynch (2018).

22. L. L. Miller and Eisenstein (2005).

23. L. L. Miller and Eisenstein (2005, 248).

24. Sawyer and Wagner (2020).

25. As of December 2022, the Biden administration is considering the rescheduling of cannabis.

26. United States Attorney's Office for the District of New Hampshire (2020).

27. G. R. Schmitt and Russell (2021, 14); Taxy et al. (2015).

28. G. R. Schmitt and Russell (2021, 14).

29. See, for example, Quinones (2015).

30. Barkow (2011, 525).

31. Lynch (2016; 2018).

32. United States Attorney's Office for the District of New Hampshire (2020).

33. Lynch (2018).

34. Lynch (2018). See, in general, Merton (1948).

35. Mandel (1924, 193).

36. See, in general, T. Lewis (1997) and Swift (2011).

37. Heitmann and Morales (2014, 22).

38. Langum (1994, ch. 2).

39. Langum (1994, 27).

40. Langum (1994, ch. 2).

41. Langum (1994, 43).

42. Langum (1994, 43).

43. Langum (1994, 44).

44. Langum (1994, 45–46).

45. Langum (1994, 46).

46. Langum (1994, 49).

47. Langum (1994, 49).

48. Langum (1994, 111).

49. Langum (1994, 113).

50. Langum (1994, 169–71).

51. Langum (1994, 180).

52. Langum (1994, 185).

53. Langum (1994).

54. United Nations Office on Drugs and Crime (2021).

55. A. Farrell et al. (2019, 650).

56. A. Farrell et al. (2019, 650).

57. A. Farrell et al. (2019, 650).

58. See Connell et al. (2018), Diaz et al. (2022), Mletzko et al. (2018), and A. Wilson (2013).

59. US Department of Transportation (2021).

60. A. Farrell et al. (2019, 652).

61. A. Farrell et al. (2019, 652).

62. A. Farrell et al. (2019, 652).

63. A. Farrell et al. (2019, 661).

64. A. Farrell et al. (2019).

65. A. Farrell et al. (2019).

66. A. Farrell et al. (2019).

67. A. Farrell et al. (2019, 662).

68. A. Farrell et al. (2019, 659).

69. See Blunt and Wolf (2020), Chamberlain (2019), and Tripp (2019).

70. See Langum (1994, 130–31).

71. L. L. Miller and Eisenstein (2005); S. F. Smith (2019).

Chapter 8

1. Gusfield (1984, 1).

2. Bureau of Transportation Statistics (2021).

3. Bureau of Transportation Statistics (2021).

4. National Safety Council (2021). There is also reason to believe that official statistics significantly undercount traffic collisions that cause injuries. See Kaufman (2018).

5. National Highway Traffic Safety Administration (2021).

6. Fell et al. (2009, 64); B. H. Lerner (2011, 3).

7. Fell et al. (2009, 63).

8. "Motoring Laws and Their Enforcement," *Automobile Journal* 34(11) (1912): 137.

9. "Motoring Laws and Their Enforcement," 136; B. H. Lerner (2011, 17–18).

10. "Motoring Laws and Their Enforcement," 137.

11. B. H. Lerner (2011, 18).

12. B. H. Lerner (2011, 28).

13. B. H. Lerner (2011, 28).

14. B. H. Lerner (2011, 28).

15. B. H. Lerner (2011).

16. B. H. Lerner (2011, 61).

17. B. H. Lerner (2011, 61).

18. B. H. Lerner (2011, 62).

19. B. H. Lerner (2011, 71).

20. Fell et al. (2009, 64); B. H. Lerner (2011, 71).

21. Gusfield (1984, 80–81).

22. Gusfield (1984, 79).

23. Gusfield (1984, 112).

24. Becker (1963, 147).

25. Becker (1963, 147–48).

26. Becker (1963, 147, 155).

27. Becker (1963, 156).

28. Besharov (1981, 221).

29. B. H. Lerner (2011, 64).

30. Hingson and Winter (2003, 72).

31. B. H. Lerner (2011, 72).

32. B. H. Lerner (2011, 83).

33. B. H. Lerner (2011, 77).

34. B. H. Lerner (2011, 80).

35. B. H. Lerner (2011, 78).

36. B. H. Lerner (2011, 78).

37. B. H. Lerner (2011, 79).

38. B. H. Lerner (2011, 84).

39. B. H. Lerner (2011, 85).

40. B. H. Lerner (2011, 85).

41. B. H. Lerner (2011, 87).

42. B. H. Lerner (2011, 87).

43. B. H. Lerner (2011, 88).

44. B. H. Lerner (2011, 89).

45. B. H. Lerner (2011, 90).

46. B. H. Lerner (2011, 89). All states have subsequently lowered their maximum legal BAC to 0.08%.

47. Dang (2008, 8–9).

48. Jacobs and Strossen (1985, 596). See also L. Fernandez (1986).

49. Jacobs (1988, 173).

50. Office of Juvenile Justice and Delinquency Prevention (2020).

51. Hingson and Winter (2003, 72).

52. Hingson and Winter (2003, 72).

53. Foundation for Advancing Alcohol Responsibility (2020).

54. A. J. Davis (2007).

55. Forst (2004, 115); Spohn (2018, 329).

56. Green (2019, 606–9).

57. Forst (2004, 116).

58. Spohn (2018, 325); Tonry (2011, 71–73). See also Gershman (2010, 1277–79).

59. Spohn (2018, 325–26).

60. Quoted in Forst (2004, 112).

61. A. J. Davis (2007).

62. Gershman (2010, 1260).

63. Misner (1996, 746).

64. A. J. Davis (2007, ch. 3).

65. Vogel (2007, 3).

66. Subramanian et al. (2020).

67. Quoted in Spohn (2018, 326).

68. B. H. Lerner (2011, 77–80).

69. B. H. Lerner (2011, 79).

70. McCoy et al. (2012).

71. McCoy et al. (2012).

72. Dietrich (1997); Luria (1988).

73. Bailey (1998, 249).

74. See Dietrich (1997).

75. J. Barker (1962, 795–96).

76. Luria (1988).

77. Luria (1988, 816).

78. Luria (1988, 816).

79. Gusfield (1984).

80. Dietrich (1997); Luria (1988); Mahoney (2008, 1552–53).

81. J. Barker (1962, 796).

82. J. Barker (1962, 796).

83. Nye (1986, 184).

84. J. Barker (1962, 797, 800).

85. J. Barker (1962, 802–3).

86. Millum (1990, 188).

87. Millum (1990, 189).

88. Dietrich (1997, 33).

89. White (1995, 1433–44).

90. See Millum (1990, 189).

91. Glaeser and Sacerdote (2003, 376–77).

92. Dietrich (1997, 32).

93. Luria (1988, 814).

94. Dietrich (1997, 32).

95. MADD (2018).

96. MADD (2018).

97. Mahoney (2008, 1538).

98. White (1995).

99. Chalikian (2001, 145).

100. Levin (1983); White (1995, 1452–54).

101. Freestone (2011, 243).

102. Freestone (2011, 244).

103. Freestone (2011, 244). In other ways, motorists enjoy advantageous treatment under the criminal law (Shill 2020, 576–77).

104. Bailey (1998, 249).

105. See Dietrich (1997).

106. See Dietrich (1997).

107. See Chalikian (2001).

108. See Dietrich (1997).

109. See Dietrich (1997).

110. Dietrich (1997, 32).

111. Jacobs (1988, 185).

112. Gusfield (1984).

113. B. H. Lerner (2011). See also Becker (1963).

114. Dietrich (1997).

Chapter 9

1. K. D. Martin et al. (2018).

2. Joyce et al. (2020).

3. See Jain (2016), Manza and Uggen (2008), and McElhattan (2022b).

4. Demleitner (1999, 154).

5. McElhattan (2022b); Pinard (2010); Travis (2002).

6. Logan (2013).

7. Logan (2013). See also Garland (2001) and L. L. Miller (2016).

8. Lageson (2016); Logan (2013, 1108–9); Pattillo et al. (2004).

9. Western (2006, 109).

10. D. Kirk and Wakefield (2018).

11. McElhattan (2022b).

12. Pager (2003); Stoll and Bushway (2008).

13. Pager (2007, 4–5).

14. Travis (2002, 15).

15. Travis (2002, 15–16).

16. Jain (2016).

17. Reich (1964, 741–42).

18. Shill (2020).

19. Seo (2019, 130).

20. Barber (1931, 14).

21. McElhattan (2022a).

22. McElhattan (2022a).

23. See, for example, Exotech Systems Inc. (1970).

24. McElhattan and Headworth (2022).

25. McElhattan and Headworth (2022).

26. McElhattan (2018).

27. Ewald (2012, 223), emphasis in original; Marcus (2003, 559).

28. Marcus (2003, 559).

29. Marcus (2003, 557).

30. Ulmer et al. (2001, 22–25).

31. Marcus (2003, 560).

32. McElhattan and Headworth (2022).

33. McElhattan and Headworth (2022).

34. Crozier and Garrett (2020, 1593).

35. Crozier and Garrett (2020, 1593).

36. Schwier and James (2016, 22).

37. McElhattan and Headworth (2022).

38. Schwier and James (2016, 22).

39. Marcus (2003, 557).

40. National Inventory of Collateral Consequences of Conviction (2021).

41. Schwier and James (2016, 6).

42. Crozier and Garrett (2020, 1606).

43. Marsh (2017, 21).

44. Marsh (2017, 21).

45. K. D. Martin et al. (2018, 475).

46. Marsh (2017, 21).

47. Marsh (2017, 21).

48. Marsh (2017, 21).

49. Marsh (2017, 21).

50. Federal Reserve (2019).

51. Federal Reserve (2019, 21).

52. Federal Reserve (2019, 21–22).
53. Federal Reserve (2019, 21).
54. Harris et al. (2010).
55. McElhattan and Headworth (2022).
56. Schwier and James (2016, 6).
57. Schwier and James (2016, 6).
58. See Harris et al. (2010).
59. Schwier and James (2016, 10–11).
60. Joyce et al. (2020).
61. Carnegie (2007, 2).
62. Carnegie (2007, 38).
63. McKenzie (2015).
64. See Harris et al. (2010, 1781).
65. Marsh (2017, 22).
66. Marsh (2017, 22).
67. Marsh (2017, 22).
68. Crozier and Garrett (2020, 1607).
69. Marsh (2017, 22).
70. Marsh (2017, 23).
71. Marsh (2017, 23).
72. Marsh (2017, 23).
73. Marsh (2017, 23–24).
74. Crozier and Garrett (2020, 1591).
75. Crozier and Garrett (2020, 1592).
76. Marsh (2017, 24–25).
77. Marsh (2017, 25).
78. R. Lewis (2021).
79. Marsh (2017, 25).
80. Love and Schlussel (2020, 37–38).
81. Love and Schlussel (2020, 38).
82. May (2021).
83. May (2021).
84. Indiana Senate Republicans (2021).
85. May (2021).
86. Indiana Senate Republicans (2021).
87. May (2021).
88. Indiana Senate Republicans (2021).
89. May (2021).
90. May (2021).
91. May (2021).
92. See Harris et al. (2010).
93. Fernandes et al. (2019); Marsh (2017).
94. Page and Soss (2021, 291).
95. See Pager (2007).

Chapter 10

1. See Clemens et al. (2014, 4).

2. Cassella (2018); Challener (1996).

3. Piety (1991); Stillman (2013); Worrall (2001, 174).

4. Challener (1996, 198).

5. Dery (2012, 1).

6. "More Than $100k Seized After K-9 Officer at Dallas Love Field Airport Sniffs Out Bag," CBS Dallas–Fort Worth, December 7, 2021, https://dfw.cbslocal.com/2021/12/07/100k-seized-k9-officer-dallas-love-field-airport-sniffs-bag/; Lucia (2021).

7. Worrall (2001, 171).

8. Quoted in Stillman (2013).

9. B. Kelly (2021, 620).

10. Drug Policy Alliance (2019, 1).

11. Cassella (2018, 9–10).

12. Teigen and Bragg (2018).

13. Teigen and Bragg (2018).

14. *Austin v. United States*, 613.

15. *Austin v. United States*, 613.

16. *Lisa Olivia Leonard v. Texas*, 4.

17. *Austin v. United States*, 614.

18. *Austin v. United States*, 611–12.

19. *United States v. The Cargo of the Brig Malek Adhel*, 238.

20. *United States v. The Cargo of the Brig Malek Adhel*, 233.

21. Challener (1996, 201). See also Rolland (1999). James R. Maxeiner describes "the concept of 'offending' property" as the "personification fiction," indicating similar skepticism about the notion of legal actions directed at pieces of property (Maxeiner 1977, 768).

22. Maxeiner (1977, 785–88).

23. Maxeiner (1977, 788).

24. *Dobbins' Distillery v. United States*, 401.

25. *J. W. Goldsmith, Jr.-Grant Company v. United States*, 508.

26. See Challener (1996).

27. Seo (2019, 118).

28. Seo (2019, 133).

29. Finder (1999).

30. Challener (1996, 203).

31. Seo (2019, 134).

32. Seo (2019, 134).

33. Maxeiner (1977).

34. Pimentel (2012, 12).

35. Pimentel (2012, 12).

36. Pimentel (2012, 12–13).

37. Pimentel (2012, 13).

38. Blumenson and Nilsen (1998, 55).

39. Drug Policy Alliance (2019, 1).

40. As of 2019, seven states and the District of Columbia do not use forfeiture funds for law enforcement purposes. Other states' laws direct between 50% and 100% of forfeiture proceeds to law enforcement (Drug Policy Alliance, 2019, 1).

41. Drug Policy Alliance (2019, 1).

42. Drug Policy Alliance (2019, 1).

43. Pimentel (2012, 14).

44. Challener (1996, 204).

45. Challener (1996, 204).

46. Stillman (2013).

47. Drug Policy Alliance (2019, 1).

48. Stillman (2013).

49. Stillman (2013).

50. Drug Policy Alliance (2019, 1).

51. Knepper et al. (2020).

52. Federal Bureau of Investigation (2014); Knepper et al. (2020).

53. Federal Bureau of Investigation (2015); Knepper et al. (2020).

54. Pimentel (2012, 13).

55. B. Kelly (2021, 621).

56. Finder (1999).

57. Dery (2012).

58. Pimentel (2012, 15).

59. O'Connell (2018, 238).

60. Pimentel (2012, 15).

61. Only some of the changes that CAFRA brought about are listed here. For more comprehensive accounts, see Cassella (2001) and Pimentel (2012).

62. Cassella (2001, 108); Pimentel (2012, 15).

63. Cassella (2001, 106–7); Pimentel (2012, 18).

64. Pimentel (2012, 20).

65. Cassella (2001, 114–15).

66. Cassella (2001, 116).

67. Cassella (2001, 116).

68. Crepelle (2017, 331); Pimentel (2012, 16–17).

69. Cassella (2018, 10).

70. Crepelle (2017, 331).

71. Crepelle (2017, 327).

72. In 2015 Attorney General Eric Holder significantly limited federal adoption of assets confiscated by state and local authorities. In 2017 Attorney General Jeff Sessions undid that change, authorizing federal authorities to adopt assets seized at the local or state level, so long as a violation of federal law was implicated.

73. Pimentel (2012, 25).

74. Pimentel (2012, 25–26).

75. Cassella (2001, 110); Pimentel (2012, 25).

76. Crepelle (2017, 327).

77. Crepelle (2017, 327).

78. *Lisa Olivia Leonard v. Texas*; Legal Information Institute (2021a; 2021b).

79. Pimentel (2012, 17).
80. Crepelle (2017, 330).
81. Crepelle (2017, 330).
82. *Calero-Toledo et al. v. Pearson Yacht Leasing Co.*, 683.
83. See Ferris (1989).
84. Dery (2012, 1–2).
85. Cassella (2001, 115); Dery (2012, 1).
86. See, for example, Crepelle (2017).
87. Blumenson and Nilsen (1998).
88. See Page and Soss (2021) and Snow (2017).
89. Pimentel (2012, 14).
90. Crepelle (2017, 339).
91. Teigen and Bragg (2018).
92. Teigen and Bragg (2018).
93. Crepelle (2017, 336; reference citations omitted from quote).
94. Holcomb et al. (2011); Holcomb et al. (2018).
95. Drug Policy Alliance (2019, 2).
96. Blumenson and Nilsen (1998).
97. Worrall (2001).
98. Worrall (2001, 172).
99. Worrall (2001).
100. Worrall (2001, 178, Table 1).
101. Crepelle (2017, 337–38).
102. Crepelle (2017, 338).
103. Crepelle (2017, 338).
104. J. M. Miller and Selva (1994).
105. Pimentel (2012, 32).
106. Crepelle (2017, 354).
107. Crepelle (2017, 354–55).
108. Crepelle (2017, 355).
109. Fritz (2021); Snow (2017).
110. Crepelle (2017, 349).
111. Crepelle (2017, 349–50).
112. Snow (2017).
113. Worrall (2001, 171).
114. Challener (1996, 206).
115. Challener (1996).
116. Challener (1996, 195–96).
117. Challener (1996, 196–97).
118. Pimentel (2017, 559).
119. Quoted in Pimentel (2017, 560).
120. B. Kelly (2021, 615); Rolland (1999, 1399).
121. Rolland (1999, 1399).
122. B. Kelly (2021, 615).
123. K. Fernandez (2019, 2); B. Kelly (2021, 614).

124. K. Fernandez (2019, 2).

125. B. Kelly (2021, 614).

126. B. Kelly (2021).

127. Cassella (2001, 109); B. Kelly (2021, 616).

128. B. Kelly (2021).

129. B. Kelly (2021, 615).

130. Challener (1996, 198); Maxeiner (1977, 770); Rolland (1999, 1372).

131. Challener (1996).

132. *Lisa Olivia Leonard v. Texas*, 2.

133. Challener (1996, 206).

134. Quoted in Snow (2017, 92).

135. See, for example, Blumenson and Nilsen (1998), Crepelle (2017), Fritz (2021), Knepper et al. (2020), Maxeiner (1977), J. M. Miller and Selva (1994), O'Connell (2018), Piety (1991), Skolnick (2008), Snow (2017), Stillman (2013), and Worrall (2001).

Chapter 11

1. Christensen (2010, 452).

2. Christensen (2010, 452).

3. Gatso USA (2017).

4. Blackburn and Gilbert (1995, 1).

5. Haynes (1986).

6. Haynes (1986).

7. J. W. Peters (2009).

8. Retting et al. (1999, 30).

9. See National Conference of State Legislatures (2021). Governments, of course, also use traffic cameras in other applications, such as assessing tolls and studying traffic patterns.

10. National Conference of State Legislatures (2021).

11. National Conference of State Legislatures (2021).

12. Diamond (2021d).

13. Diamond (2021d).

14. Diamond (2021b).

15. Diamond (2021b).

16. Wilber and Willis (2005).

17. Parness (2011, 263).

18. Centers for Disease Control and Prevention (2015).

19. Wilber (2005).

20. Wilber (2005).

21. Kidwell (2017); Kidwell and Meisner (2016).

22. Kidwell (2017).

23. Sanchez and Kambhampati (2018).

24. Shannon (2007, 609).

25. Shannon (2007, 609).

26. Wilber (2005).

27. Wilber (2005).

28. Wilber (2005).

29. Diamond (2009).

30. Kidwell and Richards (2014).

31. Shannon (2007, 613).

32. Shannon (2007, 614).

33. Diamond (2021c).

34. Diamond (2021c).

35. Diamond (2021c).

36. Diamond (2021c).

37. Kidwell and Meisner (2016).

38. US Department of Justice, Office of Public Affairs (2016).

39. Kidwell (2017). In 2017 Chicago agreed to pay almost $39 million to settle another camera-related lawsuit. Brought on behalf of violators ticketed by traffic cameras, this suit alleged that Chicago violated procedural rules in issuing tickets and imposing fines (Byrne 2017).

40. See Mercer (2012).

41. Byrne (2020).

42. Diamond (2021a).

43. Wilber (2005).

44. Hu and McCartt (2015).

45. Pilkington and Kinra (2005).

46. Pilkington and Kinra (2005).

47. Retting, Kyrychenko et al. (2008); Shin et al. (2009).

48. Cunningham et al. (2008).

49. See, for example, Hu and Cicchino (2017).

50. Retting, Ferguson et al. (2008).

51. Retting and Kyrychenko (2002).

52. Retting et al. (1999).

53. Hu et al. (2011).

54. Cohn et al. (2020).

55. Cohn et al. (2020). Observed increases in rear-end collisions where automated red-light enforcement is in effect presumably result from drivers slamming on their brakes at yellow lights to avoid the possibility of a citation. Arguing against red-light cameras, former House majority leader Dick Armey referred to these situations as "panic stops" (Lehman 2002, 832).

56. Gallagher and Fisher (2020).

57. Wilber (2005).

58. Wilber (2005).

59. Wilber and Willis (2005).

60. Wilber and Willis (2005).

61. Wilber and Willis (2005).

62. Kidwell and Richards (2014).

63. Pulugurtha and Otturu (2014).

64. Kidwell and Richards (2014).

65. Kidwell and Richards (2014).

66. Mahr and Walberg (2017).

67. Morris et al. (2016). The Minnesota researchers did find some evidence that pairing automated speed enforcement with dynamic speed display signs ("YOUR SPEED" signs) increased drivers' attentiveness.

68. Parness (2011, 260).

69. See Mercer (2012, 382).

70. Morris et al. (2016).

71. Morris et al. (2016, 13–14).

72. Mercer (2012).

73. Mercer (2012).

74. Mercer (2012, 391).

75. See, for example, Samuels (2016).

76. See, for example, Simpson (2021). The city council of Berkeley, California, recently endorsed this line of thinking by passing a measure authorizing Department of Transportation personnel to enforce traffic laws rather than police (Simpson 2021).

77. Cunningham et al. (2008); Hu and McCartt (2015); Retting, Kyrychenko et al. (2008).

78. See Christensen (2010, 455) and Mercer (2012).

79. See Chapter 6.

80. See, for example, J. Fox (2020).

81. W. Farrell (2018).

82. W. Farrell (2018).

83. Sanchez and Kambhampati (2018).

84. Sanchez and Kambhampati (2018).

85. Hopkins and Sanchez (2022).

86. Shannon (2007, 609).

87. Parness (2011, 268); Shannon (2007, 614–15).

88. Parness (2011, 267).

89. Tarr (2002, 1886).

90. Christensen (2010, 463).

91. Mercer (2012, 382).

92. See, for example, Christensen (2010, 463).

93. Samuels (2016); Toler (2015).

94. Christensen (2010, 452).

95. Parness (2011).

96. Shannon (2007, 616).

97. Christensen (2010, 457).

98. Toler (2015). The relevant ordinances "explicitly presume[d] that ownership of a vehicle is conflatable with driving the vehicle at a given time" (Christensen 2010, 463).

99. Thorsen (2015).

100. Schlinkmann (2017).

101. See, for example, Lehman (2002, 829).

102. Lehman (2002, 819–20).

103. Lehman (2002, 824–25).

104. See J. W. Peters (2009).

105. Foster (2019).

106. Zmud et al. (2021).

107. Zmud et al. (2021).

108. Frankel (2018).

109. Zmud et al. (2021).

110. Alm (2015); Foster (2019).

111. Foster (2019).

112. Zmud et al. (2021, 10–11).

113. Christensen (2010, 452).

114. Christensen (2010, 452).

115. Haynes (1986); National Conference of State Legislatures (2021).

116. See Mercer (2012).

117. Headworth (2021, 23).

118. Baxandall et al. (2009).

119. Kaplan (2012).

120. Headworth and Zaborenko (2021, 1198).

Chapter 12

1. Black and Smith (2003, 1); Gable (1986, 169).

2. Lilly (2006, 95–96). See also Eason (2017) and Hagan et al. (2015).

3. Satellite communications can be interrupted in dead zones, under bridges, in tunnels, and so on (Janicki 2007, 297). On the other hand, neither weather nor congestion affects GPS (Hutchins 2007, 418; Jallad 2010, 358).

4. Hutchins (2007, 414); NASA (2012).

5. "Robert 'Bob' Martinez," Museum of Florida History, 2021, https://museumoffloridahistory.com/collections/governors-portraits/robert-bob-martinez/ (accessed December 20, 2021).

6. "Offender Monitoring Technology Goes into Orbit," *Corrections Professional* 1(12) (March 4, 1996): 9.

7. While serving as president of Pro Tech Monitoring, Martinez was also running consulting services through another business, Bob Martinez and Co. (BMC) (Trigaux 1997).

8. Pietrucha (1997).

9. "Crime Fighting Satellite Surveillance Tool Unveiled," Pro Tech Monitoring Inc. press release, *Business Wire*, May 2, 1996.

10. Abbate (2001).

11. Cloud (2002).

12. Pietrucha (1997).

13. Trigaux (1997).

14. Layson (1998).

15. Layson et al. (1999).

16. Layson (2000).

17. "Offender Monitoring Technology Goes into Orbit."

18. Christie (1994).

19. Christie (1994, 106).

20. Christie (1994, 114–16).

21. Christie (1994, 116–17).

22. "Crime Fighting Satellite Surveillance Tool Unveiled."

23. For example, "Offender Monitoring Technology Goes into Orbit" (1996).

24. Pietrucha (1997); Proctor (1996).

25. Lilly (2006, 97).

26. "Offender Monitoring Technology Goes into Orbit."

27. Trigaux (1997).

28. Lilly (2006, 97).

29. Trigaux (1997).

30. Ibarra and Erez (2005).

31. Hoshen and Drake (2001, 8).

32. Meloy and Coleman (2009, 251).

33. Forms of monitoring other than GPS tracking include RF EM, home visits, mandatory treatment programs, polygraph tests, and supervision of online activity (Markon 2009).

34. Janicki (2007, 294).

35. Meloy and Coleman (2009, 251–54).

36. See J. Kelly (2020) and Robertson (2019).

37. J. Miller (2015, 587).

38. G. Kirk (2021, 643).

39. Eife and Kirk (2021); McNeill (2018); R. J. Miller and Stuart (2017).

40. Law Enforcement Associates Inc., now known as LEA-AID, sold an RF vehicle tracker known as the Birddog, which was the specific device in question in *United States v. Knotts*. In 2007 LEA relaunched the Birddog as a GPS tracker (Herbert 2011, 486).

41. Jallad (2010, 355).

42. Ganz (2005, 1328).

43. Jallad (2010, 355).

44. J. Miller (2015, 557).

45. Ganz (2005, 1343).

46. Ganz (2005, 1344–45).

47. Ganz (2005, 1329).

48. J. Miller (2015, 563).

49. Herbert (2011, 500).

50. The matter of whether a tracker relies on its own battery or taps into a car's electrical system raises interesting Fourth Amendment issues of its own (Herbert 2011, 500–503).

51. Ganz (2005, 1330–31); Kerrane (2011, 1702); *United States v. Jones*.

52. Ganz (2005, 1332).

53. Ganz (2005, 1331); Hutchins (2007, 419).

54. K. George (2003).

55. L. Gelman (2003).

56. Ganz (2005, 1330); Kerrane (2011, 1702).

57. Herbert (2011, 478).

58. Herbert (2011, 479).

59. Herbert (2011, 478).

60. Herbert (2011, 480).

61. Gee (2020, 307); Ram (2018, 667); Zimmer (2018, 120).

62. Gee (2020, 306–7).

63. McMahon (2020).

64. See Hutchins (2007, 427).

65. *United States v. Knotts*.

66. *United States v. Knotts*, 281.

67. *United States v. Knotts*.

68. *United States v. Karo*.

69. In this specific case, however, the Court ruled that, even after excluding information related to monitoring the device inside the home to be searched, the warrant affidavit contained enough other information to constitute probable cause for a search warrant. *United States v. Karo*.

70. See Hutchins (2007).

71. Ganz (2005, 1326); Herbert (2011, 444–45).

72. Ganz (2005, 1339–41); Hutchins (2007, 446); Kerrane (2011, 1723).

73. Hutchins (2007, 446); Kerrane (2011, 1723).

74. Foster (2019, 233).

75. See Herbert (2011, 443).

76. Kerrane (2011, 1727).

77. Herbert (2011, 443).

78. *United States v. Jones*.

79. Foster (2019, 232).

80. See, in general, Herbert (2011).

81. *Riley v. California*, 9.

82. *Riley v. California*.

83. *Carpenter v. United States*, 22.

84. Zimmer (2018, 108).

85. See Gray (2017).

86. Jones (2019).

87. Tau and Hackman (2020).

88. J. Russell George to Senators Wyden and Warren, February 18, 2021, https://s .wsj.net/public/resources/documents/Response.pdf. The government's use of location tracking is a long-standing interest of Senator Wyden's (see Herbert 2011, 446).

89. Hecht-Felella (2021, 16).

90. Harvard Law Review Editors (2021, 2509).

91. Hecht-Felella (2021, 16).

92. Harvard Law Review Editors (2021, 2512).

93. Graham (2010).

94. Herbert (2011, 450–54).

95. Ganz (2005).

96. See Brayne (2020), Gray (2017), Joh (2014, 2016), and Ridgeway (2018).

97. J. Miller (2015, 562–63).

Conclusion

1. K. Barker et al. (2021).

2. Epstein and Mazzei (2021); C. Peters (2021).

3. C. Peters (2021).

4. See Simpson (2021).

5. Goodman (2021).

6. Office of Management and Budget (2022).

7. Friess (2022); Rosario (2021).

8. National Highway Traffic Safety Administration (2021).

9. National Highway Traffic Safety Administration (2021; 2022).

10. National Highway Traffic Safety Administration (2022).

11. Macek (2022, 4).

12. National Highway Traffic Safety Administration (2021).

13. Rosenfeld et al. (2021).

14. Piquero et al. (2021).

15. Rosenfeld et al. (2021).

16. Rosenfeld et al. (2021).

17. Rosenfeld et al. (2021).

18. Rosenfeld et al. (2021, 17).

19. Piquero et al. (2021, 10).

20. Rosenfeld et al. (2021, 17).

21. J. Q. Wilson and Kelling (1982).

22. Schnepel (2020).

23. Ng (2022).

REFERENCES

Abbate, Janet. 2001. "Government, Business, and the Making of the Internet." *Business History Review* 75(1): 147–76.

Adair, Cassius. 2019. "Licensing Citizenship: Anti-Blackness, Identification Documents, and Transgender Studies." *American Quarterly* 71(2): 569–94.

Albanese, Jay S. 2014. "The Italian-American Mafia." In *The Oxford Handbook of Organized Crime*, ed. L. Paoli, 142–58. New York: Oxford University Press.

Alm, Jessica Gutierrez. 2015. "The Privacies of Life: Automatic License Plate Recognition Is Unconstitutional Under the Mosaic Theory of Fourth Amendment Privacy Law." *Hamline Law Review* 38(1): 127–60.

American Automobile Association. 2021. "Our History." https://www.hoosier.aaa.com/about-us/our-history.

Archer, Deborah N. 2020. "'White Men's Roads Through Black Men's Homes': Advancing Racial Equity Through Highway Reconstruction." *Vanderbilt Law Review* 73(5): 1259–330.

Archer, Deborah N. 2021. "Transportation Policy and the Underdevelopment of Black Communities." *Iowa Law Review* 106: 2125–51.

Association of Centers for the Study of Congress. 2021. "Department of Transportation Act." Newark: University of Delaware Library. http://acsc.lib.udel.edu/exhibits/show/legislation/department-of-transportation-a.

Austen, Ben. 2018. *High-Risers: Cabrini-Green and the Fate of American Public Housing*. New York: HarperCollins.

Bahn, Charles. 1974. "The Reassurance Factor in Police Patrol." *Criminology* 12(3): 338–45.

Bailey, Greg. 1988. "Death by Automobile as First Degree Murder Utilizing the Felony Murder Rule." *West Virginia Law Review* 10(1): 235–52.

Baker, James Stannard. 1958. "Driver Licensing." *Annals of the American Academy of Political and Social Science* 320: 53–62.

Baldeck, Brett. 2021. "911 Centers Seeing Thousands of Accidental Calls and Volume Continues to Increase." FOX 46 Charlotte, April 27. https://www.fox46.com/news/local-news/911-centers-seeing-thousands-of-accidental-calls-and-volume-continues-to-increase/.

Barber, A. B. 1931. "Why Drivers' License Laws with Examination Are Needed." *Georgia Lawyer* 2(1): 14–19.

Barker, Jack. 1962. "The Fallacy and Fortuity of Motor Vehicle Homicide." *Nebraska Law Review* 41(4): 793–815.

Barker, Kim, Mike Baker, and Ali Watkins. 2021. "In City After City, Police Mishandled Black Lives Matter Protests." *New York Times*, March 20. https://www.nytimes.com/2021/03/20/us/protests-policing-george-floyd.html.

Barker, Matthew Jude. 2014. *The Irish of Portland, Maine: A History of Forest City Hibernians*. Charleston, SC: History Press.

Barker, Vanessa. 2009. *The Politics of Imprisonment: How the Democratic Process Shapes the Way America Punishes Offenders*. New York: Oxford University Press.

Barkow, Rachel E. 2011. "Federalism and Criminal Law: What the Feds Can Learn from the States." *Michigan Law Review* 109(4): 519–80.

Bartlett, Arthur. 1949. "Can We Afford Young Drivers?" *Nation's Business* 37(9): 31.

Baumgartner, Frank R., Kate Bell, Luke Beyer, Tara Boldrin, Libby Doyle, Lindsey Govan, Jack Halpert, Jackson Hicks, Katherine Kyriakoudes, and Cat Lee. 2021. "Intersectional Encounters, Representative Bureaucracy, and the Routine Traffic Stop." *Policy Studies Journal* 49(3): 860–86.

Baumgartner, Frank R., Leah Christiani, Derek A. Epp, Kevin Roach, and Kelsey Shoub. 2017. "Racial Disparities in Traffic Stop Outcomes." *Duke Forum for Law Social Change* 9: 21–54.

Baumgartner, Frank R., Derek A. Epp and Kelsey Shoub. 2018. *Suspect Citizens: What 20 Million Traffic Stops Tell Us About Policing and Race*. New York: Cambridge University Press.

Baxandall, Phineas, Kari Wohlschlegel, and Tony Dutzik. 2009. *Private Roads, Public Costs: The Facts About Toll Road Privatization and How to Protect the Public*. Boston: US PIRG Education Fund.

Becker, Howard S. 1963. *Outsiders: Studies in the Sociology of Deviance*. Glencoe, IL: Free Press.

Bejarano, David. 2001. *Vehicle Stop Study Year End Report: 2000*. San Diego: San Diego Police Department.

Bell, Monica C. 2016. "Situational Trust: How Disadvantaged Mothers Reconceive Legal Cynicism." *Law and Society Review* 50(2): 314–47.

Besharov, Douglas J. 1981. "Terminating Parental Rights: The Indigent Parent's Right to Counsel After *Lassiter v. North Carolina*." *Family Law Quarterly* 15(3): 205–21.

Bhagat, Nikhil. 2011. "Filling the Gap? Non-Abrogation Provisions and the Assimilative Crimes Act." *Columbia Law Review* 111(1): 77–120.

Billock, Jennifer. 2017. "How Moonshine Bootlegging Gave Rise to NASCAR." *Smithsonian Magazine*, February 10. https://www.smithsonianmag.com/travel/how-moonshine-bootlegging-gave-rise-nascar-180962014/.

Black, Matt, and Russell G. Smith. 2003. *Electronic Monitoring in the Criminal Justice System.*" Trends and Issues in Crime and Criminal Justice no. 254. Canberra: Australian Institute of Criminology.

Blackburn, Robert R., and Daniel T. Gilbert. 1995. *Photographic Enforcement of Traffic Laws: A Synthesis of Highway Practice.* Washington, DC: National Academy Press.

Blumenson, Eric, and Eva Nilsen. 1998. "Policing for Profit: The Drug War's Hidden Economic Agenda." *University of Chicago Law Review* 65(1): 35–114.

Blunt, Danielle, and Ariel Wolf. 2020. "Erased: The Impact of FOSTA-SESTA and the Removal of Backpage on Sex Workers." *Anti-Trafficking Review* 14: 117–21.

Bock, Robert, and John McGrath. 2011. "Graduated Drivers Licensing Programs Reduce Fatal Teen Crashes." NIH news release, November 4. Bethesda, MD: National Institutes of Health. https://www.nih.gov/news-events/news-releases/graduated-drivers-licensing-programs-reduce-fatal-teen-crashes.

Bottles, Scott L. 1987. *Los Angeles and the Automobile: The Making of the Modern City.* Berkeley: University of California Press.

Brayne, Sarah. 2020. *Predict and Surveil: Data, Discretion, and the Future of Policing.* New York: Oxford University Press.

Broadhead, Robert S., and Ray C. Rist. 1976. "Gatekeepers and the Social Control of Social Research." *Social Problems* 23(3): 325–36.

Bureau of Transportation Statistics. 2021. *Transportation Fatalities by Mode.* Washington, DC: US Department of Transportation. https://www.bts.gov/content/transportation-fatalities-mode.

Burnham, John Chynoweth. 1961. "The Gasoline Tax and the Automobile Revolution." *Mississippi Valley Historical Review* 48(3): 435–59.

Byrne, John. 2017. "City Reaches $38.75 Million Settlement in Red Light Ticket Lawsuit." *Chicago Tribune*, July 20. https://www.chicagotribune.com/politics/ct-rahm-emanuel-red-light-tickets-lawsuit-settlement-met-20170720-story.html.

Byrne, John. 2020. "Mayor's Transportation Pick: Red-Light Cameras 'a Deterrent.'" *Chicago Tribune*, January 9.

Calder, Lendol. 1999. *Financing the American Dream: A Cultural History of Consumer Credit.* Princeton, NJ: Princeton University Press.

Campeau, Holly, Ron Levi, and Todd Foglesong. 2021. "Policing, Recognition, and the Bind of Legal Cynicism." *Social Problems* 68(3): 658–74.

Carnegie, Jon A. 2007. *Driver's License Suspensions, Impacts, and Fairness Study.* New Brunswick, NJ: Alan M. Voorhees Transportation Center, Rutgers University.

Caro, Robert A. 1974. *The Power Broker: Robert Moses and the Fall of New York.* New York: Knopf.

Cassella, Stefan D. 2001. "The Civil Asset Forfeiture Reform Act of 2000: Expanded Government Forfeiture Authority and Strict Deadlines Imposed on All Parties." *Journal of Legislation* 27(1): 97–152.

Cassella, Stefan D. 2018. "Asset Forfeiture Law in the United States." In *The Palgrave Handbook of Criminal and Terrorism Financing Law*, ed. Colin King, Clive Walker, and Jimmy Gurulé, 427–46. London: Palgrave Macmillan.

Centers for Disease Control and Prevention. 2015. *Automated Speed-Camera Enforcement*. Washington, DC: US Department of Health and Human Services. https://www.cdc.gov/motorvehiclesafety/calculator/factsheet/speed.html.

Centers for Disease Control and Prevention. 2016. *Graduated Driver Licensing*. Washington, DC: US Department of Health and Human Services. https://www.cdc.gov/phlp/publications/topic/gdl.html.

Chalikian, Anahid. 2001. "Charging First-Degree Murder as Opposed to Vehicular Manslaughter." *Journal of Legal Advocacy and Practice* 3: 143–46.

Challener, Deborah J. 1996. "Note, Civil Forfeiture, and Innocent Owners." *Tennessee Law Review* 64: 195–213.

Chamberlain, Lura. 2019. "FOSTA: A Hostile Law with a Human Cost." *Fordham Law Review* 87: 2171–211.

Chenane, Joselyne L., Emily M. Wright, and Chris L. Gibson. 2020. "Traffic Stops, Race, and Perceptions of Fairness." *Policing and Society* 30(6): 720–37.

Childress, Sarah. 2016. "The Problem with 'Broken Windows' Policing." *Frontline*, June 28. https://www.pbs.org/wgbh/frontline/article/the-problem-with-broken-windows-policing/.

Christensen, Joel O. 2010. "Wrong on Red: The Constitutional Case Against Red-Light Cameras." *Washington University Journal of Law and Policy* 32(1): 443–66.

Christie, Nils. 1994. *Crime Control as Industry: Towards Gulags, Western Style*, 2nd ed. New York: Routledge.

Clemens, Austin, Miner P. Marchbanks III, and Dottie Carmichael. 2014. *Asset Forfeiture in Texas: DPS and County Interactions*. Austin, TX: Office of Court Administration.

Cloud, John. 2002. "American Cartographic Transformations During the Cold War." *Cartography and Geographic Information Science* 29(3): 261–82.

Cohn, Ellen G., Suman Kakar, Chloe Perkins, Rebecca Steinbach, and Phil Edwards. 2020. "Red Light Camera Interventions for Reducing Traffic Violations and Traffic Crashes: A Systematic Review." *Campbell Systematic Reviews* 16(2): e1091. https://doi.org/10.1002/cl2.1091.

Coleman, C. Vernon, II. 2016. "Denzel Curry Opens Up About His Brother's Death in 'Knotty Head' Documentary." *XXL*, May 7. https://www.xxlmag.com/denzel-curry-knotty-head-documentary/.

Connell, Elizabeth, Steven Jones, and Javonda Williams. 2018. "Human Trafficking and the Transportation Profession: How Can We Be Part of the Solution?" *ITE Journal* 88(7): 45–49.

Crepelle, Adam. 2017. "Probable Cause to Plunder: Civil Asset Forfeiture and the Problems It Creates." *Wake Forest Journal of Law and Policy* 7(2): 315–64.

Cressey, Donald R. 1974. "Law, Order, and the Motorist." In *Crime, Criminology, and Public Policy: Essays in Honour of Sir Leon Radzinowicz*, ed. R. Hood, 213–34. New York: Free Press.

Cronon, William. 1991. *Nature's Metropolis: Chicago and the Great West*. New York: Norton.

Crozier, William E., and Brandon L. Garrett. 2020. "Driven to Failure: An Empirical

Analysis of Driver's License Suspension in North Carolina." *Duke Law Journal* 69(7): 1585–642.

Cunningham, Christopher M., Joseph E. Hummer, and Jae-Pil Moon. 2008. "Analysis of Automated Speed Enforcement Cameras in Charlotte, North Carolina." *Transportation Research Record* 2078: 127–34.

Dang, Jennifer N. 2008. *Statistical Analysis of Alcohol-Related Driving Trends, 1982–2005*. Washington, DC: National Highway Traffic Safety Administration.

Darden, Joe T., Richard Child Hill, June Thomas, and Richard Thomas. 1997. *Detroit: Race and Uneven Development*. Philadelphia: Temple University Press.

Davis, Angela J. 2007. *Arbitrary Justice: The Power of the American Prosecutor*. New York: Oxford University Press.

Davis, Charles Henry. 1914. "Foreword." *Proceedings of the Academy of Political Science in the City of New York* 4(2): 241–45.

Demleitner, Nora V. 1994. "Organized Crime and Prohibition: What Difference Does Legalization Make?" *Whittier Law Review* 15(3): 613–45.

Demleitner, Nora V. 1999. "Preventing Internal Exile: The Need for Restrictions on Collateral Sentencing Consequences." *Stanford Law and Policy Review* 11(1): 153–72.

Dery, Alice W. 2012. "Overview of Asset Forfeiture." *Business Law Today* 2012(6): 1–5.

Diamond, Richard. 2009. "Washington Deploys Work Zone Cams Despite No Worker Fatalities: Washington State Department of Transportation Uses Highway Worker Deaths as Excuse to Deploy Freeway Speed Cameras Despite Lack of Worker Deaths." *TheNewspaper.com*, April 27. https://www.thenewspaper.com/news/27/2759.asp.

Diamond, Richard. 2021a. "President Biden Signs Federal Speed Camera Subsidy Bill: New Infrastructure Law Provides Speed Camera Companies with Subsidies for Photo Radar." *TheNewspaper.com*, November 16. https://www.thenewspaper.com/news/70/7098.asp.

Diamond, Richard. 2021b. "Red Light Camera Industry Returns to Profitability: Company with Near-Monopoly in the US Automated Ticketing Market Plans to Roll Out 650 New Speed Cameras This Year." *TheNewspaper.com*, August 18. https://www.thenewspaper.com/news/70/7072.asp.

Diamond, Richard. 2021c. "Top Twenty-One Photo Enforcement Felons: Twenty Politicians, Lobbyists, and Photo Enforcement Executives Have Been Convicted of Felony Crimes Ranging from Forgery to Bribery." *TheNewspaper.com*, November 2, 2018. Updated 2021. https://www.thenewspaper.com/news/64/6450.asp.

Diamond, Richard. 2021d. "Verra Mobility Loses Money, Buys Its Main Money-Losing Rival: Verra Mobility Wins Approval of Deal to Buy Redflex, Though Both Photo Ticketing Companies Continue to Lose Cash." *TheNewspaper.com*, May 27. https://www.thenewspaper.com/news/70/7048.asp.

Diaz, Madelyn, Lin Huff-Corzine, and Jay Corzine. 2022. "Demanding Reduction: A County-Level Analysis Examining Structural Determinants of Human Trafficking Arrests in Florida." *Crime and Delinquency* 68(1): 28–51.

Dietrich, James J. 1997. "Problems and Charging Choices in Prosecuting Vehicular Fatalities." *The Prosecutor* 31(1): 32–37.

Divine, Joshua M. 2020. "Statutory Federalism and Criminal Law." *Virginia Law Review* 106(1): 127–98.

Dobson, Kenneth S. 2001. "How Detroit Police Reinvented the Wheel." *Detroit News*, December 21. http://blogs.detroitnews.com/history/2001/12/21/how-detroit -police-reinvented-the-wheel/.

Domonoske, Camila. 2021. "'Tragic': Driving Was Down in 2020, but Traffic Fatality Rates Surged." *NPR*, March 5. https://www.npr.org/2021/03/05/974006735/ tragic-driving-was-down-in-2020-but-traffic-fatality-rates-surged.

Douglass, R. Bruce. 2016. "'Shell as Hard as Steel' (or, 'Iron Cage'): What Exactly Did That Imagery Mean for Weber?" *Journal of Historical Sociology* 29(4): 503–24.

Drug Policy Alliance. 2019. *Civil Asset Forfeiture.* New York: Drug Policy Alliance. https://drugpolicy.org/sites/default/files/civil-asset-forfeiture-january2019_0 .pdf.

Dupnack, Jessica. 2019. "Detroit Police Sergeant Who Failed to Respond to Officer Shooting Retiring, Had PTSD, Attorney Says." FOX 2 Detroit, December 5. https:/ /www.fox2detroit.com/news/detroit-police-sergeant-who-failed-to-respond-to -officer-shooting-retiring-had-ptsd-attorney-says.

Eason, John M. 2017. *Big House on the Prairie: Rise of the Rural Ghetto and Prison Proliferation.* Chicago: University of Chicago Press.

Eife, Erin, and Gabriela Kirk. 2021. "'And You Will Wait . . .': Carceral Transportation in Electronic Monitoring as Part of the Punishment Process." *Punishment and Society* 23(1): 69–87.

Elias, Norbert. 1995. "Technization and Civilization." *Theory, Culture, and Society* 12: 7–42.

Engel, Robin Shepard. 2005. "Citizens' Perceptions of Distributive and Procedural Injustice During Traffic Stops with Police." *Journal of Research in Crime and Delinquency* 42(4): 445–81.

Engel, Robin Shepard, and Jennifer M. Calnon. 2004. "Examining the Influence of Drivers' Characteristics During Traffic Stops with Police: Results from a National Survey." *Justice Quarterly* 21(1): 49–90.

Epp, Charles R., Steven Maynard-Moody, and Donald Haider-Markel. 2014. *Pulled Over: How Police Stops Define Race and Citizenship.* Chicago: University of Chicago Press.

Epstein, Reid. J., and Patricia Mazzei. 2021. "GOP Bills Target Protesters (and Absolve Motorists Who Hit Them)." *New York Times*, April 21. https://www.nytimes .com/2021/04/21/us/politics/republican-anti-protest-laws.html.

Ewald, Alec C. 2012. "Collateral Consequences in the American States." *Social Science Quarterly* 93(1): 211–47.

Exotech Systems Inc. 1970. *Improving the Enforcement of Driver License Denials, Suspensions, and Revocations.* Washington, DC: National Highway Safety Bureau, US Department of Transportation.

Farber, David. 2002. *Sloan Rules: Alfred P. Sloan and the Triumph of General Motors.* Chicago: University of Chicago Press.

Farrell, Amy, Meredith Dank, Ieke de Vries, Matthew Kafafian, Andrea Hughes, and Sarah Lockwood. 2019. "Failing Victims? Challenges of the Police Response to Human Trafficking." *Criminology and Public Policy* 18(3): 649–73.

Farrell, William. 2018. "Predominantly Black Neighborhoods in DC Bear the Brunt of Automated Traffic Enforcement." DC Policy Center, June 28. https://www.dcpolicycenter.org/publications/predominately-black-neighborhoods-in-d-c-bear-the-brunt-of-automated-traffic-enforcement/.

Federal Bureau of Investigation. 2014. *Crime in the United States 2014*. Washington, DC: US Department of Justice.

Federal Bureau of Investigation. 2015. *Crime in the United States 2015*. Washington, DC: US Department of Justice.

Federal Bureau of Investigation. 2019. "Curbing Car Crimes: How a 100-Year-Old Car Theft Law Led to the Modern FBI." FBI, October 31. https://www.fbi.gov/news/stories/how-100-year-old-car-theft-law-led-to-modern-fbi-103119.

Federal Bureau of Investigation. 2020. "The Bureau and the Great Experiment: How Prohibition Fueled Bootleggers, Mobsters, and Corruption." FBI, January 24. https://www.fbi.gov/news/stories/the-bureau-and-the-great-experiment-012420.

Federal Bureau of Investigation. 2021. "Bonnie and Clyde." https://www.fbi.gov/history/famous-cases/bonnie-and-clyde.

Federal Bureau of Prisons. 2021. "Historical Information." https://www.bop.gov/about/history/.

Federal Highway Administration. 1997. "Year of First State Driver License Law and First Driver Examination." https://www.fhwa.dot.gov/ohim/summary95/dl230.pdf.

Federal Reserve. 2019. *Report on the Economic Well-Being of U.S. Households in 2018*. Washington, DC: Board of Governors, Federal Reserve System. https://www.federalreserve.gov/publications/files/2018-report-economic-well-being-us-households-201905.pdf.

Feldman, Leslie Dale. 2001. *Freedom as Motion*. Lanham, MD: University Press of America.

Fell, James C., A. Scott Tippetts, and Robert B. Voas. 2009. "Fatal Traffic Crashes Involving Drinking Drivers: What Have We Learned?" *Annals of Advances in Automotive Medicine* 53: 63–76.

Ferdinand, Theodore N. 1989. "Juvenile Delinquency or Juvenile Justice: Which Came First?" *Criminology* 27(1): 79–106.

Fernandes, April D., Michele Cadigan, Frank Edwards, and Alexes Harris. 2019. "Monetary Sanctions: A Review of Revenue Generation, Legal Challenges, and Reform." *Annual Review of Law and Social Science* 15: 397–413.

Fernandez, Kris. 2019. "*Timbs v. Indiana*: The Constitutionality of Civil Forfeiture When Used by States." *Duke Journal of Constitutional Law and Public Policy Sidebar* 14: 1–18.

Fernandez, Lazaro. 1986. "DUI Roadblocks: Drunk Drivers Take a Toll on the Fourth Amendment." *John Marshall Law Review* 19(4): 983–1006.

Ferrandino, Joseph. 2015. "Minority Threat Hypothesis and NYPD Stop and Frisk Policy." *Criminal Justice Review* 40(2): 209–29.

Ferris, Janet E. 1989. *Starting Forfeiture Programs: A Prosecutors' Guide*. Washington, DC: US Department of Justice.

Finder, Alan. 1999. "Drive Drunk, Lose the Car? Principle Faces a Test." *New York Times*, February 24, p. B1.

Finley, Ben, and Jonathan Drew. 2021. "Prosecutor Finds Deputies Justified in Shooting of Black Man." Associated Press, May 19. https://www.wate.com/news/national-world/prosecutor-finds-deputies-justified-in-shooting-of-black-man/.

Flink, James J. 1988. *The Automobile Age*. Cambridge, MA: MIT Press.

Ford, Henry, with Samuel Crowther. 2005. "My Life and Work." https://www.gutenberg.org/cache/epub/7213/pg7213.html.

Forst, Brian. 2004. *Errors of Justice: Nature, Sources, and Remedies*. New York: Cambridge University Press.

Foster, Stephanie. 2019. "Should the Use of Automated License Plate Readers Constitute a Search After *Carpenter v. United States*?" *Washington University Law Review* 97(1): 221–44.

Foucault, Michel. 1979. *Discipline and Punish: The Birth of the Prison*, trans. A. Sheridan. New York: Vintage Books.

Foundation for Advancing Alcohol Responsibility. 2020. *2018 State of Drunk Driving Fatalities in America*. Arlington, VA: Foundation for Advancing Alcohol Responsibility. https://www.responsibility.org/wp-content/uploads/2020/02/2018_Drunk-Driving-Stats-Book.pdf.

Fox, Justin. 2020. "Traffic Cameras Could Help Reduce Racism in Traffic Enforcement: Opinion." *Insurance Journal*, July 13. https://www.insurancejournal.com/news/national/2020/07/13/575227.htm.

Fox, Sanford J. 1970. "Juvenile Justice Reform: An Historical Perspective." *Stanford Law Review* 22(6): 1187–239.

Frankel, Todd C. 2018. "The Surprising Return of the Repo Man." *Washington Post*, May 15. https://www.washingtonpost.com/business/economy/the-surprising-return-of-the-repo-man/2018/05/15/26fcd30e-4d5a-11e8-af46-b1d6dcod9bfe_story.html?utm_term=.e1bbc60f0a23.

Freestone, Tobias. 2011. "Elementary My Dear Watson: The Evolution to Strict Liability Murder Thirty Years After *People v. Watson*." *Whittier Law Review* 33(1): 243–74.

Friess, Steve. 2022. "'Defund the Police' Is Dead but Other Reform Efforts Thrive in US Cities." *Newsweek*, June 24. https://www.newsweek.com/2022/06/24/defund-police-dead-other-reform-efforts-thrive-us-cities-1709393.html.

Fritz, Dawn. 2021. "*Timbs v. Indiana*: Civil Forfeiture, Racism, and the War on Drugs." *Denver Law Review*, https://denverlawreview.org/dlr-online-article/timbs.

Gable, Ralph Kirkland. 1986. "Application of Personal Telemonitoring to Current Problems in Corrections." *Journal of Criminal Justice* 14(2): 167–76.

Gaines, Larry K. 2004. *An Analysis of Traffic Stop Data in the City of Riverside (Third Year Report)*. Riverside, CA: City of Riverside.

Gallagher, Justin, and Paul J. Fisher. 2020. "Criminal Deterrence When There Are Offsetting Risks: Traffic Cameras, Vehicular Accidents, and Public Safety." *American Economic Journal: Economic Policy* 12(3): 202–37.

Ganz, John S. 2005. "It's Already Public: Why Federal Officers Should Not Need Warrants to Use GPS Vehicle Tracking Devices." *Journal of Criminal Law and Criminology* 95(4): 1325–62.

Garland, David. 2001. *The Culture of Control: Crime and Social Order in Contemporary Society.* Chicago: University of Chicago Press.

Gatso USA. 2017. "History." https://www.gatso-usa.com/about/history.

Gee, Harvey. 2020. "Last Call for the Third-Party Doctrine in the Digital Age After *Carpenter?*" *Boston University Journal of Science and Technology Law* 26(2): 286–323.

Gelman, Andrew, Jeffrey Fagan, and Alex Kiss. 2007. "An Analysis of the New York City Police Department's 'Stop-and-Frisk' Policy in the Context of Claims of Racial Bias." *Journal of the American Statistical Association* 102(479): 813–23.

Gelman, Lauren. 2003. "Attachment of GPS Devices to Private Vehicles Requires a Warrant." Blog post, October 7. http://cyberlaw.stanford.edu/packets001557.shtml.

George, Kathy. 2003. "Court Will Decide If Police Need Warrant for GPS 'Tracking.'" *Seattle Post-Intelligencer,* May 11. https://www.seattlepi.com/news/article/Court-will-decide-if-police-need-warrant-for-GPS-1114503.php.

Gershman, Bennett L. 2010. "Prosecutorial Decisionmaking and Discretion in the Charging Function." *Hastings Law Journal* 62(5): 1259–84.

Gilsinan, James F. 1989. "They Is Clowning Tough: 911 and the Social Construction of Reality." *Criminology* 27(2): 329–44.

Glaeser, Edward L., and Bruce Sacerdote. 2003. "Sentencing in Homicide Cases and the Role of Vengeance." *Journal of Legal Studies* 32(2): 363–82.

Go, Julian. 2020. "The Imperial Origins of American Policing: Militarization and Imperial Feedback in the Early 20th Century." *American Journal of Sociology* 125(5): 1193–254.

Goodman, J. David. 2021. "A Year After 'Defund,' Police Departments Get Their Money Back." *New York Times,* October 10. https://www.nytimes.com/2021/10/10/us/dallas-police-defund.html.

Gotham, Kevin Fox. 2014. *Race, Real Estate, and Uneven Development: The Kansas City Experience, 1900–2010,* 2nd ed. Albany: State University of New York Press.

Graham, Stephen. 2010. *Cities Under Siege: The New Military Urbanism.* New York: Verso.

Gray, David. 2017. *The Fourth Amendment in an Age of Surveillance.* New York: Cambridge University Press.

Green, Bruce A. 2019. "Prosecutorial Discretion: The Difficulty and Necessity of Public Inquiry." *Dickinson Law Review* 123(3): 589–626.

Gusfield, Joseph R. 1984. *The Culture of Public Problems: Drinking-Driving and the Symbolic Order,* rev. ed. Chicago: University of Chicago Press.

Hagan, John, Gabriele Plickert, Alberto Palloni, and Spencer Headworth. 2015. "Making Punishment Pay: The Political Economy of Revenue, Race, and Regime in the California Prison Boom." *Du Bois Review: Social Science Research on Race* 12(1): 95–118.

Haigh, Susan. 2021. "State Lawmakers Work to Strip Old 'Whites Only' Covenants."

Associated Press, July 28. https://apnews.com/article/whites-only-property-cov enants-race-ethnicity-56d67ad0dff72e8b71de768a24c90274.

Hamilton, Vivian E. 2014. "Liberty Without Capacity: Why States Should Ban Adolescent Driving." *Georgia Law Review* 48: 1019–84.

Harcourt, Bernard E. 2001. *Illusion of Order: The False Promise of Broken Windows Policing*. Cambridge, MA: Harvard University Press.

Harcourt, Bernard E., and Jens Ludwig. 2006. "Broken Windows: New Evidence from New York City and a Five-City Social Experiment." *University of Chicago Law Review* 73(1): 271–320.

Harris, Alexes, Heather Evans, and Katherine Beckett. 2010. "Drawing Blood from Stones: Legal Debt and Social Inequality in the Contemporary United States." *American Journal of Sociology* 115(6): 1753–99.

Harvard Law Review Editors. 2021. "Geofence Warrants and the Fourth Amendment." *Harvard Law Review* 134: 2508–29.

Haynes, Gary. 1986. "Red Light Camera Could Put Stop to One Traffic Problem." *Chicago Tribune*, September 19. https://www.chicagotribune.com/news/ct-xpm -1986-09-19-8603100585-story.html.

Headworth, Spencer. 2019. "Getting to Know You: Welfare Fraud Investigation and the Appropriation of Social Ties." *American Sociological Review* 84(1): 171–96.

Headworth, Spencer. 2021. *Policing Welfare: Punitive Adversarialism in Public Assistance*. Chicago: University of Chicago Press.

Headworth, Spencer, and Viridiana Ríos. 2021. "Listening to Snitches: Race/Ethnicity, English Proficiency, and Access to Welfare Fraud Enforcement Systems." *Law and Policy* 43: 319–47.

Headworth, Spencer, and Callie Zaborenko. 2021. "Legal Reactivity: Correctional Health Care Certifications as Responses to Litigation." *Law and Social Inquiry* 46(4): 1173–205.

Hecht-Felella, Laura. 2021. *The Fourth Amendment in the Digital Age*. New York: Brennan Center for Justice, New York University School of Law.

Hegman, Gregg. 1972. "Taking Cars: Ethnography of a Car Theft Ring." In *The Cultural Experience: Ethnography in a Complex Society*, ed. J. P. Spradley and D. W. McCurdy, 169–75. Prospect Heights, IL: Waveland Press.

Heitmann, John A. 2018. *The Automobile and American Life*, 2nd ed. Jefferson, NC: McFarland.

Heitmann, John A., and Rebecca H. Morales. 2014. *Stealing Cars: Technology and Society from the Model T to the Gran Torino*. Baltimore: Johns Hopkins University Press.

Herbert, Ian. 2011. "Where We Are with Location Tracking: A Look at the Current Technology and the Implications on Fourth Amendment Jurisprudence." *Berkeley Journal of Criminal Law* 16(2): 442–505.

Hingson, Ralph, and Michael Winter. 2003. "Epidemiology and Consequences of Drinking and Driving." *Alcohol Research and Health* 27(1): 63–78.

Hinkle, Joshua C., and David Weisburd. 2008. "The Irony of Broken Windows Policing: A Micro-Place Study of the Relationship Between Disorder, Focused Police Crackdowns, and Fear of Crime." *Journal of Criminal Justice* 36: 503–12.

Holcomb, Jefferson E., Tomislav V. Kovandzic, and Marian R. Williams. 2011. "Civil Asset Forfeiture, Equitable Sharing, and Policing for Profit in the United States." *Journal of Criminal Justice* 39(3): 273–85.

Holcomb, Jefferson E., Marian R. Williams, William D. Hicks, Tomislav V. Kovandzic, and Michele Bisaccia Meitl. 2018. "Civil Asset Forfeiture Laws and Equitable Sharing Activity by the Police." *Criminology and Public Policy* 17(1): 101–27.

Holmes, Joseph Austin. 1901. "Road Building with Convict Labor in the Southern States." *Yearbook of the Department of Agriculture* 1901: 319–32.

Hopkins, Emily, and Melissa Sanchez. 2022. "Chicago's 'Race-Neutral' Traffic Cameras Ticket Black and Latino Drivers the Most." ProPublica, January 11. https://www.propublica.org/article/chicagos-race-neutral-traffic-cameras-ticket-black-and-latino-drivers-the-most.

Hoshen, Joseph, and George Drake. 2001. *Offender Wide Area Continuous Electronic Monitoring Systems.* National Institutes of Justice Grant Report. Washington, DC: US Department of Justice. https://www.ojp.gov/pdffiles1/nij/grants/187101.pdf.

Hu, Wen, and Jessica B. Cicchino. 2017. "Effects of Turning On and Off Red Light Cameras on Fatal Crashes in Large US Cities." *Journal of Safety Research* 61: 141–48.

Hu, Wen, and Anne T. McCartt. 2015. *Effects of Automated Speed Enforcement in Montgomery County, Maryland, on Vehicle Speeds, Public Opinion, and Crashes.* Arlington, VA: Insurance Institute for Highway Safety.

Hu, Wen, Anne T. McCartt, and Eric R. Teoh. 2011. "Effects of Red Light Camera Enforcement on Fatal Crashes in Large US Cities." *Journal of Safety Research* 42(4): 277–82.

Hunter, George. 2019. "Detroit Police Sergeant Accused of Failing to Act in Officer Shooting Retires." *Detroit News*, December 5. https://www.detroitnews.com/story/news/local/detroit-city/2019/12/05/detroit-police-sergeant-accused-of-failing-to-act-retires/2623392001/.

Hutchins, Renée McDonald. 2007. "Tied Up in *Knotts*? GPS Technology and the Fourth Amendment." *UCLA Law Review* 55(2): 409–66.

Ibarra, Peter R., and Edna Erez. 2005. "Victim-Centric Diversion? The Electronic Monitoring of Domestic Violence Cases." *Behavioral Sciences and the Law* 23(2): 259–76.

Indiana Senate Republicans. 2021. "Messmer: Bill Reinstating Certain Suspended Driver's Licenses Passes Senate Committee 3.17.2021." https://www.indianasenaterepublicans.com/messmer-bill-reinstating-certain-suspended-driver-s-licenses-passes-senate-committee-3-17-2021.

Jackson, Kenneth T. 1985. *Crabgrass Frontier: The Suburbanization of the United States.* New York: Oxford University Press.

Jacobs, James B. 1988. "The Law and Criminology of Drunk Driving." *Crime and Justice* 10: 171–229.

Jacobs, James B., and Nadine Strossen. 1985. "Mass Investigations Without Individualized Suspicion: A Constitutional and Policy Critique of Drunk Driving Roadblocks." *UC Davis Law Review* 18(3): 595–680.

Jager, Eric. 2004. *The Last Duel: A True Story of Crime, Scandal, and Trial by Combat in Medieval France*. New York: Broadway Books.

Jain, Eisha. 2016. "Prosecuting Collateral Consequences." *Georgetown Law Journal* 104(5): 1197–244.

Jallad, Tarik N. 2010. "Old Answers to New Questions: GPS Surveillance and the Unwarranted Need for Warrants." *North Carolina Journal of Law and Technology* 11(2): 351–76.

Janicki, Megan A. 2007. "Better Seen than Herded: Residency Restrictions and Global Positioning System Tracking Laws for Sex Offenders." *Public Interest Law Journal* 16: 285–311.

Jenkins, Brian Michael, and Bruce R. Butterworth. 2019. *"Smashing into Crowds": An Analysis of Vehicle Ramming Attacks*. San Jose, CA: Mineta Transportation Institute, San Jose State University. https://transweb.sjsu.edu/sites/default/files/SP-1119-Vehicle-Ramming-Attacks.pdf.

Joh, Elizabeth E. 2014. "Policing by Numbers: Big Data and the Fourth Amendment." *Washington Law Review* 89: 35–68.

Joh, Elizabeth E. 2016. "The New Surveillance Discretion: Automated Suspicion, Big Data, and Policing." *Harvard Law and Policy Review* 10: 15–42.

Jones, Matthew DeVoy. 2019. "Cell Phones Are Orwell's Telescreen: The Need for Fourth Amendment Protection in Real-Time Cell Phone Location Information." *Cleveland State Law Review* 67(4): 523–58.

Joyce, Nina R., Melissa R. Pfeiffer, Andrew R. Zullo, Jasjit Ahluwalia, and Allison E. Curry. 2020. "Individual and Geographic Variation in Driver's License Suspensions: Evidence of Disparities by Race, Ethnicity, and Income." *Journal of Transport and Health* 19: e100933. https://doi.org/10.1016/j.jth.2020.100933.

Kagan, Robert A. 2001. *Adversarial Legalism: The American Way of Law*. Cambridge, MA: Harvard University Press.

Kaplan, Ivan. 2012. "Does the Privatisation of Publicly Owned Infrastructure Implicate the Public Trust Doctrine? *Illinois Central* and the Chicago Parking Meter Concession Agreement." *Northwestern Journal of Law and Social Policy* 7(1): 136–69.

Kaufman, Maya. 2018. "The Silence After the Hit-and-Run." *New York Times*, August 31. https://www.nytimes.com/2018/08/31/nyregion/police-inaction-after-hit-and-run-crashes.html.

Kearney, Paul W. 1948. "Are You a Deadly Driver?" *Redbook* 91(4): 34–37, 113.

Kelly, Brian. 2021. "An Empirical Assessment of Asset Forfeiture in Light of *Timbs v. Indiana*." *Alabama Law Review* 72(3): 613–40.

Kelly, Joe. 2020. "Seventh Circuit Examines Lifetime GPS Tracking of Sex Offenders." *Courthouse News Service*, September 18. https://www.courthousenews.com/seventh-circuit-examines-lifetime-gps-tracking-of-sex-offenders/.

Kerrane, Kaitlyn A. 2011. "Keeping Up with Officer Jones: A Comprehensive Look at the Fourth Amendment and GPS Surveillance." *Fordham Law Review* 79(4): 1695–742.

Kidwell, David. 2017. "Redflex to Pay $20 Million to Chicago to Settle Lawsuit over Red-Light Camera Bribery." *Chicago Tribune*, February 6. https://www.chicago

tribune.com/investigations/ct-red-light-cameras-lawsuit-settled-met-20170206
-story.html.

Kidwell, David, and Jason Meisner. 2016. "City Insider Given 10 Years in Prison
for Red Light Cameras Scandal." *Chicago Tribune*, August 29. https://www.chi
cagotribune.com/investigations/ct-red-light-cameras-john-bills-sentencing
-20160828-story.html.

Kidwell, David, and Alex Richards. 2014. "Tribune Study: Chicago Red Light Cameras Provide Few Safety Benefits." *Chicago Tribune*, December 19. https://www
.chicagotribune.com/suburbs/lake-county-news-sun/ct-red-light-camera
-safety-met-20141219-story.html.

Kim, Young-An, and John R. Hipp. 2018. "Physical Boundaries and City Boundaries:
Consequences for Crime Patterns on Street Segments?" *Crime and Delinquency*
64(2): 227–54.

Kim, Young-An, and John R. Hipp. 2022. "Both Sides of the Street: Introducing Measures of Physical and Social Boundaries Based on Differences Across Sides of the
Street, and Consequences for Crime." *Journal of Quantitative Criminology* 38:
75–103. https://doi.org/10.1007/s10940-020-09484-4.

Kirk, David S., and Sara Wakefield. 2018. "Collateral Consequences of Punishment:
A Critical Review and Path Forward." *Annual Review of Criminology* 1: 171–94.

Kirk, Gabriela. 2021. "The Limits of Expectations and the Minimization of Collateral
Consequences: The Experience of Electronic Home Monitoring." *Social Problems* 68(3): 642–57.

Kling, Samuel. 2013. "Wide Boulevards, Narrow Visions: Burnham's Street System
and the Chicago Plan Commission, 1909–1930." *Journal of Planning History* 12(3):
245–68.

Kneebone, Elizabeth, and Alan Berube. 2013. *Confronting Suburban Poverty in
America*. Washington, DC: Brookings Institution Press.

Knepper, Lisa, Jennifer McDonald, Kathy Sanchez, and Elyse Smith Pohl. 2020. *Policing for Profit: The Abuse of Civil Asset Forfeiture*, 3rd ed. Arlington, VA: Institute
for Justice.

Kohler-Hausmann, Issa. 2018. *Misdemeanorland: Criminal Courts and Social Control in an Age of Broken Windows Policing*. Princeton, NJ: Princeton University
Press.

Krisher, Tom. 2021. "NTSB Chief: Focus on Road Safety Must Shift to Entire System."
Associated Press, September 13. https://apnews.com/article/joe-biden-business
-transportation-transportation-safety-national-transportation-safety-board
-b84c28c5c1631b3d69b97bef9c9e2177.

Lageson, Sarah Esther. 2016. "Found Out and Opting Out: The Consequences of
Online Criminal Records for Families." *Annals of the American Academy of Political and Social Science* 665(1): 127–41.

Langum, David J. 1994. *Crossing Over the Line: Legislating Morality and the Mann
Act*. Chicago: University of Chicago Press.

Layson, Hoyt M., Jr. 1998. "Portable Tracking Apparatus for Continuous Position
Determination of Criminal Offenders and Victims." US Patent 5,731,757, filed
August 19, 1996, and issued March 24, 1998.

Layson, Hoyt M., Jr. 2000. "Body Worn Active and Passive Tracking Device." US Patent 6,014,080, filed October 28, 1998, and issued January 11, 2000.

Layson, Hoyt M., Jr., David S. Segal, and Peter Lefferson. 1999. "Tamper Detection for Body Worn Transmitter." US Patent 5,959,533, filed May 27, 1997, and issued September 28, 1999.

Leff, Carol Skalnik, and Mark H. Leff. 1981. "The Politics of Ineffectiveness: Federal Firearms Legislation, 1919–38." *Annals of the American Academy of Political and Social Science* 455(1): 48–62.

Legal Information Institute. 2021a. "In Personam." https://www.law.cornell.edu/wex/in_personam.

Legal Information Institute. 2021b. "In Rem." https://www.law.cornell.edu/wex/in_rem.

Lehman, Mary. 2002. "Comment: Are Red Light Cameras Snapping Privacy Rights?" *University of Toledo Law Review* 33: 815–45.

Leonard, V. A. 1938. *Police Communication Systems*. Berkeley: University of California Press.

Lerman, Amy E., and Vesla M. Weaver. 2014. *Arresting Citizenship: The Democratic Consequences of American Crime Control*. Chicago: University of Chicago Press.

Lerner, Barron H. 2011. *One for the Road: Drunk Driving Since 1900*. Baltimore: Johns Hopkins University Press.

Lerner, Michael A. 2007. *Dry Manhattan: Prohibition in New York City*. Cambridge, MA: Harvard University Press.

Levchak, Philip J. 2021. "Stop-and-Frisk in New York City: Estimating Racial Disparities in Post-Stop Outcomes." *Journal of Criminal Justice* 73: art. 101784. https://doi.org/10.1016/j.jcrimjus.2021.101784.

Levin, Mark S. 1983. "*People v. Watson*: Drunk Driving Homicide—Murder or Enhanced Manslaughter." *California Law Review* 71(4): 1298–323.

Levine, Harry G., and Craig Reinarman. 1991. "From Prohibition to Regulation: Lessons from Alcohol Policy for Drug Policy." *Milbank Quarterly* 69(3): 461–94.

Lewis, Robert. 2021. "State Lifts Suspensions of Half a Million Driver's Licenses." CalMatters, January 29. https://calmatters.org/justice/2021/01/california-drivers-licenses-traffic-ticket/.

Lewis, Tom. 1997. *Divided Highways: Building the Interstate Highways, Transforming American Life*. New York: Viking.

Lichtenstein, Alex. 1993. "Good Roads and Chain Gangs in the Progressive South: 'The Negro Convict Is a Slave.'" *Journal of Southern History* 59(1): 85–110.

Lichtenstein, Alex. 1996. *Twice the Work of Free Labor: The Political Economy of Convict Labor in the New South*. New York: Verso.

Lilly, J. Robert. 2006. "Issues Beyond Empirical EM Reports." *Criminology and Public Policy* 5(1): 93–101.

Lipsky, Michael. 2010. *Street-Level Bureaucracy: Dilemmas of the Individual in Public Services*, updated ed. New York: Russell Sage Foundation.

Litman, Todd. 2011. *Mobility as a Positional Good: Implications for Transport Policy and Planning*. Victoria, Canada: Victoria Transport Policy Institute.

Litwin, Kenneth J., and Yili Xu. 2007. "The Dynamic Nature of Homicide Clearances: A Multilevel Model Comparison of Three Time Periods." *Homicide Studies* 11(2): 94–114.

LoFaso, Charles A. 2020. "Solving Homicides: The Influence of Neighborhood Characteristics and Investigator Caseload." *Criminal Justice Review* 45(1): 84–103.

Logan, Wayne A. 2013. "Informal Collateral Consequences." *Washington Law Review* 88(3): 1103–18.

Love, Margaret, and David Schlussel. 2020. *Pathways to Reintegration: Criminal Record Reforms in 2019*. Washington, DC: Collateral Consequences Resource Center. https://ccresourcecenter.org/wp-content/uploads/2020/02/Pathways -to-Reintegration_Criminal-Record-Reforms-in-2019.pdf.

Lucia, Andrea. 2021. "Dallas Police Oversight Board Wants to Know Why Officers Seized Woman's Bag of Cash at Love Field." CBS DFW, December 15. https://dfw .cbslocal.com/2021/12/15/dallas-police-oversight-board-love-field/.

Lundman, Richard J., and Robert L. Kaufman. 2003. "Driving While Black: Effects of Race, Ethnicity, and Gender on Citizen Self-Reports of Traffic Stops and Police Actions." *Criminology* 41(1): 195–220.

Lundman, Richard J., and Meghan Myers. 2012. "Explanations of Homicide Clearances: Do Results Vary Dependent upon Operationalization and Initial (Time 1) and Updated (Time 2) Data?" *Homicide Studies* 16(1): 23–40.

Luria, David. 1988. "Death on the Highway: Reckless Driving as Murder." *Oregon Law Review* 67(4): 799–836.

Lynch, Mona. 2009. *Sunbelt Justice: Arizona and the Transformation of American Punishment*. Stanford, CA: Stanford University Press.

Lynch, Mona. 2016. *Hard Bargains: The Coercive Power of Drug Laws in Federal Court*. New York: Russell Sage Foundation.

Lynch, Mona. 2018. "Prosecutorial Discretion, Drug Case Selection, and Inequality in Federal Court." *Justice Quarterly* 35(7): 1309–36.

Lynd, Robert S., and Helen Merrell Lynd. 1929. *Middletown: A Study in American Culture*. San Diego: Harcourt Brace Jovanovich.

Macek, Kara. 2022. *Pedestrian Traffic Fatalities by State*. Washington, DC: Governors Highway Safety Association.

MADD. 2018. *Penalties for Drunk Driving Vehicular Homicide*. Washington, DC: Mothers Against Drunk Driving National Office. https://www.madd.org/wp -content/uploads/2018/07/Vehicular-Homicide.pdf.

Magee, Lauren A., J. Dennis Fortenberry, Wanzhu Tu, and Sarah E. Wiehe. 2020. "Neighborhood Variation in Unsolved Homicides: A Retrospective Cohort Study in Indianapolis, Indiana, 2007–2017." *Injury Epidemiology* 7(1): 1–10.

Mahoney, Ryan J. 2008. "Depraved Indifference Murder in the Context of DWI Homicides in New York." *St. John's Law Review* 82(4): 1537–88.

Mahr, Joe, and Matthew Walberg. 2017. "10 Years After Red Light Cameras Came to Suburbs, State Hasn't Assessed Whether They've Improved Safety." *Chicago Tribune*, November 7. https://www.chicagotribune.com/investigations/ct-met-red -light-cameras-studies-20171107-story.html.

Mancini, Matthew J. 1996. *One Dies, Get Another: Convict Leasing in the American South*. Columbia: University of South Carolina Press.

Mandel, Arch. 1924. "The Automobile and the Police." *Annals of the American Academy of Political and Social Science* 116: 191–94.

Manning, Peter K. 1988. *Symbolic Communication: Signifying Calls and the Police Response*. Cambridge, MA: MIT Press.

Manning, Peter K. 1992. "Information Technologies and the Police." *Crime and Justice* 15: 349–98.

Manning, Peter K. 2003. *Policing Contingencies*. Chicago: University of Chicago Press.

Manza, Jeff, and Christopher Uggen. 2008. *Locked Out: Felon Disenfranchisement and American Democracy*. New York: Oxford University Press.

Marcus, Aaron J. 2003. "Are the Roads a Safer Place Because Drug Offenders Aren't on Them: An Analysis of Punishing Drug Offenders with License Suspensions." *Kansas Journal of Law and Public Policy* 13(4): 557–84.

Markon, Jeremy. 2009. "Tracking Sex-Crime Offenders Gets Trickier." *Washington Post*, November 23.

Marsh, Andrea M. 2017. "Rethinking Driver's License Suspensions for Nonpayment of Fines and Fees." In *Trends in State Courts 2017*, ed. D. W. Smith, C. F. Campbell, and B. P. Kavanagh, 20–26. Williamsburg, VA: National Center for State Courts.

Martin, Alison. 2020. "John Dillinger's Escape from a Crown Point Jail Cell Made Headlines 86 Years Ago This Week." *Chicago Sun-Times*, March 4. https://chica go.suntimes.com/2020/3/4/21161878/john-dillinger-crown-point-escape-jail -chicago-daily-news-jon-seidel.

Martin, Karin D., Bryan L. Sykes, Sarah Shannon, Frank Edwards, and Alexes Harris. 2018. "Monetary Sanctions: Legal Financial Obligations in US Systems of Justice." *Annual Review of Criminology* 1: 471–95.

Martin, Ryan, Andrew Fan, Ellen Glover, and Dana Brozost-Kelleher. 2020. "IMPD Dogs Bite Far More Often." *Journal and Courier* (Lafayette, IN), October 11, p. 1A.

Massey, Douglas S., and Nancy A. Denton. 1993. *American Apartheid: Segregation and the Making of the Underclass*. Cambridge, MA: Harvard University Press.

Maxeiner, James R. 1977. "Bane of American Forfeiture Law: Banished at Last?" *Cornell Law Review* 62: 768–802.

May, Ethan. 2021. "Holcomb Signs Bill Looking to Get Suspended Drivers Back on the Road Legally." *Indianapolis Star*, March 2. https://www.indystar.com/story /news/local/transportation/2021/03/02/indiana-drivers-license-suspensions -could-change-under-house-bill/4291634001/.

Maynard-Moody, Steven, and Michael Musheno. 2003. *Cops, Teachers, Counselors: Stories from the Front Lines of Public Service*. Ann Arbor: University of Michigan Press.

McAfee, Ward M. 1990. "A History of Convict Labor in California." *Southern California Quarterly* 72(1): 19–40.

McCoy, Tana, Patti Ross Salinas, Jeffrey T. Walker, and Lance Hignite. 2012. "An Examination of the Influence of Strength of Evidence Variables in the Prosecution's Decision to Dismiss Driving While Intoxicated Cases." *American Journal of Criminal Justice* 37(4): 562–79.

McCutcheon, James C. 2021. "The Impact of the Interstate on Violent Crime in Three Southern States: Do Drugs Play a Role?" *Criminal Justice Studies* 34(2): 156–72.

McCutcheon, James C., Greg S. Weaver, Lin Huff-Corzine, Jay Corzine, and Bert Burraston. 2016. "Highway Robbery: Testing the Impact of Interstate Highways on Robbery." *Justice Quarterly* 33(7): 1292–310.

McElhattan, David. 2018. "'$40 to Make Sure': Background Check Laws and the Endogenous Construction of Criminal Risk." *Studies in Law, Politics, and Society* 77: 99–121.

McElhattan, David. 2022a. "The Exception as the Rule: Negligent Hiring Liability, Structured Uncertainty, and the Rise of Criminal Background Checks in the United States." *Law and Social Inquiry* 47(1): 132–61.

McElhattan, David. 2022b. "The Proliferation of Criminal Background Check Laws in the United States." *American Journal of Sociology* 127(4): 1037–93.

McElhattan, David, and Spencer Headworth. 2022. "Immobilized: The Proliferation of Driver's License Consequences for Criminal Convictions." Unpublished manuscript.

McKenzie, Brian. 2015. *Who Drives to Work? Commuting by Automobile in the United States: 2013*. American Community Survey Reports. Washington, DC: US Census Bureau.

McLuhan, Marshall. 1966. *Understanding Media: The Extensions of Man*, 2nd ed. New York: Signet.

McMahon, Lara M. 2020. "Limited Privacy in 'Pings': Why Law Enforcement's Use of Cell-Site Simulators Does not Categorically Violate the Fourth Amendment." *Washington and Lee Law Review* 77(2): 981–1034.

McNeill, Fergus. 2018. *Pervasive Punishment: Making Sense of Mass Supervision*. Bingley, UK: Emerald.

McShane, Clay. 1994. *Down the Asphalt Path: The Automobile and the American City*. New York: Columbia University Press.

Meloy, Michelle L., and Shareda Coleman. 2009. "GPS Monitoring of Sex Offenders." In *Sex Offender Laws: Failed Policies, New Directions*, ed. R. G. Wright, 243–66. New York: Springer.

Menell, Peter S., and Ryan Vacca. 2020. "Revisiting and Confronting the Federal Judiciary Capacity 'Crisis': Charting a Path for Federal Judiciary Reform." *California Law Review* 108(3): 789–886.

Mercer, William D. 2012. "At the Intersection of Sovereignty and Contract: Traffic Cameras and the Privatization of Law Enforcement Power." *University of Memphis Law Review* 43(2): 379–418.

Merton, Robert K. 1948. "The Self-Fulfilling Prophecy." *Antioch Review* 8(2): 193–210.

Michigan Department of Transportation. 2015. "MDOT: National Firsts." https://www.michigan.gov/mdot/0,4616,7-151-9623_11154-129682--,00.html.

Miller, Jordan. 2015. "New Age Tracking Technologies in the Post–*United States v. Jones* Environment: The Need for Model Legislation." *Creighton Law Review* 48(3): 553–604.

Miller, J. Mitchell, and Lance H. Selva. 1994. "Drug Enforcement's Doubleedged

Sword: An Assessment of Asset Forfeiture Programs." *Justice Quarterly* 11(2): 313–35.

Miller, Lisa L. 2008. *The Perils of Federalism: Race, Poverty, and the Politics of Crime Control*. New York: Oxford University Press.

Miller, Lisa L. 2016. *The Myth of Mob Rule: Violent Crime and Democratic Politics*. New York: Oxford University Press.

Miller, Lisa L., and James Eisenstein. 2005. "The Federal/State Criminal Prosecution Nexus: A Case Study in Cooperation and Discretion." *Law and Social Inquiry* 30(2): 239–68.

Miller, Reuben Jonathan, and Forrest Stuart. 2017. "Carceral Citizenship: Race, Rights, and Responsibility in the Age of Mass Supervision." *Theoretical Criminology* 21(4): 532–48.

Millum, Deborah A. 1990. "The Other Tragedy of Vehicular Related Deaths in Ohio's Criminal Statutes." *University of Dayton Law Review* 16(1): 183–220.

Misner, Robert L. 1996. "Recasting Prosecutorial Discretion." *Journal of Criminal Law and Criminology* 86(3): 717–77.

Missouri Attorney General's Office. 2021. *Missouri Vehicle Stops 2020 Annual Report*. https://ago.mo.gov/docs/default-source/vsr/2020-vehicle-stops-annual-report .pdf?sfvrsn=ffd40b8a_2.

Mletzko, Deborah, Lucia Summers, and Ashley N. Arnio. 2018. "Spatial Patterns of Urban Sex Trafficking." *Journal of Criminal Justice* 58: 87–96.

Morgan, Kimberly J., and Ann Shola Orloff, eds. 2017. *The Many Hands of the State: Theorizing Political Authority and Social Control*. New York: Cambridge University Press.

Morris, Nichole L., Jennifer L. Cooper, Alice Ton, Peter Easterlund, and John Paul Plummer. 2016. *Examining the Impact of ASE (Automated Speed Enforcement) in Work Zones on Driver Attention*. St. Paul: Minnesota Department of Transportation.

Moskos, Peter. 2008. *Cop in the Hood: My Year Policing Baltimore's Eastern District*. Princeton, NJ: Princeton University Press.

Myers, Wayne. 2006. "*Roper v. Simmons*: The Collision of National Consensus and Proportionality Review." *Journal of Criminal Law and Criminology* 96(3): 947–94.

NASA. 2012. "Global Positioning System History." https://www.nasa.gov/ directorates/heo/scan/communications/policy/GPS_History.html.

National Auto Auction Association. 2017. "History of Auto Theft." https://www.naaa .com/NAAA_Legislative/HistoryOfAutoTheft.html.

National Commission on Law Observance and Enforcement. 1931. *Report on the Enforcement of the Prohibition Laws of the United States*. Washington, DC: National Commission on Law Observance and Enforcement.

National Conference of State Legislatures. 2021. "Automated Enforcement Overview." https://www.ncsl.org/research/transportation/automated-enforcement -overview.aspx.

National Conference on Street and Highway Safety. 1924. *First National Conference on Street and Highway Safety*. Washington, DC: US Department of Commerce.

National Conference on Street and Highway Safety. 1926. *Final Text of Uniform Vehicle Code*. Washington, DC: US Department of Commerce.

National Emergency Number Association. 2021. "9-1-1 Statistics." https://www.nena.org/page/911Statistics.

National Highway Traffic Safety Administration. 2021. "2020 Fatality Data Show Increased Traffic Fatalities During Pandemic." NHTSA news release, June 3. https://www.nhtsa.gov/press-releases/2020-fatality-data-show-increased-traffic-fatalities-during-pandemic.

National Highway Traffic Safety Administration. 2022. "Newly Released Estimates Show Traffic Fatalities Reached a 16-Year High in 2021." NHTSA news release, May 17. https://www.nhtsa.gov/press-releases/early-estimate-2021-traffic-fatalities.

National Inventory of Collateral Consequences of Conviction. 2021. "Collateral Consequences Inventory." Arlington, VA: National Reentry Resource Center. https://niccc.nationalreentryresourcecenter.org/consequences.

National Safety Council. 2021. "Deaths by Transportation Mode." https://injuryfacts.nsc.org/home-and-community/safety-topics/deaths-by-transportation-mode/.

Nelson, Derek. 1995. *Moonshiners, Bootleggers, and Rumrunners*. Osceola, WI: Motorbooks International.

Ng, Alfred. 2022. "Amazon Gave Ring Videos to Police Without Owners' Permission." *Politico*, July 13. https://www.politico.com/news/2022/07/13/amazon-gave-ring-videos-to-police-without-owners-permission-00045513.

Norton, Peter D. 2007. "Street Rivals: Jaywalking and the Invention of the Motor Age." *Technology and Culture* 48(2): 331–59.

Norton, Peter D. 2008. *Fighting Traffic: The Dawn of the Motor Age in the American City*. Cambridge, MA: MIT Press.

Nye, David C. 1986. "Drunk Driving: The New Automobile Statute's Overlapping Effect." *BYU Journal of Public Law* 1: 183–92.

O'Connell, David. 2018. "Civil Asset Forfeiture: Lining Pockets and Ruining Lives." *National Lawyers Guild Review* 74(4): 237–56.

Office of Juvenile Justice and Delinquency Prevention, US Department of Justice. 2020. "Estimated Number of Arrests by Offense and Race, 2019." https://www.ojjdp.gov/ojstatbb/crime/ucr.asp?table_in=2&selYrs=2019&rdoGroups=3&rdoData=c.

Office of Management and Budget. 2022. "Fact Sheet: President Biden's Budget Invests in Reducing Gun Crime to Make Our Communities Safer." March 28. https://www.whitehouse.gov/omb/briefing-room/2022/03/28/fact-sheet-president-bidens-budget-invests-in-reducing-gun-crime-to-make-our-communities-safer/.

Oliver, Willard M. 2017. *August Vollmer: The Father of American Policing*. Durham, NC: Carolina Academic Press.

Olney, Martha L. 1989. "Credit as a Production-Smoothing Device: The Case of Automobiles, 1913–1938." *Journal of Economic History* 49(2): 377–91.

Olney, Martha L. 1991. *Buy Now, Pay Later: Advertising, Credit, and Consumer Durables in the 1920s*. Chapel Hill: University of North Carolina Press.

Ousey, Graham C., and Matthew R. Lee. 2010. "To Know the Unknown: The Decline in Homicide Clearance Rates, 1980–2000." *Criminal Justice Review* 35(2): 141–58.

Page, Joshua. 2011. *The Toughest Beat: Politics, Punishment, and the Prison Officers Union in California*. New York: Oxford University Press.

Page, Joshua, and Joe Soss. 2021. "The Predatory Dimensions of Criminal Justice." *Science* 374(6565): 291–94.

Pager, Devah. 2003. "The Mark of a Criminal Record." *American Journal of Sociology* 108(5): 937–75.

Pager, Devah. 2007. *Marked: Race, Crime, and Finding Work in an Era of Mass Incarceration*. Chicago: University of Chicago Press.

Pagnanelli, Enrico. 2007. "Children as Adults: The Transfer of Juveniles to Adult Courts and the Potential Impact of *Roper v. Simmons*." *American Criminal Law Review* 44(1): 175–94.

Paoletti, Isabella. 2012. "The Issue of Conversationally Constituted Context and Localization Problems in Emergency Calls." *Text and Talk* 32(2): 191–210.

Parness, Jeffrey A. 2011. "Beyond Red Light Enforcement Against the Guilty but Innocent: Local Regulations of Secondary Culprits." *Willamette Law Review* 47(2): 259–86.

Pattillo, Mary, David Weiman, and Bruce Western, eds. 2004. *Imprisoning America: The Social Effects of Mass Incarceration*. New York: Russell Sage Foundation.

Perkinson, Robert. 2010. *Texas Tough: The Rise of America's Prison Empire*. New York: Picador.

Peters, Cameron. 2021. "State-Level Republicans Are Making It Easier to Run Over Protesters." *Vox*, April 25. https://www.vox.com/2021/4/25/22367019/gop-laws-oklahoma-iowa-florida-floyd-blm-protests-police.

Peters, Jeremy W. 2009. "More Red-Light Cameras on the Way." *New York Times*, City Room Blog, April 7. https://cityroom.blogs.nytimes.com/2009/04/07/more-red-light-cameras-on-the-way/.

Petersen, Nick. 2017. "Neighbourhood Context and Unsolved Murders: The Social Ecology of Homicide Investigations." *Policing and Society* 27(4): 372–92.

Pierson, Emma, Camelia Simoiu, Jan Overgoor, Sam Corbett-Davies, Daniel Jenson, Amy Shoemaker, Vignesh Ramachandran, Phoebe Barghouty, Cheryl Phillips, and Ravi Shroff. 2020. "A Large-Scale Analysis of Racial Disparities in Police Stops Across the United States." *Nature Human Behaviour* 4(7): 736–45.

Pietrucha, Bill. 1997. "Satellites to Start Tracking Criminal Offenders." *Newsbytes*, January 6.

Piety, Tamara. 1991. "Comment: Scorched Earth: How the Doctrine of Civil Forfeiture Has Laid Waste to Due Process." *University of Miami Law Review* 45: 911–78.

Pilkington, Paul, and Sanjay Kinra. 2005. "Effectiveness of Speed Cameras in Preventing Road Traffic Collisions and Related Casualties: Systematic Review." *BMJ Clinical Research* 330(7487): 331–34.

Pimentel, David. 2012. "Forfeitures Revisited: Bringing Principle to Practice in Federal Court." *Nevada Law Journal* 13(1): 1–59.

Pimentel, David. 2017. "Forfeitures and the Eighth Amendment: A Practical Approach to the Excessive Fines Clause as a Check on Government Seizures." *Harvard Law and Policy Review* 11: 541–84.

Pinard, Michael. 2010. "Reflections and Perspectives on Reentry and Collateral Consequences." *Journal of Criminal Law and Criminology* 100(3): 1213–24.

Piquero, Alex R., Wesley G. Jennings, Erin Jemison, Catherine Kaukinen, and Felicia Marie Knaul. 2021. *Domestic Violence During COVID-19: Evidence from a Systematic Review and Meta-Analysis*. Washington, DC: Council on Criminal Justice.

Poli, Joseph A. 1942. "The Development and Present Trend of Police Radio Communications." *Journal of Criminal Law and Criminology* 33(2): 193–97.

Policing Project. 2018. *An Assessment of Traffic Stops and Policing Strategies in Nashville*. New York: New York University School of Law

Post, Robert. 2006. "Federalism, Positive Law, and the Emergence of the American Administrative State: Prohibition in the Taft Court Era." *William and Mary Law Review* 48(1): 1–183.

Proctor, Paul. 1996. "GPS Against Crime." *Aviation Week and Space Technology* 144(19): 13.

Puckett, Janice L., and Richard J. Lundman. 2003. "Factors Affecting Homicide Clearances: Multivariate Analysis of a More Complete Conceptual Framework." *Journal of Research in Crime and Delinquency* 40(2): 171–93.

Pulugurtha, Srinivas S., and Ramesh Otturu. 2014. "Effectiveness of Red Light Running Camera Enforcement Program in Reducing Crashes: Evaluation Using 'Before the Installation,' 'After the Installation,' and 'After the Termination' Data." *Accident Analysis and Prevention* 64: 9–17.

Quinones, Sam. 2015. *Dreamland: The True Tale of America's Opiate Epidemic*. New York: Bloomsbury.

Ram, Natalie. 2018. "Innovating Criminal Justice." *Northwestern University Law Review* 112(4): 659–724.

Reich, Charles A. 1964. "The New Property." *Yale Law Journal* 73(5): 733–87.

Retting, Richard A., Susan A. Ferguson, and Charles M. Farmer. 2008. "Reducing Red Light Running Through Longer Yellow Signal Timing and Red Light Camera Enforcement: Results of a Field Investigation." *Accident Analysis and Prevention* 40(1): 327–33.

Retting, Richard A., and Sergey Y. Kyrychenko. 2002. "Reductions in Injury Crashes Associated with Red Light Camera Enforcement in Oxnard, California." *American Journal of Public Health* 92(11): 1822–25.

Retting, Richard A., Sergey Y. Kyrychenko, and Anne T. McCartt. 2008. "Evaluation of Automated Speed Enforcement on Loop 101 Freeway in Scottsdale, Arizona." *Accident Analysis and Prevention* 40(4): 1506–12.

Retting, Richard A., Allan F. Williams, Charles M. Farmer, and Amy F. Feldman. 1999. "Evaluation of Red Light Camera Enforcement in Fairfax, Va., USA." *ITE Journal* 69: 30–35.

Reyes, Nicholas Tucker, and Spencer Headworth. 2022. "Automobility on Installments Or: How I Learned to Stop Worrying and Love Car Loans." Unpublished manuscript.

Riccucci, Norma M. 2005. *How Management Matters: Street-Level Bureaucrats and Welfare Reform*. Washington, DC: Georgetown University Press.

Ridgeway, Cecilia L. 2011. *Framed by Gender: How Gender Inequality Persists in the Modern World*. New York: Oxford University Press.

Rivera, Lauren A. 2015. *Pedigree: How Elite Students Get Elite Jobs*. Princeton, NJ: Princeton University Press.

Roberts, Aki. 2007. "Predictors of Homicide Clearance by Arrest: An Event History Analysis of NIBRS Incidents." *Homicide Studies* 11(2): 82–93.

Robertson, Gary D. 2019. "Supreme Court Narrows Lifetime GPS Tracking of Sex Offenders." *Associated Press*, August 16. https://apnews.com/article/78d4f8f00c e54bc0817335ca5bd755ec.

Rojek, Jeff, Richard Rosenfeld, and Scott Decker. 2012. "Policing Race: The Racial Stratification of Searches in Police Traffic Stops." *Criminology* 50(4): 993–1024.

Rolland, Melissa A. 1999. "Forfeiture Law, the Eight Amendment's Excessive Fines Clause, and *United States v. Bajakajian*." *Notre Dame Law Review* 74(4): 1371–401.

Rosario, Ariana Acevedo. 2021. "Meet Devon Moore, WLPD's First Social Worker." *Purdue Exponent*, April 15. https://www.purdueexponent.org/city_state/article_ a52c723a-a5ef-5f46-b9af-5f675556ofda.html.

Rose, Mark H., and Raymond A. Mohl. 2012. *Interstate: Highway Politics and Policy Since 1939*, 3rd ed. Knoxville: University of Tennessee Press.

Rosenfeld, Richard, Thomas Abt, and Ernesto Lopez Jr. 2021. *Pandemic, Social Unrest, and Crime in US Cities: 2020 Year-End Update*. Washington, DC: Council on Criminal Justice.

Rothstein, Richard. 2017. *The Color of Law: A Forgotten History of How Our Government Segregated America*. New York: Norton.

Rubin, Edward. 1934. "A Statistical Study of Federal Criminal Prosecutions." *Law and Contemporary Problems* 1(4): 494–508.

Rule, James B., Douglas McAdam, Linda Stearns, and David Uglow. 1983. "Documentary Identification and Mass Surveillance in the United States." *Social Problems* 31(2): 222–34.

Sampson, Robert J., and Stephen W. Raudenbush. 1999. "Systematic Social Observation of Public Spaces: A New Look at Disorder in Urban Neighborhoods." *American Journal of Sociology* 105(3): 603–51.

Samuels, Diana. 2016. "Latest Court Challenge to Redflex Traffic Cameras Is in Gretna." *New Orleans Times-Picayune*, April 28. https://www.nola.com/news/ traffic/article_9e4589e2-2b12-5362-9c2e-e3b8b1b26d07.html.

Sanchez, Melissa, and Sandhya Kambhampati. 2018. "How Chicago Ticket Debt Sends Black Motorists into Bankruptcy." ProPublica, February 27. https:// features.propublica.org/driven-into-debt/chicago-ticket-debt-bankruptcy/.

Sanders, Carrie. 2006. "Have You Been Identified? Hidden Boundary Work in Emergency Services Classifications." *Information, Communication, and Society* 9(6): 714–36.

Sawyer, Wendy, and Peter Wagner. 2019. *Mass Incarceration: The Whole Pie 2019*. Northampton, MA: Prison Policy Initiative. https://www.prisonpolicy.org/ reports/pie2019.html.

Sawyer, Wendy, and Peter Wagner. 2020. *Mass Incarceration: The Whole Pie 2020*. Northampton, MA: Prison Policy Initiative. https://www.prisonpolicy.org/reports/pie2020.html.

Scharff, Virginia. 1991. *Taking the Wheel: Women and the Coming of the Motor Age*. New York: Free Press.

Schlinkmann, Mark. 2017. "Red Light Cameras in Missouri Are Down—But not Necessarily Out." *St. Louis Post-Dispatch*, June 18. https://www.stltoday.com/news/traffic/along-for-the-ride/red-light-cameras-in-missouri-are-down-but-not-necessarily-out/article_c7519772-9e63-51d1-a590-7e4aa358c72f.html.

Schmitt, Angie. 2020. *Right of Way: Race, Class, and the Silent Epidemic of Pedestrian Deaths in America*. Washington, DC: Island Press.

Schmitt, Glenn R., and Amanda Russell. 2021. *Fiscal Year 2020 Overview of Federal Criminal Cases*. Washington, DC: United States Sentencing Commission. https://www.ussc.gov/sites/default/files/pdf/research-and-publications/research-publications/2021/FY20_Overview_Federal_Criminal_Cases.pdf.

Schnepel, Kevin T. 2020. *COVID-19 in U.S. State and Federal Prisons: December 2020 Update*. Washington, DC: Council on Criminal Justice.

Schwier, Ryan T., and Autumn James. 2016. *Roadblock to Economic Independence*. Indianapolis: Indiana University, Robert H. McKinney School of Law. https://mckinneylaw.iu.edu/practice/clinics/_docs/DL_Rpt_2-1-16.pdf.

Seiler, Cotten. 2008. *Republic of Drivers: A Cultural History of Automobility in America*. Chicago: University of Chicago Press.

Sentencing Project. 2020. "The Facts: State-by-State Data." https://www.sentencingproject.org/the-facts/#map.

Seo, Sarah A. 2013. "Antinomies and the Automobile: A New Approach to Criminal Justice Histories." *Law and Social Inquiry* 38(4): 1020–40.

Seo, Sarah A. 2019. *Policing the Open Road: How Cars Transformed American Freedom*. Cambridge, MA: Harvard University Press.

Shannon, Kevin P. 2007. "Speeding Towards Disaster: How Cleveland's Traffic Cameras Violate the Ohio Constitution." *Cleveland State Law Review* 55(4): 607–36.

Sheller, Mimi, and John Urry. 2000. "The City and the Car." *International Journal of Urban and Regional Research* 24(4): 737–57.

Shill, Gregory H. 2020. "Should Law Subsidize Driving?" *New York University Law Review* 95: 498–579.

Shin, Kangwon, Simon P. Washington, and Ida van Schalkwyk. 2009. "Evaluation of the Scottsdale Loop 101 Automated Speed Enforcement Demonstration Program." *Accident Analysis and Prevention* 41(3): 393–403.

Shoub, Kelsey, Derek A. Epp, Frank R. Baumgartner, Leah Christiani, and Kevin Roach. 2020. "Race, Place, and Context: The Persistence of Race Effects in Traffic Stop Outcomes in the Face of Situational, Demographic, and Political Controls." *Journal of Race, Ethnicity, and Politics* 5(3): 481–508.

Simpson, Brett. 2021. "Why Cars Don't Deserve the Right of Way." *The Atlantic*, October 15. https://www.theatlantic.com/ideas/archive/2021/10/end-police-violence-get-rid-traffic-cop/620378/.

Skolnick, Jerome H. 2008. "Policing Should Not Be for Profit." *Criminology and Public Policy* 7(2): 257–62.

Slobogin, Christopher. 2020. "The Case for a Federal Criminal Court System (and Sentencing Reform)." *California Law Review* 108(3): 941–64.

Smith, Stephen F. 2019. "Federalization's Folly." *San Diego Law Review* 56(1): 31–72.

Smith, William R., Donald Tomaskovic-Devey, Matthew T. Zingraff, H. Marcinda Mason, Patricia Y. Warren, Cynthia Pfaff Wright, Harvey McMurray, and C. R. Felnon. 2003. *The North Carolina Highway Traffic Study: Final Report.* Washington, DC: National Institute of Justice.

Snow, Vanita Saleema. 2017. "From the Dark Tower: Unbridled Civil Asset Forfeiture." *Drexel Law Review* 10: 69–125.

Sommers, Roseanna, and Vanessa K. Bohns. 2019. "The Voluntariness of Voluntary Consent: Consent Searches and the Psychology of Compliance." *Yale Law Journal* 128: 1962–2033.

Sorin, Gretchen. 2020. *Driving While Black: African American Travel and the Road to Civil Rights.* New York: Liveright.

Spohn, Cassia. 2018. "Reflections on the Exercise of Prosecutorial Discretion 50 Years After Publication of *The Challenge of Crime in a Free Society*." *Criminology and Public Policy* 17(2): 321–40.

Stevenson, Megan, and Sandra Mayson. 2018. "The Scale of Misdemeanor Justice." *Boston University Law Review* 98(3): 731–78.

Stillman, Sarah. 2013. "Taken: Under Civil Forfeiture, Americans Who Haven't Been Charged with Wrongdoing Can Be Stripped of Their Cash, Cars, and Even Homes. Is That All We're Losing?" *New Yorker*, August 12 and 19. https://www.newyorker.com/magazine/2013/08/12/taken.

Stoll, Michael A., and Shawn D. Bushway. 2008. "The Effect of Criminal Background Checks on Hiring Ex-Offenders." *Criminology and Public Policy* 7(3): 371–404.

Subramanian, Ram, Léon Digard, Melvin Washington II, and Stephanie Sorage. 2020. *In the Shadows: A Review of the Research on Plea Bargaining.* Brooklyn, NY: Vera Institute of Justice.

Swift, Earl. 2011. *The Big Roads: The Untold Story of the Engineers, Visionaries, and Trailblazers Who Created the American Superhighways.* Boston: Houghton Mifflin Harcourt.

Tanenhaus, David S. 2004. *Juvenile Justice in the Making.* New York: Oxford University Press.

Tarr, Andrew W. J. 2002. "Picture It: Red Light Cameras Abide by the Law of the Land." *North Carolina Law Review* 80(5): 1879–96.

Tau, Byron, and Michelle Hackman. 2020. "Federal Agencies Use Cellphone Location Data for Immigration Enforcement." *Wall Street Journal*, February 7. https://www.wsj.com/articles/federal-agencies-use-cellphone-location-data-for-immigration-enforcement-11581078600.

Taxy, Sam, Julie Samuels, and William Adams. 2015. *Drug Offenders in Federal Prison: Estimates of Characteristics Based on Linked Data.* Washington, DC: Bureau of Justice Statistics, US Department of Justice.

Teigen, Anne, and Lucia Bragg. 2018. "Evolving Civil Asset Forfeiture Laws." *Legis-Brief* 26(5).

Thorsen, Leah. 2015. "Missouri Supreme Court Strikes Down Red-Light Ordinances." *St. Louis Post-Dispatch*, August 19. https://www.stltoday.com/news/local/metro/missouri-supreme-court-strikes-down-red-light-ordinances/article_f5967dba-5e9a-5e22-9682-b3cc9ed89f35.html.

Toler, Lindsay. 2015. "Why You Don't Have to Pay Your Red-Light Camera Tickets Anymore, St. Louis." *St. Louis Magazine*, August 18. https://www.stlmag.com/news/why-you-don%E2%80%99t-have-to-pay-your-red-light-camera-tickets/.

Tonry, Michael. 2011. *Punishing Race: A Continuing American Dilemma*. New York: Oxford University Press.

Tracy, Karen, and Sarah J. Tracy. 1998. "Rudeness at 911: Reconceptualizing Face and Face Attack." *Human Communication Research* 25(2): 225–51.

Tracy, Sarah J., and Karen Tracy. 1998. "Emotion Labor at 911: A Case Study and Theoretical Critique." *Journal of Applied Communication Research* 26: 390–411.

Travis, Jeremy. 2002. "Invisible Punishment: An Instrument of Social Exclusion." In *Invisible Punishment: The Collateral Consequences of Mass Imprisonment*, ed. M. Mauer and M. Chesney-Lind, 15–36. New York: New Press.

Trigaux, Robert. 1997. "'Orbiting Warden' Watches Offenders." *St. Petersburg Times*, January 7.

Tripp, Heidi. 2019. "All Sex Workers Deserve Protection: How FOSTA/SESTA Overlooks Consensual Sex Workers in an Attempt to Protect Sex Trafficking Victims." *Penn State Law Review* 124(1): 219–46.

Tyler, Tom R. 2006. *Why People Obey the Law*, rev. ed. Princeton, NJ: Princeton University Press.

Ulmer, R. G., V. I. Shabanova, and D. F. Preusser. 2001. *Evaluation of Use and Lose Laws*. Washington, DC: National Highway Traffic Administration, US Department of Transportation.

United Nations Office on Drugs and Crime. 2021. "Human Trafficking." https://www.unodc.org/unodc/en/human-trafficking/human-trafficking.html.

United States Attorney's Office for the District of New Hampshire. 2020. "Frequently Used Federal Drug Statutes." https://www.justice.gov/usao-nh/frequently-used-federal-drug-statutes.

United States Courts. 2019. *Judicial Business 2019*. Washington, DC: Administrative Office of the United States Courts. https://www.uscourts.gov/statistics-reports/judicial-business-2019.

United States Courts. 2020. *Judicial Business 2020*. Washington, DC: Administrative Office of the United States Courts. https://www.uscourts.gov/statistics-reports/judicial-business-2020.

Urry, John. 2000. *Sociology Beyond Societies: Mobilities for the Twenty-First Century*. New York: Routledge.

Urry, John. 2004. "The 'System' of Automobility." *Theory, Culture, and Society* 21(4–5): 25–39.

US Department of Justice. 2020. "Motor Vehicle Theft Prevention Statutes: General

Overview." In *Criminal Resource Manual*. Washington, DC: US Department of Justice. https://www.justice.gov/archives/jm/criminal-resource-manual-1359 -motor-vehicle-theft-prevention-statutes-general-overview.

US Department of Justice, Office of Public Affairs. 2016. "Redflex Traffic Systems Enters into Non-Prosecution Agreement with United States." Justice News, November 27. https://www.justice.gov/opa/pr/redflex-traffic-systems-enters-non -prosecution-agreement-united-states.

US Department of Transportation. 2021. "DOT's Commitment to Prevent Human Trafficking." https://www.transportation.gov/briefing-room/dots-commitment -prevent-human-trafficking.

VanSickle, Abbie, and Challen Stephens. 2020. "Police Use Painful Dog Bites to Make People Obey." The Marshall Project, December 14. https://www .themarshallproject.org/2020/12/14/police-use-painful-dog-bites-to-make -people-obey.

Van Wagenen, Juliet. 2017. "The First Police Radio Stopped Bootleggers in Their Tracks." *StateTech*, June 9. https://statetechmagazine.com/article/2017/06/first -police-radio-stopped-bootleggers-their-tracks.

Vogel, Mary E. 2007. *Coercion to Compromise: Plea Bargaining, the Courts, and the Making of Political Authority*. New York: Oxford University Press.

Wagner, Dennis. 2021. "US Sees Rise of 'Vehicle Ramming.'" *Indianapolis Star*, November 24, p. 11A.

Ware, Leland. 2021. "*Plessy*'s Legacy: The Government's Role in the Development and Perpetuation of Segregated Neighborhoods." *RSF: The Russell Sage Foundation Journal of the Social Sciences* 7(1): 92–109.

Watkins-Hayes, Celeste. 2009. *The New Welfare Bureaucrats: Entanglements of Race, Class, and Policy Reform*. Chicago: University of Chicago Press.

Weber, Joe. 2017. "Continuity and Change in American Freeway Networks." *Journal of Transport Geography* 58: 31–39.

Weber, Max. 1978. *Economy and Society: An Outline of Interpretive Sociology*, ed. G. Roth and C. Wittich. Berkeley: University of California Press.

Weber, Max. 2003. *The Protestant Ethic and the Spirit of Capitalism*. Mineola, NY: Dover.

Wells, Christopher W. 2012. *Car Country: An Environmental History*. Seattle: University of Washington Press.

Western, Bruce. 2006. *Punishment and Inequality in America*. New York: Russell Sage Foundation.

White, Katherine M. 1995. "Drunk Driving as Second-Degree Murder in Michigan." *Wayne Law Review* 41(3): 1433–68.

Whitlatch, Walter G. 1967. "The Juvenile Court: A Court of Law." *Case Western Reserve Law Review* 18(4): 1239–50.

Wilber, Del Quentin. 2005. "D.C. Police Plan More Speed Cameras." *Washington Post*, February 21.

Wilber, Del Quentin, and Derek Willis. 2005. "D.C. Red-Light Cameras Fail to Reduce Accidents." *Washington Post*, October 4.

Wilmot, Sydney. 1914. "The Use of Convict Labor for Highway Construction in the North." *Proceedings of the Academy of Political Science in the City of New York* 4(2): 246–308.

Wilson, Alicia. 2013. "Using Commercial Driver Licensing Authority to Combat Human Trafficking Related Crimes on America's Highways." *University of Memphis Law Review* 43: 969–1012.

Wilson, James Q., and George L. Kelling. 1982. "Broken Windows: The Police and Neighborhood Safety." *Atlantic Monthly* 249(3): 29–38. https://www.theatlantic.com/magazine/archive/1982/03/broken-windows/304465/.

Wilson, William Julius. 1987. *The Truly Disadvantaged: The Inner City, the Underclass, and Public Policy*. Chicago: University of Chicago Press.

Worrall, John L. 2001. "Addicted to the Drug War: The Role of Civil Asset Forfeiture as a Budgetary Necessity in Contemporary Law Enforcement." *Journal of Criminal Justice* 29(3): 171–87.

Xu, Yili. 2008. "Characteristics of Homicide Events and the Decline in Homicide Clearance: A Longitudinal Approach to the Dynamic Relationship, Chicago 1966–1995." *Criminal Justice Review* 33(4): 453–79.

Zimmer, Samantha G. 2018. "Cell Phone or Government Tracking Device? Protecting Cell Site Location Information with Probable Cause." *Duquesne Law Review* 56(1): 107–40.

Zimring, Franklin E. 2005. *American Juvenile Justice*. New York: Oxford University Press.

Zmud, Johanna, Troy Walden, Ben Ettelman, Laura Higgins, Jon Graber, Robert Gilbert, and David Hodges. 2021. *State of Knowledge and Practice for Using Automated License Plate Readers for Traffic Safety Purposes*. Washington, DC: National Highway Traffic Safety Administration.

Cases and Statutes Cited

Austin v. United States, 509 U.S. 602 (1993)
Barrows v. Jackson, 346 U.S. 249 (1953)
Bell v. Burson, 402 U.S. 535 (1971)
Bennis v. Michigan, 516 U.S. 442 (1996)
Brinegar v. United States, 338 U.S. 160 (1949)
Brown v. Board of Education of Topeka, 347 U.S. 483 (1954)
Buchanan v. Warley, 245 U.S. 60 (1917)
Calero-Toledo et al. v. Pearson Yacht Leasing Co., 416 U.S. 663 (1974)
Caminetti v. United States, 242 U.S. 470 (1917)
Carpenter v. United States, 585 U.S. —— (2018)
Carroll v. United States, 267 U.S. 132 (1925)
Corrigan et al. v. Buckley, 271 U.S. 323 (1926)
Dobbins' Distillery v. United States, 96 U.S. 395 (1877)
Gideon v. Wainwright, 372 U.S. 335 (1963)
Grady v. North Carolina, 575 U.S. 306 (2015)
Illinois v. Caballes, 543 U.S. 405 (2005)

In re Gault, 387 U.S. 1 (1967)

Jones v. Mississippi, 593 U.S. —— (2021)

J. W. Goldsmith, Jr.-Grant Company v. United States, 254 U.S. 505 (1921)

Katz v. United States, 389 U.S. 347 (1967)

Kent v. United States, 383 U.S. 541 (1966)

Kyllo v. United States, 533 U.S. 27 (2001)

Lawrence v. Texas, 539 U.S. 558 (2003)

Lisa Olivia Leonard v. Texas, Statement of Thomas, J. on Petition for Writ of Certiorari to the Court of the Appeals of Texas, Ninth District, 580 U.S. —— (2017)

Mapp v. Ohio, 367 U.S. 643 (1961)

Mendenhall v. Akron, 117 Ohio St. 3d 33, 2008-Ohio-270 (2008)

Miller v. Alabama, 567 U.S. 460 (2012)

Miranda v. Arizona, 384 U.S. 436 (1966)

Olmstead v. United States, 277 U.S. 438 (1928)

The Palmyra, 25 U.S. 1 (1827)

Plessy v. Ferguson, 163 U.S. 537 (1896)

Riley v. California, 573 U.S. 373 (2014)

Rodriguez v. United States, 575 U.S. 348 (2015)

Roper v. Simmons, 543 U.S. 551 (2005)

Shelley v. Kraemer, 334 U.S. 1 (1948)

Stanford v. Kentucky, 492 U.S. 361 (1989)

State v. Hall, 19 S.E. 602 (1894)

State v. Kuhlman, 729 N.W.2d 577 (2007)

Terry v. Ohio, 392 U.S. 1 (1968)

Timbs v. Indiana, 586 U.S. —— (2019)

United States v. $38,005 in United States Currency, No. 5: 15-CV-27-REW, E.D. Ky. (Jun. 22, 2016)

United States v. Approximately 64,695 Pounds of Shark Fins, 520 F.3d 976 (2008)

United States v. Bajakajian, 524 U.S. 321 (1998)

United States v. Jones, 565 U.S. 400 (2012)

United States v. Karo, 468 U.S. 705 (1984)

United States v. Knotts, 460 U.S. 276 (1983)

United States v. Maynard, 615 F.3d 544 (2010)

United States v. One 1987 Mercedes 560 SEL, 919 F.2d 327 (1990)

United States v. One Parcel of Property Located at 508 Depot Street, Garretson, Minnehaha County, South Dakota, 964 F.2d 814 (1992)

United States v. One Pearl Necklace, 105 F. 357 (1900)

The United States v. The Cargo of the Brig Malek Adhel, 43 U.S. 210 (1844)

Van Oster v. Kansas, 272 U.S. 465 (1926)

Weeks v. United States, 232 U.S. 383 (1914)

Whren v. United States, 517 U.S. 806 (1996)

Yates v. United States, 574 U.S. 528 (2015)

Anti-Car Theft Act, Pub. L. no. 102-519 (1992)

Bank Secrecy Act, Pub. L. no. 91-508 (1970)

Civil Asset Forfeiture Reform Act, Pub. L. no. 106-185 (2000)

Combating Human Trafficking in Commercial Vehicles Act, Pub. L. no. 115-99 (2018)

Comprehensive Crime Control Act, Pub. L. no. 98-473 (1984)

Comprehensive Drug Abuse Prevention and Control Act, Pub. L. no. 91-513 (1970)

Destruction, Alteration, or Falsification of Records in Federal Investigations and Bankruptcy, 18 U.S.C. §1519 (2002)

Federal Aid Highway Act of 1921, Pub. L. no. 67-87 (1921)

Federal-Aid Highway Act of 1956, Pub. L. no. 84-627 (1956)

Federal Aid Road Act, Pub. L. no. 64-156 (1916)

Federal Motor Vehicle Theft Prevention Standard, 49 CFR Part 541 67(123): 43075–87 (1984)

Harrison Narcotics Tax Act, Pub. L. no. 63-223 (1914)

Infrastructure Investment and Jobs Act, Pub. L. no. 117-58 (2021)

Liquor Enforcement Act, 27 U.S.C. 9 (1936)

Motor Vehicle Theft Law Enforcement Act, Pub. L. no. 98-547 (1984)

National Firearms Act, Pub. L. no. 73-474 (1934)

National Motor Vehicle Theft Act, 18 U.S.C.A. § 2311 et seq. (1919)

National Prohibition Act, Pub. L. no. 66-66 (1919)

No Human Trafficking on Our Roads Act, Pub. L. no. 115-106 (2018)

Racketeer Influenced and Corrupt Organizations Act, Pub. L. no. 91-452 (1970)

Servicemen's Readjustment Act, Pub. L. no. 78-346 (1944)

Trafficking Victims Protection Act, Pub. L. no. 106-386 (2000)

Vehicle Identification Number Requirements, 49 CFR Part 565 73(84): 23367–85 (2008)

White-Slave Traffic Act, Pub. L. no. 61-277 (1910)

INDEX

accidents. *See* deaths and accidents

accountability: of juveniles, 71, 73, 76; of police/law enforcement, 87–90

Addams, Jane, 72

Advanced Business Sciences, 199

African Americans: access of, to mobilities offered by automobiles, 62–63, 66; capabilities as drivers, 66; convict labor performed by, 12; housing discrimination against, 83–84; investigatory stops of, 5, 105–7; policing practices experienced by, 103–4; prosecutorial discretion involving, 139; suspension of driver's licenses of, 154; urban planning's impact on, 81. *See also* marginalized groups; racial disparities

age. *See* juveniles

Aiken, Doris, 136–37, 141

alcohol. *See* drunk driving; Prohibition

Alcohol Safety Action Projects, 134

ALPRs. *See* automated license plate readers

Amazon, 216

American Automobile Association (AAA), 11, 67

American Bar Association Task Force on the Federalization of Criminal Law, 117–18

American Medical Association, 133

American Traffic Solutions, 182–84, 191

Anti-Car Theft Act (1992), 10, 21

Anti-Saloon League (ASL), 45

Armed Career Criminal Act (1984), 123

Articles of Confederation, 112–13

ASL. *See* Anti-Saloon League

Association of Casualty and Surety Companies, 70

Austin v. United States (1993), 163, 176, 178

automated license plate readers (ALPRs), 4, 192–93

automated traffic enforcement. *See* traffic cameras

automobile exception, 3, 45, 55–56, 59, 78, 88, 89, 94, 192

Automobile Journal, 133

Automobile Protective and Information Bureau, 20

automobiles: autonomy associated with, 61–67; cost and financing of, 61–62, 226n4; crime in relation to, 2, 4, 9, 17–25, 87; manufacturing of, 18–19;

The authorized representative in the EU for product safety and compliance is:
Mare Nostrum Group
B.V Doelen 72
4831 GR Breda
The Netherlands

www.ingramcontent.com/pod-product-compliance
Lightning Source LLC
Chambersburg PA
CBHW020338270326
41926CB00007B/232